Multimedia Programming Using Max/MSP and TouchDesigner

A step-by-step guide to designing, building, and refining immersive audio-visual applications and performance environments using Max and TouchDesigner

Patrik Lechner

[PACKT]
PUBLISHING
BIRMINGHAM - MUMBAI

Multimedia Programming Using Max/MSP and TouchDesigner

Copyright © 2014 Packt Publishing

All rights reserved. No part of this book may be reproduced, stored in a retrieval system, or transmitted in any form or by any means, without the prior written permission of the publisher, except in the case of brief quotations embedded in critical articles or reviews.

Every effort has been made in the preparation of this book to ensure the accuracy of the information presented. However, the information contained in this book is sold without warranty, either express or implied. Neither the author, nor Packt Publishing, and its dealers and distributors will be held liable for any damages caused or alleged to be caused directly or indirectly by this book.

Packt Publishing has endeavored to provide trademark information about all of the companies and products mentioned in this book by the appropriate use of capitals. However, Packt Publishing cannot guarantee the accuracy of this information.

First published: November 2014

Production reference: 1191114

Published by Packt Publishing Ltd.
Livery Place
35 Livery Street
Birmingham B3 2PB, UK.

ISBN 978-1-84969-971-6

www.packtpub.com

Cover image by Patrik Lechner

Credits

Author
Patrik Lechner

Reviewers
Richard Burns
Shawn Faherty
Dr. Joel W. Matthys
Adam Murray
Matthew Ragan
Roy Vanegas

Acquisition Editor
Vinay Argekar

Content Development Editors
Poonam Jain
Priya Singh

Technical Editor
Indrajit A. Das

Copy Editors
Sayanee Mukherjee
Alfida Paiva

Project Coordinator
Mary Alex

Proofreaders
Simran Bhogal
Maria Gould
Ameesha Green
Paul Hindle

Indexers
Monica Ajmera Mehta
Priya Sane

Graphics
Sheetal Aute

Production Coordinator
Shantanu N. Zagade

Cover Work
Shantanu N. Zagade

About the Author

Patrik Lechner started making electronic music at the age of 16, and soon discovered environments such as Pure Data and Max/MSP. From then on, he developed many tools for his own experimental music, and it wasn't long after this that he started creating generative 3D visualizations of audio material. Since then, he has devoted nearly all his life to real-time audio/video processing and generation.

Patrik worked as an audio engineer for an Austrian TV station for years, and taught Max/MSP both privately and at institutions. For instance, he conducted workshops for the audio engineers of the Burgtheater Vienna, and since 2012, he has been working for the University of Applied Sciences in St. Pölten (FH St. Pölten).

Patrik has worked on many multimedia projects, for example, an installation at the Festspielhaus Baden-Baden for the Institut für Creative\Media/Technologies, FH St. Pölten, and an interactive audio installation in Dubai. As an artist, he did audiovisual performances in Austria, Italy, Germany, Mexico, Canada, and Dubai, and regularly played at the Austrian Pavilion at the world exhibition in Shanghai 2010. He worked a lot with classically trained musicians, developed a real-time scoring system/piece for a string quartet that premiered in 2012, and frequently works with painters and artists from other fields.

> I would like to thank the University of Applied Sciences, St. Pölten, for their continued support. I'd especially like to thank Alex Harker, Aya Georgieva, Brigitte Lechner, Camilo Ocampo, Cycling '74, Darwin Grosse, Derivative, Emmanuel Andel, Hannes Raffaseder, Isabelle Rousset, Jakob Doppler, Julian Rubisch, Martina Assum, Mathias Husinsky, Nathanaël Lécaudé, Peter Wyskovsky, Patrick Hollinsky, Pierre Alexandre Tremblay, Sebastian Zeiner, Thomas Seelig (MVC), Wolfgang Seierl (and institutions), and everyone on the Cycling '74 and Derivative.ca forums since they either technically or personally greatly supported this book.

About the Reviewers

Richard Burns is an interactive developer who specializes in the field of projection mapping. At Projection Artworks in London, he has worked along with numerous musicians and bands on live music visuals, projection mapping systems, and social media integration. In his spare time, he performs as a VJ at various locations in the UK and teaches TouchDesigner.

Shawn Faherty is a 3D visual artist living near Boston, MA. He is currently a member of CEMI and can be found VJing, making music videos, and collaborating with other local artists.

Dr. Joel W. Matthys is a composer and multimedia artist who specializes in networked musical ensembles, data sonification, and live coding. He is the founder of CiCLOP, the Cincinnati Composers Laptop Orchestra Project, and has presented his works at major electronic music conferences across the US, including SEAMUS, Studio 300, and Applause! New Music Festival. Matthys earned his doctorate at the University of Cincinnati College-Conservatory of Music, and teaches Composition, Theory, and Electronic Arts at Carroll University in Waukesha, WI.

Adam Murray is a software engineer and music technology enthusiast from San Francisco. He has been programming with Max for over 10 years and doing amateur computer music production for over 20 years. You can find some of his work on his website at `http://compusition.com`.

Matthew Ragan is a native of California, and he earned his Bachelor of Arts degree from the California State University in Fresno and his Master of Fine Arts degree from Arizona State University's Interdisciplinary Digital Media and Performance Program. Focused on the intersection of digital media and live performance, his artistic practice and research have often explored the complexities of media interactivity in the context of performance.

Matthew has recently contributed to the design and implementation of the media in WonderDome, Before You Ruin It, Asylum, The Fall of the House of Escher, Neuro, X-Act: Commons, Half-Way House, Sparrow Song, and ¡Bocón!, and his work was recently published in *Research Perspectives and Best Practices in Educational Technology Integration*.

Roy Vanegas is a programmer, composer, and educator based in New York City who specializes in full MAMP stack web programming. He has earned degrees in Music, Math, Computer Science, and Design, and teaches at various graduate schools throughout NYC and the American Northeast. A CSS and JavaScript specialist, he started programming in 1996 and took up Max/MSP/Jitter programming in 2005. His website is `http://roy.vanegas.org`.

He currently works as a senior web developer at a private university in NYC and is working on his first Google Glass project.

www.PacktPub.com

Support files, eBooks, discount offers, and more

For support files and downloads related to your book, please visit www.PacktPub.com.

Did you know that Packt offers eBook versions of every book published, with PDF and ePub files available? You can upgrade to the eBook version at www.PacktPub.com and as a print book customer, you are entitled to a discount on the eBook copy. Get in touch with us at service@packtpub.com for more details.

At www.PacktPub.com, you can also read a collection of free technical articles, sign up for a range of free newsletters and receive exclusive discounts and offers on Packt books and eBooks.

PACKTLIB

https://www2.packtpub.com/books/subscription/packtlib

Do you need instant solutions to your IT questions? PacktLib is Packt's online digital book library. Here, you can search, access, and read Packt's entire library of books.

Why subscribe?
- Fully searchable across every book published by Packt
- Copy and paste, print, and bookmark content
- On demand and accessible via a web browser

Free access for Packt account holders

If you have an account with Packt at www.PacktPub.com, you can use this to access PacktLib today and view 9 entirely free books. Simply use your login credentials for immediate access.

Table of Contents

Preface   1
Chapter 1: Getting Started with Max   7
  Understanding the basic concepts of Max   7
  Modular basis for expressions   10
  When to use Max   11
    Max – the message domain   12
    Max Signal Processing   14
    Jitter, Matrix, and video processing   16
      Jitter data format   17
  Summary   19
  Exercises   19
Chapter 2: Max Setup and Basics   21
  Setting things up   21
    Getting help   22
      The Max-integrated help system   22
      The forums   22
      Externals   23
      Other resources   23
    Setting up Max   23
      The audio status window   24
      Setting up MIDI   28
      Other preferences   28
      Object defaults   29
      File preferences   30
      Installing externals   30
    Other setup tips   31
    Organizing finished code   33
      Abstractions   33
      Extras   36
      Clippings   36
      Packages   38

Projects	39
Prototypes	39
Basic Max patching and GUI	**39**
Objects in Max	39
Arguments	40
Attributes	43
Creating our Hello World program	**45**
Dissection and construction	46
Contents	47
The [print] object	47
The message box	48
The MSP-Hello World	50
A quick overview of GUI	**51**
Summary	**53**

Chapter 3: Advanced Programming Techniques in Max — 55

Introducing the synthesizer example	**56**
Initializing a patcher	**57**
Excursus of microscopic timing and message ordering	**60**
A bpatcher for MIDI input	**62**
Sending and receiving data	**64**
The #n notation	**66**
Collections of data	**67**
More message box magic	**70**
Structuring our patches	**70**
The pattr family – a communication system	74
Timing in Max	**78**
The event priority	**82**
Debugging	**82**
Smart ways to debug	83
The debugger	83
Optimizing	84
Scripting and the this patcher	**86**
Summary	**88**

Chapter 4: Basic Audio in Max/MSP — 89

Basic audio principles	**89**
Audio synthesis	**90**
Amplitude modulation	91
Ring modulation versus amplitude modulation	94
Tremolo	95
Feedback	96

[ii]

Frequency modulation	98
Controlling FM	100
Feedback	103
Phase modulation	104
The poly~ object	106
Managing instances and patcher loading	109
Polyphony and voice allocation	110
Additive synthesis	112
Discrete Summation Formulae	114
Subtractive synthesis and filtering	116
The classic approach	118
Building an equalizer	120
The filter theory: an introduction	121
Waveshaping	126
Sampling and audio file playback	**128**
Mixing and signal routing	**132**
Conventional mixing	134
Summary	**135**
Chapter 5: Advanced Audio in Max/MSP	**137**
More sampling	**138**
Granular sampling	143
FX	**146**
Stutter	147
Dynamics	149
Noise gate	149
Working with expanders	151
Limiter	152
Compressor	154
Reverberation	157
Poly as a cascade	161
Convolution	165
Taking a room's impulse response	166
FFT	**167**
Drawing a signal's spectrum	169
Simple convolution	171
An FFT filter	172
Spectral reverb and freezing	173
Recording and playback of FFT data	175
Transient detection	176
Sample-accurate sequencing	**178**
Summary	**181**

Chapter 6: Low-level Patching in Gen — 183
- Introducing Gen — 183
- The Gen workspace — 184
  - Exploring the differences between Max and Gen — 185
    - Parameters through param — 185
    - Buffers and data — 186
    - Subpatchers and abstraction inside Gen — 187
    - Genexpr and the CodeBox — 188
    - Efficiency — 190
- Examples — 190
  - The Karplus-Strong synthesis — 191
  - A mass-spring system — 196
  - Waveguides and scattering junctions — 198
- Further reading — 203
- Summary — 203

Chapter 7: Video in Max/Jitter — 205
- Inputting and outputting Jitter data — 205
- Getting started with the Jitter matrix — 208
  - Matrix processing — 209
  - Feedback and delay — 210
- Using OpenGL in Jitter — 212
  - Geometry manipulation — 214
  - Shaders and FX — 215
- Summary — 218

Chapter 8: Max for Live — 219
- Introducing the fundamentals of Max for Live — 219
  - MIDI in/out — 222
  - Audio in/out — 222
  - Synchronization — 223
- Parameters and saving — 224
- The Live API — 226
- An example device – a parameter modulator — 228
- Summary — 231

Chapter 9: Basic Visualization Using TouchDesigner — 233
- The need for TouchDesigner — 234
- How to get help — 234
- Basics and UI of TouchDesigner — 235
  - A scripting prologue — 236
  - Hello World — 237
    - COMPs — 238

TOPs	239
CHOPs	240
SOPs	240
MATs	241
DATs	242
The operators	245
The viewer flag	246
The clone immune flag	246
The cooking flag	247
The bypass flag	247
The lock flag	247
The viewer active flag	247
The parameter dialog	249
Wires and links	251
The select OP	253
A closer look at timeslicing, CHOPs, and exporting	254
Panes	257
Components – structuring a project	259
Where am I?	259
Creating our first UI	262
Hierarchy	263
Abstraction	265
Palette	266
Local	267
Clones	268
What's happening in root?	268
Assign a text editor to TouchDesigner	269
Summary	**269**
Chapter 10: Advanced Visualization Using TouchDesigner	**271**
The basic audio-reactive video	**272**
A 2D composting example	**278**
Replicator COMP	**280**
The me.digits expression as a way to individualize replicants	282
Connecting Max and TD	**284**
A component for lots of movies	**289**
Converting between OP families	**290**
Dealing with time	**291**
The Animation component	294
Using the animation COMP for nonlinear purposes	296
Synchronization	297
SMPTE LTC	299
Audio ramp	300
UDP	301

Introducing 3D rendering	**302**
SOPs	304
Assigning a material	306
The data inside SOPs	308
Summary	**314**
Chapter 11: 3D Rendering and Examples	**315**
Interactive and non-procedural tools	**315**
The geometry viewer	316
Grouping by selection	318
The Modeler	319
The Geo COMP	**319**
Instancing	320
Camera, light, and shading	**321**
Cameras	321
A camera path	322
Cut and blend	322
Fog and FOV	324
Lights and shadows	325
Materials	327
Transparency	328
Render passes	329
Render picking and 3D GUIs	329
Examples of procedural modeling	334
A speaker	334
Structure	335
Modeling	336
Rendering	337
A waterfall plot	338
Structure	338
Modeling	339
A fractal texture	339
Modeling	340
Liquid	340
Structure	341
Modeling	341
Rendering	341
A house in a landscape	342
Structure	342
Modeling	343
Rendering	344
Summary	**344**

Chapter 12: Connecting Our Software to the World — 345
Analog synths and control voltage — 346
Arduino and microcontrollers — 347
An Arduino example project — 349
Hardware requirements for the Arduino project — 349
The Arduino code — 351
Pure Data — 354
Multi-touch screens — 355
The TUIO protocol — 356
Interfacing other programs — 357
Open Sound Control (OSC) — 357
MIDI — 358
Keystrokes and simulated user activity — 358
Audio and video — 358
Multispeaker setups — 360
Exhibitions — 361
Exporting an application — 365
Customizing an application — 368
Collaborative work — 370
Summary — 371
Index — 373

Preface

This book is about the creation of multimedia content with a strong emphasis on real-time generation of content. The two software packages, Max/MSP and TouchDesigner, are chosen as specialized tools to make the generation of audio and video material as flexible and intuitive as possible. Programming inside these languages/tools makes it easy to come up with any tool you might need in order to realize most abstract visions of artistic expression or simply to automate a process that needs to be done regularly. Have you ever lacked control over one of your favorite audio or video effects? Well, let's just build it ourselves! Have you always had an idea for your perfect individual synthesizer? By the end of this book, you'll be able to build it! Both artists and technically interested people are addressed, as the goals of the provided code are not only always headed towards practical needs of multimedia arts but also explained technically.

This book attempts to provide all the necessary tools and crafts in order to enable you to achieve both technical and artistic aims. All of them? Both software packages, Max/MSP and TouchDesigner, are well documented. Trying to replace this documentation of two fast-changing pieces of software would be inappropriate. This book relies on you to consult this documentation, and therefore, the content of this book will go a lot further. While the initial chapters will address people who have never worked with the software, at the end of this book, very advanced topics will be covered. The idea is to not only provide a very profound basis to start with multimedia programming, but also to rely on the documentation and integrated help systems of the software packages, thereby covering as much material as possible. This idea of both providing a solid basis and reaching for advanced techniques also makes it a good repository of concepts, techniques, and best practices. This is even true for me, the author, as I have also learned a lot during the course of writing this book, and have already found myself using it to look up techniques I forgot.

Preface

What this book covers

Chapter 1, Getting Started with Max, will allow us to learn what Max/MSP is about, what we can use it for, why we use it, and how to use it.

Chapter 2, Max Setup and Basics, will allow us to set up our custom Max system, go through the relevant settings, and start diving into programming with Max.

Chapter 3, Advanced Programming Techniques in Max, starts with building a simple synthesizer, and then covers advanced techniques and introduces topics such as parameter saving, structuring our programs, and how to use Max in a professional manner.

Chapter 4, Basic Audio in Max/MSP, starts with how to specifically deal with audio, as the previous chapters dealt with Max in a more general way. Various synthesis techniques, sampling, and some digital signal processing theory is introduced.

Chapter 5, Advanced Audio in Max/MSP, takes a deeper look at audio-processing techniques. More sampling, granular sampling, and effects such as compression and reverbs are introduced, and spectral techniques are also discussed.

Chapter 6, Low-level Patching in Gen, specifically deals with audio in Max/MSP's Gen. Filters as well as simple physical modeling networks are discussed.

Chapter 7, Video in Max/Jitter, explores Max/MSP's video engine, Jitter, which is used to generate some simple 3D scenery.

Chapter 8, Max for Live, is about how Max and Ableton Live are a match made in heaven. We'll learn how to make this match for our patches, how to use Max for Live, and how to prepare our patches to be used inside Live.

Chapter 9, Basic Visualization Using TouchDesigner, introduces TouchDesigner to create real-time visualizations of our audio processes.

Chapter 10, Advanced Visualization Using TouchDesigner, discusses topics such as 2D compositing, time syncing, and 3D rendering.

Chapter 11, 3D Rendering and Examples, explains in more detail how TouchDesigner is used for more complex and bigger 3D scenes and 3D rendering.

Chapter 12, Connecting Our Software to the World, explains how after creating complex programs we might want to connect them to the outside world using sensors, motors, multi-touch screens, and multispeaker setups. Some techniques for addressing such situations are explained.

What you need for this book

To get the most out of this book, Cycling '74 Max/MSP 6 or later is needed as well as Derivative's free software TouchDesigner FTE 088.

Who this book is for

This book is for a beginner in both Max/MSP and TouchDesigner, or more broadly speaking, for a beginner in multimedia programming. Due to the advanced nature of later chapters, it can also be very helpful even for experienced users and programmers.

Conventions

In this book, you will find a number of styles of text that distinguish between different kinds of information. Here are some examples of these styles, and an explanation of their meaning.

Code words in text, database table names, folder names, filenames, file extensions, pathnames, dummy URLs, user input, and Twitter handles are shown as follows: "We can use the `me.time.frame` parameter to get the frame number."

A block of code is set as follows:

```
add_1 = in1 + 1;
mul_2 = add_1 * 0.5;
sub_3 = mul_2 - 0.2;
out1 = sub_3;
```

New terms and **important words** are shown in bold. Words that you see on the screen, in menus or dialog boxes for example, appear in the text like this: "Change the view of the sidebar to the **Explorer**, **Inspector**, **Reference**, or **Max** window."

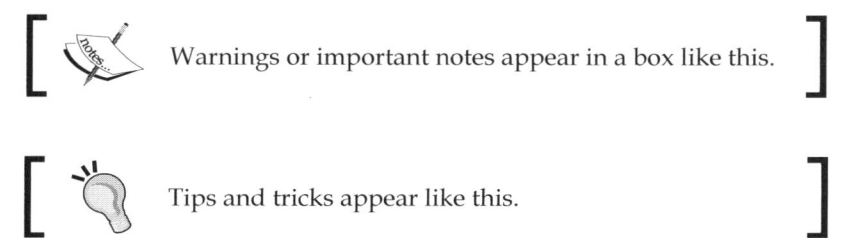

> Warnings or important notes appear in a box like this.

> Tips and tricks appear like this.

Reader feedback

Feedback from our readers is always welcome. Let us know what you think about this book—what you liked or may have disliked. Reader feedback is important for us to develop titles that you really get the most out of.

To send us general feedback, simply send an e-mail to `feedback@packtpub.com`, and mention the book title via the subject of your message.

If there is a topic that you have expertise in and you are interested in either writing or contributing to a book, see our author guide on `www.packtpub.com/authors`.

Customer support

Now that you are the proud owner of a Packt book, we have a number of things to help you to get the most from your purchase.

Downloading the example code

You can download the example code files for all Packt books you have purchased from your account at `http://www.packtpub.com`. If you purchased this book elsewhere, you can visit `http://www.packtpub.com/support` and register to have the files e-mailed directly to you. In case of Max examples, all examples (except for the first two chapters) are provided as so called Max projects. For each chapter, just open the corresponding *.maxproj file.

Downloading the color images of this book

We also provide you a PDF file that has color images of the screenshots/diagrams used in this book. The color images will help you better understand the changes in the output. You can download this file from:

`https://www.packtpub.com/sites/default/files/downloads/9716OT_ColoredImages.pdf`

Errata

Although we have taken every care to ensure the accuracy of our content, mistakes do happen. If you find a mistake in one of our books—maybe a mistake in the text or the code—we would be grateful if you would report this to us. By doing so, you can save other readers from frustration and help us improve subsequent versions of this book. If you find any errata, please report them by visiting http://www.packtpub.com/submit-errata, selecting your book, clicking on the **Errata Submission Form** link, and entering the details of your errata. Once your errata are verified, your submission will be accepted and the errata will be uploaded on our website, or added to any list of existing errata, under the Errata section of that title.

To view the previously submitted errata, go to https://www.packtpub.com/books/content/support and enter the name of the book in the search field. The required information will appear under the Errata section.

Piracy

Piracy of copyright material on the Internet is an ongoing problem across all media. At Packt, we take the protection of our copyright and licenses very seriously. If you come across any illegal copies of our works, in any form, on the Internet, please provide us with the location address or website name immediately so that we can pursue a remedy.

Please contact us at copyright@packtpub.com with a link to the suspected pirated material.

We appreciate your help in protecting our authors, and our ability to bring you valuable content.

Questions

You can contact us at questions@packtpub.com if you are having a problem with any aspect of the book, and we will do our best to address it.

Getting Started with Max

In this chapter, we will explore the fundamentals of Max. We will see what it is, how to use it, what we can use it for, and what Max is not capable of, or for which tasks it would be cumbersome to use it. You'll understand when it's appropriate to use Max and when it could lead to frustration. Max is quite different in comparison to other (text-oriented) programming languages. It has the strength of being very intuitive as you will see; it can do a lot in real time, so we can get very direct feedback to what we do. In this chapter, we will try to get a feeling of what Max is and what comes with it, and start looking at the general workflow. We will cover the following topics:

- Understanding Max and how it works
- MSP (audio and signal processing in Max)
- Jitter (video and matrix processing in Max)

Understanding the basic concepts of Max

Cycling'74, the company that produces the software, defines it as a toolkit for audiovisual/multimedia expressions that don't demand much knowledge about programming. In fact, Max is a graphical programming language that lets us avoid the traditionally steep learning curve of text-oriented programming languages to some extent. We simply put boxes into an empty canvas, called a **patcher** or a **patch**, and connect them, patching them together.

> **Downloading the example code**
> You can download the example code files for all Packt books you have purchased from your account at http://www.packtpub.com. If you purchased this book elsewhere, you can visit http://www.packtpub.com/support and register to have the files e-mailed directly to you. In case of Max examples, all examples (except for the first two chapters) are provided as so called Max projects. For each chapter, just open the corresponding *.maxproj file.

Getting Started with Max

Let's compare graphical programming with other representations of code for a minute. Look at this patcher:

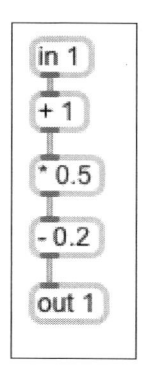

Don't bother about the *vocabulary*, that is the object names, too much. This is a special patcher. It is also called a gen~ patcher, and we use it here since it allows us to see the code generated under the hood. However, this gen~ patcher is using a somewhat different vocabulary (object names). So, don't try to implement this right away; we'll have a slightly theoretical start for now. Can you already see what's happening? Imagine a number, say 0, coming into our patcher at [**in 1**]. You can see that first, we add 1 to our incoming number, resulting in 1. Then, we multiply it with 0.5 (or divide it by 2), resulting in 0.5. Afterwards, we subtract 0.2 and get 0.3, which will be sent to the output of our little patcher. The program we see here doesn't do anything very useful, but it will hopefully illustrate differences in representing mathematical operations. By now, you have seen two representations of what's happening; the last few sentences describe what's happening in the patcher and the patcher itself. In essence, these sentences are like a recipe for cooking. Let's add another equation for reference:

$$y[n] = (X[n]+1) \cdot 0.5 - 0.2$$

Don't be afraid of the notation. For simplicity, you can simply ignore the **n** subscriptions, but this is a common notation that you will encounter very often. The **x** parameter usually denotes an incoming value, and it corresponds to our [**in 1**] in our patcher; **y** corresponds to the output, [**out 1**]. The **n** parameter stands for a running index. Since we are usually dealing with a sequence of incoming numbers, we have to be able to address this fact. In some cases, we would, for example, like to combine the input with the previous input in some way. To give an example for this case, let's think of an expression that outputs the input plus the previous number's input:

$$y[n] = x[n] + x[n-1]$$

You don't have to understand what this is actually doing right now; this is just to make you familiar with another way of representing our code. We will later see how to create an **n-1** term in max (a one-sample delay), but now, let's concentrate on another form of representing our first patcher:

```
add_1 = in1 + 1;
mul_2 = add_1 * 0.5;
sub_3 = mul_2 - 0.2;
out1 = sub_3;
```

This might look a bit overcomplicated for such a simple operation. It is the code that Max automatically generated for us when we created our patch. You can see that we are constantly assigning values to variables, for example the variable `sub_3` is assigned the value `mul_2 - 0.2`, which is referring to the variable `mul_2` and so on, until we reach `in1`. One can certainly write this program in a more elegant way, but let's stick to this version for now.

Think about the differences in these four representations of a system:

- Mathematical (the previous equation)
- Code (C++, as in the previous code)
- Data flow (Max patch) / block diagram (as in our patcher depicted previously)
- Text (a recipe that explains what to do in natural human language)

Each one of them has its strengths and weaknesses. A mathematical expression is concise and precise. On the other hand, mathematical expressions that describe a system can be declarative (meaning not giving us a recipe to get from the input to output but only describing a relation as it's the case for differential equations). Code, Max patches, and written recipes, on the other hand, are always imperative. They tell us what to do with the input so as to get the output. A Max patch has the advantage that the flow of data is always obvious. We always go from the outlets of an object to the input of another, typically using a line, going from top to bottom. A traditionally coded program doesn't need to be that way. This, for example, looks much like our mathematical representation and does not provide us with an impression of the order of operations as quickly as a Max patch does:

```
out1 = (in1+1)*0.5-0.2
```

It is yet another valid version of our code, a bit tidier than the automatically generated code of course.

Getting Started with Max

So, we can see that one major advantage of Max patching is that we can quickly see the order of operations, just like when we connect the guitar stomp boxes' input to the output, as shown in the following figure:

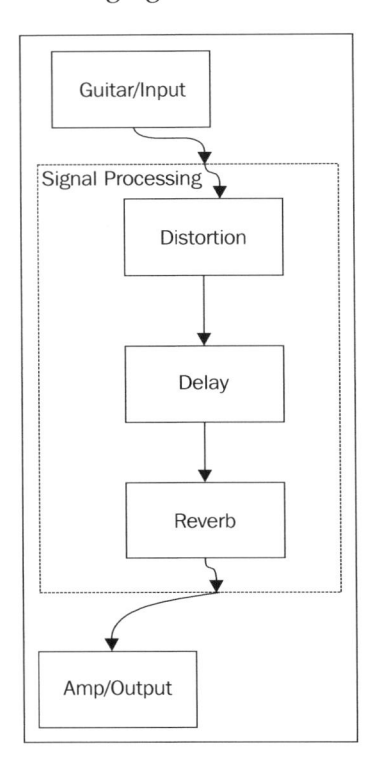

```
Guitar/Input
    |
    v
Signal Processing
    Distortion
        |
        v
    Delay
        |
        v
    Reverb
        |
        v
Amp/Output
```

I leave it to you to reflect on the differences of these representations in our text recipe.

Modular basis for expressions

We saw that Max can create code for us that looks very much like C++. There are some special cases, namely the gen domain, which we will see in *Chapter 6*, *Low-level Patching in Gen*, in which we can actually see and also export the code that Max is creating from our visual programming. You can think of Max as a high-level programming language in which we put together code we don't quite know. The details of this are both an advantage and a disadvantage of Max, but often, we won't care about the code itself.

We lose some control over what's actually happening, but there are lots of things we don't want to see and don't want to care about in typical multimedia programming. We usually don't want to deal with memory allocation when our aim is to quickly build a synthesizer, for example. A good tool for a certain task allows us to control all parameters that are of any interest for a certain task, not less and not more. For multimedia programming, Max is very close to this objective.

The real power of Max is in its modularity. Think of it like a basis, an infrastructure where you can not only patch but also embed text-oriented programming very easily. Numerous programming languages such as JavaScript, Java, Python, and others can be used within Max if we believe that a task requires these or is simply achieved quicker or better with a different approach than patching. Many people learned, for example, JavaScript simply because they wanted to improve their Max patching, so Max can serve you as a starting point to get into programming in general if you like, but only if you like. Of course, in general, it can be considered a good thing to be able to achieve a result in various ways by using different programming languages because you can always choose, and also because you have the opportunity to get many perspectives on programming methodology, problem solving, and problems themselves.

When to use Max

If you think of our previous different representations, you might notice that the last version might be the one that could be created in the fastest fashion. It's simply faster to type the following than it is to put objects in a Max patch, hopefully in a tidy way, and connect them:

```
out1 = (in1+1)*0.5-0.2
```

If we know exactly what we want to achieve and how to achieve it, meaning we have a picture in our minds of all operations needed to accomplish a calculation, we will typically be faster in a text-programming language than in a graphical one. However, as soon as there is some doubt about how we want to do things, or what our objective really is, a graphical programming language that also doesn't need to compile each time we want to test the result will be more inspiring and faster. We can just try out things a lot quicker, which might inspire us. If you think about experimental music for example, the word suggests it's all about trying things out, doing experiments. With Max, we get our results really fast.

A word of caution should be said though. If we are working in Max, the target is often an aesthetic one, be it music, video art, or dancing robots. If we do so, there is often a fair amount of technical interest or necessity that drives us; otherwise, we could have done the job in a higher-level application. A very common danger is to lose the target of creating beautiful things while programming the tools for them night and day. In this regard, Max is also more dangerous than a **Digital Audio Workstation (DAW)** but a lot less than traditional programming languages.

It's hard to find general rules when the Max/MSP/Jitter package is the best tool for a problem, mainly because it is highly individualistic. If you just started Max and are a Java professional, it does not make sense to recommend using Max for everything it can do. Mostly, we use Max when it's the most efficient solution, meaning we can get the task at hand done in the fastest way and with the most satisfying overall result within Max. However, there are problems that have a structure that is very close to a Max way of thinking and others that don't. Real-time signal-processing certainly is one of the strengths of Max since it generally follows a block diagram form and is optimized for real-time processing. Don't forget that Max is designed to do signal-processing particularly well. Also, the ease with which we can often design an appealing GUI is an advantage. Problems that are easily solved in other programming languages (but partly can be done in Max) include recursive algorithms, problems that ask for object-oriented programming, database management, optimization problems, large-scale logical systems, and web-related problems. Some of these can of course be solved with a different language and can be embedded within Max.

Max – the message domain

Max is only one part of what you get when you purchase it. The full package actually consists of Max, MSP, Jitter, and Gen (optional). Max was the first building block and will usually serve as our infrastructure and control surface. It will handle data flying through our patches and sequence events, control the others (MSP, Jitter, and Gen), handle user input, handle the GUI, and so to speak the desk on which everything else is lying around. We'll now go through a simple Max patch, and later, a similar MSP and Jitter one, and we'll see what these are good at. For everything else in general, it's a good idea to use plain Max within the Max/MS/Jitter universe. Let's consider our first Max-only patch:

Chapter 1

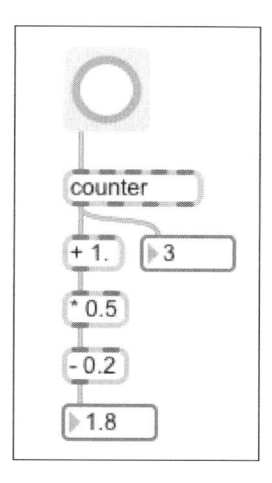

You could say that this patch is made up of the following three elements:

- Input (a button we can click on)
- Processing
- Output (the float number box, [flonum], at the bottom that lets us see the result)

So **[counter]** counts how many times we clicked on the button; then, we do some calculations on that number (you might see that it's the same calculation we looked at before) and output the result to the screen.

> Notice that this patch isn't doing anything unless we click the button. This is an important concept and a major difference between the Max realm and the MSP and Gen~ domains.

We call the message that comes out of the button a **bang**. It is nothing more than an event. You could say it is how one Max object (one of the boxes) shouts to another: now! and the receiving object knows what to do if we patched everything together correctly. In the example given along with the counter, the bang message that comes from the button object simply tells the counter to increase the number output by one. You will meet this event-based concept everywhere in Max and it will be worthwhile to understand it thoroughly and have it in the back of your head while programming, but we will come to this again later in *Chapter 2, Max Setup and Basics* and in *Chapter 3, Advanced Programming Techniques in Max*.

Getting Started with Max

Max Signal Processing

Without further investigation, we'll dive into analogies for the example we just looked at in all the other worlds; first, let's look at **Max Signal Processing (MSP)**:

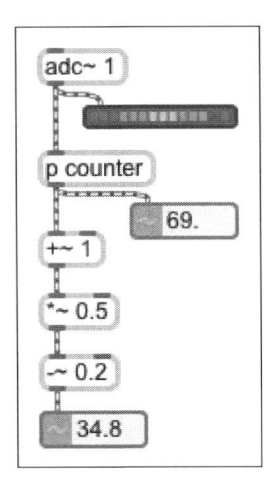

As you can see, we are still doing the same small calculation. MSP is the audio part of Max, and so all the operations that we are applying are suited for audio signals but can be used for all sorts of things, such as doing this calculation. You can recognize an MSP object by its little tilde (~) at the end of its name. The tilde isn't used a lot in many languages, which results in partly strange locations on computer keyboards. Please refer to the English Wikipedia entry on the tilde to find a key combination to create a tilde on your keyboard.

This time, our input is an [adc~ 1] object. The adc term stands for analog to digital conversion; it's just our audio input. Beware, this is a tricky patcher; I've hidden many things for didactical reasons, but if you wish, go ahead and look at the patcher itself (by double-clicking on **p counter**). Instead of monitoring whether a button has been pushed, we are checking whether the audio input level is high. Essentially, you can clap your hands instead of pushing a button (this is a very primitive **clap detector** though). Again, we count how often we clapped, process that count, and output a number.

The important difference to the Max version is that we are always dealing with streams of numbers in MSP, namely we are getting sample rate number of values every second, even if nothing is happening, for example, adding two constants. Refer to the following screenshot:

[14]

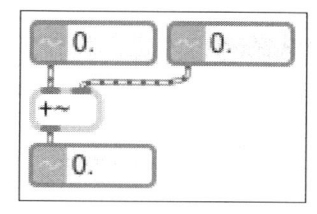

Here, we are adding 0 and 0 and as a result, we get 0 of course. Seems like an inexpensive process regarding CPU right? Well it is, but bear in mind that we are calculating *0 + 0 = 0* 44,100 times per second in my case of a 44.1 kHz sample rate. So, the takeaway message here really is that in MSP, if we have a static input, it doesn't mean that we are not processing, so it doesn't mean we are not crunching numbers all the time. We will learn how to deal with this problem using the [poly~] object in a later chapter.

This difference in the Max world is one reason why this simple patch became complicated (the things I have hidden in the screenshot). To really stick to the analogy instead of outputting a number, we can have an output sound, for example, a sine wave with the resulting number as audible sound, but let's keep things simple here for now.

To sum it up, we can say that we use MSP when we want to process audio (there are exceptions, though). However, there are other situations in which we would want to use MSP due to the way in which it treats data. MSP processes floating-point numbers with a 64-bit resolution called double precision, whereas Max represents floats with 32-bits (the MSP [buffer~] object also stores its values *only* with 32-bits). So we essentially have more precision and can represent both bigger and smaller numbers in MSP than in Max. Also, and this is maybe even more important, we not only have a bigger resolution of our values but in time as well. The default scheduler interval of Max runs at 1 ms, so at 1000 Hz it is able to represent signals with a maximum frequency of 500 Hz, in theory. Without going into that theory too deep (Sampling theory and the Nyquist rate), you can imagine that if we process 1,000 values per second, we can't work with signals at higher frequencies. However, that's the job of MSP, and we tend to use MSP for all time-critical processes such as drum sequencers and everything where timing should be really tight. We'll use MSP simply for all high frequency ($\geq$ 100 Hz might be a good border here) data that we manage to create in or get into our software.

Getting Started with Max

Jitter, Matrix, and video processing

Let's take a look at the Jitter version:

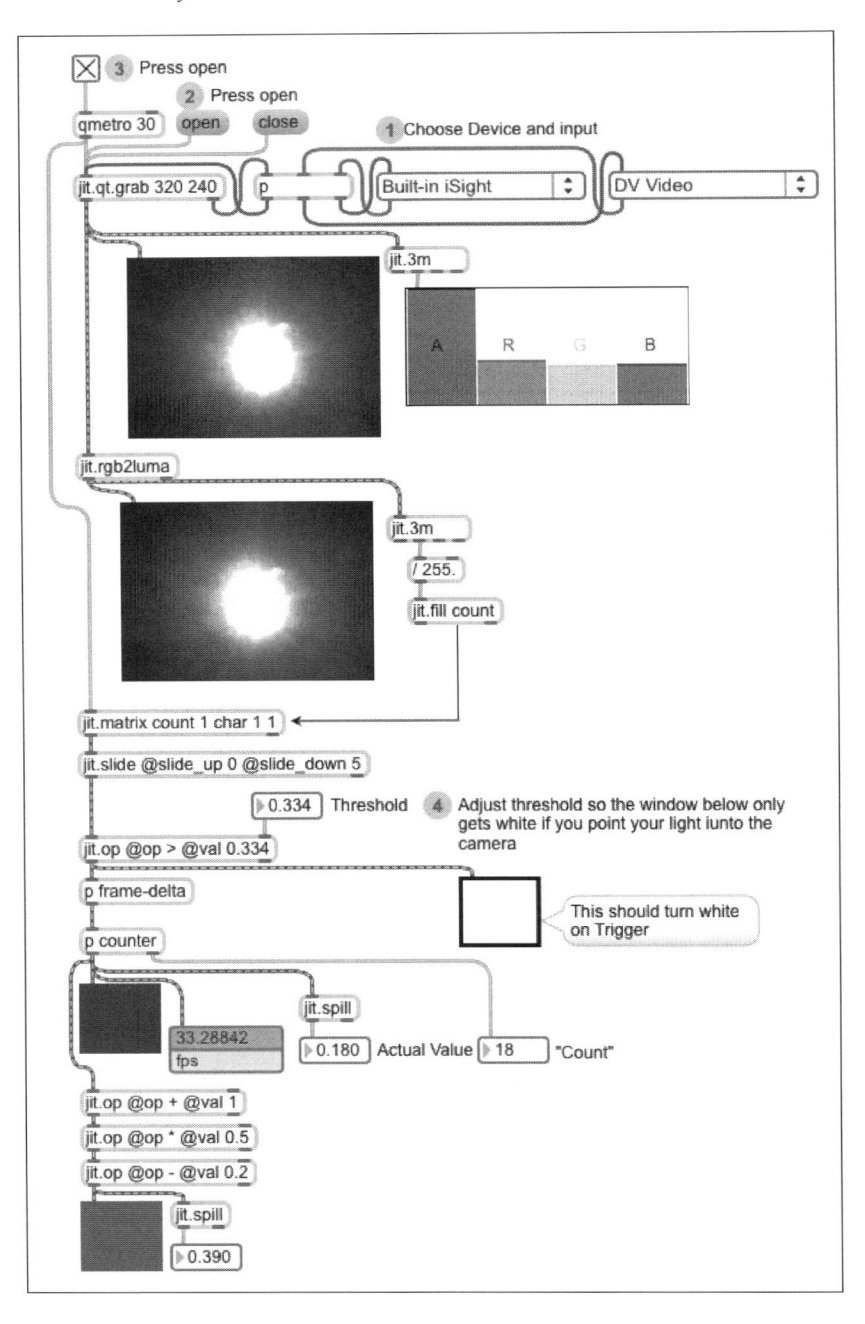

Don't be afraid! I know it looks complicated and we won't go over every detail since it's needless to understand everything at this point. The difficulty here is only that if we still follow our analogy, we have to analyze incoming video as the input of our system. It actually still is our senseless small calculation, but since Jitter is made for matrix calculation and especially for video material, we do everything in matrices here. Our clap detector becomes a flash light detector, and doing the actual counting in Jitter is also not a task you should start with when learning Jitter. However, if you look closely, you can see that at the very bottom, there are three [jit.op] objects that are doing the actual processing. Everything else is just to get a trigger signal out of our video input and to also count these triggers within this video context. This is a highly complicated way to achieve our initial goal, but it should show you that we can also calculate anything with matrices. Many things are hidden in there, which you can take a look at later.

Jitter processes are somewhat similar to Max processes. It runs at the scheduler rate (see *Chapter 2, Max Setup and Basics* and *Chapter 3, Advanced Programming Techniques in Max*) that Max does, in contrast to MSP that runs at audio rate. Also, nothing is processing if the input is static or if we trigger calculations. Usually, if we are really working with video signals, we want to achieve frame rates between 25 and 60 fps; therefore, it's also similar to how things work in MSP: a stream of data. The difference in MSP is that we are in more direct control of the rate; we have to drive the system with a [metro] object that is sending out bangs at a given rate. In the Jitter context, we will typically use a [qmetro] object. It's the same as the [metro] object with the difference that it waits for other processes (like drawing the last frame) to get completed. Refer to *Chapter 2, Max Setup and Basics* for the scheduler and priority. In this case, it's our [qmetro] object that is sending out a bang (resulting in the computation of the next frame), each of which is 30 milliseconds; therefore, we are running our computations at ~33 fps (1/interval in seconds = fps or also Hz).

Jitter data format

Jitter matrices are divided into planes. Planes are similar to what one often calls a channel (for example, an alpha channel, a red channel, and so on) in video technique. Let's consider the format of a standard video signal in Jitter; we have an alpha plane, a red plane, a green, and a blue one for video. Each of these planes is a two-dimensional matrix in itself; it has, for example, 1,080 columns and 720 rows, so one cell per pixel. Or you could think of it this way; each cell or pixel, in the case of a video signal, needs to store four values; therefore, we represent each pixel with 4 cells each on an individual plane. This leads us to an imagination that is depicted later; take it with a grain of salt.

Getting Started with Max

The plane count is something different than the dimensions of a matrix. As soon as we have a plane count greater than 1, we can think of it as adding one dimension, independent of what the plane count might be. For a detailed explanation on Jitter matrices, refer to `http://cycling74.com/docs/max5/tutorials/jit-tut/jitterwhatisamatrix.html`.

The following diagram shows a two-dimensional Jitter matrix with 4 planes illustrated in three dimensions. If our plane count is greater than one, then we can imagine our matrix to have one additional dimension:

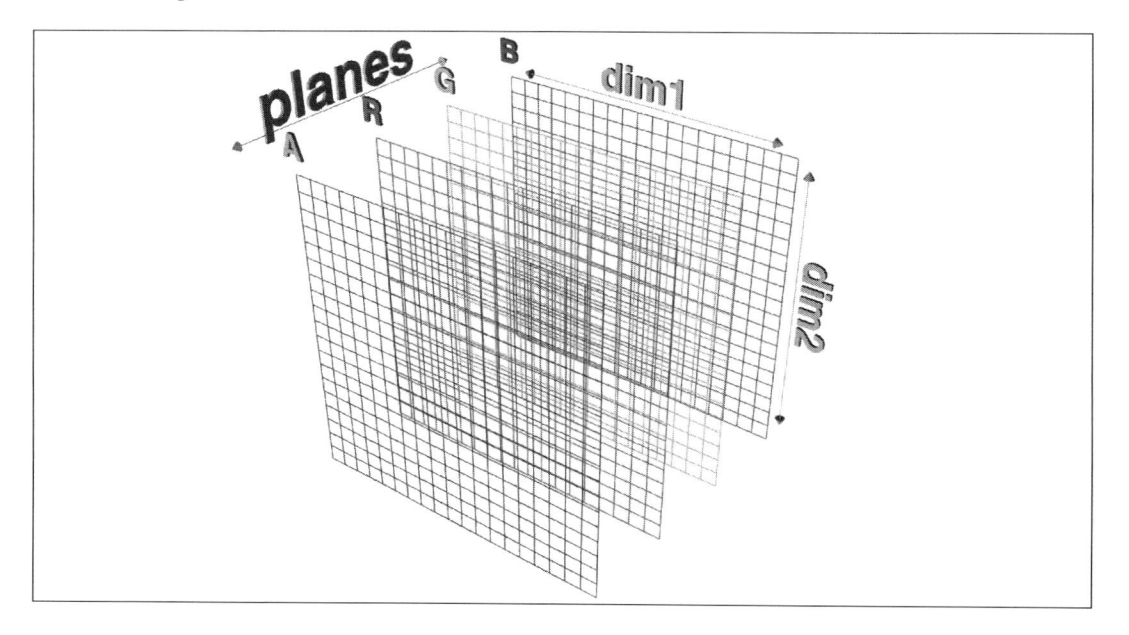

Now, since you have an idea of how Jitter handles data, you can imagine that as soon as we are confronted with multidimensional data, it's a good idea to do processing with Jitter (or even with a shader). We have tools to process arrays or lists in Max and MSP, but as soon as data gets two or more dimensions, we'll tend to use Jitter. We can have up to 32 planes and use up to 32 dimensions. Obviously, this data can grow quite quickly; therefore, we have the advantage of having great control over the bit depth, but we'll take a look at this in more detail in *Chapter 7, Video in Max/Jitter* of this book.

Summary

We have seen that Max is inspired by block diagrams and an *I connect one device to another* workflow that is reinforcing experimentation and visual thinking. Being familiar with Max helps us sometimes to choose between Max/MSP/Jitter for a certain task or use something different. I didn't outline differences between Max and other visual programming languages, concentrating on multimedia expressions like Max's brother environment Pd, Reaktor, vvvv, Usine, Bidule, SynthMaker, TouchDesigner Audulus, and others. There are simply way too many out there. However, we made some progress on understanding the different territories within Max and what their advantages and disadvantages are. In short, we learned that high frequency or very high-timing accuracy leads us to MSP and multidimensional (>2) data that tends to ask for the use of Jitter. The Max domain itself is here for everything else and often it's used to build bridges between the other environments as well.

In the next chapters, we will dive right into Max, and we'll see how to configure it to our needs and customize it, and get some small projects going. We'll get to know Max a lot more and soon, we will build a simple synthesizer, getting ready for more audio processing.

Exercises

1. Try to think of your projects, ideas, and reasons why you actually want to learn Max and why you bought this book. Take the project apart in your head or think of some bits of code necessary to achieve the whole idea if you put them together the right way. In what environments (Max, MSP, Jitter, or something else) would these be written? Try to think of cases where it's not as clear as in a simple synthesizer.

2. Think about a project that incorporates audio and video. What processes are done in which environment? Draw a simple flowchart and think about where it's best to go from Jitter to MSP or the other way around.

3. Open our MSP counter/processing patch from the beginning of this chapter. Go inside **[p counter]** (a subpatcher, we'll learn about this shortly) by double-clicking on it. Try to think about what's happening in there and why it's necessary.

2
Max Setup and Basics

In this chapter, we'll get ourselves ready for patching. Get ourselves ready? If you really want to start immediately, then go ahead and jump right to the middle of this chapter where we start off. Getting a bit of an overview of what we'll achieve in the beginning of this chapter, it is going to help us and make us work:

- Faster
- With less effort
- With fewer problems
- In a more efficient way
- With a general idea of problem solving in Max

In this chapter, we will learn the following topics:

- Setting up Max
- Basic Max patching and GUI
- Creating our Hello World program
- A quick overview of GUI

Setting things up

Max comes in two flavors: 32-bit and 64-bit. What you choose really depends on what you want to do with Max, given that you have a 64-bit OS and therefore have a choice. A major advantage of the 32-bit version is that there are way many more externals (third-party Max objects) compiled for this version. In this book, we will make use of some externals that are not yet compatible with the 64-bit version, so I actually recommend that you go for the 32-bit one.

Getting help

So, I guess you've installed Max and have tested it out, but as the first step, we actually need you to know where you can get help if you are stuck in any way. There are several places where you can get help.

The Max-integrated help system

Max comes with an exceptionally good built-in help system. Use it whenever you have any doubt about what you are doing. There are the tutorials, the reference pages, and the object help patches. The first two can, for example, be accessed via the help menu of Max, while the latter one can be accessed simply by pressing *Alt/option* + clicking on an object. These help files are patchers themselves, and therefore, it's a common practice to copy-paste parts of them when working with an unfamiliar object or when we simply need exactly what's built in there already. A slightly hidden help are the examples. In our Max application folder, we find a folder called `examples`, which is a huge repository of partly very advanced patches.

Also, there is the **clue** window. You can find it in the menu by navigating to **window | clue window**. A floating window opens and offers you hints about many things if you roll over them with the cursor.

The forums

The Max/MSP forums, which can be found at `http://cycling74.com/newest-topics/`, are places full of interesting and competent people willing to help. To increase your chances of getting help, there are at least three things you have to consider:

- Search the forum before you post.
- Be concrete and, if possible, post a tidy patch that illustrates your problem or question as isolated as possible.
- If you post a patch, select all the objects in your patch, use the **copy-compressed** option from the **Edit** menu in Max, and paste the code as text into your post. This is the easiest and most common method of sharing patches.

Externals

Externals are Max objects made by third parties. We can often download them for free, or sometimes pay for them. Shortly, in this chapter, we are going to cover how to install externals. After installation, they behave just like normal Max objects. Externals can help us if we are confronted with a higher-level problem that we assume somebody has solved already, for example pitch tracking, an ambisonics toolset, or classic music notation tools and GUI objects. A good place to look for externals is the C '74 forum; another place is http://www.maxobjects.com/.

Other resources

It might be obvious, but if you are programming with Max/MSP, you often need additional information on the topic in which you are programming. Don't forget that whether you want to find out how **Fast Fourier Transform** (**FFT**) works, render OpenGL content, or do algorithmic composition, there are tons of resources out there that are completely independent of Max but more or less ready to be applied in it. For example, the open online courses that many universities provide also offer Computer Science classes, courses on digital signal processing, and even audio engineering. What one learns there can help a lot when dealing with Max.

> The following are some articles that help us with Max more directly (although some of these use a different language or no specific programming language at all):
> - Alessandro Cipriani and Mauricio Giri's *Electronic Music and Sound Design*
> - Miller Puckette's *The Theory and Technique of Electronic Music* at http://crca.ucsd.edu/~msp/techniques/latest/book-html/
> - Curtis Roads's *Computer Music Tutorial*
> - Andy Farnell's *Designing Sound*
> - http://www.dspguide.com/
> - http://algorithmiccomposer.com/

Setting up Max

So after installing Max, we should go through a couple of things. Depending on how deep you want to go with this, feel free to jump over some parts, but audio is going to be an important part for us, so let's start here.

The audio status window

Let's first check whether audio is set up correctly. This won't be such a big deal; you'll typically have audio running in no time, but you might think about tuning it at some point, optimizing it for a certain patch, and this section should support you if you do so. If you just want to get audio up and running quickly, then proceed with the following steps:

1. Navigate to **Extras | Audiotester**, so you can check all your input and output immediately while setting it up.
2. Then, while leaving the other window open, which provides us with test signals and metering, configure audio and navigate to **Options | Audio Status**.

You'll get this window:

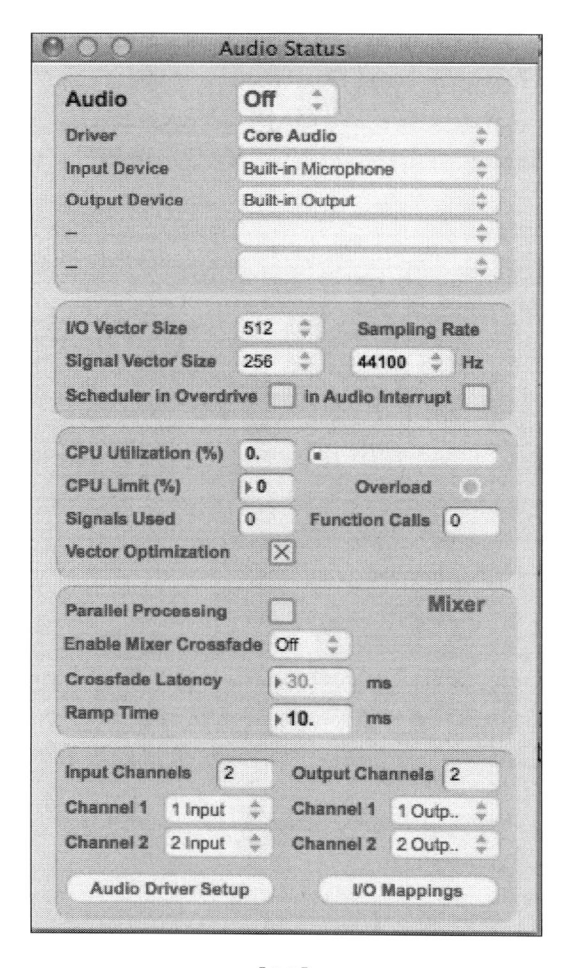

Here, you'll quickly find what to do, but let's look at it in more detail. The audio status window actually is a Max patcher, and you can press *command/control + e* to get into edit mode, and then press *command/control* + click on the **view toggle** box that suddenly appears to inspect the patcher (we will go through these mysterious keystrokes more slowly and in a structured manner later in the Hello World section of this chapter). The audio status window being a patch means that we can access and reconfigure all these settings within our patchers also if we like. Let's have a look at all the settings for a moment. Some of these are simple while some are quite complex. For a thorough description, refer to `http://cycling74.com/docs/max6/dynamic/c74_docs.html#mspaudioio`. Here, we'll just try to get an overview and go through the more important ones:

- **Audio**: Here, we can switch global audio processing in Max on and off.
- **Driver**: This is the audio driver of course. On a Mac, we'll typically use **Core Audio**; on Windows, we'll strive to use ASIO (your sound card needs to support ASIO for this to be available).
- **Input Device**: This is your audio input device.
- **Output Device**: This is your audio output device.
- **I/O Vector Size**: This is also referred to as the buffer size or block size. It's the number of samples that are passed between the audio interface and Max at a time (as a block). Increasing this number not only gives more input/output latency but also more CPU cycles left for your computations. Decreasing it naturally causes the opposite; the input/output delay decreases at the cost of some CPU processing power. Often, you might encounter clicks in your audio output if you demand too much of your system. You can check whether this is the problem here in the status window during the CPU utilization, and if it's the case, you can try to increase the buffer size and/or decrease the sampling rate if possible to treat the problem. However, this is a bit of a simplification; too large vector sizes can also cause clicks. For more detailed information, refer to `http://cycling74.com/docs/max6/dynamic/c74_docs.html#mspaudioio`. As it's also stated there, optimizing a system's parameters for a certain patcher is a process of trial and error. Also, this setting affects the timing accuracy of Max messages if the audio is on, overdrive is on, and the scheduler in audio interrupt is on (which is a very typical situation). Decreasing this value will improve the timing accuracy in this case; the details of this are explained later in the *In Audio interrupt* point of this list.

- **Signal Vector Size**: This is the size of the buffers that MSP is processing at a time. MSP objects don't process each sample individually, but chunks of samples and this is the amount of samples. Decreasing the number costs more CPU cycles, but this setting has nothing to do with audio latency. Some applications in audio demand the use of very short delays and feedback, and in MSP, our shortest delay (with feedback) is equal to this number of samples (luckily, there is gen~ in which we can have single sample delays that allow for feedback, but since this is an optional package and we might want to stay out of gen~ sometimes, this number is still important). If you are running patches with very small delays that are really at these limits, changing this number can effectively change how your patches sound. Also, this setting can be set locally for parts of our patches using [poly~]. Therefore, we will have a tendency to put in the largest number possible here.
- **Sampling rate**: This is the sample rate of both Max and your audio device. The sampling theorem tells us that we can represent any frequency up to half of the sampling rate (the Nyquist frequency), so with a sampling rate of 44.1 kHz, we can work with frequencies up to 22.05 kHz. Many processes in synthesis and processing generate frequencies beyond this (which, in short, causes noise or aliasing), so we tend to either use higher sampling rates for the overall processing or up sample locally and only those processes where we think it's important. We'll see how this works using [poly~] later. The Nyquist frequency, however, will be the highest frequency you'll be able to input into Max or output from your sound card. To put it simply, here, we can trade audio quality against CPU usage.
- **Scheduler in Overdrive**: This setting is pretty important. If active, Max prioritizes timing accuracy and MIDI input over user interaction, such as mouse clicks and GUI redraw. If your work will concentrate on audio and MIDI processing, you should activate overdrive. If you are mainly using Jitter, it should be turned off.
- **In Audio interrupt (Scheduler)**: This setting will force Max to compute the max event scheduler right before processing each signal sample block (only available when **Scheduler In Overdrive** is active). This can greatly improve the timing of audio triggered by the Max scheduler (not only Max processing but also MIDI), but the improvement is dependent on your I/O vector size setting. The actual resulting scheduler interval can be calculated as follows:

$$I = \frac{v_s}{f_s}$$

Here, **I** is the scheduler interval in seconds **vs** the I/O vector size in samples, and **fs** is the sampling rate in Hz.

Anyway, you can always open the `Timing_accuracy.maxpat` patcher that is also depicted in the following screenshot, to inspect the timing accuracy with different settings:

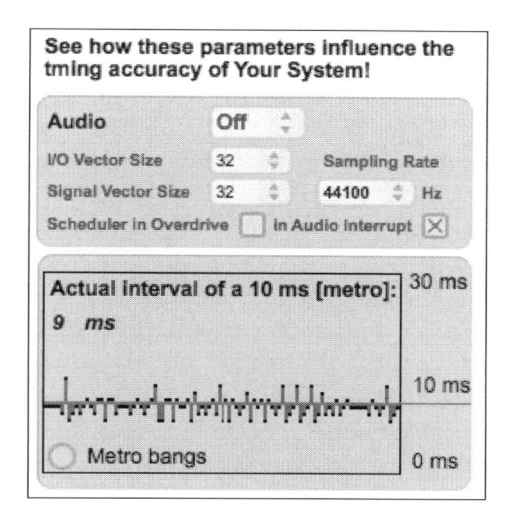

The following are important points worth mentioning:

- **CPU utilization**: CPU utilization is calculated by taking the amount of time required to calculate a signal vector's worth of audio divided by the amount of real time taken up by the signal vector. So this only takes the MSP portion of your patches into account.
- **Signals used**: This simply is the amount of internal buffers needed to send signals between MSP objects.
- **Function calls**: This number gives an approximate idea of how many calculations are needed for one sample of audio in the current network.
- **Parallel processing**: This enables Max to distribute the audio processing of multiple top-level patchers over multiple CPU cores.

Max Setup and Basics

Setting up MIDI

Setting up MIDI is quite straightforward. Go to **Options | MIDI Setup** and you will be presented with the window shown in the following screenshot:

Type	On	Name	Abbrev	Offset
input	✓	to Max 1	‌	0
input	✓	to Max 2	‌	0
output	✓	AU DLS Synth 1	‌	0
output	✓	from Max 1	‌	0
output	✓	from Max 2	‌	0

If you are on a Mac and have no MIDI device connected, it's likely to look exactly like what is shown in the previous screenshot. Max automatically created some virtual MIDI ports for you to be used in other applications that can communicate with Max. On Windows, this doesn't happen automatically, but you can use applications such as loopMIDI to achieve similar setups. I highly recommend that you assign abbreviations for your MIDI devices and use them; beware, though, as Max tends to forget them if it's started without your device being connected. The offset parameter simply allows us to add an offset to the outgoing or incoming MIDI channel. This way, we can identify the incoming MIDI messages sent from different devices just by the channel number, regardless of them being sent on the same channel. This, therefore, is an alternative to the abbreviation/naming method.

Other preferences

So now, let's take a moment to configure Max in order to work with it more efficiently. Go to **Max | Preferences** on a Mac and **Options | Preferences** on Windows.

The default preferences are fine for most things, but here are some settings that might come in handy:

- **Debug | Probing | enable**: This enables little help bubbles to pop up if you hover over an MSP cord. This again is very helpful for debugging signal processing. We can very easily detect **Not a Number** (**NaN**), infinity values, or DC offset at any point in the signal flow.

- **Font | Native Text Rendering | enable**: This is particularly helpful on Windows machines. Often, Max's text is rendered in a strange way on Windows, and switching to native text rendering fixes these problems. So only enable this if you encounter problems.

- **Patching | Grid Size**: Experiment with this setting over time. We will soon see how we can move around objects via a keyboard, and a good value here can make us a lot faster. I personally use a grid size of 18 x 15.
- **Patching | Show Grid (default for new patchers) | enable**: Try this out; it has a tendency to encourage a tidier patching.
- **Patching | Segmented patch cords | enable**: This may be a question of taste, so try it out. Instead of having to drag each patch cord, you can just click on an inlet or outlet, route it in a tidy way while connecting, and lead it to its end with another click (cancel the connecting process with *command* + click on Mac and *Ctrl* + click on Windows)
- **Scheduler | Refresh Rate**: This only applies if the **Refresh** option under **Scheduler** is enabled and is Macintosh only. Play around with this setting too. It determines how often Max redraws the GUI. The parameter is in ms, although the **clue** window tells us it's in Hertz. Anyway, if you concentrate on audio and want to squeeze out more processing power one can easily live with 10 FPS or less, therefore less than 100 ms. If you prefer a very snappy interface, you can even lower the default value of 33 ms. Since your computer screen probably has a refresh rate of 60 Hz, values above 17 ms make sense.

Object defaults

Last but not least, there are the object defaults. Under **Options**, we find the object defaults. Here, we can define, save, and load color schemes. Of course, you can configure this to your personal preferences, but there is one preference I want to recommend; put the background color of the [multislider] option to an opacity of zero. We often layer [multislider] options for complex signal displays, and therefore, this makes a lot of sense. Also, beware that you can always switch these object defaults and embed them in a saved patcher. Therefore, if you are creating a user interface that should look somewhat coherent and consistent, you might define colors here instead of defining them for each object in your patcher. Beware though that these settings will also affect the already created objects. Therefore, you can globally change your colors when you're done creating a GUI. Finally, to fix the colors, you have to go to the patcher inspector (*Shift* + *command* / *Ctrl* + *I*) and enable **Save Default-Valued Object Attributes** to bake your colors. This cannot be reverted, so do a backup beforehand!

File preferences

File references is where we can tell Max where to search for things we want it to find. The folders included in this list are part of the Max search path. It does make a lot of sense to think not only about the file and folder structures for all our Max-related work, but also for the individual projects. We'll talk about this later anyway, but if you already have in mind to create some sort of toolset of your own, which consists of lots of Max patches, you might go ahead and create a folder and add it there. Also, media such as WAVE files and so on are easier to work with if you have them somewhere Max can see them. It's quite typical to add a folder called `samples` in here where we store some files we regularly work with. If this list of folders gets too crowded over time, or if you decide to add huge sample libraries in here, it can happen that Max starts up quite slow, so beware. We can always load any media file by using its full path, and with the new projects feature in Max 6, we can also have project-specific search paths.

The global search path should mainly point to your abstractions, externals, and frequently used files.

Installing externals

We have mentioned externals already; we typically find them online, install them, and then they behave like Max objects. There are many reasons for using them; they help us a lot if we don't want to reinvent the wheel, if processes are too complex for us and somebody else solved them already, or if their greater efficiency makes a real difference for a certain task. We also saw in *Chapter 1, Getting Started with Max*, that sometimes, it makes more sense to solve a problem with text programming rather than in Max, and in these cases, we can embed the code in Max as an external.

Installing these externals is simple; we just follow the instructions that (hopefully) come with the package. Now, let's walk-through one installation.

Go to `http://www.thehiss.org/` and download **HIRT (HISSTools Impulse Response Toolbox)** created by Alex Harker and Pierre Alexandre Tremblay. This is a great toolbox that includes tools used for impulse response creation and convolution. The main reason why we are downloading it at this early stage is that it also contains a very flexible spectrum display that will find great usage throughout this book.

After downloading, we have to extract the files from the ZIP file and locate the actual externals (the `.mxo` files for Mac or `.mxe` or `.mxe64` for Windows) and their help files (the `.maxhelp` files). In the case of HIRT, everything is really tidy and we'll just take the corresponding folders and put them into the Max search path. For example, we know from the file menu that the `Max 6.1/patches` folder is in our search path. We'll just create a folder there that we'll call `externals` for example, and put everything in there, the `externals` folder as well as the help files folder we downloaded, that's the whole installation (you can consider using the packages feature discussed later instead).

Some other highly recommended additions (not necessarily externals) to Max are as follows:

- The Max package downloader
- The Max toolbox
- The CNMAT library
- The BEAP library
- [shell]/[DOSHack]

You can easily find all of them by doing a quick search on the Cycling '74 forums.

Other setup tips

Now that we have configured Max, we have an idea of how to handle Max files, where to put them, and how everything should be set up. Max and TouchDesigner are often used in audiovisual installations to increase maintainability and stability, and to improve the overall workflow on site. There is a lot we can consider to install or configure to give us and Max/TD a better environment to work with. Here is a small list of things we might consider in this case. You can treat it as a checklist and an overview; some of these are highly recommended to be done, and others relate to personal preference, particularity, or exaggeration. I tried to put them in order of the most important things to rather negligible ones:

- Make an image of your disk when everything is up and running finally. You never know; maybe one day the PC running your installation suddenly explodes for no reason after you are finally finished.
- Install a VNC server; remote maintenance saves our lives.

- **Restart On Crash and ReStartMe**: These are both little programs that check whether our Max patch just crashed and will restart it, or even restart our system if it hangs.

- Consider exporting our Max patch(es) as an application(s). We will learn more about this topic in a later chapter.

- Often, we will want our system to start automatically at a certain time of the day, so don't forget to configure the BIOS that way.

- Get the [shell] or [DOSHack] external. This way, you can give Max a lot more control over your system and also shut it down in the evening from within Max.

- Uninstall everything you don't need. Do this before everything else because you might run into problems if you notice that you do need some of those things after all and something stops working. If you do it beforehand, you'll have probably more time to cope with these problems.

- Deactivate unnecessary services, processes, and applications that start with the system. Keep an eye on automatic software and OS updates. You know those public screens used for advertisements that show a window about software updates being ready to install; we'd like to avoid that. Also, our system should just stay the same; never change a running system, they say; letting itself change automatically over time is like running around with a blindfold.

- Sometimes, we really need to emulate user interaction (keystrokes, mouse clicks, and so on) if there is additional software in use that isn't scriptable. For these situations, there are externals such as [aka.keyboard], the Autobot Java class for Max (as mxj), and applications such as **AutoIt** and **AutoHotkey**.

- Install bginfo/geektool/bginfo4x or similar software. It allows the IP address (and other information) of our system to be shown on the desktop wallpaper. This is incredibly handy with multi-machine setups.

- Install SoX and ffmpeg. These are both command-line conversion and editing tools that can do things really quickly. If you suddenly find that all the hundred samples you use in your installation should be EQed and a little more compressed to meet on-site room acoustics and so on and there is no CPU overhead to do it at runtime, you can batch-preprocess them with SoX. Finally, if you need a different video format, you will love the ffmpeg video format.

- Install Wireshark. We often deal with information transmitted via networks. Wireshark is a great debugging tool for these things.
- This is some useful hardware advice; for bigger jobs or in environments where you can't know whether somebody has pulled the power plug out of your system (so nearly everywhere!), you might consider getting a battery backup/uninterruptible power supply.
- Having a good text editor at hand will speed up things a lot. We can also edit Max patches with text editors, for example, to search for and replace a lot of objects. Sublime Text and Notepad++ are very powerful text editors for instance.
- Last but not least, sometimes, we have to deal a lot with moving files around and so on. There are a lot of alternatives to Windows Explorer and Apple's Finder that can help us do things a lot faster. muCommander is one of those.

Organizing finished code

When installing externals or other additional material, you might stumble upon one of these concepts. However, they are all very useful even if we just coded some small Max patch ourselves that we plan to use regularly, so let's see what they are exactly.

Abstractions

Abstractions will become increasingly important for us over the time we work with Max. Suppose we want an object to square an incoming number. Now, there is [pow], but this object is capable of doing more (taking the *n*th power) than just squaring, and we just want to square the input and nothing more. We'll need that a lot and having an *object* that just does this might be handy.

Max Setup and Basics

Alright, so we'll make a new patcher (jump ahead to basic patching if you don't feel ready and revisit this section afterwards). We'll create an [inlet] object, a [* 0.] object (don't be too confused about the zero now; we'll learn about this in arguments and attributes), and an [outlet] object. Inlet and outlet magically transform into the boxes you see on the top and bottom of the screenshot after writing, for example, inlet in an empty object box and hitting *Enter*. So we'll arrive here:

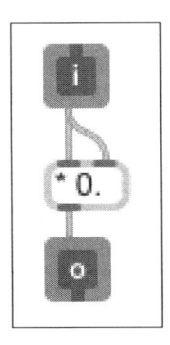

Now, we'll save this patcher in a folder within the Max search path; ideally, we have/create one called abstractions (it's really up to you how you organize your files and folder structures, but you might consider taking the advantage of the packages system we'll go through in this chapter) and save it there with the name square.maxpat. We close that patcher, forget about it, and make a new patcher as follows:

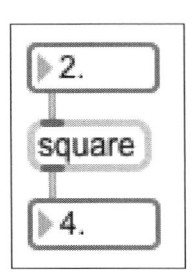

You can get these float boxes by just hitting the *f* key, or by typing flonum into an empty object box. Since Max is aware of the fact that there is a patcher called square somewhere in its search path, it will automatically insert it for us. If you double-click on [square], you can actually see the contents of it, finding our previously created abstraction.

> In order to prevent ambiguity, try to make sure there is no object or abstraction that already has the name you choose for a new abstraction. Just try it out before you save; make a new patcher and try creating an instance of your new abstraction. If you get an error, you are fine; if an object or abstraction gets loaded, you should make up a different name!

We said we shall forget about it; this is one advantage of abstraction. We can hide complexity we don't care about. You can easily imagine that if our abstraction contains more than one object, we are making things a lot tidier using abstraction. There is an easier way (encapsulation/subpatchers/bpatchers) of doing this, which we will learn in the section about advanced patching, but abstraction also has another advantage; assume we use our new `square` abstraction in multiple patches many times. Then, it strikes us that there is an error in the abstraction all over the place. However, we don't have to (in fact, can't) correct the mistake a hundred times if we use abstractions. We just have to correct our mistake in the original file and all instances get updated!

So you see, making lots of abstractions might seem like an advanced topic, but for beginners and intermediates working with Max and fighting with bugs, it's especially useful because we can reduce the time we spend on debugging.

So the takeaway message is start using abstractions early, use them a lot, and build up a library of things you need often.

One more thing about abstractions: we should follow all the guidelines of tidy patching (and so on) that apply for normal patching; we'll go through them later on. But one of them is particularly recommended for abstractions; remember the inlets and outlets we created? And remember that we do want to forget what's in there? So what about an abstraction with multiple inlets and outlets, or just one that's a bit more complex? If we don't want to look inside what's actually in the abstractions, we should give ourselves some hints like this:

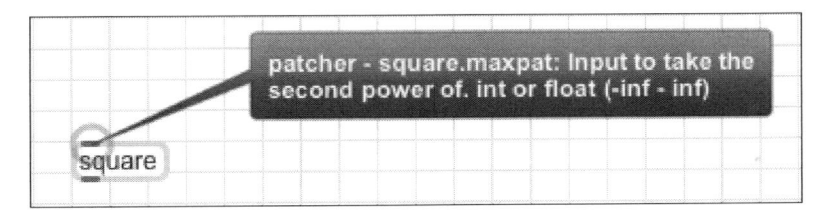

The hints appears when we hover over the input of our abstraction; my cursor just vanished while taking the screenshot. It's what I typed into the comment field in the inspector of the [inlet] object (select the inlet and press *command/Ctrl + I*). This may be a bit overdone in this case, but it's a very good practice to state all of these in this place:

- What parameter do I control when I send something in the specific inlet? Take a filter, for example; is this the frequency or resonance?
- What datatypes are accepted? Int, Float, Signal, Strings, Lists, and so on? What range makes sense? What are the units? For example, a delay might be controlled in samples, milliseconds, seconds, or even Hertz. So, which one is it? Or if we control the amplitude with this inlet, is it dB? Is it linear? Is it linear from 0 to 1 or did we decide it should be from 0 to 127 to stick to MIDI conventions?

This will make our abstractions a lot more usable because obviously if we don't do it, we will be forced to go through the hidden code again to see what all these properties could be. Of course, all this is true for outlets as well.

Extras

You might have noticed the **Extras** menu in Max. We can find a lot of helpful things there, and they are all patchers. The nice thing is you can add your own patchers there. It's quite simple; just save your patcher in Max 6.1/patchers/extras, restart Max, and it should be there. This can be quite handy; for example, you could put your patch that we used to measure our system's timing accuracy there in order to be able to tweak performance slightly. Also, CPU and RAM measurements are a good thing to have there, and we'll go through how to measure these in a more advanced chapter later.

> **Exercise**
>
> You may often need to just send the input of your audio interface out to your speakers. You may need a certain MIDI connection between a keyboard and outboard equipment all the time. Try to think of something useful that will make your life easier when you get it at hand in the **Extras** menu and place it there!

Clippings

Clippings are great. Essentially, they are also just patchers we can save somewhere and access in a specific way, but this is something special. We'll create one right away that you'll need a lot and make the development of audio effects and processors a lot more convenient.

Make a new patcher. Create a new [degrade] object. We are going to steal something from its help file and afterwards delete the object again. I just happen to know that degrade is one of the many objects whose help file we want. Press *Alt* + click on **[degrade]** to get its help patcher. Here you'll find this:

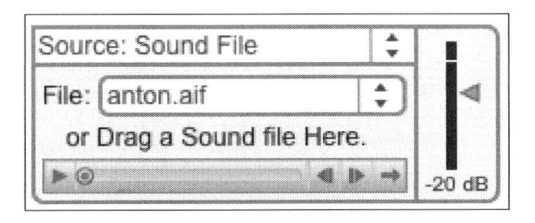

Unlock the help patch (*command/Ctrl + e*) and copy this little field (it's called bpatcher, and we'll also learn about these soon). Paste this into our patcher. Delete the [degrade] object as we don't need it anymore. Now, we'll save our patcher under Max 6.1/patchers/clippings/AudioTestInput.maxpat. Restart Max. Make a new patcher, and while it's unlocked, right-click on an empty area of your patcher:

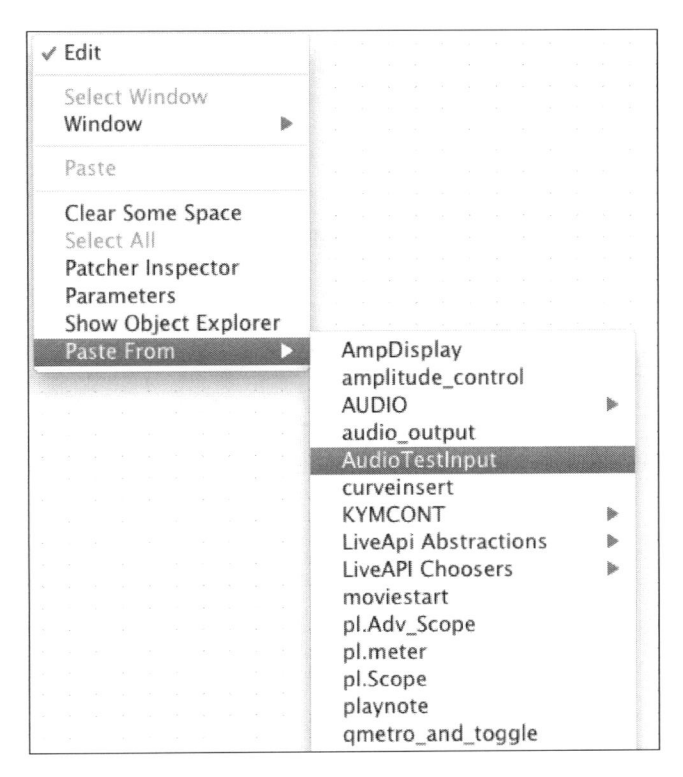

Max Setup and Basics

In the context menu, you can find our patch; choose it and you'll see that it's pasted into our new patch. The neat thing about this really is this `bpatcher` has output (and can have input), so we can actually build small modules that can be interconnected and have their own GUI. This little patch will serve us well since it provides a variety of test signals that will come in handy when we'll be designing signal-processing algorithms.

Although we now created a clipping out of an existing `bpatcher` object, we can make our own also, and that way build up, for example, modular synth-like environments very conveniently. You can take a look at the VIZZIE clippings that come with Max and are suited for simple video processing, or try out the BEAP library (the BEAP library can be downloaded at `https://github.com/stretta/BEAP/wiki/BEAP-Modular---Overview-and-Install`), which works in a similar way with the aim of replicating a modular synth-style workflow.

> Consider deleting some of the preinstalled clippings to make your **Paste from** menu cleaner. It's about accessing things quickly right? So we don't want to have all kinds of stuff lying around that we don't need. Some of the ones that come with Max are really not very useful in the long run. Have a look through them and see which ones make sense for you. In this occasion, you might notice that some menu items are somewhat mysteriously just there, although there are no `according` files in the `clippings` folder this has to do with packages.

Packages

So now, we've seen externals, abstractions, extras, and clippings that moved to special places in our filesystem, and after a year, we really lost track of everything. We probably have two or three different abstraction folders by now; we've had multiple updates of Max each time the standard clippings get restored that we delete each time because we want to keep our clippings menu clean. Also, at a certain point, you'd like to share a patch that contains all sorts of references to files and patches on your system. All this sounds pretty messy and confusing right? Here come packages to our rescue!

Go to `Max 6.1/packages` and take a look inside the `Vizzie` folder there. We find some folders called `extras`, `clippings`, and `patchers`, and some other stuff. These folders just work the same way as the folders in the `Max 6.1/` directory. So if we create a folder called `My first project`, `my general stuff`, or something similar, inside the `packages` folder and create these subfolders, we can use these instead of having our files spread out over the system. Within the `packages` folder, you'll also find an `about packages.txt` file, which describes what types of folders are supported and how to use them.

Projects

Projects are a feature that allows us both to keep track of all the dependencies a patcher might have and also to easily pack those together. We can view it as the dependant of the packages feature. If we plan a complex patcher, we might save it as a project, consolidate everything (media, abstractions, code, and so on) automatically, and open the whole thing on another computer without worrying about dependencies.

Prototypes

Prototypes are saved versions of a specific object. Most of its attributes are saved and we can load them at any time. Take, for example, a `[led]` object; if we create it, we can right-click on it and select **prototypes** and can choose different styles. Since we can also save our own, and many objects have many attributes that define their overall behavior, we might consider building up our own library of prototypes that show up more complex configurations than just a single color. Also, for a consistent GUI design, this comes in handy.

Basic Max patching and GUI

Now, we'll finally go ahead and start patching. In this section, we'll go through the basic functionality of Max and we will talk a bit about the craft of patching. It's an easy thing, but we will try to explore a lot about shortcuts and ways to go about things faster. Additionally, we will of course get to know the GUI in more detail. Nearly all patches you see here can of course be used readily as they are from your download. On the other hand, you will learn more if you just replicate them quickly, or even better, understand them and rebuild the principle without looking at them more than once. Often, there are many ways to achieve a goal and the number of ways to achieve the goal increases with the complexity of the goal.

Objects in Max

Before we dive into patching, let's just very briefly think about the Max objects that we have been talking about. We can imagine them as small virtual machines (Cipriani and Giri 2010, 51) that fulfill different tasks for us. I think you have a basic understanding of what they are by now, but there is something left to say about how they work. Look at the following screenshot. We see an `[int]` object. The bubbles appear when you hover over the corresponding inlets and outlets but of course, usually not all at the same time, as shown here. As you can see, there is a red ring on the left hot inlet and a blue one on the right cold inlet.

Max Setup and Basics

These are called hot and cold and also illustrated that way (as shown in the following screenshot) because if we send a message, for example, an integer into the right or cold inlet, there won't be any output. It will be stored there as it says in the bubble, whereas if we send an integer or bang message into the left or hot inlet, it will output the integer or the last stored integer in the case of the bang message:

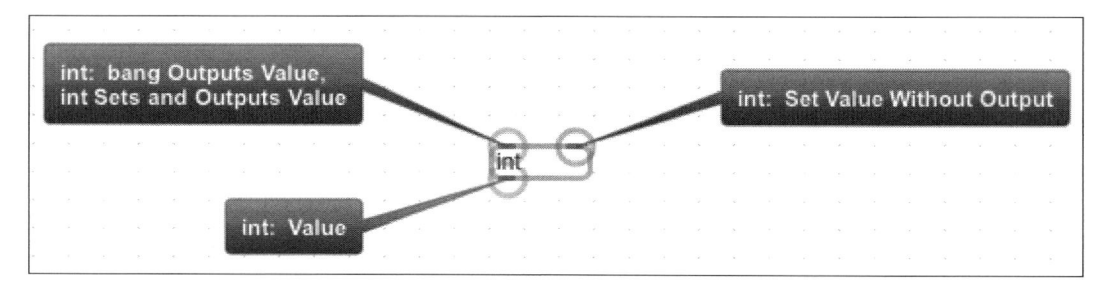

The concept of hot and cold inlets is everywhere in Max, and we will encounter it at the beginning or maybe later when we discuss message ordering. The important thing is to keep this idea in mind.

> **Technical detail**
>
> Max objects are written in C. When we create a Max object, we create an instance of the compiled C code that represents that object. If we send a message into it, we are simply calling a function within that code.

Arguments

You have already seen arguments, for example, in an previous illustration. There, we saw a [* 0.] object. It is, in fact, a [*] object with the argument 0. In general, arguments can fulfill two purposes:

- To initialize a variable
- To set a constant regarding the object's behavior

In the case of our [* 0.] object, we do both at the same time. When we start up our patcher and just send something into the left inlet, we do a multiplication by 0. As soon as we send another number, for example, 5 into the right inlet, the zero is overridden and we multiply by 5. So here, we initialized one of the factors. However, what constant did we set at the same time?

We didn't just initialize the multiplication with 0. Guess what's the default initial value; 0 of course. So why did we do it? Because we didn't put 0 in there but 0. Many math (and other) objects operate with integers by default. If we initialize them with a float argument, we tell the object to do floating point calculations, thereby defining its internal behavior constantly, shown as follows:

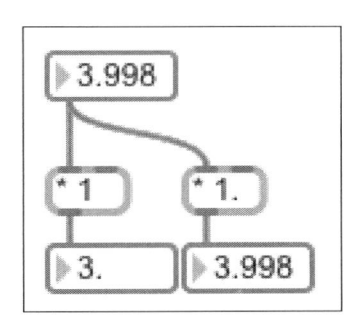

In the preceding screenshot, you can see the different behavior of two differently initialized [*] objects. The integer one simply performs a floor operation, cutting way everything behind the decimal point. Remember that this is one of the most common mistakes both for beginners and advanced users. It is recommended that you initialize everything explicitly (instead of relying on the default value because we know or believe it will suit our needs) because it makes patches more readable. Also, it's a psychological trick; we at least think about the value very shortly and state it explicitly instead of hiding it, setting the value implicitly, and maybe a little more unconsciously.

Max Setup and Basics

We can find what arguments are obligatory or optional for any given object in its help patch, in the object's reference, or in the descriptions that pop up after you typed a space after the object name of the object you are creating, as shown in the following screenshot:

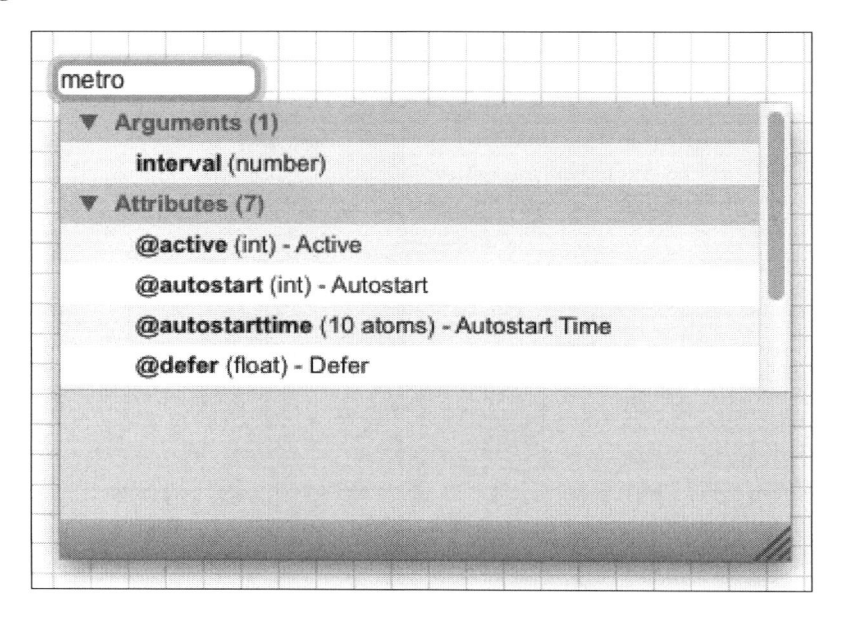

The syntax is important here; we always get the object name, a single space, the arguments separated by spaces, and the attributes afterwards, whereas each attribute is preceded by @, and all of them are also separated by spaces:

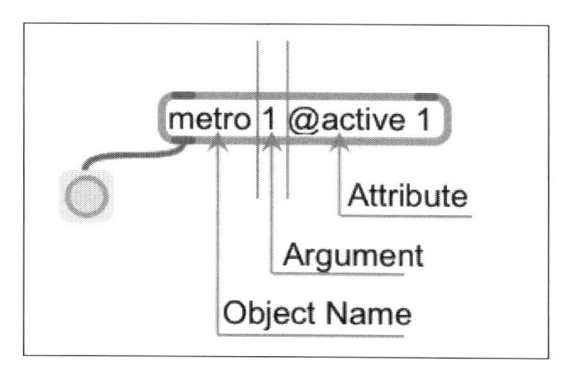

In the previous screenshot, we can see a [metro] object that has been given one argument, its interval in ms, and with one attribute set, active 1, which means it is switched on. Before we go looking at attributes, we will consider another example of arguments, that is, the ones of the [counter] object:

[counter 1 0 5]

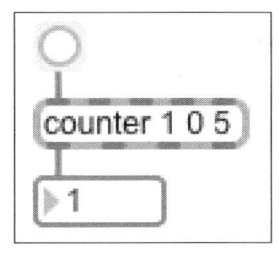

In this case, we are provided with three arguments: **1, 0, 5**. These are as follows:

- The mode of the counter where **0** means count forwards, **1** means backwards, and **2** means back and forth
- The minimum of the count
- The maximum of the count

So this counter counts from **5** down to **0**. Most of the time, we need something that counts from **0** to some number, so up, not down. In this case, we can provide only one argument and it will be taken as the maximum. If we provide two arguments, it will be taken as minimum and maximum. Pretty confusing, right? That's something we will get used to, but if there are more parameters, nobody wants to count how many arguments are provided to identify their function. That's where attributes come into play.

Attributes

As we have seen, attributes are like arguments, but they have the advantage of being able to be addressed by writing their name instead of knowing (or looking up often) that the property we are searching for can be set via, say, the third argument.

For example, the [dosomething 1000 0.5 0.9] object won't mean a lot to us in a couple of weeks, whereas [dosomethin @cutoff 1000 @resonance 0.5 @gain 0.9] is a lot more descriptive.

Most of the time, we cannot choose whether we address something as an attribute or an argument (for our own abstractions we can!); some properties can be set via one while some by the other. The [metro] object's interval can be set via the first argument or the argument @interval n, but that's an exception. For the sake of completeness, the attribute overrides the argument in the rare case in which we will provide both [metro] and @interval n at the same time. It might seem that arguments and attributes are doing more or less the same work, but internally, they are substantially different. Their actual difference doesn't matter for us too much, but we just want to get a feeling of whether a property is an attribute or an argument. Arguments initialize and attributes configure an object.

Max Setup and Basics

All attributes are collected in the inspector. Remembering the shortcut for the inspector, the shortcut is *command/Ctrl + I* (this only works if we have an object selected), will help us a lot since we can then also select an attribute by typing the name of the attribute, then hit *Enter*, and configure everything as we like in a very fast manner. The following screenshot shows the inspector window:

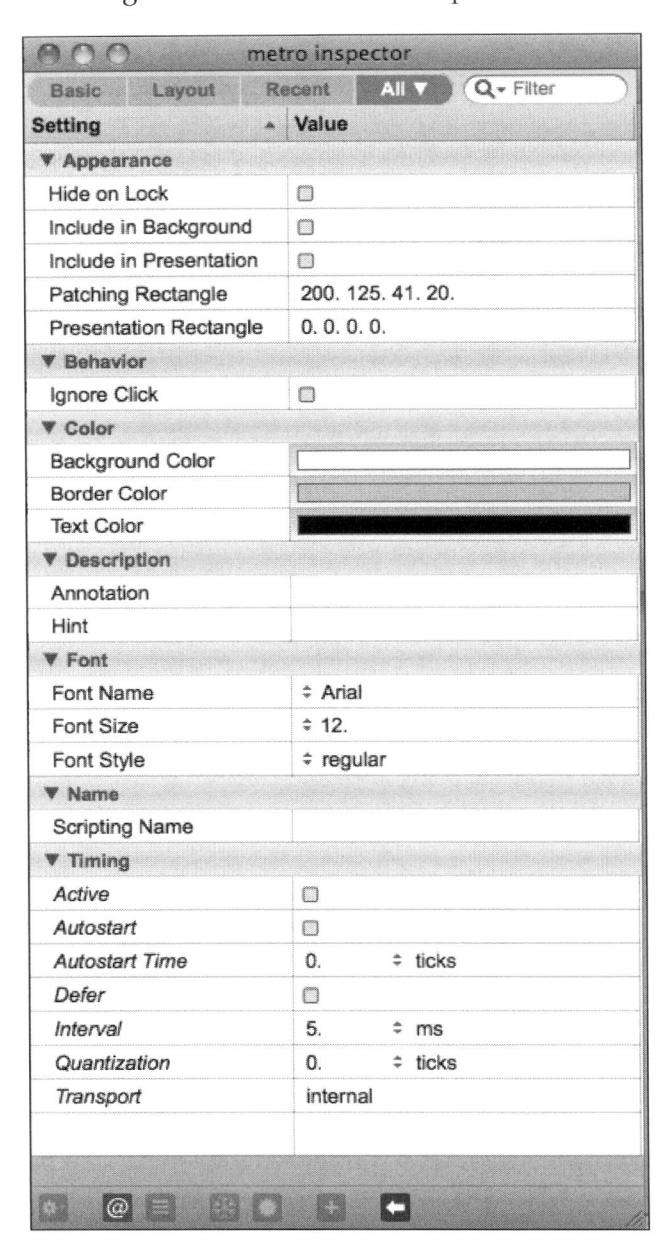

Setting	Value
▼ Appearance	
Hide on Lock	☐
Include in Background	☐
Include in Presentation	☐
Patching Rectangle	200. 125. 41. 20.
Presentation Rectangle	0. 0. 0. 0.
▼ Behavior	
Ignore Click	☐
▼ Color	
Background Color	
Border Color	
Text Color	
▼ Description	
Annotation	
Hint	
▼ Font	
Font Name	⇕ Arial
Font Size	⇕ 12.
Font Style	⇕ regular
▼ Name	
Scripting Name	
▼ Timing	
Active	☐
Autostart	☐
Autostart Time	0. ⇕ ticks
Defer	☐
Interval	5. ⇕ ms
Quantization	0. ⇕ ticks
Transport	internal

The inspector has a couple of built-in gadgets that help us a lot. By pressing the little @ sign at the bottom of the inspector's screen. We can see the attribute names, so we can remember it and type it into the object box next time we need it. Also, we can just drag-and-drop attributes out of the inspector into our patches. This will cause a little pop up to open, asking us what should be done. Try out these options; they are all made to interact with the chosen attribute in a manual or programmatic manner or to monitor it. This saves us a lot of typing.

> You can set all attributes with the inspector but you can't access all of them with the @ notation or dynamically using messages. There are ways around this limitation, which we will cover in the section on scripting using the [thispatcher] object.

If we configure a certain attribute in the inspector, it can happen that our newly set value is not saved. Some attributes are simply not saved by default, but we can change this by freezing the attribute. We can find out whether an attribute is being saved if we look at their names. Those that are written in italics won't be saved; those that are not will be. Those that are written in italics will also be available through the @ notation and therefore can be set permanently this way as well.

Creating our Hello World program

So let's start up Max, close the splash screen if you haven't got rid of it already, and make a new patch (*command/Ctrl + N*). You will see something like what's shown in the following screenshot; without the objects, the cords, the message box, and the sidebar might not be open or it might be in another mode. You don't need to open the sidebar for now, but if you like it, press the button with the number 11 in the following screenshot. We can have the Max window in a separate window. Either way, free floating or in the side bar, open it and I highly recommend that you remember the shortcut for it, which is *command/Ctrl + M*. Now, we have everything set up to write the obligatory Hello World program:

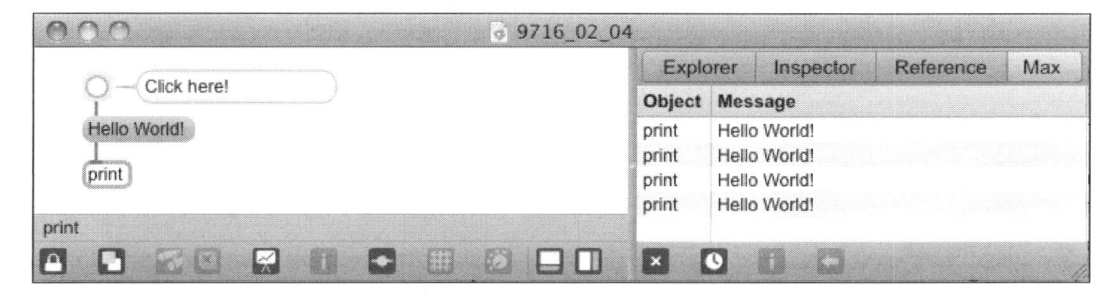

So this is our Hello World program. How was this created? What do we see here?

Dissection and construction

First of all, we see three objects here. A [button], a [message], and a [print] object (and of course, a comment object that reads **click here!**). So we can create them just like that; we create a new object in the patch by just hitting *n* and start writing. In one object, we write button; in the second one, we write message; and in the third one, we write print. The purpose of this little patch is obviously to print the **Hello World** message to the Max window, which in this case is attached and not a separate window. Then, we interconnect these objects.

Now, here is the ninja way to do it:

1. Make a new patcher: (*command/Ctrl + N*).
2. Hit *B* to get the button right away.
3. Hit *M* to get a message box and position the message box below the button object using arrow keys on the keyboard. Use *Shift* + arrow keys for momentary toggling snap to grid on and off. Hit *Enter* again to edit the contents of the message box and hit *Shift + Enter* to finish editing it.
4. Hit *N* for a new object, type print, hit *Enter*, and position it below.
5. If you want to get the selection back on another object to edit or reposition it again, you can use *command/Ctrl* + the arrow keys.
6. Now, if you have the max toolbox (mentioned in the externals section) installed, select them all and hit *Shift + C*. Otherwise, just connect them manually, and we are done! Now, this sounds pretty complicated, and you don't have to remember all these shortcuts, but if you know some of them, you'll have a better time coding with Max, I promise. Just try it out, it's not so hard!

> There are two files that mainly define our keyboard shortcuts: Max 6.1/Cycling '74/interfaces/maxinterface.json and Max 6.1/Cycling '74/init/max-keycommands.txt.
> Be sure to take a backup when redefining things there.

If you try out your patcher, you might need to **Lock** the patcher before the button reacts to your clicks in the expected way. In Max, there are two modes of interaction with your patcher: the edit mode and the locked mode. Naturally, one is for editing your program and one is for actual interaction. So in order to be able to click on the button, we have four ways to enter the locked mode:

- Clicking on the little lock icon on the bottom left of the patcher window
- Using the shortcut *command/Ctrl + E* to toggle between the modes

- Using *command/Ctrl* + left mouse button to click into an empty area of the patcher to toggle the modes
- Pressing and holding *command/Ctrl* during the interaction with the GUI

The last option is the preferred one during development since one often needs to only adjust one value or quickly click a button, but actually, one is still patching and not performing.

Contents

Let's think about the actual contents of this patcher. We have a user interface object, namely a button. We have a message box and the `print` object. If we click on the button, it actually sends a message out of its outlet, called a **bang** message. We discussed this in *Chapter 1, Getting Started with Max*. It tells the next object to act now and to do whatever it is supposed to do, nearly always to output data.

> **Exercise**
> Prove that the message that goes from the button to the message box actually is a bang message.

The [print] object

Before we go over the message box, there are a couple of things we need to go over in relation to the `print` object. When programming with Max, we must always remember that `print` is one of our best friends. As in many other programming languages, there are various ways to output data or debug processes, but the `print` statement/object is at the heart of debugging. Whenever we aren't sure what's happening, we put `print` objects everywhere.

> **Caution**
> Printing a lot to the max window drains more performance than you might think! Keep track of your `print` objects that lie around and consider using mechanisms such as [gate] and the [send]/[receive] system to deactivate printing globally.

The `print` object takes an argument that will show up in the Max window's object column instead of **print**, so we can design our printouts to be a bit more informative, as in the following screenshot. Also, if we double-click on a line in the Max window, Max highlights the corresponding print object.

> Many beginners struggle with errors in their patchers although Max is actually telling them what's wrong or at least gives a hint. Max also communicates with us through the **Max** window (not only `print` objects), so keep an eye on it. A typical window layout to do standard work in Max has a patcher window, an **Inspector** window, and the **Max** window open and visible.

Look at the following screenshot to see an example of printing:

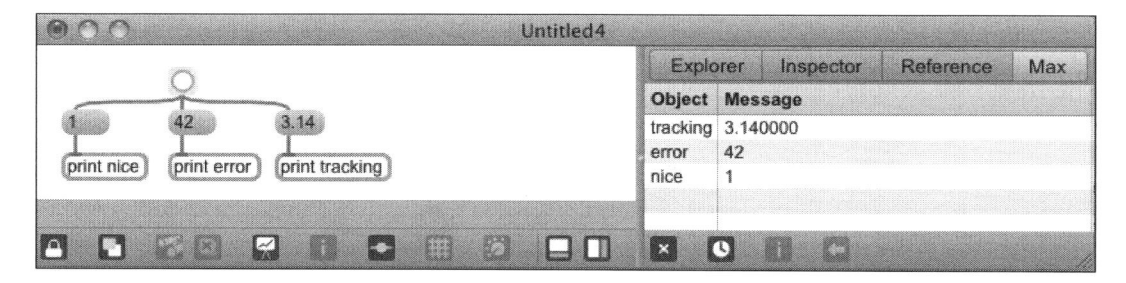

The debugging facilities of printing might also be the reason why the Hello World program is so popular for starting to program in a specific language. We will need a simple debugging tool right at the beginning, so we can always see what we are doing. Debugging is not the most exciting topic in the world and nobody wants to learn a lot about how to treat the mistakes before starting to do anything. This book contains a section on debugging, and I invite you to refer to it whenever you feel the need for it. We'll cover this rather late and you might want to avoid the situation in which you say "Well, great, why didn't you tell me this earlier?"

The message box

The `message box` object is a very versatile special object. You will find it everywhere, and while we will use it in various ways in this book, not all of its functionality is covered here. As you know, you can always get help if you press *Alt* + click on an object. Here are some of its main features:

- We can edit the content and write any message in there that we would want to send anywhere.
- We can set the contents of it dynamically by sending anything into the right inlet.

- We can, as you have seen, send out the contents by sending a bang into its left inlet.
- Moreover, if we click on it (when in locked mode), it also sends out its contents, so it's also a basic text button.

You see it's an object that helps us in many situations and the following screenshot shows of some more advanced features of it. We can use it for the basic formatting of messages and lists and even ordering things in time.

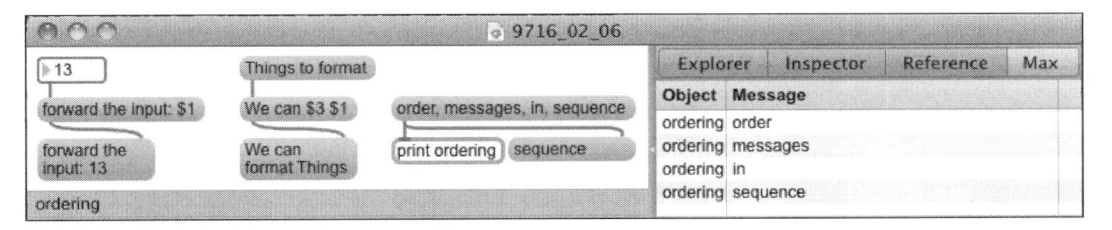

Using the $n object (where *n* is a number between 1 and 9) notation enables us to generate compound messages on the fly as you can see. Also, the use of commas is important to notice here. Commas divide the contents up into several messages in sequence. These messages are sent in sequence, as fast as Max can.

Since we saw that we can display messages using the message box right inlet, it's also a good debugging tool. However, the patcher shown in the previous screenshot shows a subtle difference between `print` and the `message box` object. Look at the right-hand section where we used the commas. The `message box` object used for display only shows the sequence. That's not because this is a screenshot; try it out, you won't see the other messages (Max is too fast!). In contrast to that, [print] can be used very well for this task; all messages appear in chronological order (by default at least).

Max Setup and Basics

The MSP-Hello World

By now, you should be able read data from any point in Max using either the `message box` or the `print` statement. But what about streams of numbers and signals? What about MSP? Let's have a look at how to get information about an unknown signal. Depending on if it's a stream of Max messages or MSP signals, we are going to need different tools, as shown in the following screenshot:

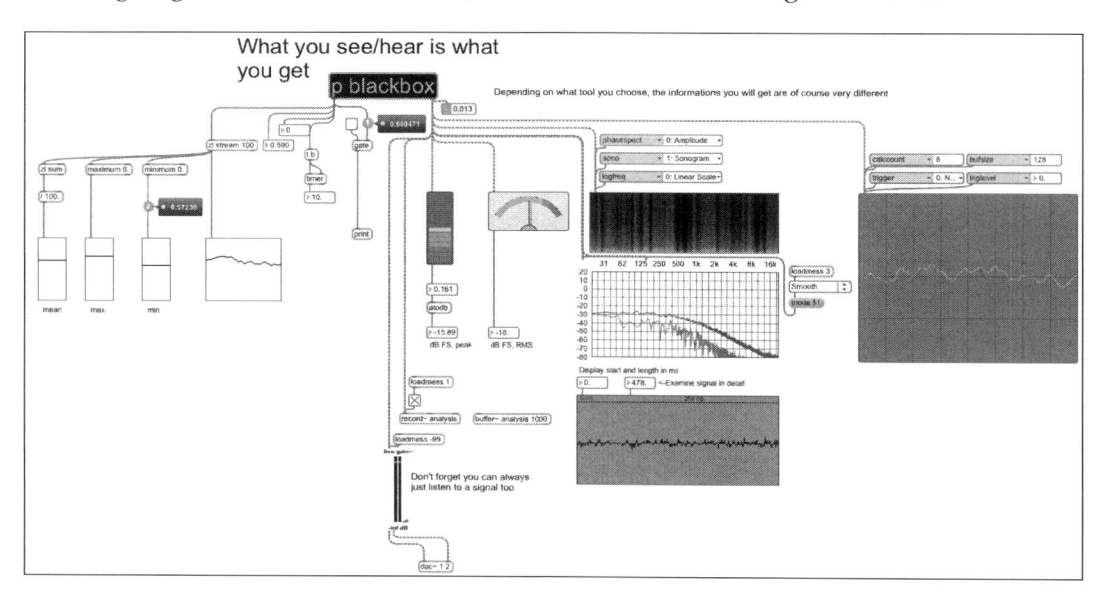

In this screenshot, you can see `patcher wysiwyg.maxpat`. Open it and play around with it. Don't look into the blackbox too soon (by double clicking it)! It generates two signals: one in the max domain, a stream of numbers of course, and the other one in the MSP domain. This patch may contain a lot of objects that are new to you, but you can just *Alt* + click on each of them to get to know them. The main point here is again to understand what we are doing. Although a signal has a lot of properties, often, the most important thing about an audio signal is how it sounds; as obvious as this sounds, don't forget this.

However, there are many other features a signal may have and many ways of looking at those. Take amplitude, for example; you can look at the numerical value, you can measure in dB or linear, or you can look at the peak value if you want to check whether your signal is clipping or use RMS, if you rather care for a rough guide of loudness. There are a number of new standards since the AES/EBU recommendation R128 that also describes properties of an audio signal that might be even more important than peak or RMS (namely LU, true peak, and dynamic range measurements).

All these more or less describe the amplitude of a signal and there are many more (for example, different frequency weighted measurements). Often, we care a lot more about the spectrum of a signal, hence the amplitudes of a signal's components, or even more sophisticated features of a signal.

The most important thing is to discover what we really want to know about a signal and how to get this information.

> **Exercise**
>
> With the given `wysiwyg.maxpat` patch, look at all the tools, get to know them, and do some research if you feel you don't understand a concept behind a measurement. Before looking into the blackbox, try to guess what's in there and build what you think might be in there, or draw a block diagram!

A quick overview of GUI

Let's get a basic overview of the GUI at this point. The Max GUI is not a static thing and we can't cover everything here, but it also is self-describing. The clue window, little pop ups, and the reference help us if there are any questions, but in order to be able to talk about things and to give some directions as to where to look for a certain thing, let's go through the interface using the following screenshot:

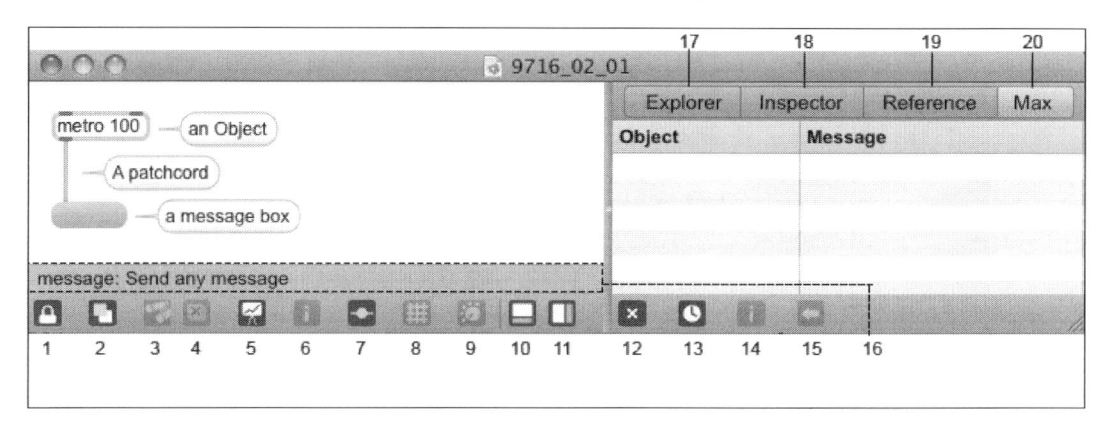

Max Setup and Basics

The following are the steps to install the Max GUI:

1. Lock/unlock the patchers / modify read-only. If the window shows a loaded abstraction, this symbol will show up. If we press the following button, then we can edit the patcher in place, loading the original temporarily:

2. The patcher windows: Here, we can access functions as opening another view of the patcher (for instance, when designing GUIs, it's really handy to have one locked view and one unlocked view open). Also, we can always open the original here if our patcher is loaded as an abstraction.
3. Open the object **Explorer**, which is also accessible via the shortcut key *P*.
4. The shortcuts menu: You can also access this via the shortcut key *X*. As stated before, we can modify these.
5. The presentation mode: You can also switch between the presentation mode and the edit mode via *command/Ctrl + Alt + E*.
6. Open the **Inspector**, which is also accessible via *command/Ctrl + I*.
7. Enable debugging. There is a section about debugging in this book.
8. Show/hide the grid.
9. Open the mixer panel. Here, we can mute the patchers' DSP, see the patchers' audio CPU usage, and so on.
10. Show/hide the status bar.
11. Open/close the side bar.

The following are Max window-specific:

1. Clear the Max window.
2. If you clicked on one of the column headings to order the printout by the Max object or message, here you can revert to ordering by time.
    - If you selected a line in the Max window, this will open the **Inspector** of the corresponding object
    - If you selected a line in the Max window, this will highlight the corresponding object
3. The status bar.
4. Change the view of the side bar to **Explorer**, **Inspector**, **Reference**, or the **Max** window.

Summary

By now, we shouldn't feel lost in the world of Max. We learned how to get help, we saw how basic patching works, and got to know the building blocks, the Max object, the message box, and some GUI elements. In the next chapter, we will start off by building patches that have more relation to praxis, and we will explore Max in depth by the use of patches that actually might be useful and are not only of theoretical interest.

3
Advanced Programming Techniques in Max

We've now got the basics out of the way. In fact, for anything that you see in the forthcoming chapters that you don't understand, you should have a couple of ideas in mind on how to get information. Therefore, we'll increase the tempo here a bit. We'll start off with getting into initialization more because it can be a frustrating thing if you aren't aware of some methods. After that, we'll cover message ordering, bpatchers, subpatchers, lists, and more. All of this will be shown using a practical example: a simple synthesizer. If you aren't interested in synthesis at all and if you are more the Musique concrete guy, to use this really old differentiation, you will learn even more if you just implement a sampler, for example, using the shown techniques!

We will be covering the following topics in this chapter:

- Initializing a patcher
- Microscopic timing and message ordering
- Sending, receiving, and collecting data
- Structuring the patchers
- Timing in Max and prioritizing events

Introducing the synthesizer example

As mentioned before, we'll start with a simple synthesizer. It's a subtractive one with two oscillators, [saw~] and [rect~]; a lowpass filter, [lores~]; and a standard ADSR, [adsr~]. In this chapter, we won't talk much about the actual synthesis or sound processing. We are going to use the synth to motivate us a bit to learn everything else that's needed around the synth and in many other occasions. While learning these methods, we are going to improve the synth in many ways, and as I said already, it doesn't really matter if it's a synth, a sampler or something else. In fact, I encourage you to build something else and apply the techniques discussed in the upcoming sections to it, rather than working with this synth. One last thing before we dive into it; don't expect this first little synth to sound unbelievably great. Again, we'll come to more sophisticated sound-processing topics in the next chapter.

So let's have a look at where we are going to start off:

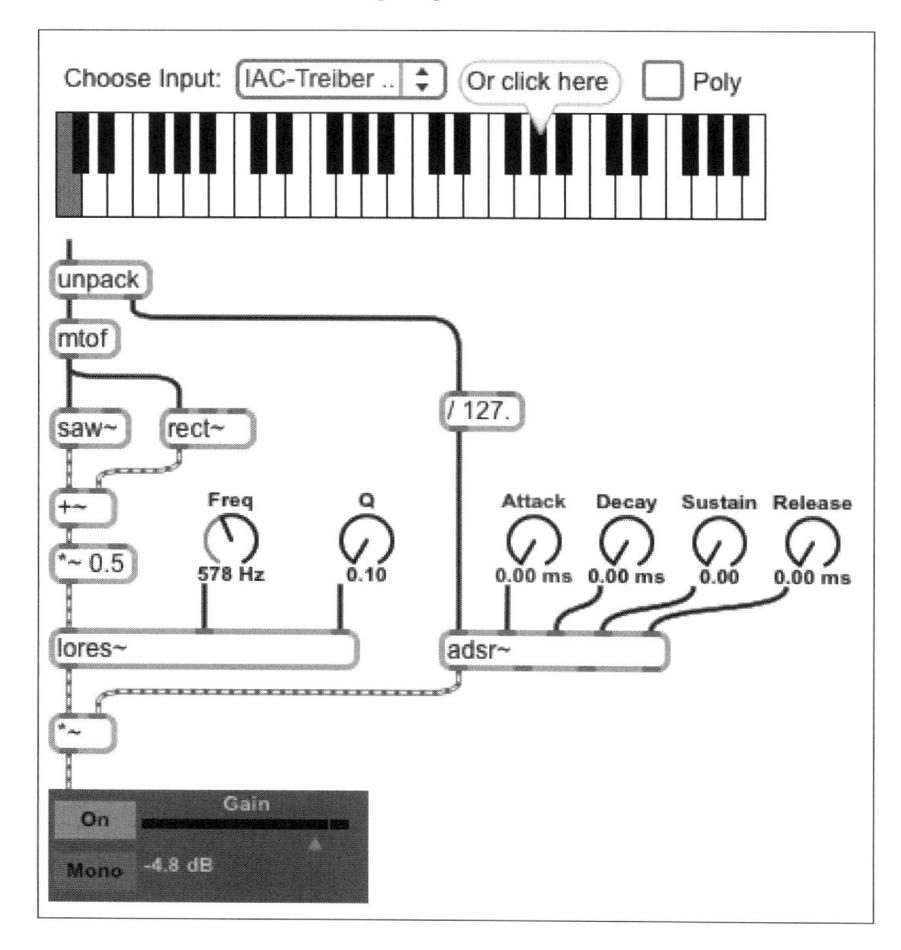

So, there are a lot of things we can talk about here. Basically, we have a MIDI input at the top and an audio output at the bottom, and more or less everything in between is our synth. If you open the patch `firstSynth_v001`, you might not quite see what is shown here. In fact, you won't even be able to get a sound when clicking on the keyboard. Why? Think about it for a moment. First of all, audio might be switched off. Secondly, the cutoff of the lowpass filter is turned down completely, so only very low frequencies will be able to pass. However, I saved it the way it is shown here, not with all `[live.dial]` objects at zero position. Why isn't that saved too?

Initializing values correctly and saving presets are two slightly different things; you can see that if we decide to manage values via presets and so on. We can also initialize them by recalling a preset. However, there are often many values that don't need to be controlled by presets or other storage management techniques but that need to be initialized. Let's first care for initialization, so when we fire up our patcher, we at least get some sound.

Initializing a patcher

Initializing means to set up parameters of our patch at startup. There are a couple of ways to initialize values. Look at the following screenshot that depicts the `initialization.maxpat` patcher:

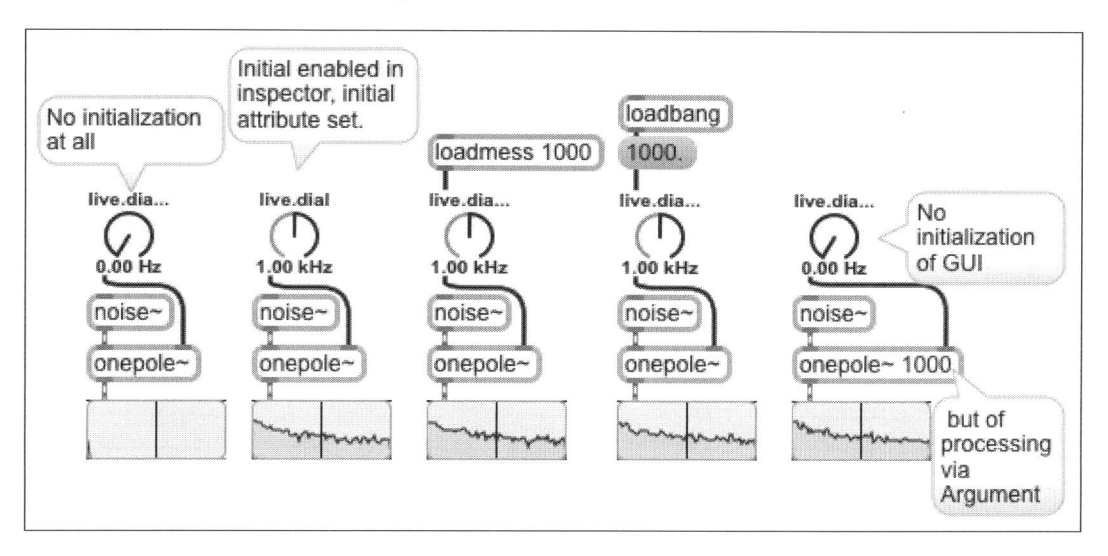

In the patch, you can see 5 differently initialized versions of the same. The **[noise]** patch is a white noise generator, and **[onepole]** is another lowpass filter (from left to right) and can be explained as follows:

- No or rather default initialization (not recommended)
- Initialization using initial attributes (through the inspector)
- The [loadmess] object that fires out its argument when the patch is opened
- The [loadbang] object that fires a bang when the patch's open end is connected to a messagebox object, which in turn contains our initial value
- Initialization of the processing part using an argument but no/default initialization of the GUI object

The last one is particularly interesting; it can actually be considered as a bug (a bug we built, not Cycling'74). It has been taken up in this list to re-emphasize the idea of initializing objects via arguments. In this case, we produced a conflict between the GUI and the processing; the GUI shows us that the filter has a cutoff of 0 Hz, but it actually has a cutoff of 1,000 Hz. As soon as we move the corresponding [live.dial] object once, everything is synced again. So if it has this disadvantage, why do we do something like this? We will revisit this idea in the *Structuring our patches* section. Essentially, it's about bidirectional communication. For now, stick to one of the other three methods, which only have minor differences from each other. Think about what's missing from the previous method and what the advantages might be.

> **Exercise**
> With the new initialization techniques at hand, try to fix our synth! To turn on audio at startup, look up the [adstatus] object or you can just send the integer 1 into [dac~]. The target is to open our patch, hit a key, and want reasonable sound right away.

Here is another neat little trick about initialization; sometimes, we need some object (especially interface objects) to be set but don't want it to output its value. For this purpose, we have the set message. Many objects behave similarly in reception of this message, as follows:

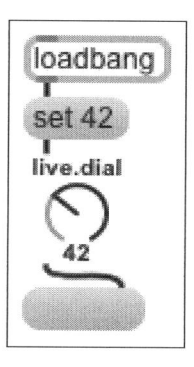

A word of caution about initialization; it can often be a source of errors. Wrong or a missing initialization can cause our patches to malfunction or even to crash on startup. To suppress the firing of all our [loadbang] and [loadmess] patchers, press and hold *command/Ctrl + shift* while opening it. Try this with the `debugging_initialization.maxpat` patcher. After that, press the button in the upper-left hand corner to fire all of them with just one click. This little trick allows us to test our startup easily. You can see the patcher in the following screenshot, and at its bottom, a more sophisticated initialization technique. If we need to order lots of processes in time on a macro level, we should consider implementing something like the startup sequence with the addition of an abstraction.

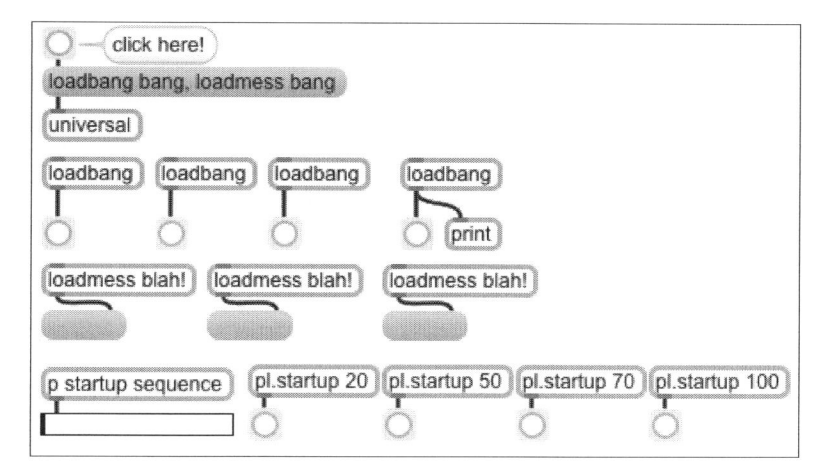

Take the bottom part of this patcher with a grain of salt. Mostly, if things have to be ordered in time, such as loading a sample and then querying its length, they shouldn't be done this way. The [buffer~] object in which we can load samples, for example, sends out a bang on its right outlet if it has finished with reading the file. So, even processes that take an indefinite amount of time should be ordered by logic and not by time. Doing things such as this startup sequence seems professional and can help if you take care of what you are doing. It's great if we load a lot of things dynamically, but we should try to stay away from these things, especially for smaller patchers. The [trigger] object is our best friend when we have to put things in order. If we want something to happen after something else in terms of initialization, simply putting in a delay is unreliable and a bad idea. In seldom cases, we are forced to make use of [defer] / [deferlow] to move things to the low priority queue if we want a process to wait for things. Refer to the *Event priority* section for more information on the event queue and the scheduler.

Excursus of microscopic timing and message ordering

We have just mentioned the timing on a macroscopic level; let's quickly introduce one of the most important things we'll learn about Max: microscopic timing, as I call it, or message ordering. Consider this situation: we'd like to use a MIDI [notein] object to trigger a custom sequence or function. So, we know that we need to construct something that takes pitch and velocity and produces a bang (always a good design strategy; think what's coming in and out, and then what needs to be in there). Simple enough. However, [notein] also sends note-off messages (a velocity of zero), so we need to filter those out. On an incoming velocity, we first need to test it (is it zero?) and then decide whether to pass it or not. That's what you can see in the following patcher; it's the contents of the ourStripnote subpatcher contained in the Micro_Timing_and_Message_Order.maxpat patcher:

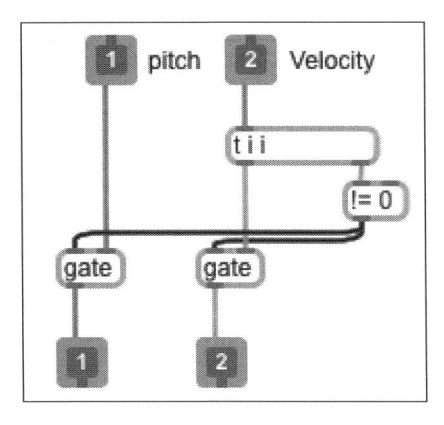

The first *do this then do that* process is expressed by [t i i]. It's an abbreviation for [trigger i i], and [trigger] is an object that lets us manage timing. It takes its input and sends it out as the given data type (**i** stands for integer) as many times as the argument is provided, in this case twice, and it sends everything in the right-to-left order, because Max is evaluating things in a right-to-left, depth-first order. So what happens here is that velocity comes in first (since [notein], as all the objects, sends out its right outlets first), then it's tested for unequality to zero, [!= 0], the result being either one or zero, which is sent to the gates and causes them to pass (or not) what's coming in their right inlets. Then, the velocity is sent to the right [gate] object and out (or not), and then the pitch comes through (or not). What if we don't care about this? Max needs to order things at least somehow if we don't state the order of things explicitly, so it does it in the right-to-left order, as shown in the following screenshot:

Object	Message
one	bang
two	bang

That's not what we want. We don't want to cause our patches to function differently if we were to move stuff around, say, for example, just to tidy up a bit. Study the mentioned patcher and the help-patcher of [trigger] carefully; there is a reason why there is an abbreviation, [t], for it; we'll need it all the time.

> **Exercise**
>
> Take another example of ordering; we want to detect the change of a running float. For example, we have somehow tracked 3D or 2D data of a person moving, and we just want to use the "how much is she or he moving" data to control the amplitude of a track or something similar. Essentially, we want to take the derivative of the data. Therefore, we'd like to always subtract the last value received from the one at the input of our imagined derivative patch and output the result. Sounds simple, right? Beware; the simple things are the most important and hard ones. Give it a try though! There are multiple solutions but here is a possible hint: you'll need these objects: [- 0.], [f], and [trigger f b], or just the [- 0.] and [t f f] objects.

The answer is also in the `Micro_Timing_and_Message_Order.maxpat` patcher. Have you been able to make it? If yes, congratulations, you have constructed a simple high-pass filter and you are far ahead in the MSP/gen~ section of the book!

But wait a moment; so all this is right to left? How unintuitive can this be for a person used to left-to-right writing systems? What's the logic here? The logic simply is that if we want the leftmost inlet to be the most important and hot one (following a left-to-right idea), the global right-to-left idea rises as a consequence. Therefore, we typically (take `[f]` or `[*]` as an example) first store a value at the right inlet and then trigger the output at the left inlet.

A bpatcher for MIDI input

Since we have fixed our initialization problems, let's look at the MIDI/GUI keyboard or what we could call the nput stage of our synthesizer patcher. For our convenience, both MIDI input and the `[kslider]` object (so the keyboard) have been packed into an object called a `bpatcher`. Bpatchers can load patchers that are saved in the search path, or they can be edited in place. To get familiar with them, create a new patcher, make a new object, and type in bpatcher. An empty square will appear. Now, we have two options. We can go to its inspector (*command/Ctrl + I*) and enable **embed patcher in parent**. Then, we can right-click on the bpatcher itself and choose **Object → New view of <none>**. Now, we can edit the contents of the patcher. The second and more common way is to leave the embed patcher in the parent unchecked and provide a patcher file in the `bpatchers` patcher attribute in its inspector. In this case, the `bpatcher` object is not embedded; let's open it and look inside by right-clicking on it and choosing **Object | new view of pl.keys.bp**, or if you'd like to edit it, choose **Open original**. If you open it, we first meet **Presentation Mode**. We can toggle **Presentation Mode** on and off using *command/Ctrl + E*. Obviously, presentation mode is made to hide our program and present a beautiful, reduced GUI. Objects can be added to presentation mode using their context menu or by selecting them and hitting *command/Ctrl + shift + P*.

> In the patcher inspector (*command/Ctrl + shift + I*), we can enable **open in presentation mode**.

So let's look at how data is coming into our synth in this case:

Chapter 3

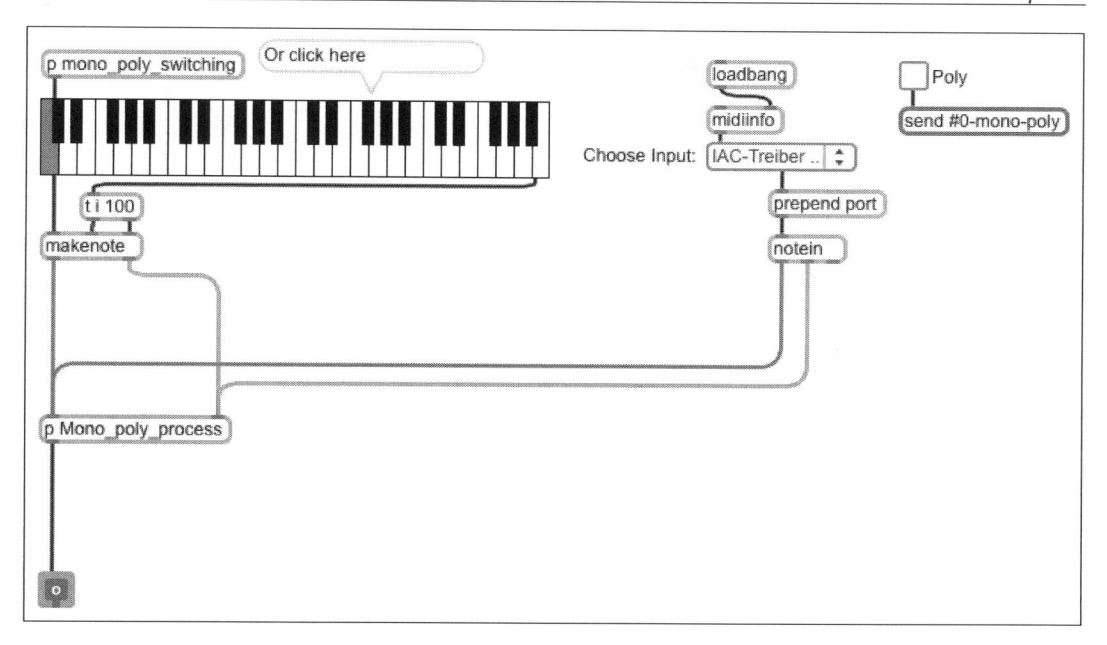

Again, we won't go over every object here in detail as you can easily find out everything about each of them. Two strange objects are here though: [p mono_poly_switching] and [p Mono_poly_process]. These aren't objects; they are what's called a subpatcher. If you double-click on them when in locked mode, you can see their contents. Subpatchers are simply encapsulated parts of a patch and we can create them by making a new object and pressing *P* or typing patcher. Optionally (highly recommended), we can give them a name as an argument. Another often used way to create these is to select a finished portion of a patch and go to **Edit | Encapsulate** or press *command/Ctrl + shift + E*. This even creates the inlets and outlets of the patcher automatically and connects them, if the selected portion is connected to things we didn't select.

As you can see, [notein] is sending two things out to one of the subpatchers. First of all, notice that the patchcords are colored; this greatly improves readability and can be done via the **context** menu of a patchcord. To select multiple patchcords, press *Alt* + box or simply press *shift* and select each of them.

> Readability is key. If you pay attention to it, you will find yourself reading and maintaining a lot more time than writing code. So keep it tidy to have an easier life! Producing chaotic code is very common when experimenting and can be very inspiring and fast. Cleaning it up afterwards makes our experiments usable in the future though.

[63]

Advanced Programming Techniques in Max

So what are those two things coming out of [notein]? They are pitch and velocity, both of which range from 0 to 127. Before we think about how these got combined (there's just one cord coming out of the bpatcher object, and we'll learn about this in the *Collections of data* section in this chapter), let's think about data coming into Max in general.

Sending and receiving data

We got a whole range of objects for this purpose, and [notein] is just one of them. In the following screenshot, you can see the most common objects in that regard:

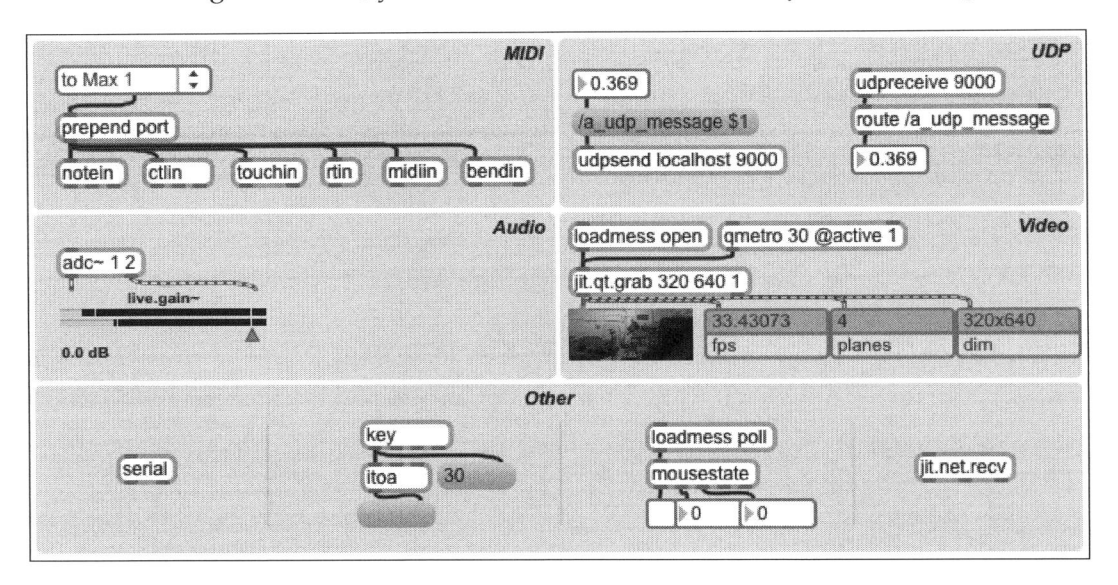

In the preceding patcher, getting_data_into_max.maxpat is presenting us with some possibilities if we want to communicate with our patchers. Very often, we will need MIDI, but the use of **Open Sound Control** (**OSC**) is increasing for good reasons; it has the potential to be faster, has a higher resolution (no limit of 7-bit messages, that is 0 to 127), and we don't need to remember that we sent the filter cutoff on CC 84 on channel 13 because the message simply might be /synth1/filter/cutoff 1000. For OSC communication over the network or locally between applications, we use [udpsend]. We'll use it later a lot also to communicate between Max and TouchDesigner. The [serial] object is used to do serial communication obviously. While **USB** stands for **Universal Serial Bus**, standard USB devices won't work unless there is a USB to serial adapter in between. Later, we will use this object when Arduino comes into play, for example (most versions of Arduino have a built-in adapter).

Sometimes, we also want to communicate from one patcher to another, although these are totally independent (they are not subpatchers in the same top-level patcher or the like, but they are both top-level patchers). Open the `open_two_independent_patchers.maxpat` patch.

> This `open_two_independent_patchers.maxpat` patch will appear only for a split second, open the two patcher files, and then close itself. Some pretty advanced techniques are used in there, but go on and inspect it! However, if you want to take a look, you'll have to suppress the [loadbang] object in there and close it. Remember how?

What we see are two patches (depicted in the following screenshot) that are independent; they could be just two .maxpat files lying around anywhere on our filesystem. However, the objects used in these are connecting them ([udpsend] and [udpreceive] could also have been used in addition).

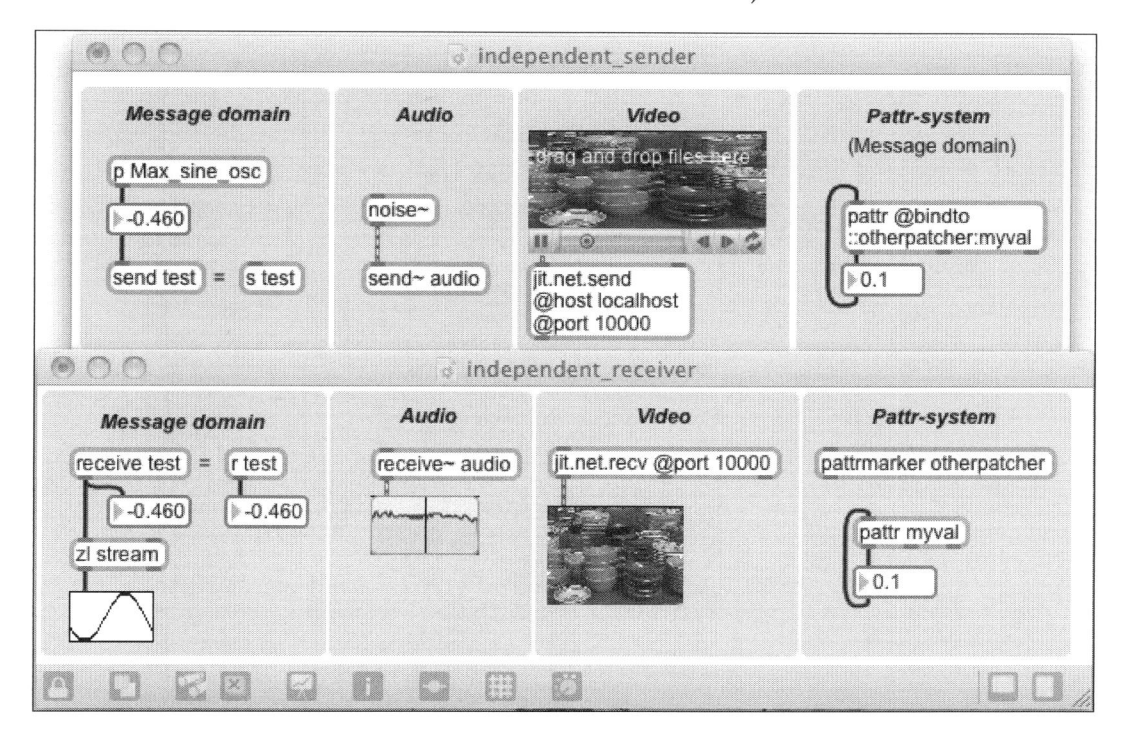

Remember the `[send]` object we saw in the patcher shown in the preceding screenshot? It also appeared in the heart of our MIDI bpatcher. There, it was used to send a value from one central place, a GUI object, to many places (in this case, just two, both within subpatchers). This is a common technique used to avoid what's called spaghetti code. I guess you can imagine what's meant by that. To improve readability of cordless connections, it's common to color both the send and receive signals with the same. Also, by double-clicking on either send or receive, you can find other occurrences of the same send/receive context.

The #n notation

The `send` and `receive` objects within the MIDI bpatcher had a strange arguments: `#0-mono-poly`. The # notation allows us to do some very neat things: `#1` to `#9` accesses the first nine arguments given to the patcher if loaded as an abstraction, and `#0` provides us with a unique random number if the patcher is loaded as an abstraction. Open the `Pound-Sign-Examples.maxpat` patcher. It doesn't do a lot but simply loads the `pound-sign-examples_abstr.maxpat` abstraction. You can see both of them in the following screenshot. However, if you double-click on the abstraction to view its interior, you shouldn't see the same thing until you unlock the patcher. This is because until you unlock the patch, it is loaded as an abstraction and therefore all the # numbers are replaced.

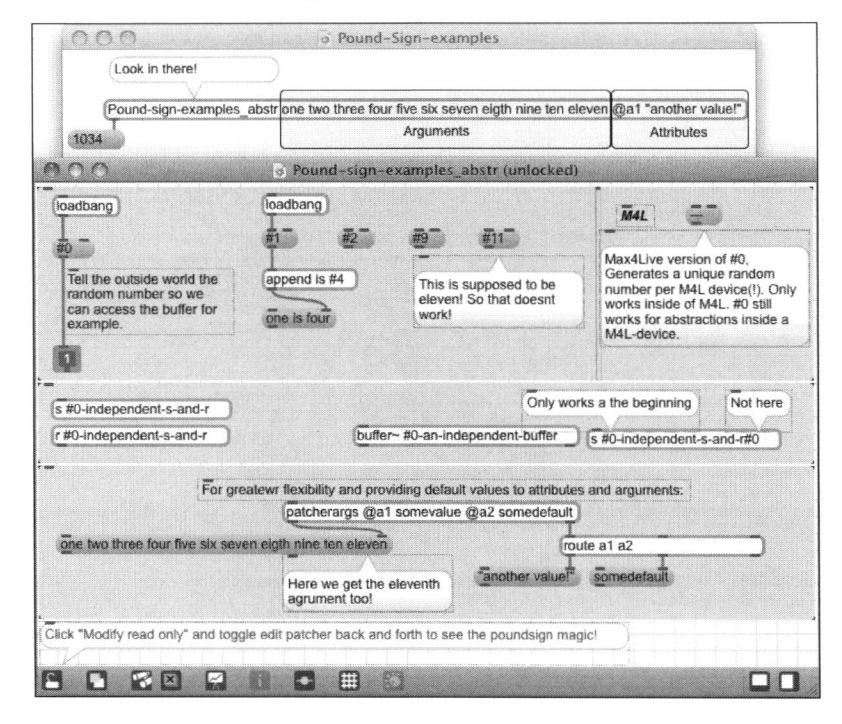

[66]

So, that's pretty handy right? However, what do we need random numbers for? We often build abstractions with the aim of loading multiple instances of them. So, if we naively used [send] and [receive] without this notation, we would create interferences between multiple instances; each send object of each instance will be sending to each occurrence of the corresponding receive object. Often, we want send and receive to only communicate within a single loaded instance.

Collections of data

Now, let's find out how our initial two patchcords (pitch and velocity) in the MIDI part of our synth became one. Of course, they were packed into a list by an object that's conveniently called [pack]. Lists are great. However, there are not only lists that consist of two integers; for example, there is the [coll] object that manages larger amounts of data, but also dictionaries in Max 6. Look at the list_examples.maxpat patchers, which are also depicted in the following screenshot, to get into lists a bit, and datatypes.maxpat (which is not depicted here) to get a feeling of datatypes and the conversion between them:

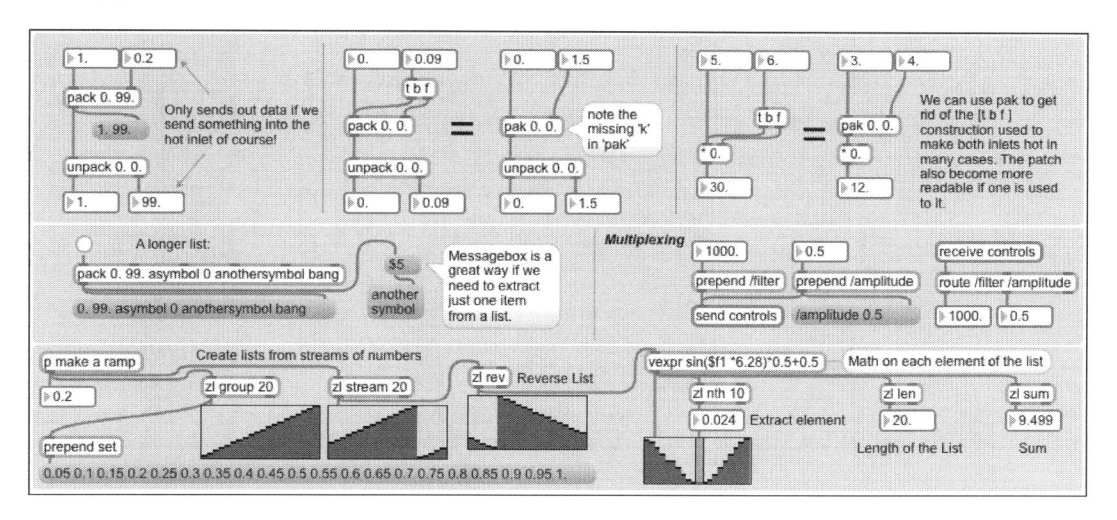

Advanced Programming Techniques in Max

We will meet lists often and get more and more familiar with them. The key objects are [pack]/[unpack], [pak], [join]/[unjoin], [vexpr], [zl], [append]/[prepend], [route], [table], [itable], [coll], and the [dict] family. To look at a more concrete and usable example of some list-related techniques, let's look at the midi_abbr_configure.maxpat patcher:

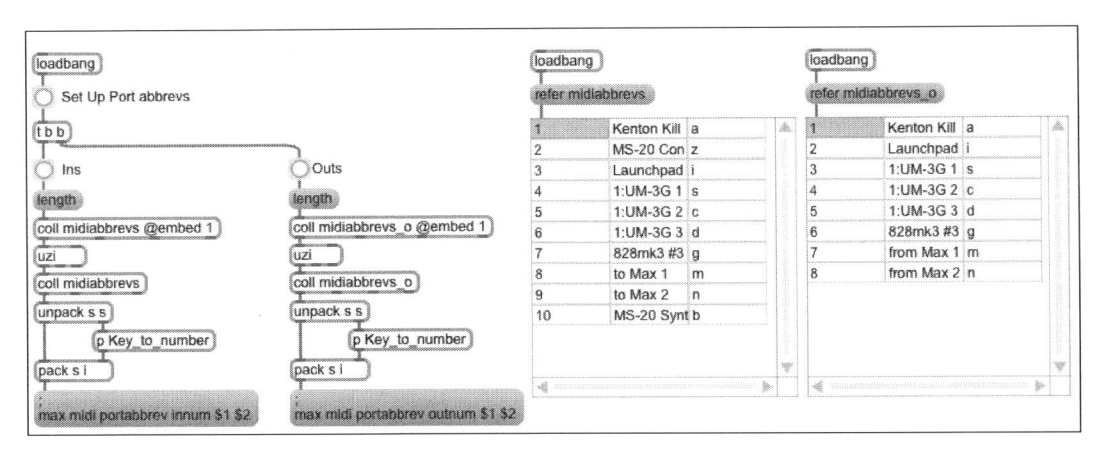

This patcher might turn out to be useful if you have a lot of MIDI devices and use abbreviations. Remember that I suggested that you use abbreviations but had to admit that Max tends to forget these? Max forgets these if we open it without the device connected, but we can remind it. We can simply write all of our abbreviations down once and can automatically restore them using this patch. Also, we can start this patch automatically before our actual performance patch, for example, just to make sure everything is configured nicely. If you look at the example with the independent top-level open_two_independent_patchers.maxpat patchers again, in combination with all the trickery we thought about audio settings, you might try to build a patch that first loads a patch that is just there to configure things properly, starts your main performance patch, and closes itself again. Let's go through this patch one by one now.

The patch consists of twice the same thing: once for MIDI inlets, and other for outlets. The core here really is the [coll] object. If you double-click on it, you can see the following code in there:

```
1, "Kenton Killamix Mini" a;
2, "MS-20 Control IN" z;
3, Launchpad i;
4, "1:UM-3G 1" s;
5, "1:UM-3G 2" c;
```

```
    6, "1:UM-3G 3" d;
    7, "828mk3 #3 MIDI Port" g;
    8, "to Max 1" m;
    9, "to Max 2" n;
    10, "MS-20 Synth IN" b;
```

It's simply a collection of port names and abbreviations I typed in there. Using the `[coll]` object's attribute `@embed 1`, the data gets saved with the patcher (we could also save it as a `.txt` file). So this essentially is the memory we added to Max. Now, we just have to get the data out and tell Max which port should have what abbreviation. We want to dump all the data. We first need to know how many items are in the list, since `coll` accepts integers to query data, and we don't want to produce errors because of querying items that don't exist. There is just one problem; `[coll]` sends out the number of items in the same outlet as the actual data. This seems to make things complicated, so we are using the fact that the named `[coll]` object contains the same data; they are instances of the same data. In the following screenshot, you can see an illustration of the concept of instancing data. We can store data in one `[coll]` object named `foo` to retrieve it from another one with the same name.

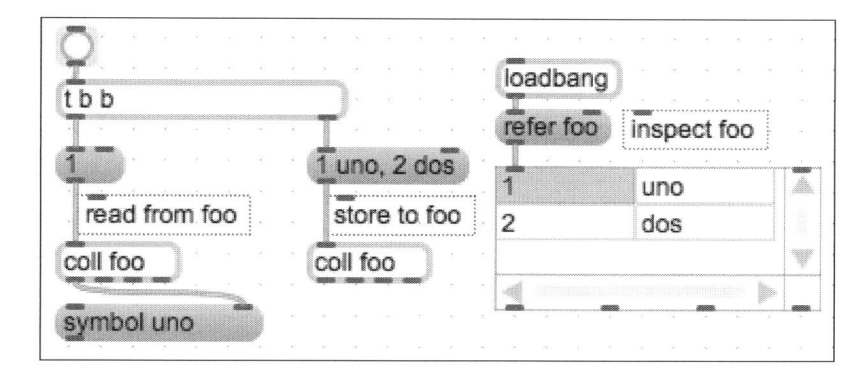

Therefore, the procedure is clear; we use one instance to query the number of lines contained in `[coll]`. We send this info to a `[uzi]` object, which in this case is used to just count to that number as fast as Max can. This count is sent to our data, querying each line and unpacking the list that is found on each line, for example, to Max 1 m is the data found in line 8. That's a list of two symbols.

[Every entry can be a list right? Therefore, `coll` can absolutely be used to store two-dimensional data, for example.]

We need to unpack the list because Max will want us to send the letter to be used as an abbreviation in the form of an integer. So **m** would, for example, need to be converted to 13. Then, we pack those things together again (the symbol and our new abbreviation integer) and send it to this weird message box that contains this:

```
;
max midi portabbrev innum $1 $2
```

This message box seems to be going nowhere.

More message box magic

What's happening is that, as we have seen already, the message box is a very special object. We can also use it to send things to the [receive] objects, or as in this instance, communicate with Max itself using the semicolon. Look at the `Message_box_morefeatures.maxpat` patcher depicted in the following screenshot:

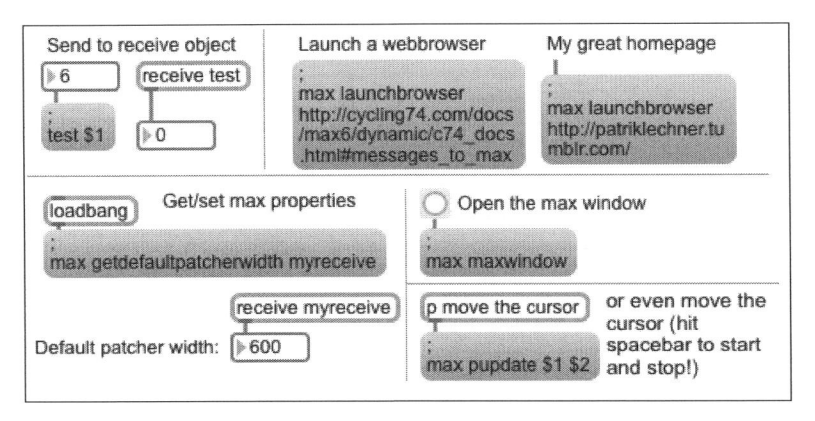

Here, some possibilities are shown that arise from the semicolon notation. For more information about what we can do by communicating with Max itself, visit http://cycling74.com/docs/max6/dynamic/c74_docs.html#messages_to_max, or simply click on the big message box on the top of the patcher; it opens your default browser, leading directly to that site.

Structuring our patches

We have now looked at a lot of techniques that will hopefully inspire you to improve our initial synthesizer patch, or your own instrument, sampler, and so on. If you haven't, I recommend that you do this. We'll now look at an upgraded version of the synth, and if you've tried it yourself already, you'll become more creative in solving Max problems.

Although the synth is a very small nice patch, we'll treat it as if it were a bigger one, and identify problems we had with the initial version, as follows:

- Initialization
- Poor overall structure, which was a bit spaghettish
- No modular, reusable parts
- No option to save and recall parameters
- No real GUI
- Besides pitch and velocity, there is no interfacing to controllers (sequencers in Max and external MIDI controllers)
- Scalability (easy to expand and duplicate without adding a great amount of chaos?)
- Debuggability

So I hope you have improved our initial patch along the way a bit already; now, let's look at the next version here, in which some of the problems have been attacked already. Open the `firstSynth_root_v002.maxpat` patch; again, it's depicted in the following screenshot too:

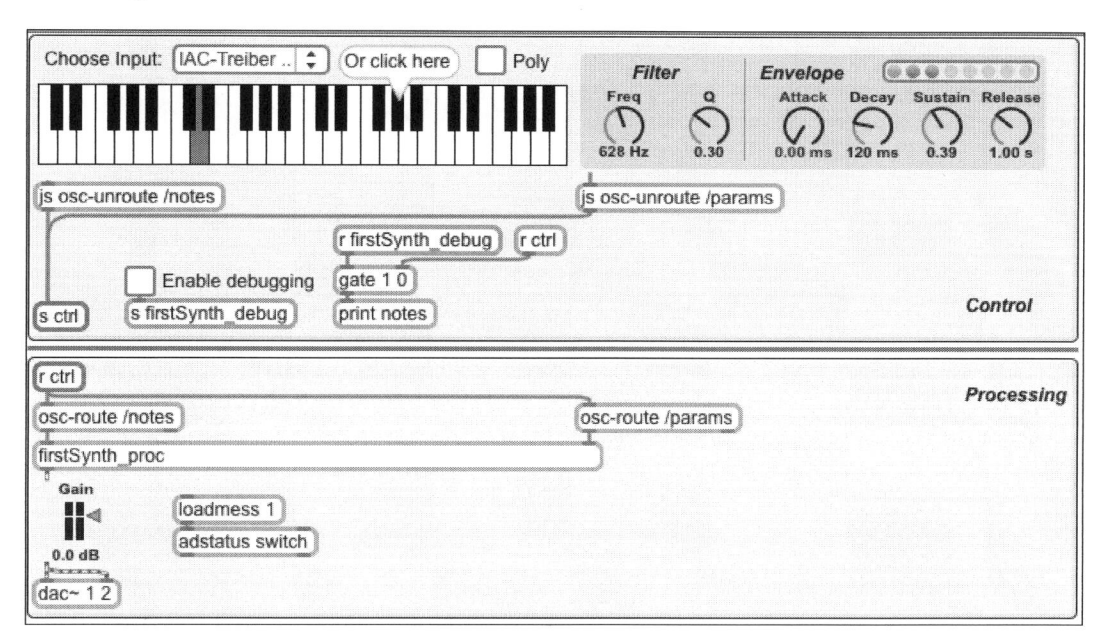

You have probably arrived at something similar already. Here, initialization has been taken care of via [loadmess] to switch audio on, always using arguments where needed, and all parameters (the dials) are given initial values via the initial attribute.

Also, the whole structure has changed. The actual synth has been packed into an abstraction called firstSynth_proc, depicted in the following screenshot:

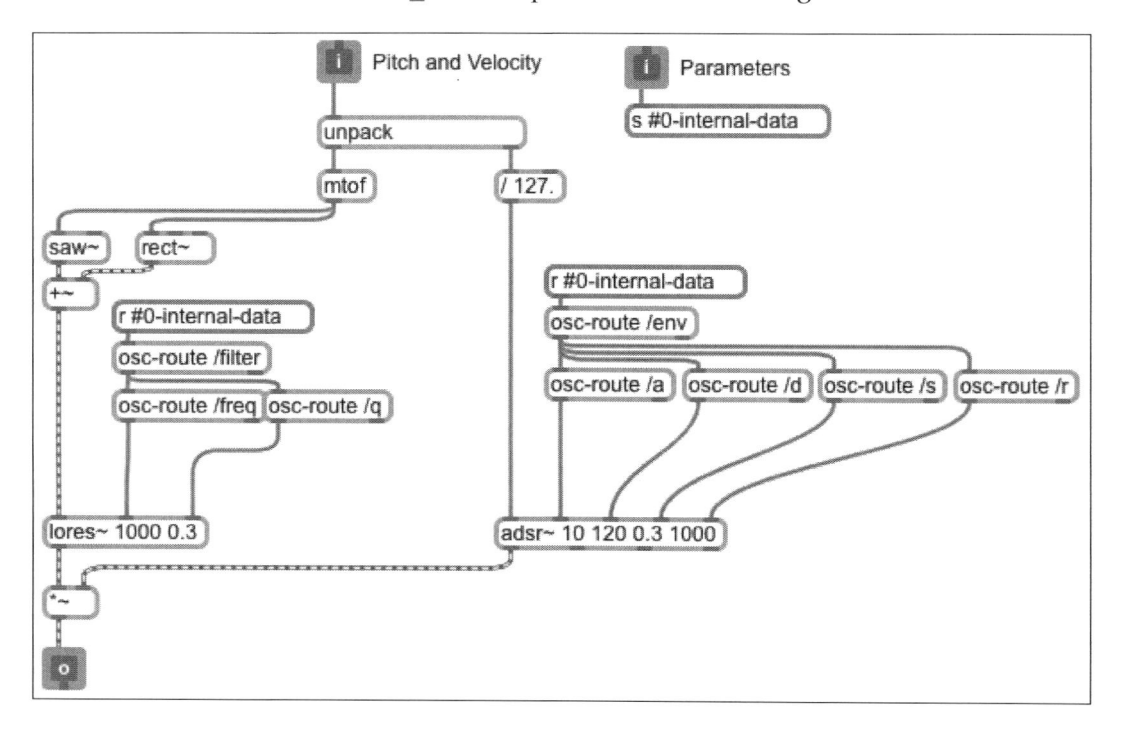

Also, the dials have been packed into an abstraction and loaded into a [bpatcher] object. This control patcher can be seen in the following screenshot and is called firstSynth_GUI.maxpat. Notice that all colors of the GUI are still at their default values. This makes it very easy to design a consistent GUI later using **object defaults**.

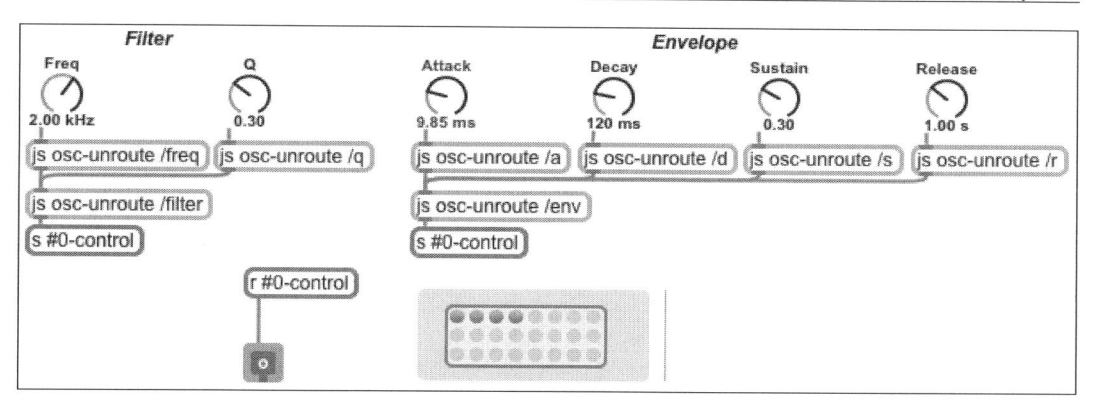

Three objects appear in these patches that haven't been introduced: [osc-route], [js], and the [preset] object (the GUI object at the bottom of the following screenshot). However, before talking about these, let's briefly think about why this has been structured this way. The structure of patches is a problem for which many strategies and opinions exist and which highly depends on the scale and idea underlying a patch. Structuring a project like this introduces a lot of objects that might seem unnecessary, and indeed, adding a huge amount of structuring to a small patcher is not a very good idea. It simply makes things more complicated than necessary. In programming, we try to write as little code as possible, as much as necessary. According to Ken Thompson:

> "One of my most productive days was throwing away 1000 lines of code."

This being said, we try to find structures for bigger-scale projects here. One of the most common principles is to at least divide a patch into processing and GUI. This is highly recommended and has been done in this case. Why? Because it makes both of them reusable and easily editable. At least three things have to be considered if we want to ensure reusability:

- **Information hiding**: This is the idea that the GUI is implementation agnostic. Our GUI in this case doesn't care if we are deciding to choose a different oscillator, filter, and so on. The important thing here is that we think about what parts are likely to change in the future. These need a communication interface to the controller (GUI) that is not likely to change.

- **A proper protocol**: The communication between the processing and the GUI should follow some standard. Sometimes, an ad hoc protocol will prepend each value with an identifier, retrieving the value using [route]. In this case, OSC has been chosen, using the [osc-route] CNMAT library external and the osc-unroute JavaScript also provided by CNMAT. The good thing is that we can simply throw away our GUI and hook up another application (that supports OSC) that controls our processing directly. Another possibility would be to completely stick to the MIDI standards, for example (which we actually partly do; we send in pitch and velocity into the MIDI range).

- **The interface**: In this case, we have chosen to give our processing part of the synth two inlets, one for the notes and another for the parameters. This is due to a variety of reasons but mainly it's due to the possibility of moving on to wrapping it into a [poly~] object, which does automatic voice allocation for us and provides other advantages as we will soon see. When working with [poly~], we'll find that it's very convenient this way. Nevertheless, as you can see, we implemented a central single communication line; the [s ctrl]-[r ctrl] send and receive pair. This makes it a lot easier to provide a different UI than if we, for example, had an inlet for each parameter in the processing patch. Also, I'm sure you have already noticed that the whole communication is sent to a print object if we choose so by checking the **enable debugging** toggle.

So now you know (if you haven't at least assumed already) what the osc objects are doing. What's [preset]? Tough question, hmm? It stores the parameters in our GUI patcher, providing us with presets (in this case, presets are stored with the GUI patcher(!) file). We can click on the little buttons to recall a preset and press *Shift* and click on it to save one. The [preset] object is nice for smaller projects but not as powerful as the [pattr] family.

The pattr family – a communication system

If you open the firstSynth_root_pattr.maxpat patch, you will hardly notice any difference. What happened is that the [preset] object is now merely a GUI object that controls a [pattrstorage] object. The [pattrstorage] object now stores our presets; if you double-click on it, you can see all the objects it is aware of, as follows:

	Name	Priority	Interp	Data
✓	GUI			
✓	Attack	0	linear	9.847684
✓	Decay	0	linear	120.
✓	Freq	0	linear	84.817253
✓	Q	0	linear	0.3
✓	Release	0	linear	1000.
✓	Sustain	0	linear	0.3

Client Objects [firstSynth]

The first line in this window, **GUI**, simply stands for our bpatcher object, which now has the scripting name, **GUI**. The [pattrstorage] object is aware of these objects, but is not aware of the menu in our bpatcher MIDI input, our [live.gain] object, and others. This is because we made it aware by modifying our initial GUI patcher. Although this new one looks nearly the same, two changes have been made; the preset object has been taken out of there and an [autopattr] object has been inserted. The [autopattr] object, by default, exposes all named objects (objects given a scripting name in their inspector) within its patcher level (not above or its subpatchers) to the pattr system. The pattrstorage object, for example, allows us to interpolate between presets, gives us more control on what values are saved, and more control in general compared to the [preset] object on its own.

Another difference in this version of our synth is that there is MIDI input that controls our attack parameter. We use [pattmarker] to make our root patch globally available for the pattr system in order to access the attack dial via a [pattr] object in the subpatcher called Midi_CC_to_Attack whose contents are depicted in the following screenshot:

```
ctlin a 25 1
scale 0 127 0 1000.
pattr @invisible 1 @bindto ::firstSynth::GUI::Attack
```

This simply sends the received value to the attack dial (after it has been brought to the appropriate range). Also, we don't want to save the value that this [pattr] object holds, since it is the same as the dial we already have on our client list of [pattrstorage]. That's why we set **@invisible 1**. However, do we really want to send our MIDI CCs to a GUI object and from there to the actual parameter? Well, we do want to save the values received or rather the parameters set by the incoming MIDI, but we don't want the values to run through a GUI object. It's not a big problem, but we'll find a different method soon, solving other problems as well.

Now, we have arrived at a point in which we can be quite happy with our structure, but what if we create an LFO that's supposed to modulate the filter and add a sequencer that produces notes? Both of these are controlled by either MIDI or the GUI, and they also control the processing or even each other. Where to put them, or how to think about such a structure?

Well, there is no definite answer. However, there are interesting systems, such as the **Model-View-Controller** (**MVC**) system. This helps us both to think about how to develop a system and gives a suggestion on how to implement it. The [pattr] family can provide us with the global communication bus. Let's first consider a most basic example, the MVC.maxpat patcher, shown in the following screenshot:

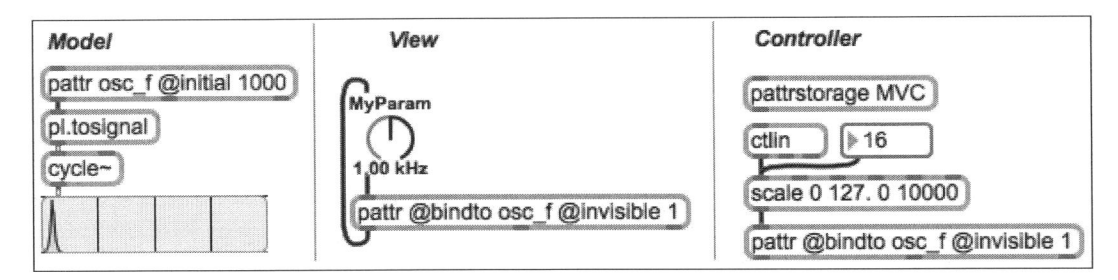

As you can see, we split up our patch in three parts instead of just two. The MVC system is a concept that is supposed to help us; there is nothing wrong with just connecting the MIDI input directly into the oscillator. However, we do have to rescale the value, and we most likely will want to save the state; we probably want to inspect its value on the screen and modify it there, but it should also react to MIDI/OSC or something similar. If we want all that, well there we are, this is a system that provides us with all that and a lot more due to the power of [pattr].

If we now add an LFO or other audio-rate modulation sources, an indicator on the dial that shows us the actual value of the parameter (the dials adjustment plus the modulation), a modulation matrix, and preset interpolation, we might end up with something like the matrix_pattr_1.maxpat patcher. Beware that, the indication of the actual value might not be that important and makes the whole construction more complicated and CPU intense (although, there is room for optimization, for example, to convert the signal to a Max domain message, which is increasing the [snapshot] object's attribute). In the following screenshot, one part of the patcher and one possible implementation of the system are shown. Both LFOs in that patcher are essentially constructed the same way as the depicted oscillator, but as much as possible has been packed into two abstractions: mod_helper and mod_param.

[76]

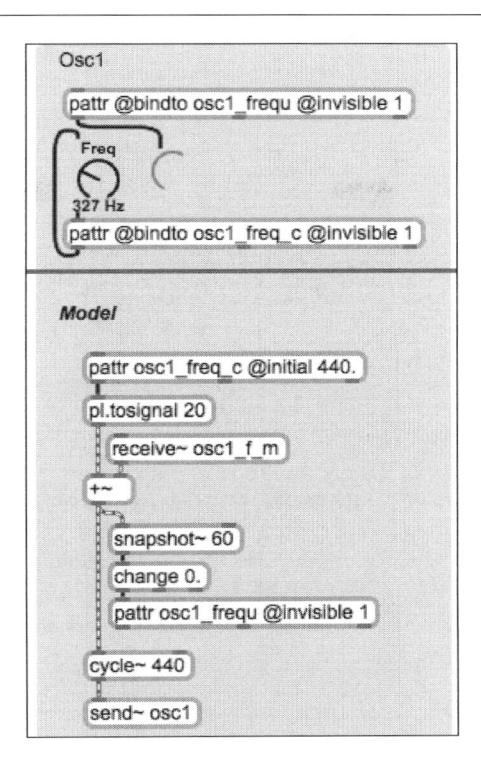

The top part of the preceding screenshot shows the **view** part of the patch; the bottom part is corresponding to the **model** part. As you can see, the small orange indicator shows a different (the actual) value of the frequency the oscillator has. I recommend that you look at the patch itself; it's a bit too big to be depicted here in a useful way. Of course, the different parts of such MVC systems can be in different abstractions too.

> As an exercise, implement a MVC system using subpatches or abstractions. Make one patch for the view, one for the model, and one for the controller. Either take the `matrix_pattr_1` patch or use one of your own. Take care, as the paths have to be changed and you have to assign scripting names to the [patch] objects that contain your abstractions/subpatchers.

Before we conclude with this section, notice both the [matrix] object used to dispatch audio signals and the [matrixctrl] GUI object. The [matrixctrl] object is very versatile; if you create it, it will look quite different and work as only binary (On/Off instead of attenuating). Study its helpfile and try to set up a [matrixctrl] object like the one in the matrix_pattr_1 patch! The key is to provide a correct file in the **Cell Image File** attribute in its inspector to activate **dial mode** and configure the **cell range** attribute. To find the correct image file, look at the one used here and the [matrixctrl] object's helpfile. Also, consider using the freeware **knobman** to create your own, which can be found at http://www.g200kg.com/en/software/knobman.html.

So, we have now seen some strategies to structure our ideas beforehand and also for implementation. The size and complexity of a project very much determines what kind of sophistication is demanded in structure. So, again, there is nothing wrong with doing things more simply. However, as soon as things can be reusable (as soon as something works properly) or scalable and expandable, one should spend some time thinking about the structure. Also, the concepts presented here are just proposals. There are many ways to structure things and there are many ways to use the pattr system. You should visit http://mspcafe.g2312.de/tLb/framework/patchdesign/ for more information on MVC by Thomas Seelig, who also was an inspiration for this section.

Timing in Max

We have mentioned sequencers and LFOs already, so let's start giving our little synth more dynamic behavior. So far, we have only worked with milliseconds as units of time but there is more: metric timing, samples, and ticks (scheduler ticks, which is the smallest available unit of time in the Max domain). Look at the following screenshot in which our metro there has been given the argument **4n**, meaning quarter notes instead of a number in milliseconds. Also, we tell it to be quantized by the same amount, so it doesn't only have the interval of a quarter note but fires on the actual quarter notes of Max's internal global transport.

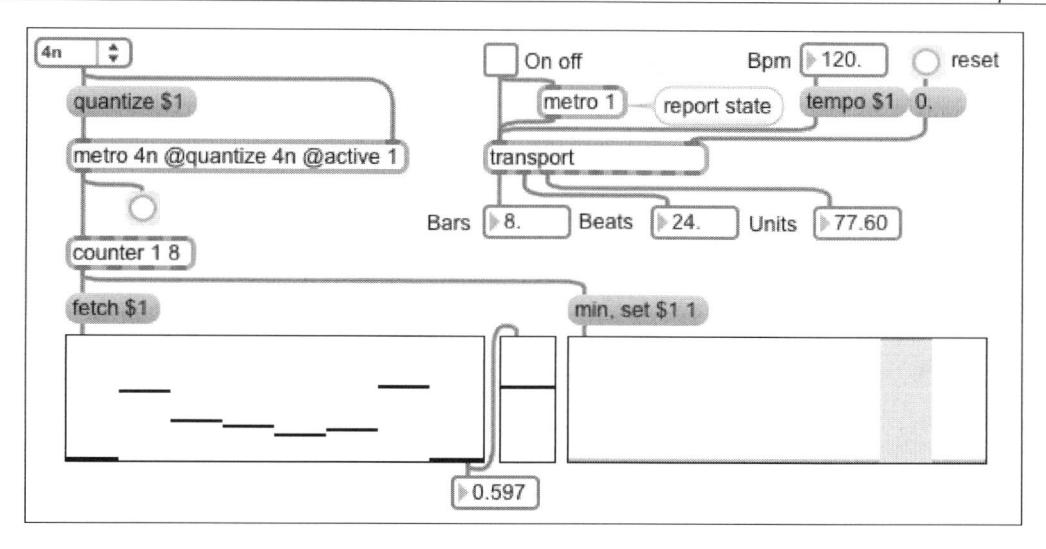

The state of global transport can be viewed by navigating to **Extras | Global transport** by double-clicking on the [transport] object or by querying a [transport] object, as shown in the following screenshot.

We can see a very basic 8-step sequencer, the seq1.maxpat patch. By layering the two [multislider] objects in presentation mode, we get a simple step indicator. If we refine this patch, we are good to go with sticking it into a bpatcher object and controlling a synth (although, I don't recommend having a sequencer's clock inside instead of keeping things more modular. However, for the sake of this tutorial, let's stick to that for now.). If you open the firstSyth_root_v003 patch, you'll see both notes and the cutoff being modulated, and hopefully at this point, you think "so that's what I'm doing this for", although the synth itself still sounds a little poor of course. We can get quite a lot of variety out of just three little basic sequencers. Note that our firstSynth_proc patch has also been modified. When we control MSP things out of the Max world, we need to smooth things a bit. This is what has been changed in there with a custom abstraction that contains a [line~] object. Why do we have to smooth things? Well, that's how audio behaves; sudden jumps are equal to high frequency content, so if we change a filter's cutoff frequency rapidly without interpolating, we are causing clicks.

Advanced Programming Techniques in Max

Now, timing in Max is quite straightforward, but how about syncing external stuff or syncing Max to external software such as a DAW? Refer to the following screenshot:

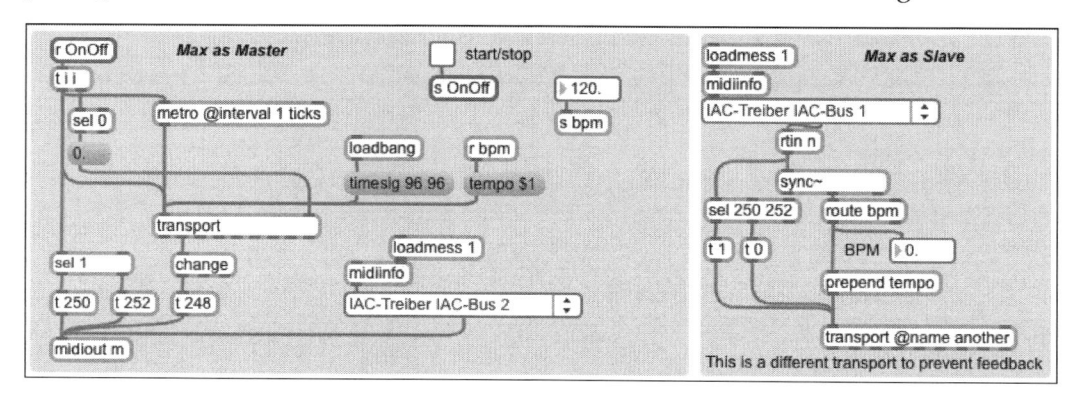

Here, we can see parts of the `clock-sync_in-out.maxpat` patcher. If you take a look at the patcher and wonder about the numbers 250, 252, and 248, refer to the Wikipedia page about the MIDI beat clock at `http://en.wikipedia.org/wiki/MIDI_beat_clock`.

These are just messages to say start, stop, and a clock tick. We can have many [transport] objects in Max, either all referring to the same transport state, or by giving them names, with which we can make them independent. Many objects can in turn be told to refer to a specific transport via the @transport attribute. There are quite a few new objects in this patch; study them carefully. Timing is an important topic and you will want to be comfortable with syncing things up. Also, when you try to sync external environments, or when working with timing in general, don't forget about the settings we discussed to get accurate timing in Max (overdrive, I/O vector size, in audio interrupt, but also the advanced scheduler settings).

> Now, look into [live.step] and try to set up a simple synth/sequencer patch that can be synced to an external clock!

Now, before finishing this part about sequencers and timing (there are many more timing-related objects we haven't talked about, such as [translate], [hostsync~] for rewire, and many more), let's look into a more generative approach to sequencers. Open the `adv_seq_1.maxpat` patch. You will be presented with a little synth and a couple of bpatchers objects. If you look into the sequencers, you will find that there is quite some list-processing happening. The idea behind the sequencer is to create an ever-changing sequence based on an adjustable one. Have a look at the sequencer in the following screenshot; we have one (green) sequence that we can adjust, but the gray one that lies behind is actually used. This gray sequence is always changing if adjusted that way, but tries to stick to the green one.

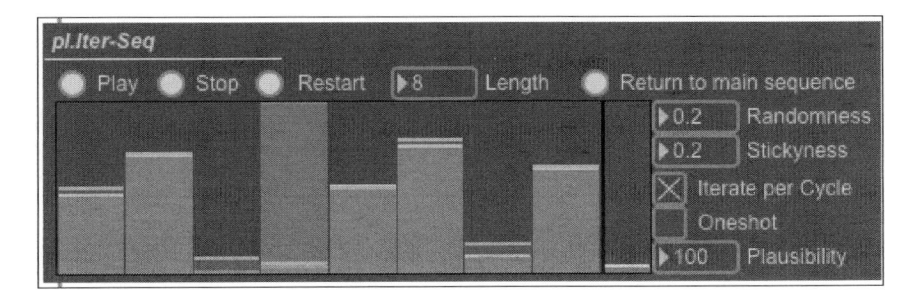

Sadly, there is not enough space here to explain the contents thoroughly, but this should motivate you to get into [uzi], [coll], and their list-processing friends. If you think "man, I'd like to create some crazy sequencers", maybe you should also think "I really have to learn some list-processing" because, well, a sequencer is something that queries entries of a possibly interesting list (or multidimensional data? Analog sequencers often output many values per step, for example, triggers, gates and multiple CVs) in a possibly interesting way. In this case, it's the sequence itself that could be described as interesting; the way it is queried is completely boring. You can probably think of a better way.

I'd like to give you an example of more interesting ways to query data. There are things such as Markov chains and other more sophisticated sequencing techniques that rely on variable data, or data that has more sophisticated features such as probabilities and so on. Look into the help-patch of the [anal] object for an example of a Markov chain. Here's an example:

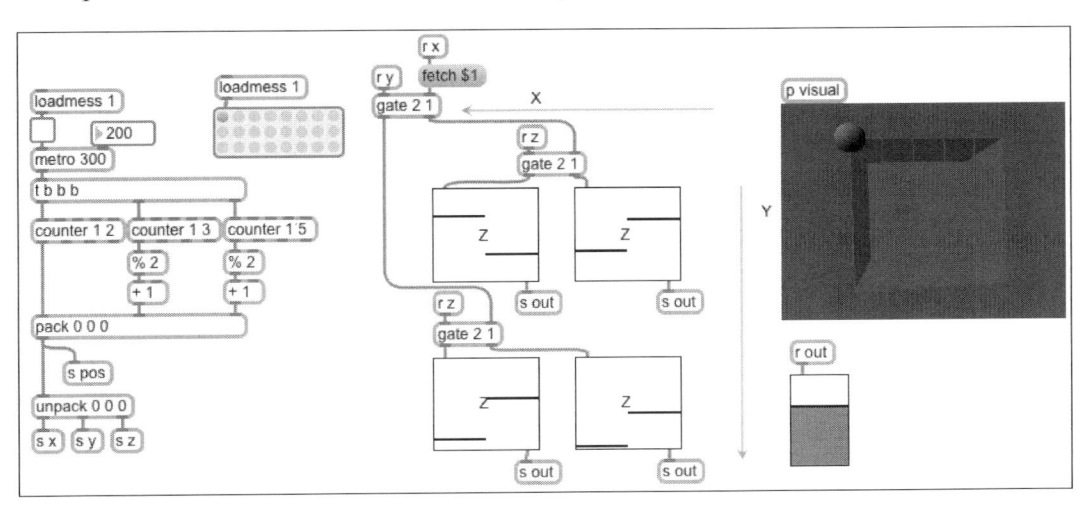

What you can see in the preceding screenshot is an attempt to think about multidimensional sequencers. Here, the sequencing is 3D; 2 to the power of 3 makes eight steps. This might not be the most usable sequencer on earth, but it probably inspires you to implement other ways of going through a couple of values also, instead of just thinking about creating interesting values.

The event priority

The event priority in Max is something one might not be aware of all the time, but having an idea about it helps a lot. To put it simply, there is a high priority thread (often called the scheduler) and a low priority thread (often called the queue) for Max messages if we turn on *Overdrive*. Otherwise, these are executed in one thread, with the same priority. Max just has two lists of things to do and does the things on both lists, but it can interrupt things being done on the low-priority list, to first finish the high-priority thread. What events are in which thread? Things such as GUI interaction get in the low-priority thread while MIDI input, for example, is in the high priority one. We can use the [deferlow] object to place an event at the end of the low-priority queue, or [defer], to put it at the top of the low-priority list. The [defer] object, therefore, might mess up the order of events since there most likely are things on the low-priority list to be done and we just jump ahead (but staying in low-priority) using [defer]. To put an event into high priority coming from low priority, we can use *(ab)use* [delay] or [pipe]. Only high-priority events contain timing information, so by adding a very small delay, we generate this information. Again, most of the time, we don't care a lot about these things, but if you are doing extremely intensive tasks very fast, the computer becomes slow and other processes get disturbed; this should ring a bell in your head. Maybe you just need to defer things. Look at the help-patcher of [defer] for a nice example with [uzi] that slows down your computer unnecessarily. For more in-depth information about the scheduler, visit http://cycling74.com/2004/09/09/event-priority-in-max-scheduler-vs-queue/.

Also, the help system provides some useful insights, which can be found at http://cycling74.com/docs/max6/dynamic/c74_docs.html#scheduler_preferences.

Debugging

Finally, let's now talk about how to fix problems. You probably arrived at this section early because you ran into problems along the way. Everything presented here is quite basic, quite boring, and very important.

Smart ways to debug

It has to be said here. Everybody produces chaos sometimes. Max is great as a rapid prototyping tool, but if we want to understand our patches in two weeks or even just after taking a break, we need to keep things tidy and add comments. I can present a completely chaotic patch here as compared to a nice and tidy one, but I think you know how they look. It has been stated already that we read a lot more code than we write, so to make things simple and tidy things up. I personally often do this when I'm stuck. I don't mean when I'm really stuck, but there are moments in which one is a bit distracted or moments in which one loses interest in a problem. These are good opportunities for you to take some time to tidy up slightly. If I'm really stuck, everything is tidy already, otherwise I'd see hope. In this case, there are some options left: go for a walk, ask somebody else, or delete everything and start from scratch. All these can lead to success in a surprisingly fast way most of the time. If you have nobody to ask, ask the forum or explain your problem to somebody you think is able to help you. Simply talking about a problem is often enough to start thinking in a different way about it.

The debugger

We already talked about the [print] object. This object and its counterparts in MSP, such as [meter~], [number~], or [jit.pwindow] and [jit.fpsgui] for Jitter are our most powerful tools in order to know what's happening. We have already mentioned that there are many ways to display features of audio and video signals. Also, don't forget to enable probing in the **debug** menu; this is really helpful. For Max processes, there is something else that might help us, especially when we deal with feedback and branching. The debugger is shown in the following screenshot:

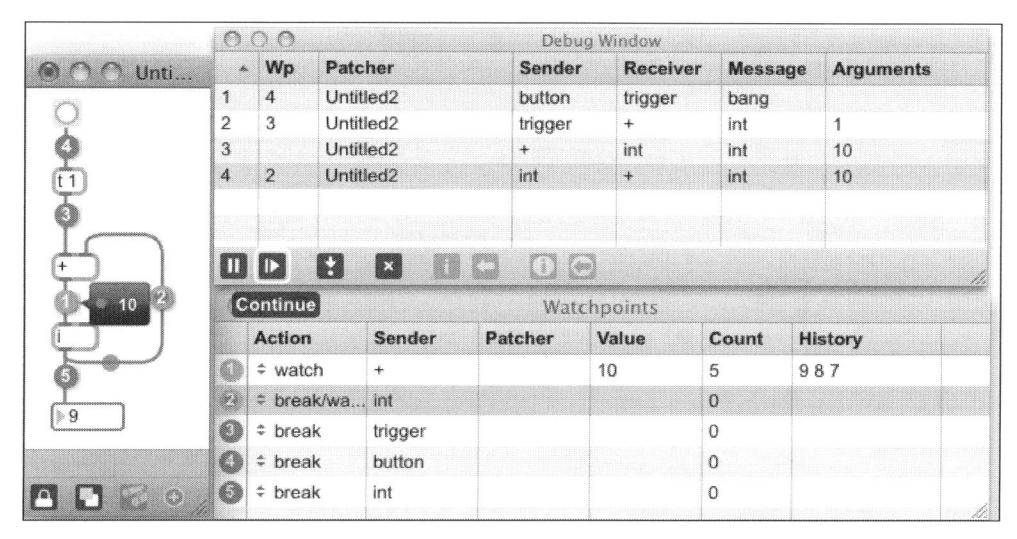

We can access the debugger by navigating to **Debug | enable debugging** and it also has a little icon in the toolbar, so we can switch it on there. To let the debugger do something, we need to add the so-called **Watchpoints**. We can do this by right-clicking on a patch cord and choose either **Add Watchpoint – Break** or **Add Watchpoint – Monitor**. All the little orange and red dots in the preceding screenshot are such Watchpoints. The red ones are break watchpoints, and the orange ones are of the watch type, as you can also see in the **Watchpoints** window. This window can be accessed by navigating to **Debug | Watchpoints**. So what does it do? The break watchpoints allow us to step through what's happening. They stop Max from executing further until we tell it to go on. Meanwhile, we can inspect values and see where the things are going and coming from. The debugger is also a great tool to understand what I call microscopic timing in the preceding screenshot. If you rebuild this little patch or a similar one, you will notice that the feedback connection going up into the cold inlet of the [+] operator is happening one step before it's going to the [number] object. The debugger is quite new to Max, and I have the impression that people who have used Max for a while have developed their bug-finding strategies already and don't use it a lot. Nevertheless, it is a very intuitive and helpful tool, so try it out!

Optimizing

Somebody once stated that optimizing is not about small details but about intelligent algorithms. While that might be true and one should sometimes question whether the whole idea behind a patch is efficient, there are most likely lots of small improvements one can make. In the Max domain, this often has something to do if things are done at the right point in time and not too often. If we need a certain number, we shouldn't be computing it all the time, but compute it once, store it, and query it as often as we like obviously. In computing, there generally is often the possibility to trade-off memory versus CPU. For example, the [cycle~] object is a wavetable. Cycling '74 decided to compute a good sine wave once and store it, and we can read it out as often as we like. Actually, computing the sine function is a very complicated CPU-intensive task. There is, however, a gen~ patch, gen~.computed_sine.maxpat, in the Max 6/examples/gen/ folder. Now, if we have no idea of which one is better performance-wise, how can we find out? This can be done by doing the things really often and comparing the results as objectively as possible, as shown in the following screenshot:

Chapter 3

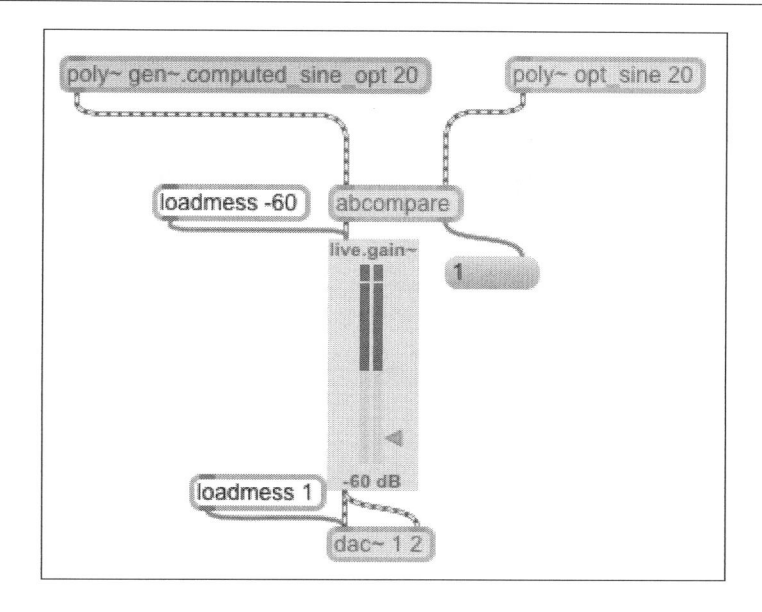

The preceding patcher, `optimization.maxpat`, shows an example from the audio realm. I've modified the original example patcher only slightly to fit inside a [poly~] object. The `poly` object, besides other great things, gives us the ability to seamlessly load any number (in this case, 20) of instances of a given patcher. So if there are any small performance differences, we just multiply them up until we see them. We can see them very clearly, nicely colored, by going to **View | Show CPU Usage**. Also, if we switch that off again, the Max window prints out the statistics. In this case, the left `poly` object consumed 81 percent of Max's total Audio CPU consumption and the right one 15 percent (to monitor non-audio CPU/memory consumption, we can use the top command in a terminal on Mac, or the task manager on Windows). Yeah, but a real sine sounds better, one might say. Often, one has ideas to do something really clever and then, when it's finished, one is definitely a bit biased towards thinking it is better. Even I, who knows he hasn't changed a thing about the DSP part during GUI design, sometimes have the impression that my stuff sounds better when I made a nice GUI, as stupid as it might be. In audio, a lot of these effects come into play all the time, so why not test it. I made the `Abcompare` abstraction exactly for this purpose and I use it all the time. It's simple; you attach a `numberbox` or `messagebox` object to see what inlet is passed through. Then, you close your eyes and hit the Space bar numerous times to switch back and forth between the inlets until you don't know anymore which input you are listening to. Then, compare, see if you like one of them better or if you can hear a difference at all, open your eyes, and see if you were right! This is just an example of trying to identify problems. One thing should be mentioned before we go to the next section: don't start to optimize too early, and if you do, try to be sure that it really helps what you are doing, so put test it out.

Scripting and the this patcher

Now, we'll come to a topic that really gives us wings. There are sometimes situations when we think "come on, doesn't this work in Max? It should!" and often, scripting is there to help us. For example, can you remember when we talked about attributes; I mentioned that some attributes can't be changed dynamically. Now, let's change them all!

Consider this situation: you build an oscillator and it doesn't have any MIDI in or the one in which you just want to give the user the possibility to determine the frequency in Hz or as a note. Simple enough. However, we don't want to have two dials and switch between them; we want one [live.dial], and we want to just switch units. Try to move the [live.dial] object's unit attribute into the patcher to create a message box; it won't work. Alright, this might have something to do with the automations in Ableton Live and Max4Live devices, but we won't use our filter mini app in Live anyway. So, let's try something different; we make one small patcher with just the live dial in one mode, and another with the dial in the other mode. Then, we make a bpatcher object and dynamically load one of the two patchers. But that won't work either; where do we send the message with the name attribute? So to give you the simplest solution for this problem, we can just include and remove these from the presentation mode. But all the other thoughts? Both of the other ideas are valid too. This is how it works; if an attribute is hidden, as shown in the following screenshot, we can still access its name by copying the attribute and pasting it into a text editor or a message box:

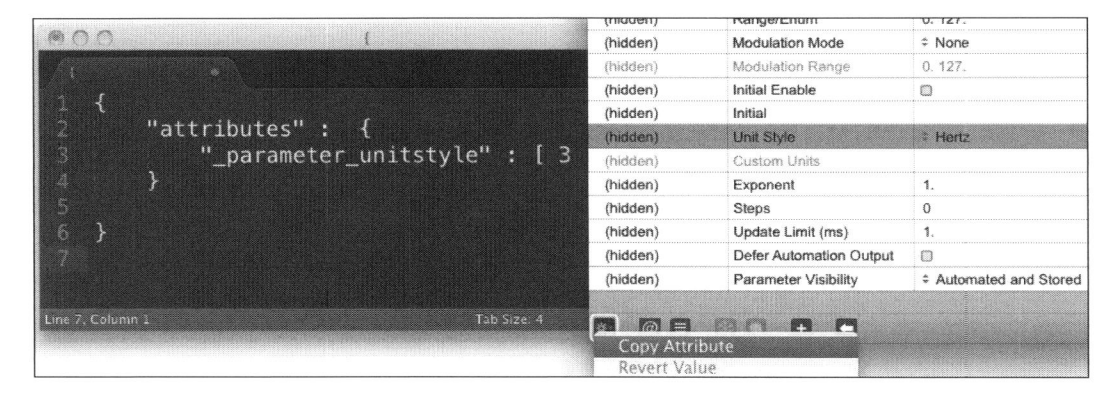

Therefore, we arrive here:

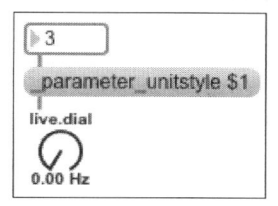

So what about `bpatcher`? Here, [thispatcher] comes to the rescue.
The [thispatcher] object can do a lot for us; it can tell us where the patcher in which it lies is located on the filesystem. It allows us to dynamically create objects, connect them, move them around, delete them, send messages to them, and much more. In this case, we are using it to send the `bpatcher` object itself a message, although our `bpatcher` object doesn't even have an inlet:

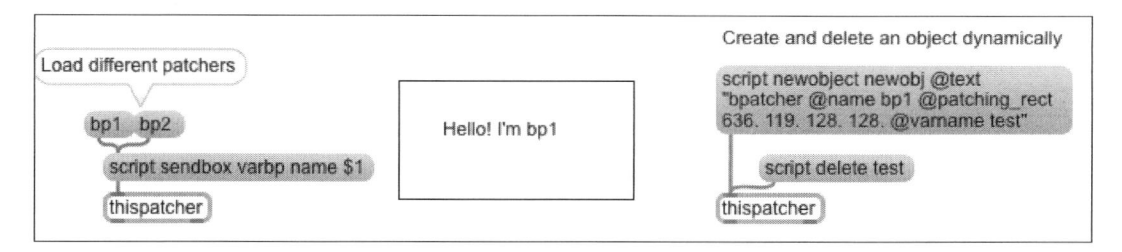

We use its scripting name, which is **varbp** in this case, to communicate with it and load a different patcher into it. We could also delete the `bpatcher` object that contains one patcher and recreate another one that contains another patcher. As you can imagine, this might be the worst way of doing it, but sometimes, it is absolutely necessary to create objects on the fly, for example, if we want to create an abstraction with a variable number of inlets based on the given argument. The [thispatcher] object allows us to do the patching automatically. Look through the [thispatcher] object's help-patch to get a feeling of what we are capable of. However, don't get too enthusiastic while spawning, deleting objects, and so on; there are often simpler solutions. For example, to have a variable GUI, a solution is presented in the same patch as all the other examples of the preceding screenshots are taken from variable `bpatcher.maxpat`. Here, the offset message is sent to a [thispatcher] object inside a `bpatcher` object to shift around what's shown by the `bpatcher` object.

Summary

So in this chapter, we learned a lot about conceptualizing and structuring patches. By now, I hope you feel comfortable with the general handling of Max and know how to go about things in a tidy, reusable, and well-structured way. Don't forget to mess around sometimes though; Max is great in helping us try out things or producing spaghetti code that makes some beautiful noise.

We covered many different topics in this chapter, such as debugging, structuring, presets, some ways to elegantly pass around data, useful GUI techniques such as the bpatcher object, and even how to create dynamic GUIs using the latter. This chapter might have seemed a bit much if you are eager to patch little experiments, but as it has been stated in the chapter many times, having some methods in mind about how to go about bigger projects is useful, but it's always a balance. It's very likely you will create more small projects than big ones, and therefore, keep in mind what we learned here, or remember to come back here when a big project comes up.

In the next chapter, we'll finally dive right into how to make some sounds instead of just thinking about how to control things.

4
Basic Audio in Max/MSP

In this chapter, we will focus on the audio-specific examples. We will take a look at the following audio processing and generation techniques:

- Additive synthesis
- Subtractive synthesis
- Sampling
- Wave shaping

One problem we will face in this and the next two chapters is that we are now working in very deep waters, so to speak. Nearly every example provided here might be understood intuitively or taken apart in hours of math and calculations. It's up to you how deep you want to go, but in order to develop some intuition; we'll have to be using some **Digital Signal Processing** (**DSP**) theory. We will briefly cover the DSP theory, but it is highly recommended that you study its fundamentals deeper to clearly understand this scientific topic if you are not familiar with it already. You will also find some references and learning material at the end of this chapter.

Basic audio principles

We already saw and stated that it's important to know, see, and hear what's happening along a signal way. If we work in the realm of audio, there are four most important ways to measure a signal, which are conceptually partly very different and offer a very broad perspective on audio signals if we always have all of them in the back of our minds. These are the following important ways:

- Numbers (actual sample values)
- Levels (such as RMS, LUFS, and dB FS)
- Transversal waves (waveform displays, so oscilloscopes)
- Spectra (an analysis of frequency components)

There are many more ways to think about audio or signals in general, but these are the most common and important ones. Let's use them inside Max right away to observe their different behavior. We'll feed some very basic signals into them: DC offset, a sinusoid, and noise. The one that might surprise you the most and get you thinking is the constant signal or DC offset (if it's digital-analog converted). In the following screenshot, you can see how the different displays react:

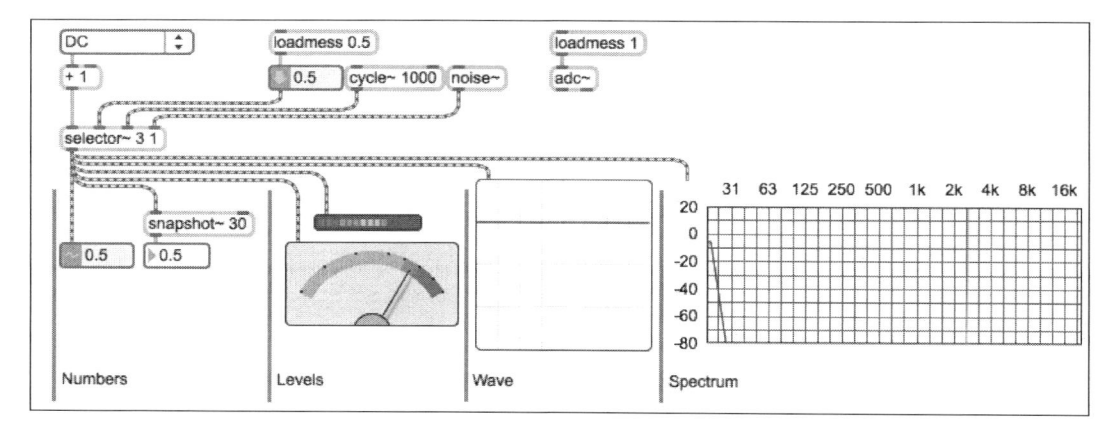

In general, one might think we don't want any constant signals at all; we don't want any DC offset. However, we will use audio signals a lot to control things later, say, an LFO or sequencers that should run with great timing accuracy. Also, sometimes, we just add a DC offset to our audio streams by accident. You can see in the preceding screenshot that a very slowly moving or constant signal can be observed best by looking at its value directly, for example, using the [number~] object. In a level display, the [meter~] or [levelmeter~] objects will seem to imply that the incoming signal is very loud, in fact, it should be at -6 dB **Full Scale** (**FS**). As it is very loud, we just can't hear anything since the frequency is infinitely low. This is reflected by the spectrum display too; we see a very low frequency at -6 dB. In theory, we should just see an infinitely thin spike at 0 Hz, so everything else can be considered an (inevitable but reducible) measuring error.

Audio synthesis

Awareness of these possibilities of viewing a signal and their constraints, and knowing how they actually work, will greatly increase our productivity. So let's get to actually synthesizing some waveforms. A good example of different views of a signal operation is **Amplitude Modulation** (**AM**); we will also try to formulate some other general principles using the example of AM.

Amplitude modulation

AM means the multiplication of a signal with an oscillator. This provides a method of generating sidebands, which is partial in a very easy, intuitive, and CPU-efficient way. Amplitude modulation seems like a word that has a very broad meaning and can be used as soon as we change a signal's amplitude by another signal. While this might be true, in the context of audio synthesis, it very specifically means the multiplication of two (most often sine) oscillators. Moreover, there is a distinction between AM and **Ring Modulation**. But before we get to this distinction, let's look at the following simple multiplication of two sine waves, and first look at the result in an oscilloscope as a wave:

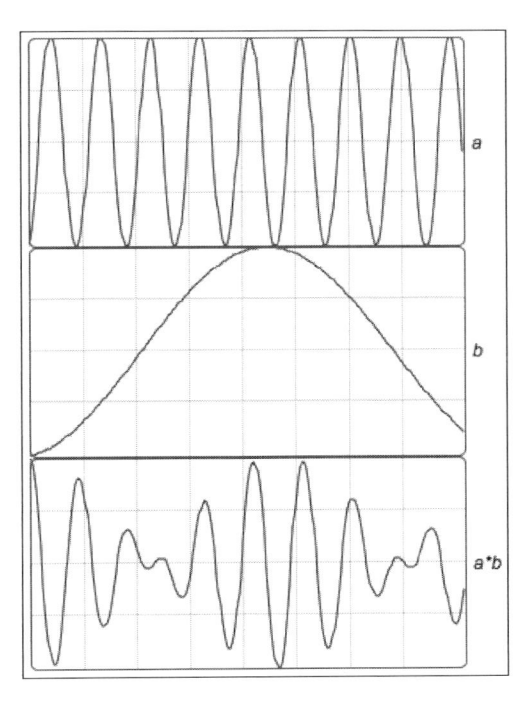

Basic Audio in Max/MSP

So in the preceding screenshot, we can see the two sine waves and their product. If we imagine every pair of samples being multiplied, the operation seems pretty intuitive as the result is what we would expect. But what does this resulting wave really mean besides looking like a product of two sine waves? What does it sound like? The wave certainly seems to have stayed in there, right? Well, viewing the product as a wave and looking at the whole process in the time domain rather than the frequency domain is helpful but slightly misleading. So let's jump over to the following frequency domain and look at what's happening with the spectrum:

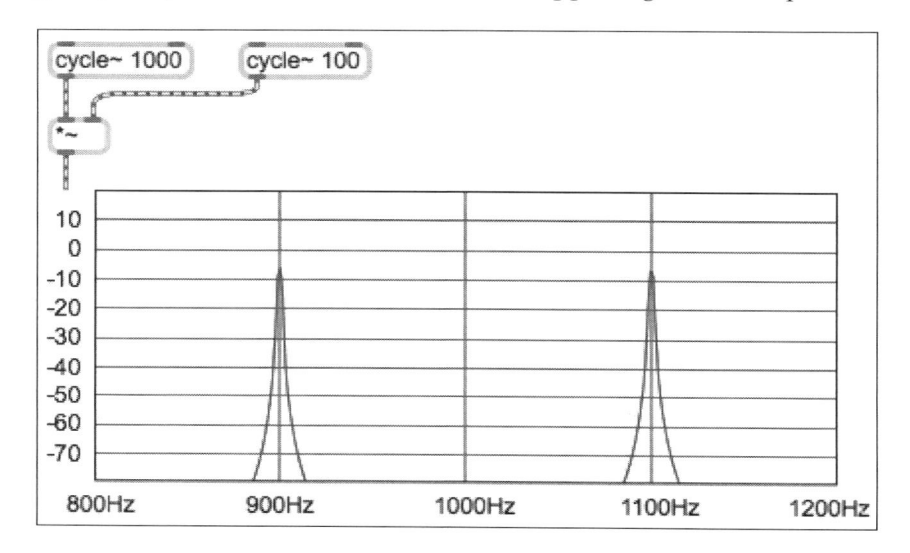

So we can observe here that if we multiply a sine wave **a** with a sine wave **b**, when **a** has a frequency of 1000 Hz and **b** has a frequency of 100 Hz, we end up with two sine waves, one at 900 Hz and another at 1100 Hz. The original sine waves have disappeared. In general, we can say that the result of multiplying **a** and **b** is equal to adding and subtracting the frequencies. This is shown in the **Equivalence to Sum and difference** subpatcher (in the following screenshot, the two inlets to the spectrum display overlap completely, which might be hard to see):

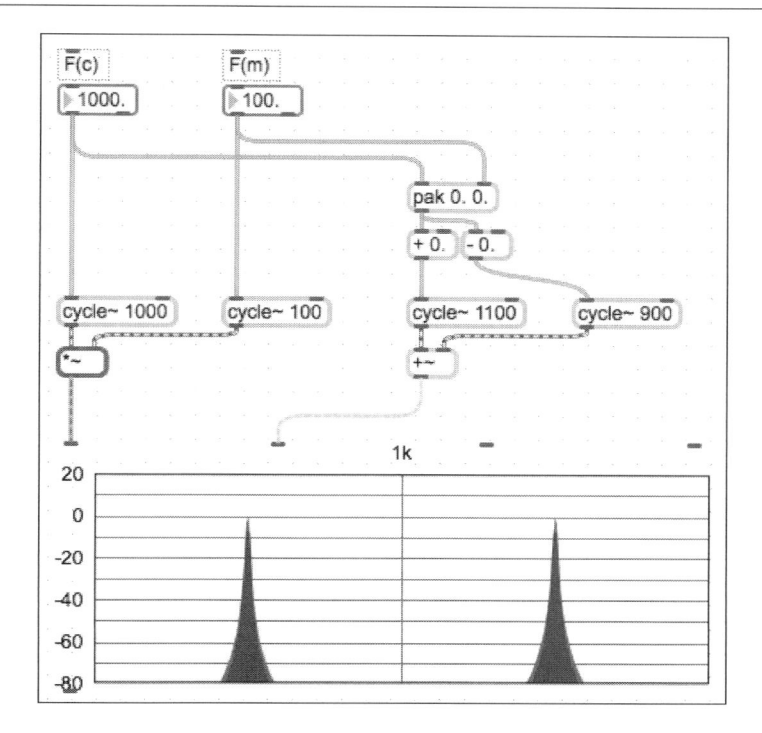

So in the preceding screenshot, you see a basic AM patcher that produces sidebands that we can predict quite easily.

> Multiplication is commutative; you will say, 1000 + 100 = 1100, 1000 - 100 = 900; that's alright, but what about 100 - 1000 and 100 + 1000? We get -900 and 1100 once again? It still works out, and the fact that it does has to do with negative frequencies, or the symmetry of a real frequency spectrum around 0.

So you can see that the two ways of looking at our signal and thinking about AM offer different opportunities and pitfalls. Here is another way to think about AM: it's the convolution of the two spectra. We didn't talk about convolution yet; we will at a later point. But keep it in mind or do a little research on your own; this aspect of AM is yet another interesting one.

Ring modulation versus amplitude modulation

The difference between ring modulation and what we call AM in this context is that the former one uses a bipolar modulator and the latter one uses a unipolar one. So actually, this is just about scaling and offsetting one of the factors. The difference in the outcome is yet a big one; if we keep one oscillator unipolar, the other one will be present in the outcome. If we do so, it starts making sense to call one oscillator on the carrier and the other (unipolar) on the modulator. Also, it therefore introduces modulation depth that controls the amplitude of the sidebands. In the following screenshot, you can see the resulting spectrum; we have the original signal, so the carrier plus two sidebands, which are the original signals, are shifted up and down:

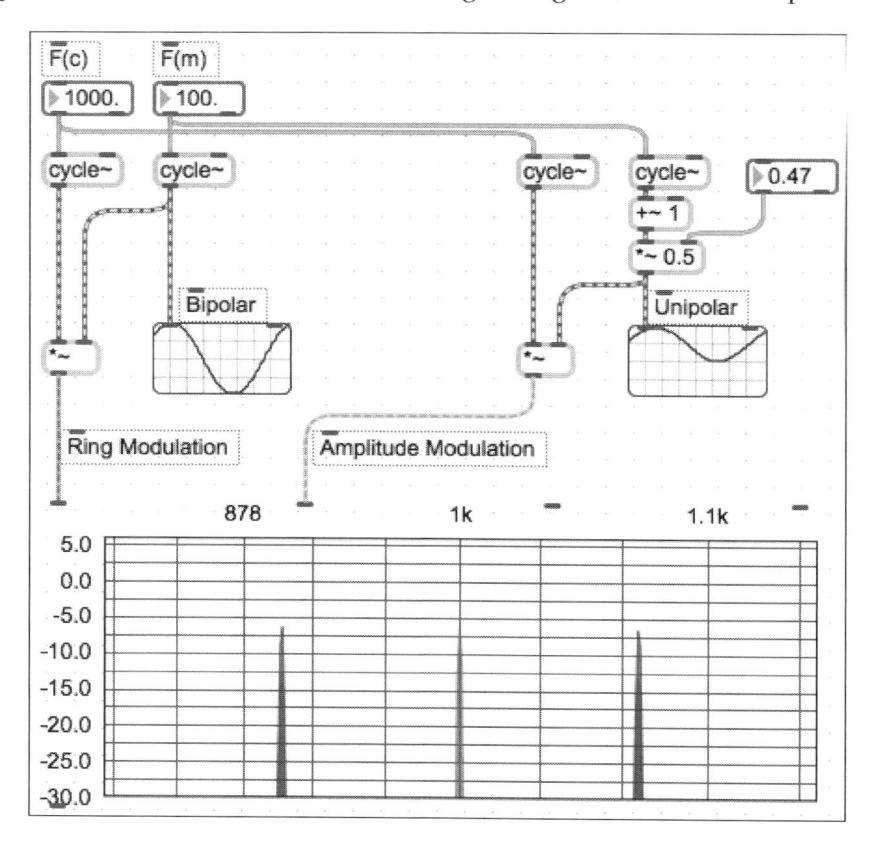

Therefore, you can see that AM has the possibility to roughen up our spectrum, which means we can use it to let through an original spectrum and add sidebands.

Tremolo

Tremolo (from the Latin word *tremare*, to shake or tremble) is a musical term, which means to change a sound's amplitude in regular short intervals. Many people confuse it with vibrato, which is a modulating pitch at regular intervals. AM is tremolo and FM is vibrato, and as a simple reminder, think that the V of vibrato is closer to the F of FM than to the A of AM.

So multiplying the two oscillators results in a different spectrum. But of course, we can also use multiplication to scale a signal and to change its amplitude. If we wanted to have a sine wave that has a tremolo, that is an oscillating variation in amplitude, with say a frequency of 1 Hertz, we would again multiply two sine waves, one with 1000 Hz for example and another with a frequency of 0.5 Hz. Why 0.5 Hz? Think about a sine wave; it has two peaks per cycle, a positive one and a negative one.

We can visualize all that very well if we think about it in the time domain, looking at the result in an oscilloscope. But what about our view of the frequency domain? Well, let's go through it; when we multiply a sine with 1000 Hz and one with 0.5 Hz, we actually get two sine waves, one with 999.5 Hz and one with 100.5 Hz. Frequencies that close create beatings, since once in a while, their positive and negative peaks overlap, canceling out each other. In general, the frequency of the beating is defined by the difference in frequency, which is 1 Hz in this case. So if we look at it this way, we come to the same result again of course, but this time, we actually think of two frequencies instead of one being attenuated.

Lastly, we could have looked up trigonometric identities to anticipate what happens if we multiply two sine waves. We find the following:

$$\cos(\theta) \cdot \cos(\varphi) = \frac{\cos(\theta - \varphi) + \cos(\theta + \varphi)}{2}$$

Here, φ and θ are the two angular frequencies multiplied by the time in seconds, for example:

$$\varphi = \omega t - 2\pi 1000 t$$

This is the equation for the 1000 Hz sine wave.

Feedback

Feedback always brings the complexity of a system to the next level. It can be used to stabilize a system, but can also make a given system unstable easily. In a strict sense, in the context of DSP, stability means that for a finite input to a system, we get finite output. Obviously, feedback can give us infinite output for a finite input. We can use attenuated feedback, for example, not only to make our AM patches recursive, adding more and more sidebands, but also to achieve some surprising results as we will see in a minute. Before we look at this application, let's quickly talk about feedback in general.

In the digital domain, feedback always demands some amount of delay. This is because the evaluation of the chain of operations would otherwise resemble an infinite amount of operations on one sample. This is true for both the Max message domain (we get a stack overflow error if we use feedback without delaying or breaking the chain of events) and the MSP domain; audio will just stop working if we try it. So the minimum network for a feedback chain as a block diagram looks something like this:

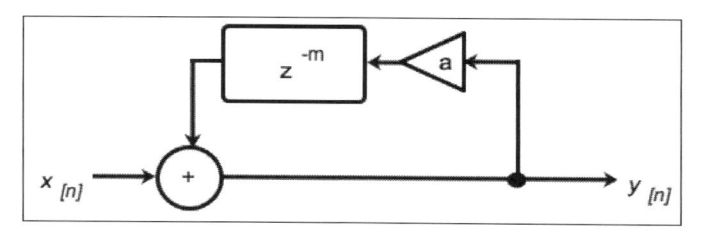

In the preceding screenshot, X is the input signal and x[n] is the current input sample; Y is the output signal and y[n] is the current output sample. In the block marked z^{-m}, **i** is a delay of **m** samples (**m** being a constant). Denoting a delay with z^{-m} comes from a mathematical construct named the Z-transform. The **a** term is also a constant used to attenuate the feedback circle. If no feedback is involved, it's sometimes helpful to think about block diagrams as processing whole signals. For example, if you think of a block diagram that consists only of multiplication with a constant, it would make a lot of sense to think of its output signal as a scaled version of the input signal. We wouldn't think of the network's processing or its output sample by sample. However, as soon as feedback is involved, without calculation or testing, this is the way we should think about the network. Remember *Chapter 1, Getting Started with Max?*, we got to know the difference equation representation of a network there, so before we look at the Max version of things, let's look at the difference equation of the network to get a better feeling of the notation. Try to find it yourself before looking at it too closely!

$$y[n] = x[n] + a \cdot y[n-m]$$

Chapter 4

In Max, or rather in MSP, we can introduce feedback as soon as we use a [tapin~] [tapout~] pair that introduces a delay. The minimum delay possible is the signal vector size. Another way is to simply use a [send~] and [receive~] pair in our loop. The [send~] and [receive~] pair will automatically introduce this minimum amount of delay if needed, so the delay will be introduced only if there is a feedback loop. If we need shorter delays and feedback, we have to go into the wonderful world of gen~. Here, our shortest delay time is one sample, and it can be introduced via the [history] object. In the Fbdiagram.maxpat patcher, you can find a Max version, an MSP version, and a [gen~] version of our diagram. For the time being, let's just pretend that the gen domain is just another subpatcher/abstraction system that allows shorter delays with feedback and has a more limited set of objects that more or less work the same as the MSP ones. In the following screenshot, you can see the difference between the output of the MSP and the [gen~] domain. Obviously, the length of the delay time has quite an impact on the output. Also, don't forget that the MSP version's output will vary greatly depending on our vector size settings.

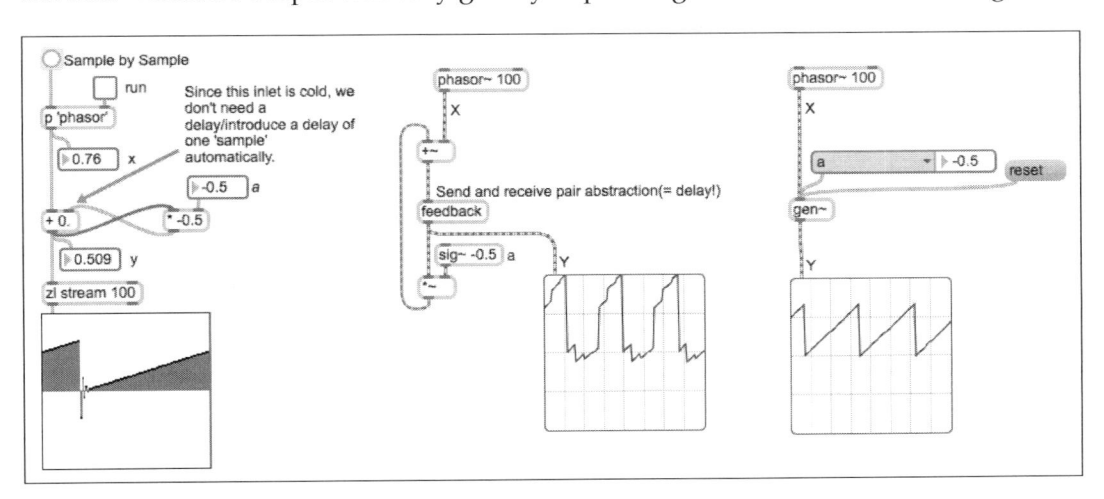

[97]

Let's return to AM now. Feedback can, for example, be used to duplicate and shift our spectrum again and again. In the following screenshot, you can see a 1000 Hz sine wave that has been processed by a recursive AM to be duplicated and shifted up and down with a 100 Hz spacing:

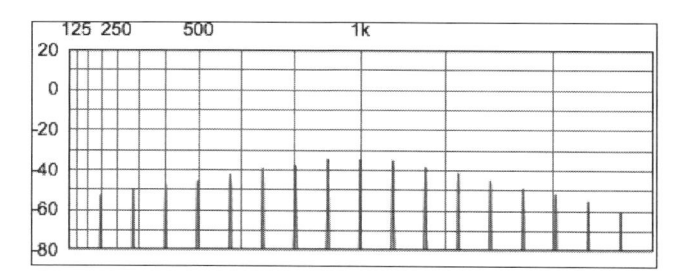

In the maybe surprising result, we can achieve with this technique is this: if the modulating oscillator and the carrier have the same frequency, we end up with something that almost sounds like a sawtooth wave.

Frequency modulation

Frequency modulation or FM is a technique that allows us to create a lot of frequency components out of just two oscillators, which is why it was used a lot back in the days when oscillators were a rare, expensive, or good, or CPU performance was low. Still, especially when dealing with real-time synthesis, efficiency is a crucial factor, and the huge variety of sounds that can be achieved with just two oscillators and very few parameters can be very useful for live performance and so on. The idea of FM is of course to modulate an oscillator's frequency. The basic, admittedly useless, form is depicted in the following screenshot:

While trying to visualize what happens with the output in the time domain, we can imagine it as shown in the following screenshot. In the preceding screenshot, you can see the signal that is controlling the frequency. It is a sine wave with a frequency of 50 Hz, scaled and offset to range from -1000 to 5000, so the center or carrier frequency is 2000 Hz, which is modulated to an amount of 3000 Hz.

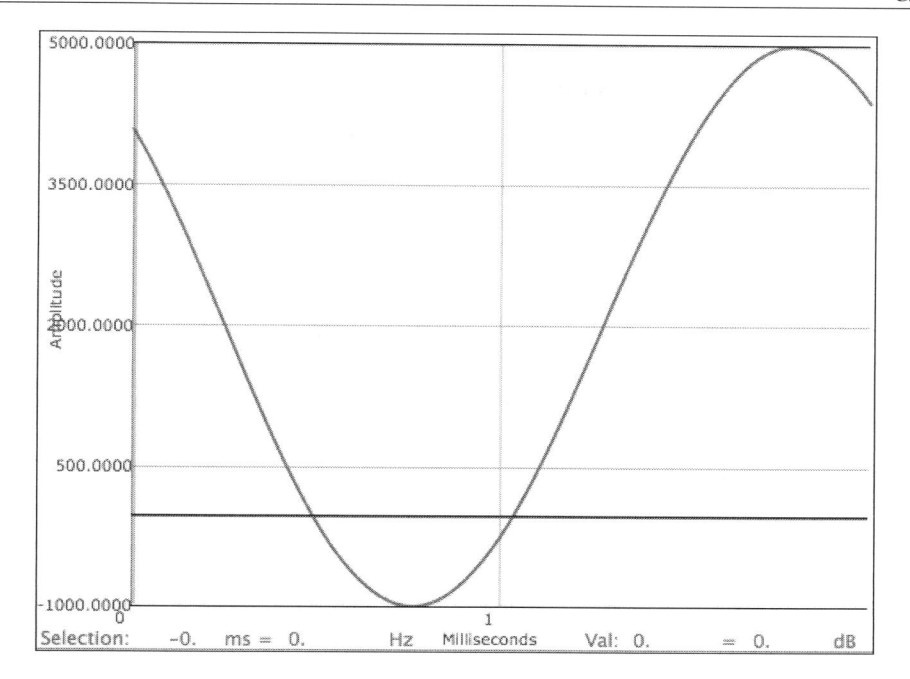

You can see the output of the modulated oscillator in the following screenshot:

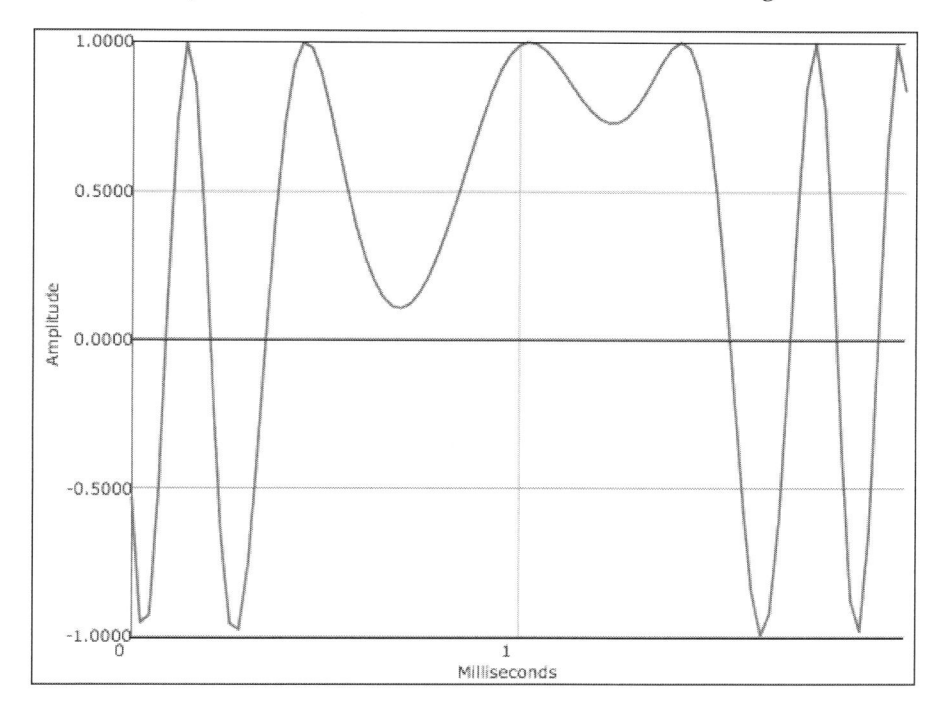

Basic Audio in Max/MSP

If we extend the upper patch slightly, we end up with this:

Although you can't see it in the screenshot, the sidebands appear with a 100 Hz spacing here, that is, with spacing equal to the modulator's frequency. Pretty similar to AM right? But depending on the modulation amount, we get more and more sidebands.

Controlling FM

If the ratio between **F(c)** and **F(m)** is an integer, we end up with a harmonic spectrum, therefore, it may be more useful to rather control **F(m)** indirectly via a ratio parameter as it's done inside the `SimpleRatioAndIndex` subpatcher. Also, an `Index` parameter is typically introduced to make an FM patch even more controllable. The modulation index is defined as follows:

$$I = \frac{A_m}{f_m}$$

Here, **I** is the index, A_m is the amplitude of the modulation, what we called amount before, and f_m is the modulator's frequency. So finally, after adding these two controls, we might arrive here:

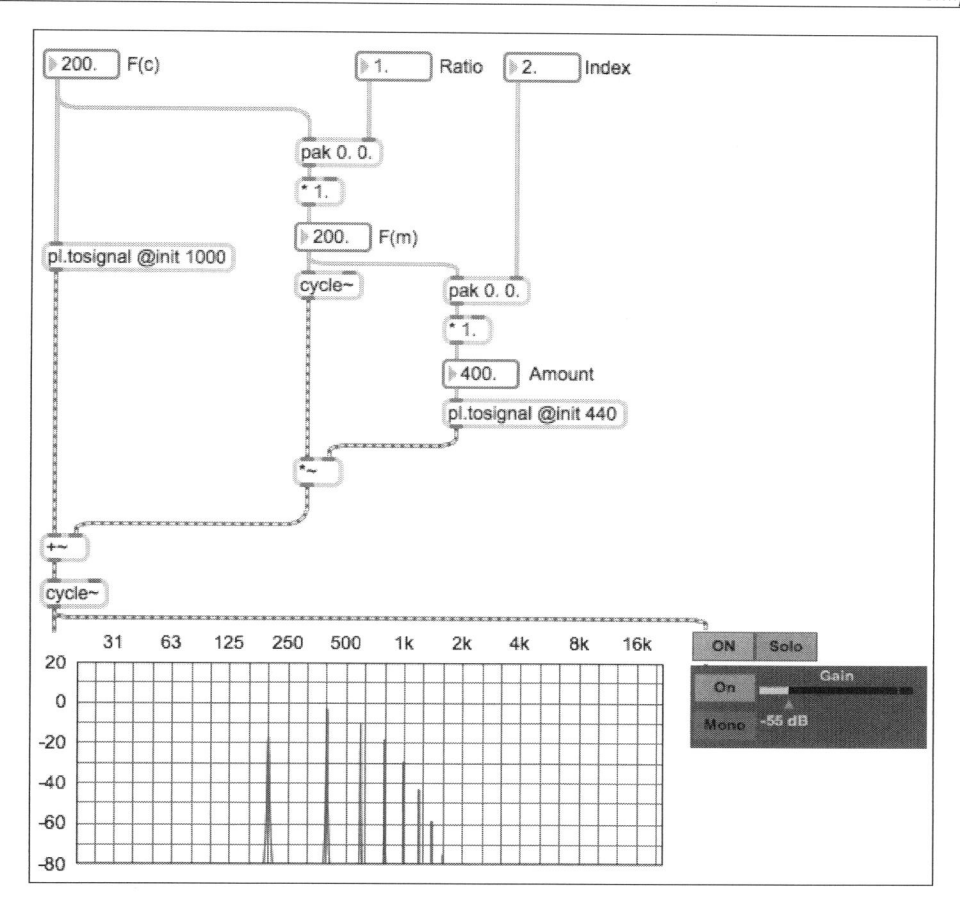

FM offers a wide range of possibilities, for example, the fact that we have a simple control for how harmonic/inharmonic our spectrum is can be useful to synthesize the mostly noisy attack phase of many instruments if we drive the ratio and index with an envelope as it's done in the `SimpleEnvelopeDriven` subpatcher. However, it's also very easy to synthesize very artificial, strange sounds. This basically is due to the following two reasons:

- Firstly, the partials that appear have amplitudes governed by Bessel functions that may seem quite unpredictable; the partials sometimes seem to have random amplitudes.

- Secondly, negative frequencies and fold back. If we generate partials with frequencies below 0 Hz, it is equivalent to creating the same positive frequency. For frequencies greater than the sample rate/2 (sample rate/2 is what's called the Nyquist rate), the frequencies reflect back into the spectrum that can be described by our sampling rate (this is an effect also called aliasing). So at a sampling rate of 44,100 Hz, a partial with a frequency of -100 Hz will appear at 100 Hz, and a partial with a frequency of 43100 kHz will appear at 1000 Hz, as shown in the following screenshot:

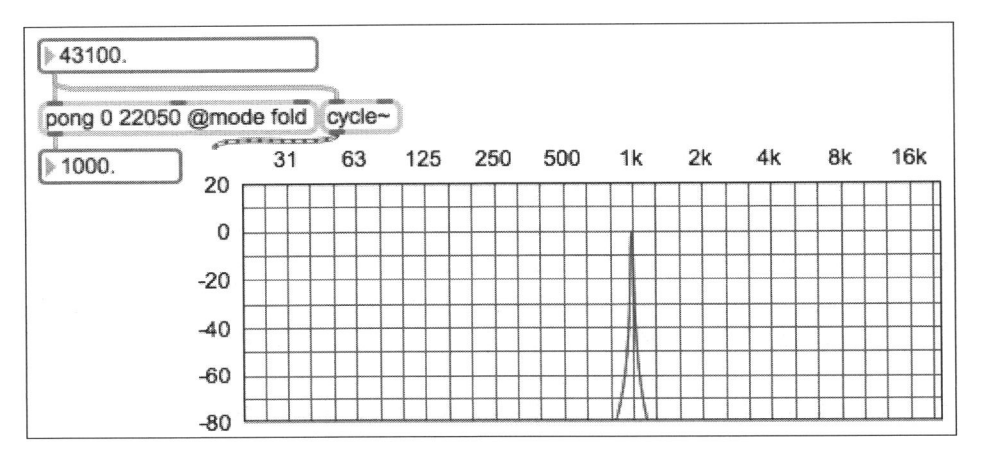

So, for frequencies between the Nyquist frequency and the sampling frequency, what we hear is described by this:

$$f_0 = f_s - f_{i|}$$

Here, f_s is the sampling rate, f_0 is the frequency we hear, and f_i is the frequency we are trying to synthesize. Since FM leads to many partials, this effect can easily come up, and can both be used in an artistically interesting manner or sometimes appear as an unwanted error. In theory, an FM signal's partials extend to even infinity, but the amplitudes become negligibly small. If we want to reduce this behavior, the [poly~] object can be used to oversample the process, generating a bit more headroom for high frequencies. The phenomenon of aliasing can be understood by thinking of a real (in contrast to imaginary) digital signal as having a symmetrical and periodical spectrum; let's not go into too much detail here and look at it in the time domain:

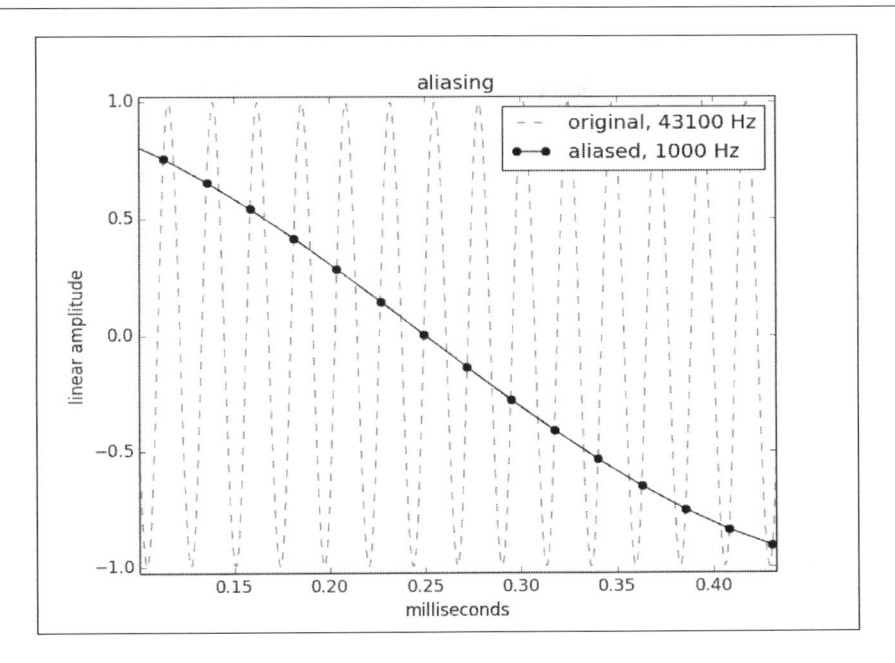

[Figure: aliasing plot showing original 43100 Hz (dashed) and aliased 1000 Hz (solid with dots), linear amplitude vs milliseconds from 0.15 to 0.40]

In the previous screenshot, we again tried to synthesize a sine wave with 43100 Hz (the dotted line) at a sampling rate of 44100 Hz. What we actually get is the straight black line, a sine with 1000 Hz. Each big black dot represents an actual sample, and there is only one single band-limited signal connecting them: the 1000 Hz wave that is only partly visible here (about half its wavelength).

Feedback

It is very common to use feedback with FM. We can even frequency modulate one oscillator with itself, making the algorithm even cheaper since we have only one table lookup. The idea of feedback FM quickly leads us to the idea of making networks of oscillators that can be modulated by each other, including feedback paths, but let's keep it simple for now. One might think that modulating one oscillator with itself should produce chaos; FM being a technique that is not the easiest to control, one shouldn't care for playing around with single operator feedback FM. But the opposite is the case.

Basic Audio in Max/MSP

A single operator FM yields very predictable partials, as shown in the following screenshot, and in the `Single OP FBFM` subpatcher:

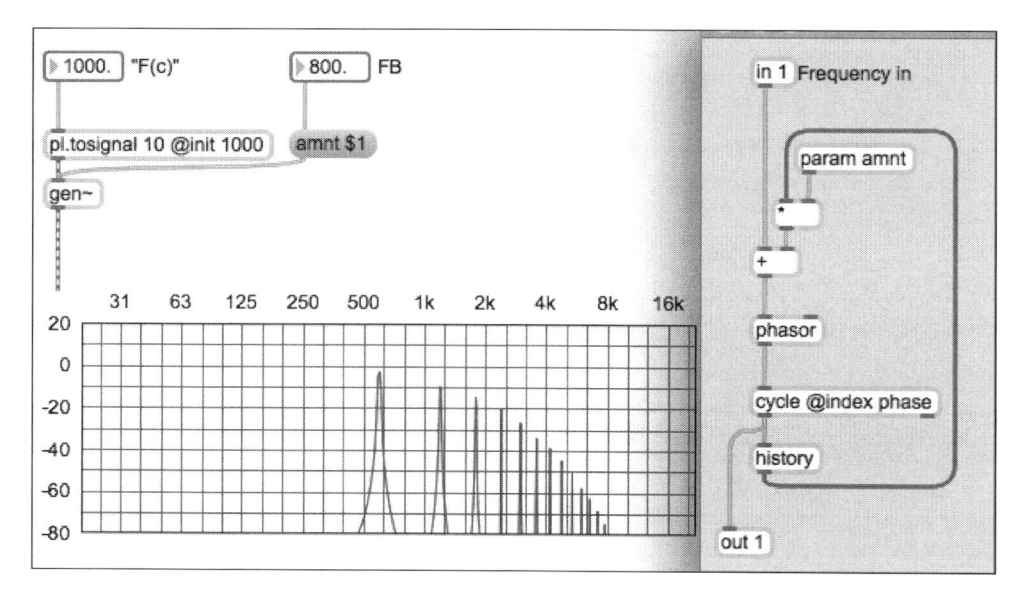

Again, we are using a gen~ patch, since we want to create a feedback loop and are heading for a short delay in the loop. Note that we are using the [param] object to pass a message into the gen~ object. What should catch your attention is that although the carrier frequency has been adjusted to 1000 Hz, the fundamental frequency in the spectrum is around 600 Hz. What can help us here is switching to phase modulation.

Phase modulation

If you look at the gen~ patch in the previous screenshot, you see that we are driving our sine oscillator with a phasor. The cycle object's phase inlet assumes an input that ranges from 0 to 1 instead of from 0 to 2π, as one might think. To drive a sine wave through one full cycle in math, we can use a variable ranging from 0 to 2π, so in the following formula, you can imagine **t** being provided by a phasor, which is the running phase. The 2π multiplication isn't necessary in Max since if we are using [cycle~], we are reading out a wavetable actually instead of really computing the sine or cosine of the input:

$$f(t) = \cos(2\pi t f_0 + \varphi)$$

This is the most common form of denoting a running sinusoid with frequency f_0 and phase φ. Try to come up with a formula that describes frequency modulation!

Simplifying the phases by setting it to zero, we can denote FM as follows:

$$f(t) = \cos\left(2\pi t \cdot \left(f_c + A \cdot \cos\left(2\pi t f_m\right)\right)\right)$$

This can be shown to be nearly identical to the following formula:

$$f(t) = \cos\left(2\pi t f_0 + A \cdot \sin\left(2\pi t f_m\right)\right)$$

Here, f_0 is the frequency of the carrier, f_m is the frequency of the modulator, and **A** is the modulation amount.

Welcome to phase modulation. If you compare it, the previous formula actually just inserts a scaled sine wave where the phase φ used to be. So phase modulation is nearly identical to frequency modulation. Phase modulation has some advantages though, such as providing us with an easy method of synchronizing multiple oscillators. But let's go back to the Max side of things and look at a feedback phase modulation patch right away (ignoring simple phase modulation, since it really is so similar to FM):

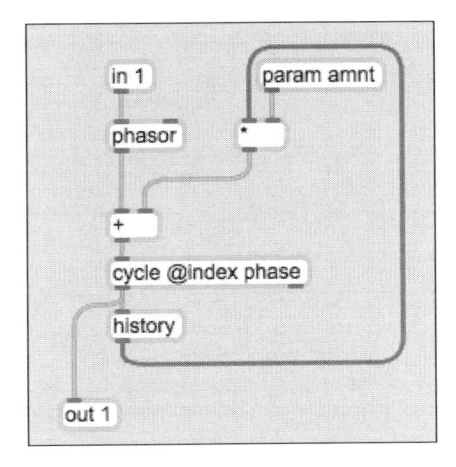

This `gen~` patcher resides inside the `One OP FBPM` subpatcher and implements phase modulation using one oscillator and feedback. Interestingly, the spectrum is very similar to the one of a sawtooth wave, with the feedback amount having a similar effect to a low-pass filter, controlling the amount of partials. If you take a look at the subpatcher, you'll find the following three sound sources:

- Our feedback FM `gen~` patcher
- A [`saw~`] object for comparison
- A `poly~` object

We have already mentioned the problem of aliasing and the [`poly~`] object has already been proposed to treat the problem. However, it allows us to define the quality of parts of patches in general, so let's talk about the object a bit before moving on since we will make great use of it throughout the audio part of this book. Before moving on, I would like to tell you that you can double-click on it to see what is loaded inside, and you will see that the subpatcher we just discussed contains a [`poly~`] object that contains yet another version of our `gen~` patcher.

The poly~ object

The `poly~` object has now been mentioned a couple of times; I hope by now you have the impression that it's pretty important, because it is, and can be a bit confusing at first. First of all, it is a container for an abstraction. We write patches, mostly knowing beforehand that we will be loading them into a `poly~` object and therefore constructing them slightly differently. Here is an overview of what `poly~` can do for us:

- The `poly~` object up sample/down sample audio in the loaded patch
- Define a different vector size for the loaded patch
- Take a patch and instantiate it multiple times
- Manage polyphony automatically (voice allocation)
- Load/unload patches dynamically
- Turn on/off audio processing for a loaded patch automatically or manually

This list seems to imply that the object is only interesting for audio purposes, but behold point three. It can be extremely useful to take any patch and load it multiple times at once. To load a patch into [`poly~`], it has to be in Max's search path or in the same folder as the host patch as it's usual for abstractions. The [`poly~`] object's first argument is the patcher to load:

Chapter 4

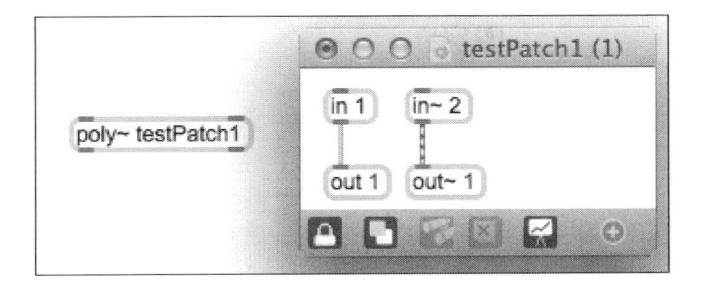

You see that the poly object shown contains a patcher called `testPatch1.maxpat`. This patcher has inlets and outlets that appear on the `[poly~]` object as usual when dealing with abstractions. Note that the inlets and outlets are not actual `[inlet]` and `[outlet]` objects. If we are dealing with poly, they need to be `[in]`/`[in~]` and `[out]`/`[out~]` objects that explicitly state whether it's a message or a signal port. Also, the numbering might lead to confusion in objects that have a running numbering scheme, so independent of a message or signal domain, we can use a running number. Our objects, on the other hand, have separate numbering for the message and signal domain, both starting at 1. Why is that?

Well, we can imagine the `poly` object's inlets and outlets managing the separation of message and signal domain automatically. We can, for example, have only one inlet to our `poly` object, but send in both messages and signals. The two in objects, one `[in 1]` and the other `[in~ 1]` in our `poly` patcher will divide these for our convenience. The `out` objects, on the other hand, are also supposed to provide us with this separation on the receiving side: the `host` patcher or the `poly~` object's actual outlets. In the following screenshot, you can see this at the beginning maybe confusing concept used to simplify things:

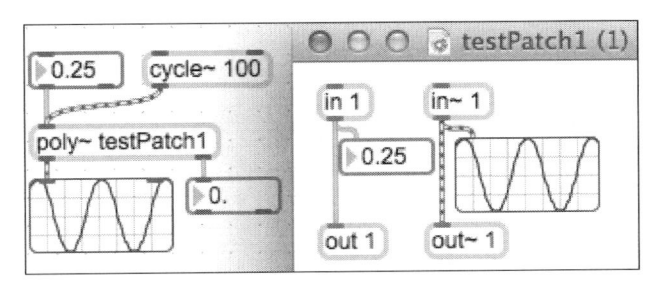

[107]

Basic Audio in Max/MSP

Up or down sampling can be achieved by providing arguments such as down 16. The amount of up or down sampling must be a power of 2. This can be extremely useful; we already saw that some processes produce a lot of high frequencies that could alias, so up sampling the process might give us more detail in the high frequency range. Also, some processes just sound better or are designed to work better at higher sampling frequencies such as many filters. What comes out of the `poly~` object is of course at our normal sampling rate, the up sampled signal that has been filtered and down sampled. You can imagine this process to be similar to an analog-to-digital conversion.

Down sampling, on the other hand, can be very useful for processes that are somewhat CPU-expensive; we would want this to happen in the signal domain without actually producing an audible signal. A good example of this is a **Low Frequency Oscillator (LFO)**. Depending on what we are controlling with the LFO, it can be down sampled a lot to save CPU cycles. But to really make this efficient, we shouldn't forget to also turn off the filter we just talked about, by using the attribute `@resampling 0`.

Before looking at what we just discussed, we'll quickly examine what it means to load multiple instance of a patcher. The first argument of `poly~` is the number of voices or instances. So `[poly~ myPatch 10]` will load the `myPatch` patch 10 times simultaneously. It simply sums up all instances' audio outputs and serializes all instances' message outputs. In the previous screenshot, you see the loaded `testPatch1` patcher; its window title also shows a **(1)**. This means we are looking at the first voice or instance. Other instances can be opened and looked at if we send the message **open n** to the `[poly~]` object, where **n** stands for the voice number of the course.

The most simple use case scenario is a really handy one: if you ever want to know in which processing audio consumes more CPU, you can just turn on **Show CPU usage**. If the processes are very lightweight and don't show a lot of differences, it's a good idea to put them into `poly`, make many instances, and compare the results. Statistically, these numbers are much more valid and reliable. Both of what we just talked about is illustrated in the following screenshot:

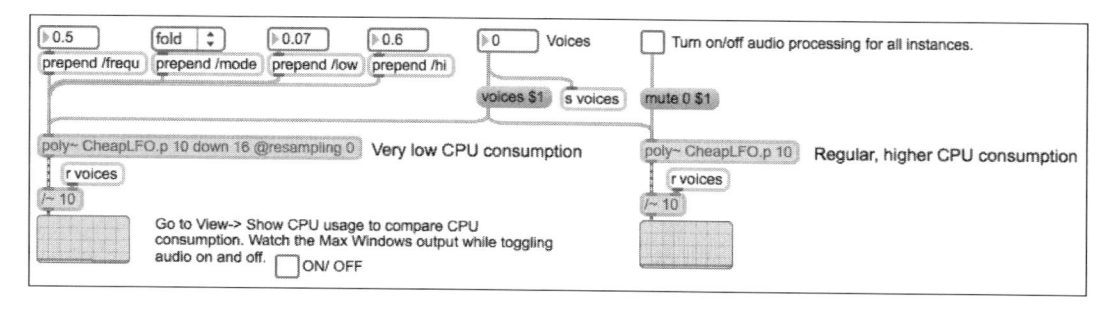

Managing instances and patcher loading

If we have, for example, ten instances of a patcher loaded, it often comes down to making small differences in the configuration of each instance. For example, we may want to create a primitive reverb-like effect with 20 delays, each delay with a slightly different delay time. We have the following two basic options to do this:

- The `target` message
- The `[thispoly~]` object

> A very common pitfall when using the `poly~` object is this: unlike signals, messages sent to the patch inside the `poly` object are by default only sent to the first instance.

As illustrated in the following screenshot, the `target` message can be used to direct a message to any instance we want:

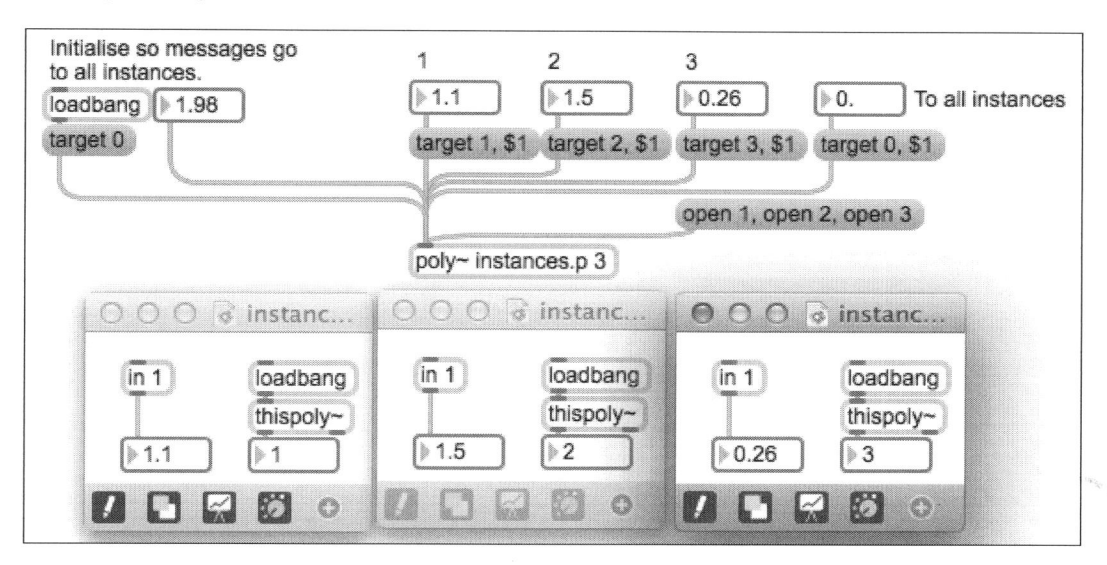

As you see, we can always know the instance number inside the instance via the `[thispoly~]` object. This can be used to access the `[coll]` objects, for example, or to pick values out of lists we are sending in and so on, to individualize each instance's parameters.

We can not only have multiple instances inside a `poly` object but also dynamically load and unload patches to switch between different processing algorithms, and we can also use the `mute` message to turn off audio processing in order to save processing power.

Basic Audio in Max/MSP

So if we only have a couple of patchers that only feature audio processing (Max processing won't be stopped using the `mute` message), it might be wiser to use muting. So we would just make, say, five `poly` objects and mute all that are not needed. If, on the other hand, we have 50 patches and always need only one of them, dynamically loading them will be more useful. The `dynamic loading` subpatcher illustrates this, although there are only three different patches to choose from. However, we may like to expand this list further. We could even go so far to make a directory in our disk with a [umenu] object referencing it, where all the patches are where we might want to load. To expand this list, we can simply drop a new patcher in that directory. In the subpatcher mentioned, we made three different oscillators and could switch between them via a [live.tab] object. Each of the oscillators uses the second inlet differently, so using a [coll] object allows us to put a name on the dial for us to always know what we are controlling. Note the [deferlow] object that makes our patch wait until the new oscillator is loaded and then updates its internal state to be in sync without [live.dial]. Refer to the following screenshot:

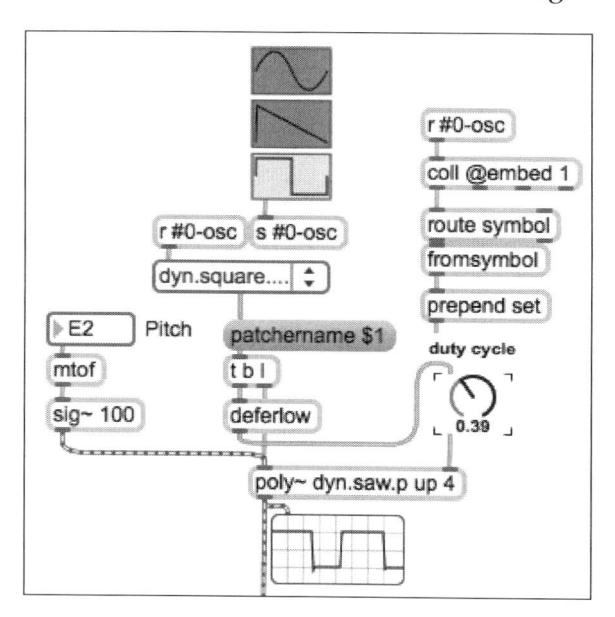

Polyphony and voice allocation

To conclude our talk about the [poly~] object, let's see what [poly~] can do for us when it comes to actual polyphony. In the next example, we are going to take our dynamic oscillator construction and put it inside another [poly~] to manage polyphony for us. So you see, we can also have the [poly~] objects inside the [poly~] objects. There are a couple of things we have to change about our original patch.

First, we will want to control it from outside the [poly~] objects, so we'll need to isolate GUI objects from sound processing/generation and think of some way in which these can communicate. Secondly, we'll need to add an envelope, namely an [adsr~] object, which goes particularly well with the [poly~] object's voice allocation capabilities. Lastly, we have to connect up the [adsr~] object with the voice allocation system via a [thispoly~] object and use a sample and hold function to actually make use of the voice allocation. You can see the result in the following screenshot:

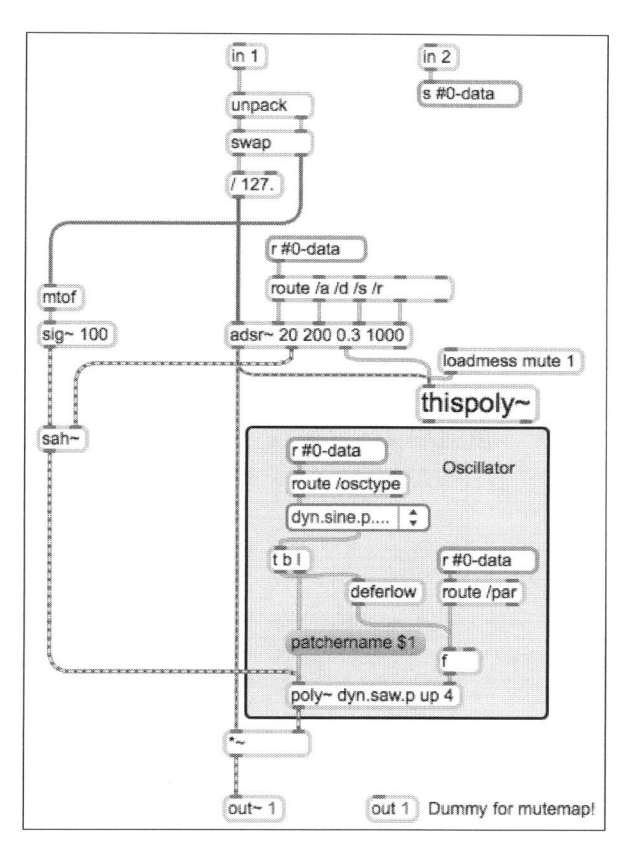

If you look at the patch and try to forget everything inside the [panel] object or substitute it in your mind with a [cycle~] object, you have the basic structure for a working polyphonic patch. The use of send and receive in combination with [route] and [prepend] is handy but optional of course. What's really important is the use of a [sah~] object to hold the pitch for this specific voice until the [adsr~] object starts a new envelope. The adsr~ object communicates with the [thispoly~] object to tell the [poly~] object's voice allocation busy states. Let's think about it more in detail.

A new note comes in at [in 1]; it's a list that contains pitch and velocity. This message needs to be prepended with midinote for [poly~] to know that this is supposed to be considered by the voice allocation system. So we, for example, send midinote 64 127, but inside, we only receive the list composed of two ints. We unpack the message and use the [swap] object. What [swap] does is just swap its two inlets, but what's important is that the order of events is therefore changed. Pack gives us the rightmost element first and the velocity, and by the use of [swap], we get the pitch first. This is important since the sample and hold need the new pitch to be present at its inlet when the new envelope is triggered.

After being brought into the range 0 to 1, the velocity goes into our envelope. On a non-zero velocity, the [adsr~] object does the following:

- It tells the [thispoly~] object to unmute the instance (the second outlet from right to left)
- It sends out a click or an impulse (the third outlet from right to left), which triggers a new value to be sampled and held by the [sah~] object unit sample
- It generates the envelope that controls our output amplitude (the fourth outlet from right to left)

Also, this envelope on the fourth outlet is being sent to the [thispoly~] object. The [thispoly~] object essentially looks at this signal, and if it is zero, [thispoly~] will automatically mute the voice.

Some last things to note; it's a good idea to mute all voices on startup, so the system doesn't consume CPU unnecessarily. On the other hand, be aware that dynamically muting and activating voices not only means that we don't process things we don't need, it also means that the overall CPU consumption of a system becomes less predictable. If we design a system that is supposed to run in real time, maybe for a concert or an installation, we definitely should try how it behaves with all active voices. If we don't try this, it might happen that we demand too much from our machine just by playing more notes at the same time than we ever tried at home.

Additive synthesis

Additive synthesis is very simple at first sight, but very deep, versatile, and complex at the second one. The basic idea is to use multiple sine waves as building blocks for more complex spectra. To put it very short, the idea of Fourier analysis, and therefore of a spectrum, is that any periodical signal can be decomposed to sum up an infinite number of sinusoids.

The only problems we face with this potentially infinitely powerful approach is that we often need a very high number of sine oscillators to create complex spectra and have to come up with some method to control their frequency, amplitude, and phase in a meaningful way. So we have an approach that can do anything but how to control it? There are several methods to do this, but let's first look at simply doing it manually. After that, we'll look at something called **Discrete Summation Formula** (**DSF**), and we'll go to inverse Fourier Transform in *Chapter 5, Advanced Audio in Max/MSP*.

We just learned how to run multiple instances of one patcher simultaneously, so a [poly~] object that contains a [cycle~] object would of course be a way of implementing an oscillator bank, which can be used for additive synthesis. Luckily, there is the [oscbank~] object, which does more or less exactly this in an optimized way. This object accepts, for example, a list that contains frequencies and amplitudes, so we can define any spectrum we like.

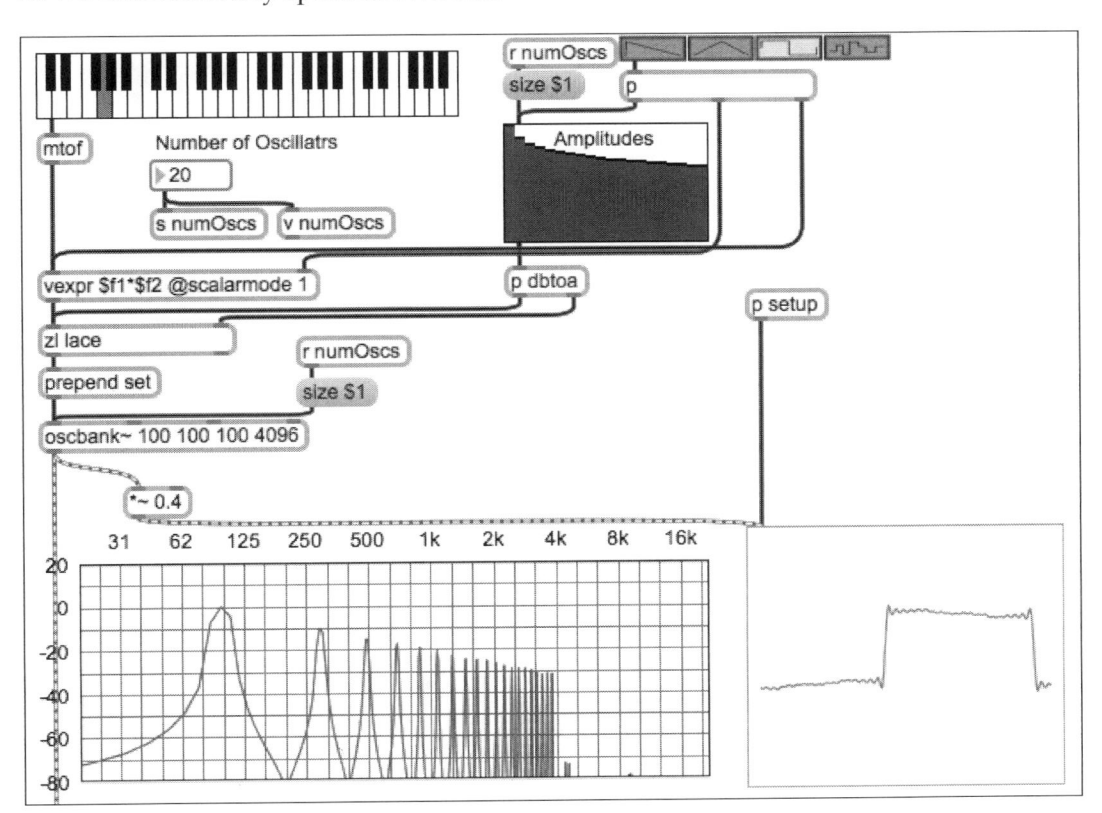

The preceding screenshot depicts the `Oscillator Bank` subpatcher inside `Additive Synthesis.maxpat`. It's a basic setup for synthesizing arbitrary waveforms. Using a [multislider] object, we can set the amplitudes of the different harmonics and implement some presets using formulas to set amplitudes and frequencies for standard waveforms such as a sawtooth, rectangle, and triangle wave. In this patch, we don't care for the phases at all, which is why our waveforms have correct spectra and sound right but don't have the right waveform (in the preceding screenshot, the rectangular wave is looking right by coincidence).

> Also, beware that although this patch sets up the oscillator bank to have a harmonic spectrum and only uses integer multiples of the fundamental frequency, this is not necessary at all. We can use any frequency and synthesize completely inharmonic spectra too.

I hope you see that this approach becomes very tedious if we set the amplitudes, frequencies, and even phases by hand, or it gets quite mathematical quickly if we try to come up with formulas that set things up for us automatically.

Discrete Summation Formulae

The idea of a DSF is to basically take a shortcut. If we want a large number of sine waves, it might not be necessary to sum all of them up; there are formulas out there that do it for us with a lot less effort and provide us with a more meaningful set of controls. The downside is that we have to go through some slightly scary-looking math. This might be the reason for this technique not being used a lot, although there are plenty of papers on the Web that contain formulas ready to be implemented in Max. In the following example, we'll use the paper, *The synthesis of complex spectra by means of discrete summation formulae* by James A. Moorer. This paper can be found at https://ccrma.stanford.edu/files/papers/stanm5.pdf.

As an example, we'll implement this formula that we found in formula 1 of the paper:

$$\sum_{k=0}^{N} a^k \cdot \sin(\theta + k\beta) = \frac{\sin(\theta) - a \cdot \sin(\theta - \beta) - a^{N+1} \cdot \left[\sin\{\theta + (N+1)\beta\} - a \cdot \sin(\theta + N\beta)\right]}{1 + a^2 - 2a \cdot \cos(\beta)}$$

I strongly recommend that you try to implement this yourself, take a look at the original paper to get some additional notes on how to actually use this formula for synthesis, and try to do the math to Max translation. The idea here really is to be able to do that translation, to find a formula, and be able to evaluate it in Max. This can help a lot in actually understanding a formula and can be done without actually understanding where it comes from.

So let's now look at the MSP version of it. Try to implement it yourself before looking at this! Generally, it will actually be easier to go from math to Max than to understand a Max patch implementing it. Max has a lot of advantages but compactness and readability are not its strongest points. Compare what space the formula takes up in this book with the space the Max patch needs. Refer to the following screenshot:

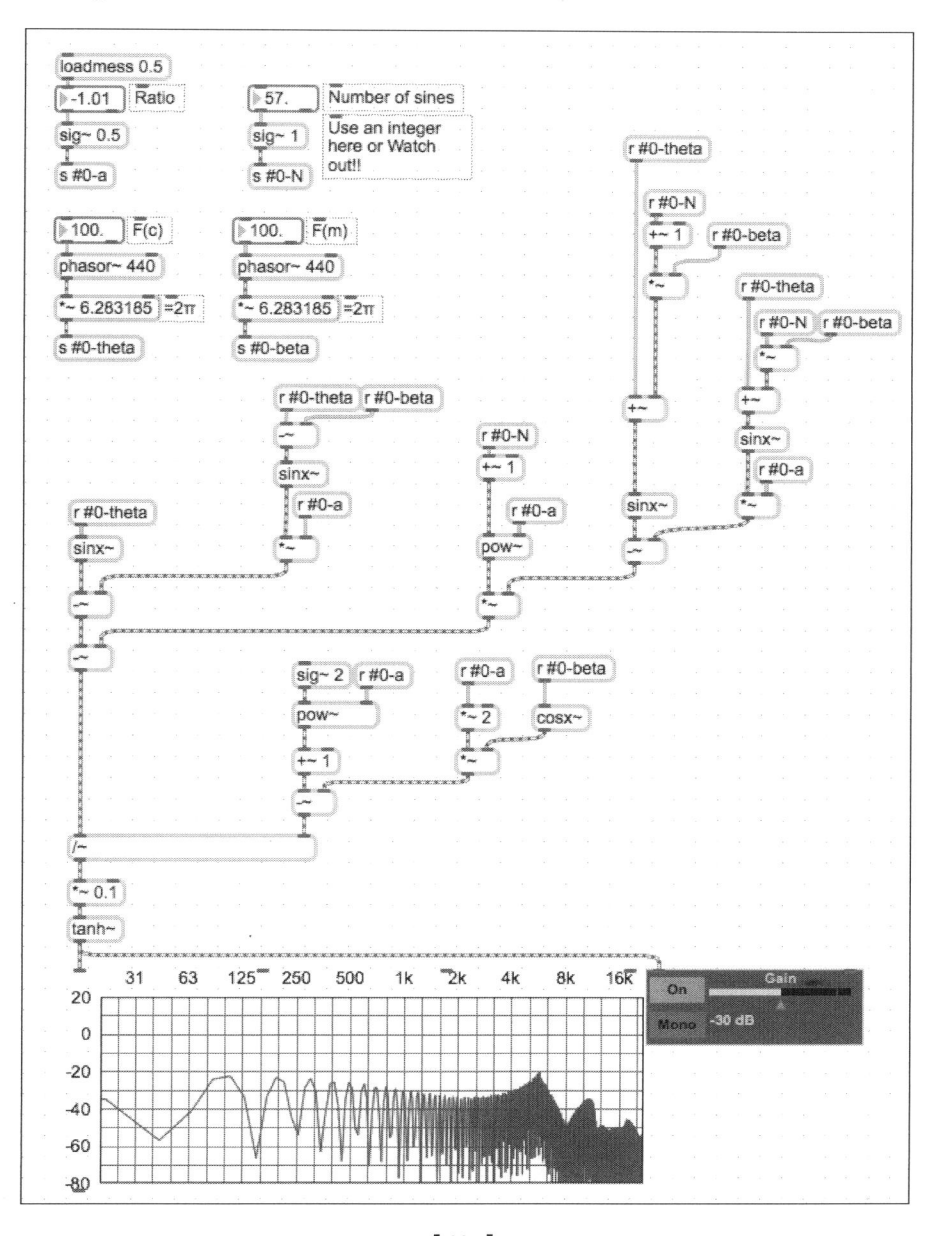

This subpatch is called DSF, and is extremely versatile in generating dynamic spectra. For more information on the parameters and their use, try it out or look at the quoted paper. As you can see, many sine waves will be required to build up such complex spectra, so we save a lot of CPU by using this approach and end up with a tiny number of parameters (compared to the number of sines x 3, for amplitude, phase, and frequency), which really allows us to control the algorithm in an intuitive way.

What's presented here is the most direct translation from the formula to the MSP domain, so lots of optimizations can be made here. We'll come to the gen~ environment soon; this will probably be easier to implement in a codebox inside gen~. If you choose to use this algorithm, think about going to the gen~ domain; think if we really need all calculations to happen in the **signal/gen~** domain or if we can do some things in the message domain, and try to move to wavetables, that is [cycle~], instead of computing the sine and cosine in real time.

DSF approaches have the problem that they need to be normalized. In the patch, [tanh~] has been used to soft clip the result after an empirical attenuation. A web search can reveal different approaches to normalizing different DSFs, and the quoted paper also provides some.

Finally, as Moorer also shows in the paper, for harmonic spectra, the formula can be greatly simplified, take a shot at this one:

$$\sum_{k=0}^{\infty} a^k \sin(\theta + k\beta) = \frac{\sin(\theta) - a \cdot \sin(\theta - \beta)}{1 + a^2 - 2a \cdot \cos(\beta)}$$

Subtractive synthesis and filtering

If what we just discussed can be compared to making a sculpture by gluing lots of tiny things (a sine wave is the most tiny thing we can find, it is a single frequency) together, now we take the approach of taking a big block of marble and cutting away everything until we are left with a beautiful sculpture. Beware though that our block of marble has to contain the beautiful sculpture beforehand. The cutting away is done using filters and the block of marble is a signal with a rich spectrum, so we have something to cut away.

In Max, we have a couple of filters that can be used right away. Before going into more detail, let's look at the following screenshot to get an overview of what we have:

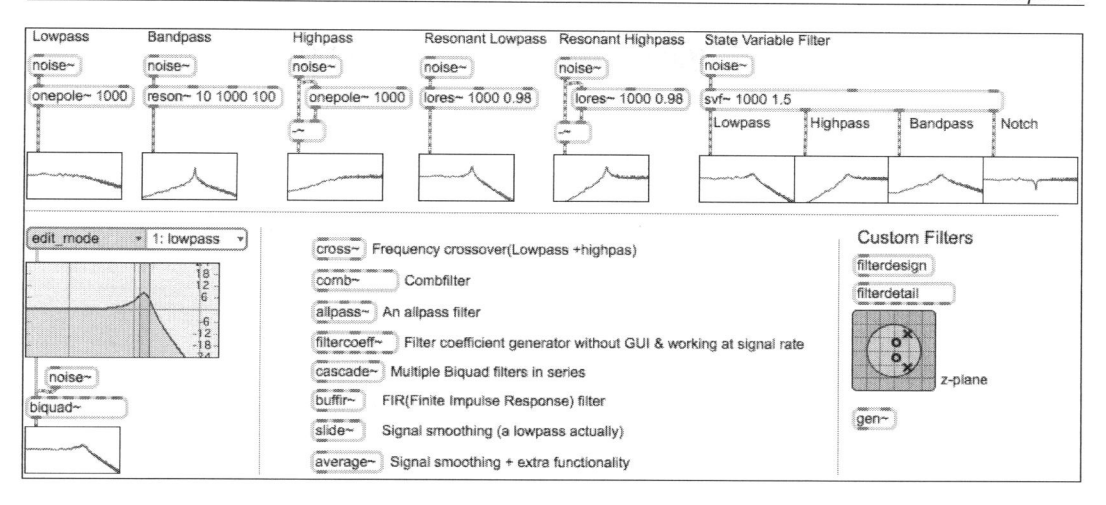

Let's quickly cover the parameters of a typical filter in order to get a more firm grasp of filter parameters in general. If we take a low-pass filter as an example, one can say that it leaves frequencies below its cutoff frequency unaltered; everything above will be increasingly attenuated. Technically speaking, it usually attenuates the cutoff frequency with -3 dB already. The resonance, or **Q**, controls the amount of feedback in a filter, emphasizing frequencies around the cutoff. The gain parameter, which is sometimes available, just allows us to regulate a gain that is constant for all frequencies.

We'll now quickly look at an example that's supposed to show that filtering is a process that also allows us to emphasize on certain frequencies so much that we won't recognize the filter's output as a filtered version of the input. Let's synthesize the sine wave out of white noise as follows:

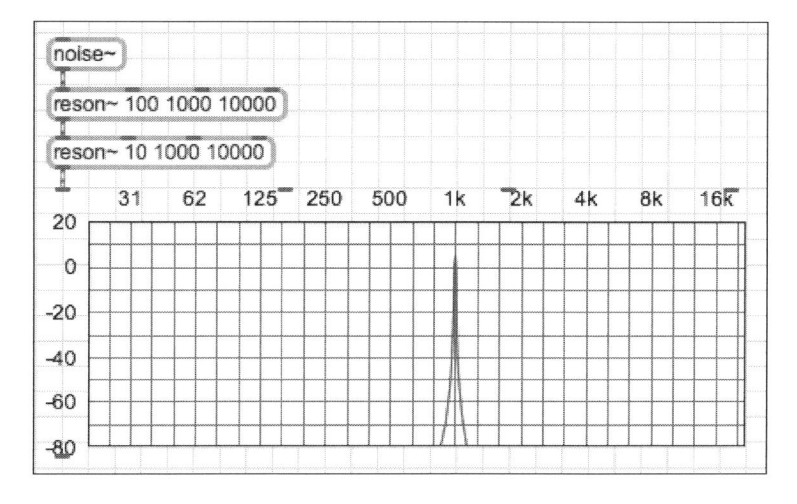

Basic Audio in Max/MSP

The values for the parameters of the two resonant bandpass filters are chosen empirically, and the sine wave at the output is not completely stable (can you think why?). Nevertheless, I hope you see that filtering can be used to design spectra in a nearly additive way too.

The classic approach

Let's practice some more and talk about the classic setup of subtractive synthesis. In general, in an analogue synthesizer, we'll find these waveforms:

- Sine
- Triangle
- Saw
- Square
- Noise

In the section about additive synthesis, we already saw a patch that implemented the formulae for these, but here are the harmonics of each of them again in detail.

When building a classic synthesizer, we can, for example, use these waveforms, which are all available in Max as bandlimited, so nearly aliasing free, versions, [cycle~], [tri~], [saw~], [rect~], and [noise~]. Loosely inspired by the legendary **Korg MS20** (choose another classic synth after this and rebuild it in Max!), we came up with a design that features a lowpass and a highpass in series, as shown in the following screenshot:

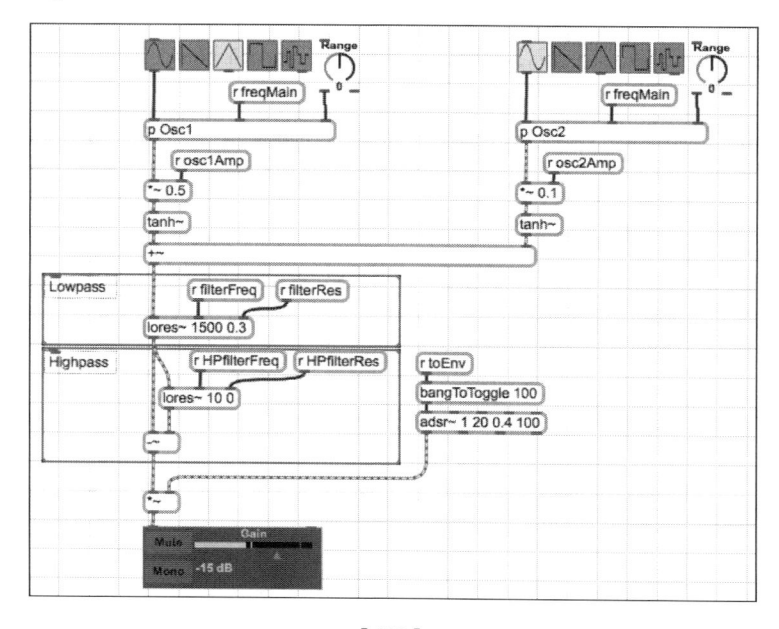

Now, this is more or less something we have already seen; you can find it as a subpatch called MS201 inside the SubractiveSynthesis.maxpat path. Let's take it a step further right away. We are going to use the [biquad~] filter, which is the most versatile filter available inside Max. Biquad stands for biquadratic, and implements a very commonly-used two-pole filter, a very generic formula, but we'll get to how to think about filters later. The [Biquad~] object is a great filter, but we have to provide it with coefficients instead of cutoff/center frequency, gain, and resonance. These coefficients can be computed manually in many programs such as Matlab or inside Max using either [filtergraph~] if we need a GUI, [filterdesign] if we want to be very explicit, or [filtercoeff~] if we want to modulate the filter's cutoff, for example, using a signal. So the next example does exactly this: a [biquad~] object is controlled via a [filtercoeff~] object in low-pass mode. These two are inside a [poly~] object, as upsampling a filter can increase sound quality quite a bit. For convenience and tidiness, the [filtercoeff] object is also inside the poly~ object. This is not optimal in terms of efficiency since upsampling the coefficient calculation won't increase audio quality, and this is quite a costly task regarding CPU consumption. The filter coefficient calculation, on the other hand, relies on the sampling frequency of the filter, so calculating the coefficients outside the upsampled process leads to faulty coefficients.

Modulation of the cutoff frequency in this patch is possible using the amplitude envelope and/or an LFO, as most conventional synthesizer designs offer. Refer to the following screenshot:

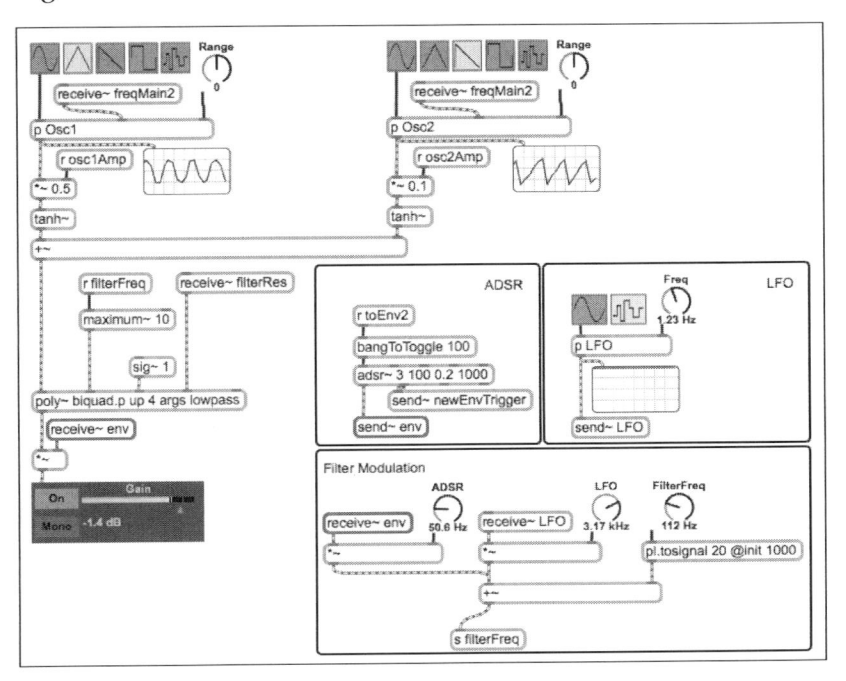

Basic Audio in Max/MSP

You already know some synthesis techniques, so go on and refine the oscillators used, implement some FM or a second filter, and introduce some slight randomness in the pitch control to make the oscillators drift out of phase a bit. There are a lot of things that can be added to this!

Building an equalizer

Quite often, we need a bread and butter EQ. This can also be done using cascaded [biquad~] objects; luckily, there is an object that combines multiple [biquad~] objects in series: the [cascade~] object. The [filtergraph~] object can be configured to contain up to 24 filters using the nfilters attribute. Its output can be sent to the cascade object and voila, we have an EQ. In the following screenshot that shows the EQgraphic subpatcher, the [filtergraph~] object that has been configured to be transparent was put over the [spectrumdraw~] external object to see a nice graph of the resulting spectrum (beware that we have to give [filtergraph~] and [spectrumdraw~] the same amplitude and frequency ranges for this to show us something useful):

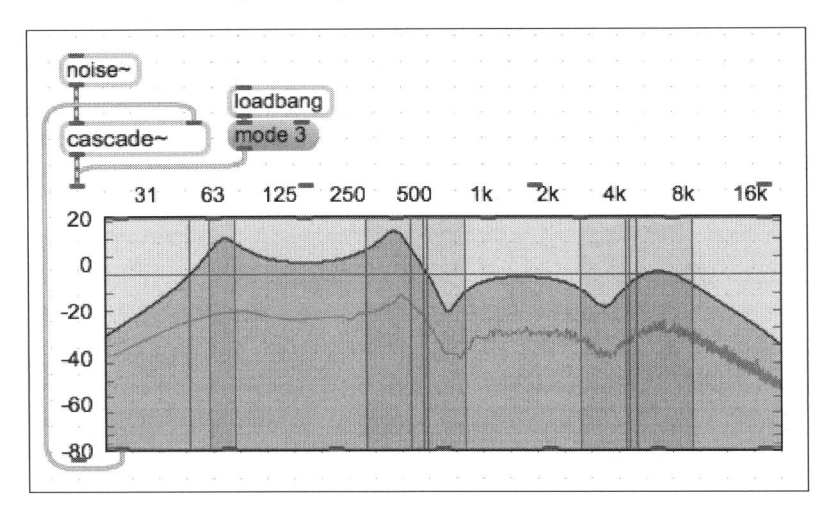

Also, a parametric EQ is created easily. There are two different versions inside the SubtractiveSynthesis.maxpat patcher, both of which are inspired by the typical channel strip EQ on a mixing desk. These can be found in the EQparametric and EQparametric2 subpatchers. One is done by cascading [biquads~] manually, and the other one is using the cascade object directly. Both make use of [poly~] for the possibility of upsampling it and since we can mute the poly~ object. By muting it automatically when the EQ is bypassed, we can make it so the EQ consumes virtually no CPU when it's bypassed. Refer to the following screenshot:

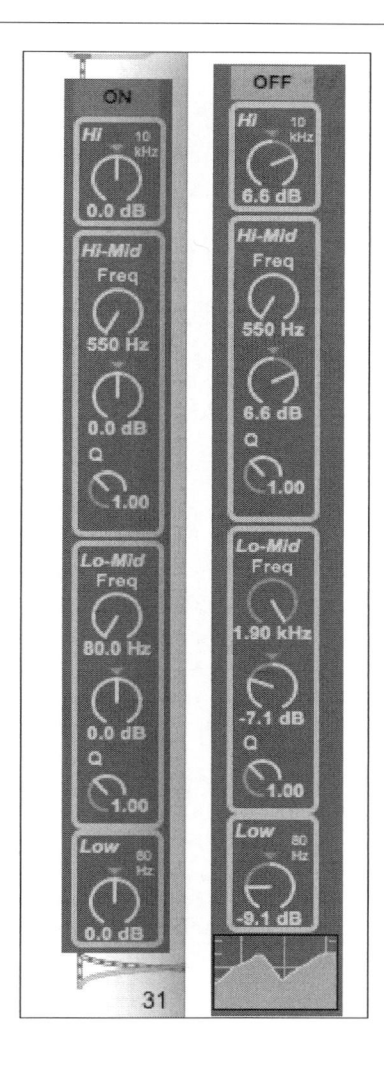

The filter theory: an introduction

Honestly, we won't be able to cover a lot of theory here. Really understanding filters just means understanding signal and system theory in general, and this is way beyond the scope of this book. Also, there are many ways to represent a given filter and fully describe it as follows:

- It is a difference equation (which we use most)
- It is a block diagram
- It is a transfer function
- It is an impulse response

Hopefully, we can obtain a feeling of how filters work, and thus how systems in general work.

Often, the following distinction between different effects is used:

- **Amplitude**: Gates, expanders, compressors, and so on
- **Time**: Delays, reverbs, and so on
- **Frequency response**: Filters

While this distinction might be useful, it is, from a technical point of view, very blurry and not very handy. A very precise and helpful distinction is to look at a system and try to find out whether it is a **Linear Time Invariant (LTI)** system or not. While we will not give a formal description of LTI systems, linearity means summing up two signals; sending them into the system results in the same single output signal as sending the two signals into the system individually and summing the outputs. You can easily see that this is, for example, not true for a compressor. A compressor reacts depending on the input's level, so it is not a linear system. Digital filters, on the other hand, most of the time, are LTI systems. Let's look at a very basic filter, that is, a running average:

$$y[n] = x[n] + x[n-1]$$

Putting it in words, the output is the input plus the last input. If you think about it, we will have to actually divide the sum by two to get the average of the last two samples, as follows:

$$y[n] = 0.5 \cdot x[n] + 0.5 \cdot x[n-1]$$

The two occurrences of **0.5** are called the coefficients. You can imagine that the more we increase the first **0.5** and the more we decrease the second **0.5**, we are reducing the effect of the filter more and more. We are weighing the input and the delayed version of the input. This is essentially all that a certain filter class does, the so-called **Finite Impulse Response (FIR)** or non-recursive filters. We can generalize the previous formula to as many terms we like, as follows:

$$y[n] = a_0 x[n] + a_1 x[n-1] + a_2[n-2] + \cdots + a_m x[n-m]$$

Or we can also put it as follows:

$$y[n] = \sum_{i=0}^{m} a_i \cdot x[n-i]$$

Here, **m** is the maximum delay in samples, and a_0 to a_m are the coefficients of the filter. We did not talk about convolution yet, but we know that what we are doing here is time-domain convolution. The coefficients of an FIR filter are the samples of its impulse response. An FIR filter has the advantage that it is simple to understand and build, and that it can be linear in phase, so the phase of an incoming signal is a linear function of frequency. However, the steepness of an FIR's frequency rolls off, so its cutoff sharpness, one could say, is dependent on the number of delays. If a sharp filter cutoff is desired, many delays, many additions, and many multiplications are needed. Thus, FIRs are very inefficient compared to an **Infinite Impulse Response (IIR)** or recursive filter. This is why most audio filters in the digital domain will be IIR filters. By the way, all analog filters feature feedback so are IIR filters.

A basic application of [buffir~] can be found in the FIR and Convolution subpatch. Here, we generate an impulse response using the sinc function, essentially making a lowpass. Below that, we find a simple convolution reverb made using the external object [multiconvolve~], which is also contained in the HIRT. Note that [buffir~] and [multiconvolve~] are actually doing (more or less) the same thing; they both convolve the input with a given impulse response, or a filter kernel, or a convolution kernel, or filter the signal with the given FIR coefficients; it's all the same. However, the implementation of these two objects is very different; [multiconvolve~] is optimized for longer impulse responses and therefore for reverb generation, as shown in the following screenshot:

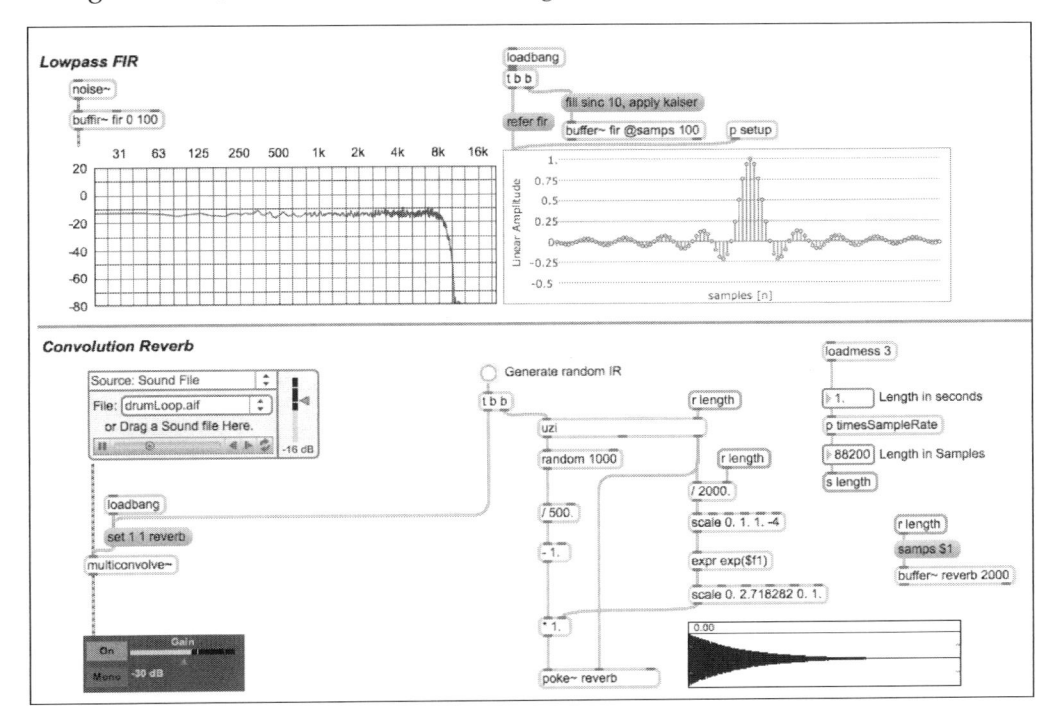

Basic Audio in Max/MSP

So you see, the distinction between a reverb and a filter can sometimes become very subtle. Let's now see what's the difference between an IIR and a delay.

We already saw the simplest IIR filter as a block diagram and difference equation in the feedback section of the AM section. The IIR filters are a lot more complex but also a lot more efficient. It can be shown that a feedback loop in a filter is equivalent to an infinite number of delay stages in an FIR. This and the fact that due to the feedback loop we can have an infinite impulse response leads to its name. Let's build a filter that blows up as soon as we send in an impulse; let's make a truly infinite impulse response filter as shown in the following screenshot:

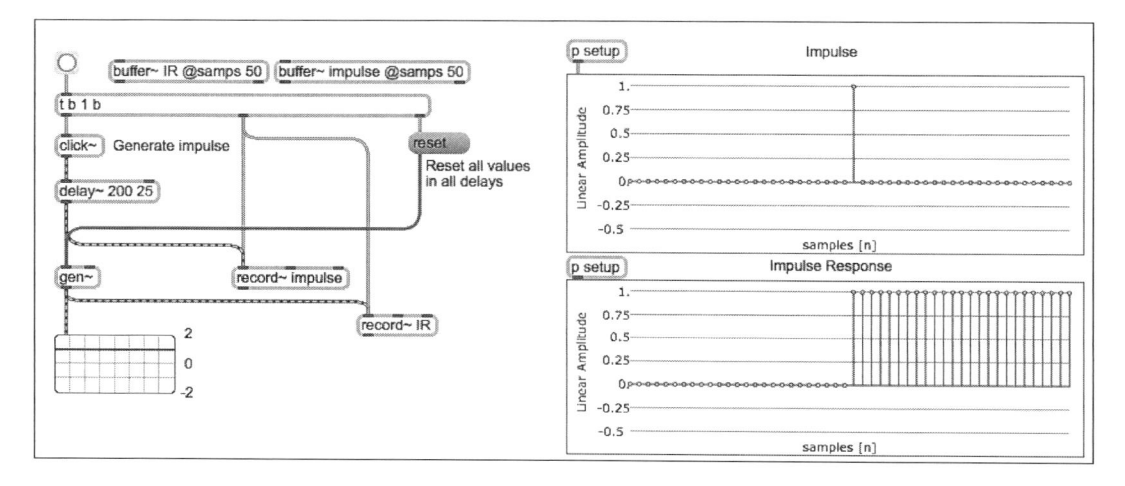

In the preceding screenshot, you can't see the actual filter. It is hidden inside the `gen~` object. However, you can see that [click~] is generating an impulse or a unit sample, and what we get on the output is what's called the unit step. Can you think of a (admittedly very primitive) filter that will do this for us? Moreover, can you think of a filter that takes the unit step function as its input and gives us the unit sample? So what is the inverse of this filter? (Hint, it's an FIR!) The solutions to both these problems are in the `Accumulator` and `Differentiator` subpatchers inside the `IIR` subpatcher.

> Take a look inside your Max application folder by navigating to /examples/gen~.filters.maxpat. Here, you will find the `gen~` versions of many MSP filters.

We will now use a very simple filter, similar to Max/MSP's [onepole~], or a one-pole filter in general. It looks like this:

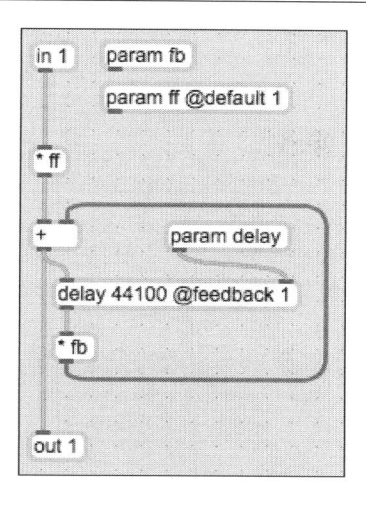

Looks pretty simple, right? We scale the input with a variable called **ff** (for feed forward) and add it to the circuit's output, scaled by **fb** (for feedback) and delayed by delay number of samples. This `gen~` patch is inside the `General` subpatcher and what shouldn't surprise you is that we can realize a lowpass and highpass with it. What might surprise you though is since we didn't fix the delay time to 1 sample, we can also achieve a comb filter and a normal audio delay with it. So we can kind of blend between all of these. Obviously, there is not much of a difference between the structure of simple delays, allpass filters, comb filters, low-pass filters, and high-pass filters. It's merely about the parameterization. Of course, there are many more complex filters and effects designs out there. Even our familiar biquad is a two-pole filter already that features two delays.

In the given subpatch, the gen patcher is there twice, so you can listen to the different effects and the impulse response is also recorded and shown. For example, here you can see the IR of the realized highpass:

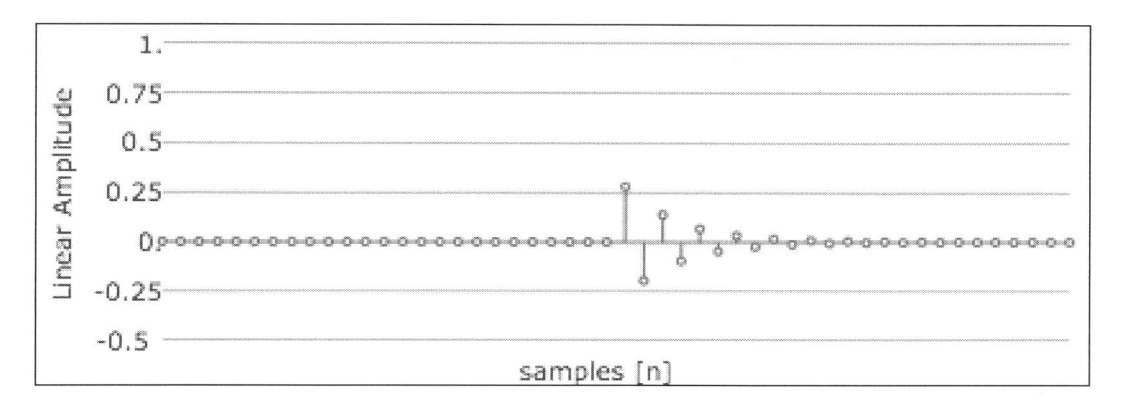

Waveshaping

In the preceding examples, we already encountered an object called [buffer~]. A [buffer~] object can hold, read, and write audio data. The creation of a buffer object means reserving a certain space in RAM that can be accessed very quickly. Therefore, this is ideal for using it as a lookup table. Let's look at the most basic example of a lookup table: the [cycle~] object. The sine wave that it's generating is not computed but read from an internal buffer. We can drive the [cycle~] object using a [phasor~] object, reading out the wavetable at the [phasor~] objects frequency. In the following screenshot, you can see two different graphical representations of the same process. Both times, we just read out the wavetable as described previously, but once we graph the two signals individually and to the right, we use the rescaled phasor driving the x axis and the output of the [cycle~] object as y.

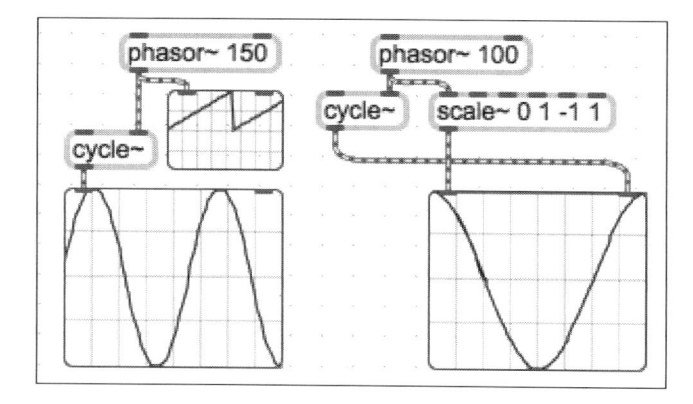

So using a [phasor~] object, we can make any stored waveform an oscillator. Note that our wavetable should start and end with the same (or a very similar) value; otherwise, we will introduce a discontinuity when looping through it with a phasor. This essentially adds a high number of harmonics, since a discontinuity in a waveform is similar to adding an impulse with an amplitude equal to the discontinuity's scale. An impulse in theory has a flat, infinite spectrum. This is simulated in the following screenshot by just scaling the phasor down a bit so it wraps around too early:

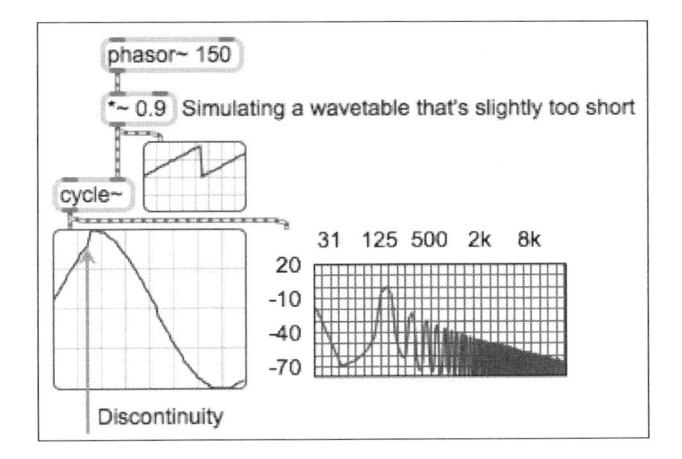

In case you are wondering, the [scope] objects here are not in phase with each other; they both react on a rising edge using the `trigger` attribute. That's why the discontinuity and the falling step of the phasor seem unaligned.

Of course, we can also use any other wave as an input to a table lookup. To get a clearer view of what happens when we use a lookup table, take a look at the interactive example `WaveshapingPlayground.maxpat`. There, you'll find the (animated) visualization of the process that is depicted in the following screenshot:

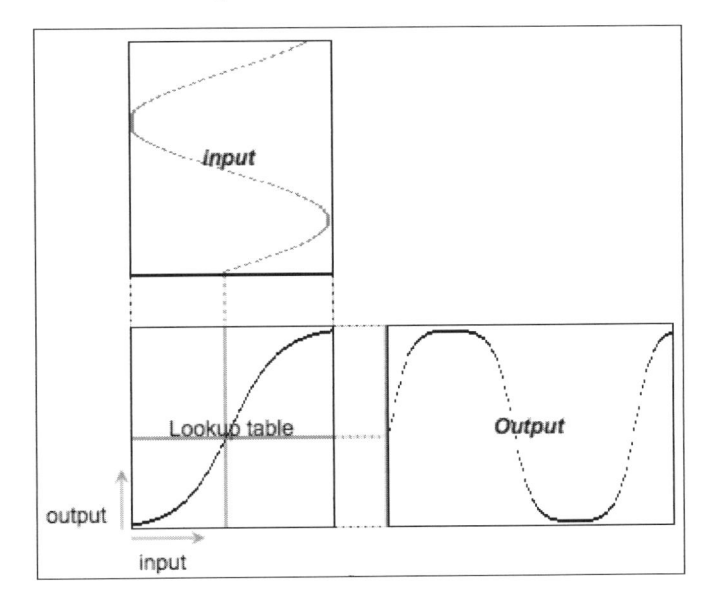

In the preceding screenshot, a sine wave is used as an input. The `tangenshyperbolicus` (tanh) function is stored in the wavetable and used as a lookup table, causing overtones or slight distortion at the output. We have used `[tanh~]` earlier too; its characteristic is very handy since it adds little harmonics when the input is low and more when the input amplitude increase.

If you've had a look at the interactive example, you'll also find what's called the **Chebyshev polynomials**. These are a number of polynomials that specifically generate a certain harmonic. A similar but different approach is to use a function directly to reshape the `input` function. The simplest form of this would be, for example, to feed a `[phasor~]` object into `[sinx~]` after multiplying with 2π to get a sine wave. In the following screenshot, you can see an implementation of the second Chebyshev polynomial:

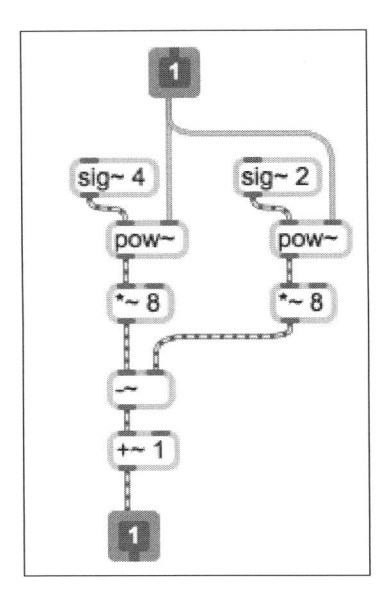

Sampling and audio file playback

We've talked a lot about samples, meaning individual values in a stream of audio. Now, we arrive at sampling, meaning recording audio, playing back of audio, and sample, which means a piece of audio. Sadly, the word sample has an ambiguous meaning in this context.

To be able to record and play something, we'll need to reference memory somehow. We have two options for this: RAM and hard disk. Playing from the hard disk and recording to it can be done using [sfplay~] and [sfrecord~] respectively. The [sfinfo~] object can be used to get additional info about the audio file such as sample rate, length, and so on. Playing from the disk is particularly useful if we need to play very long files since they would of course eat up our RAM. The same is true for recording. The big caveat here is that we don't have as much flexibility when playing from the disk, which is also the reason why we won't cover this technique any further.

Instead, let's take a look at a setup using the RAM in the following screenshot:

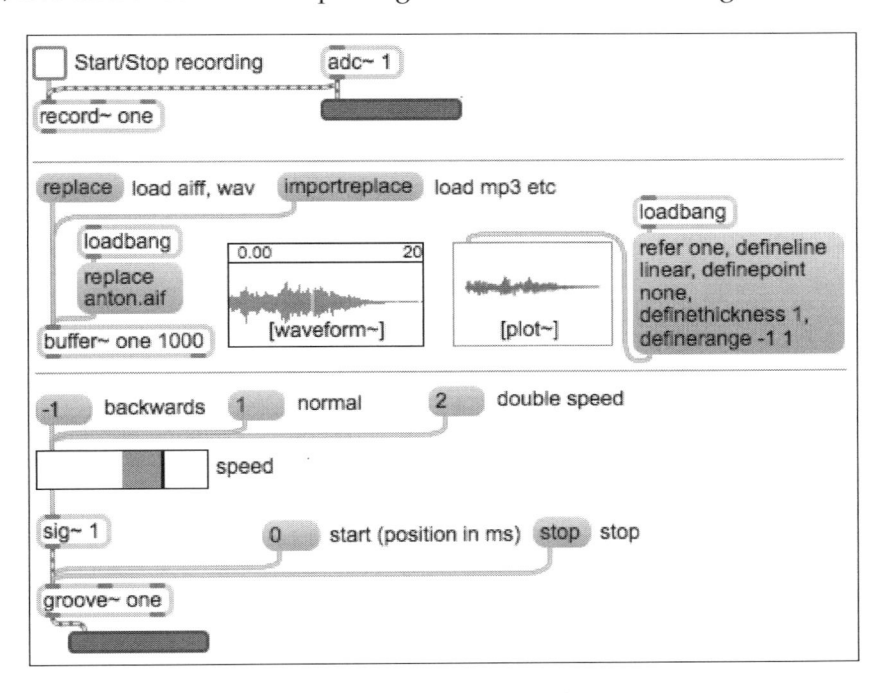

The [buffer~] object, of course, holds our sample data; [record~] is used to record (surprise); and [groove~] is one possibility to play back the data. All of these have one object as their first argument. This is the name of the [buffer~] object, which is referenced by the other two objects. To look at what's inside a buffer, we can just double-click on the [buffer~] object or on an object referencing it to have an in-patcher view of the [waveform~] contents as well as the very versatile [plot~] object can be used.

Basic Audio in Max/MSP

A slightly more advanced example can be found in the `basic record-playback` subpatcher. Here, the [waveform~] object's interactive possibilities are used in order to allow us to play around with looped regions. Get to know the [waveform] object's different modes, but also note the [info~] object. The [info~] object needs a bang at its inlet to output information about the [buffer~] object. Conveniently, the [buffer~] object outputs a bang when it has completed loading a file, so connecting these is very handy. When we work with samples, one can say that the most important thing is bookkeeping, that is, knowing the length in ms and in samples, so knowing the sample rate and knowing playback or record positions. With these basic examples, all this is not so obvious, but when we come to granular sampling, you'll see what I mean. But even here, if we want to display our playback position using the line message to the [waveform~] object, we need to use the [groove~] object's sync ramp, which is going from 0 to 1, and multiply it with the length in ms. Refer to the following screenshot:

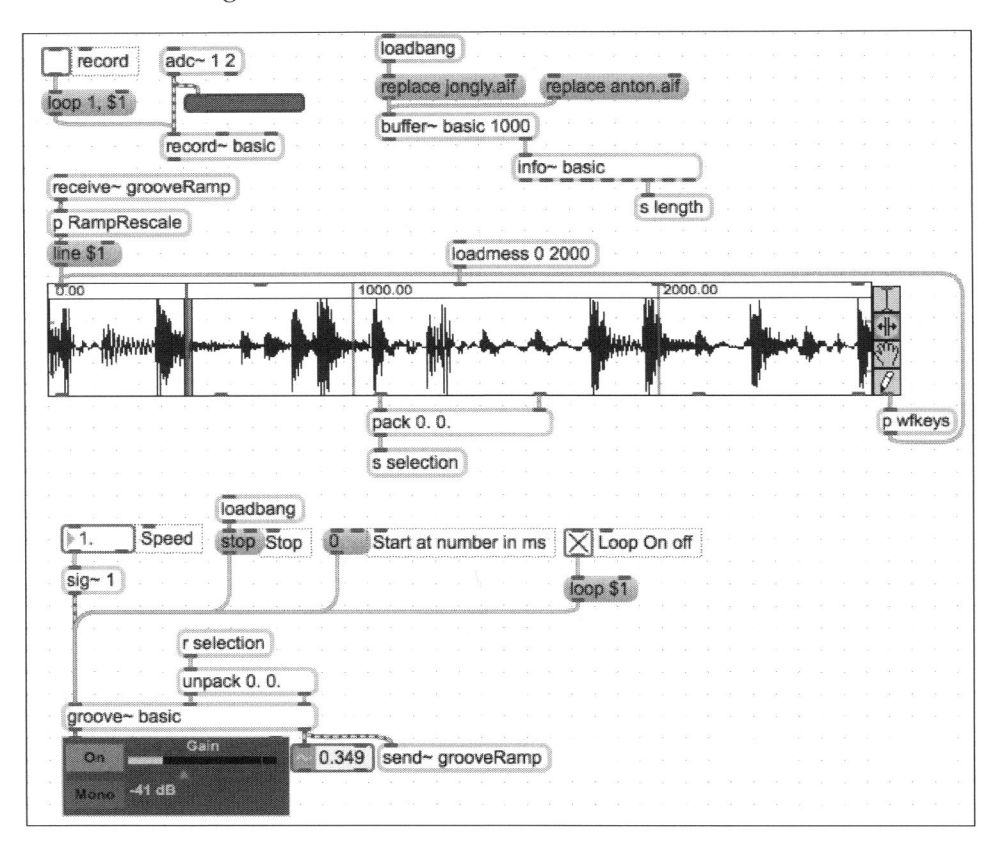

[130]

There are two other examples inside `Sampling_examples.maxpat`. One is a wave scanner, an idea that is somewhat related to granular synthesis and wave shaping. This technique does not care about the loaded file's frequencies, and just reads from a small region of it using a sine or triangle wave. When the position of this region is modulated using an LFO or a slowly moving random value, we can achieve very interesting evolving spectra.

The other example is a very basic drum machine. A small sequencer and three buffers are used in combination with a [poly~] object that contains a [groove~] object. Although we could have mixed the three drums implicitly by just sending each voice out from the same outlet, here we used a [gate~] object in combination with [thispoly~] to get each voice individually on a separate outlet. Also, each voice needs to reference a different [buffer~] object. Although we initialize all the [groove~] objects to reference the first [buffer~] object, using the set message, we assign a new one per voice. We could have built a small table using [coll], which contains all the buffer names, but using [sprintf], we can just generate the buffer names by concatenating a string with an integer, as shown in the following screenshot:

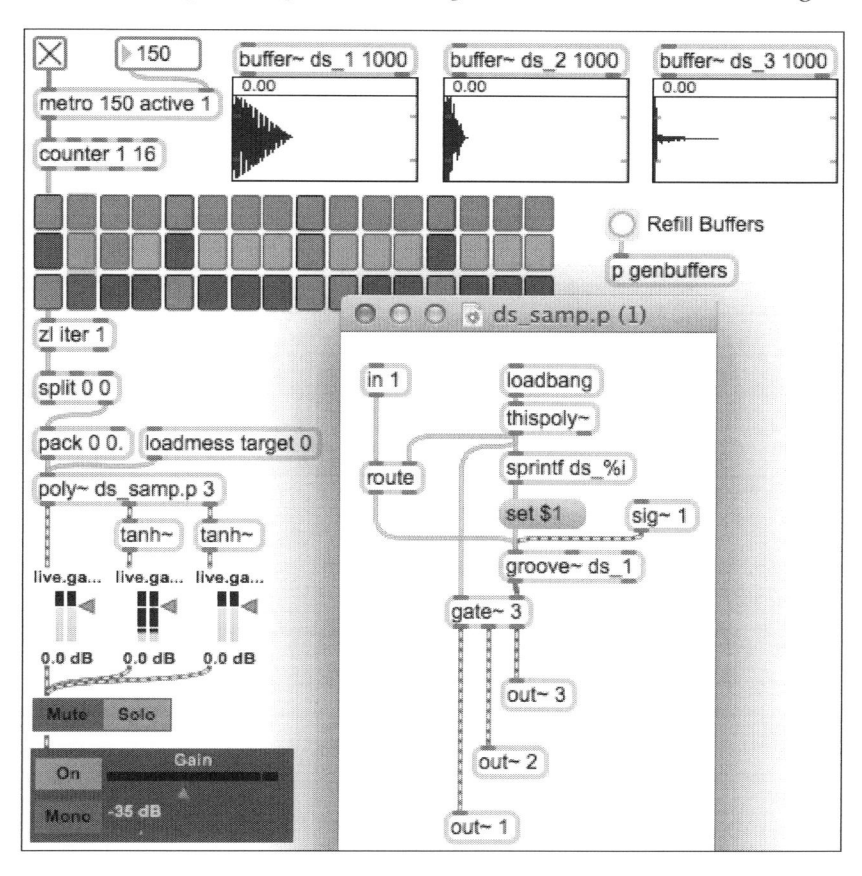

Basic Audio in Max/MSP

Now, we talked a lot about generating interesting signals and there is more to come. But let's take a break here to see how we can come up with a system that allows us to mix signals inside Max conveniently.

Mixing and signal routing

As you know, we can mix signals inside MSP implicitly by just connecting two outlets to the same inlet or by using [+~] explicitly. But there is more to routing and organizing mixes of course. Before looking at an attempt to make mixing in Max a bit more convenient, let's look at a simple mixing block that's needed quite often: a dry/wet mixer. We need this quite often; as soon as we build an effect or want to do a crossfade, we'll need to think about this. A naive approach would look like this:

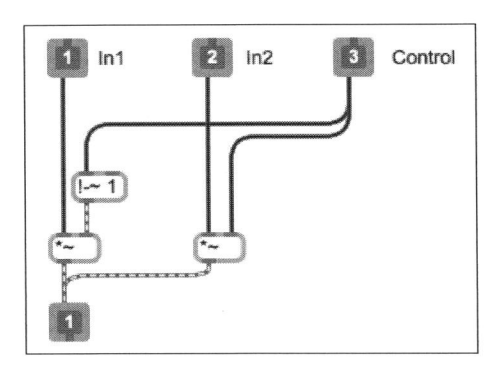

We just scale one signal by a fade value *f*, and the other one by *1-f*. However, this idea has a problem: when the signal at the control inlet is at 0.5, we multiply both inlets with 0.5 (which is equal to an attenuation by 6 dB). The problem is that adding two correlated waves is equal to an amplification by 6 dB, but by mixing two uncorrelated signals (two noise sources for example), we will only get an amplification by 3 dB. So the upshot is that we are too quiet in the middle of our fade for most practical signals and will have to compensate for that.

There are two common methods for this compensation: one is by taking the sine and the other is by using a square root of the fade value. Both of them lead to an amplification of 3 dB at fade equal to 0.5. So we can normalize the result back again by scaling the output by $\frac{1}{\sqrt{(2)}}$, which is the same as applying a gain of -3 dB. In the following screenshot, you can see a more proper cross-fade utilizing the sine:

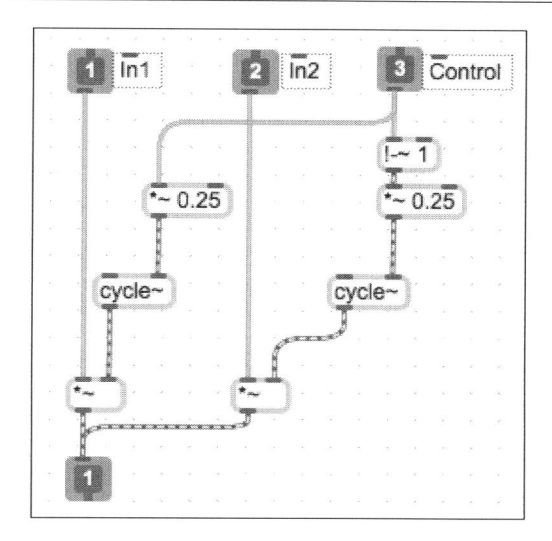

Here, the three methods are shown as diagrams; this is again a part of an interactive example that can be found in the `DryWet Methods` subpatcher inside `MixingAndRouting.maxpat`:

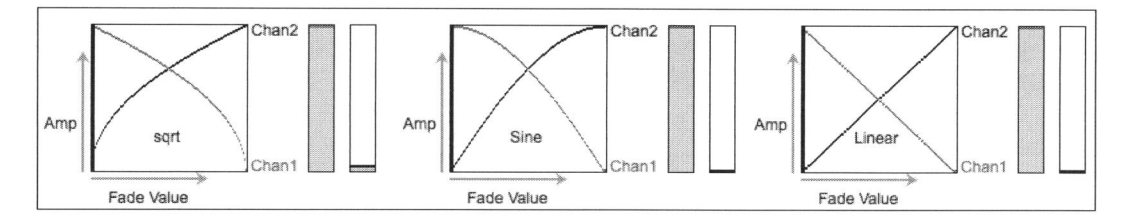

Implementations of the three methods are also inside the patcher; take a look at them and see whether you can hear the difference! The sine version has the advantage of needing less processing power since it's a lookup instead of a square root calculation as you know. Lastly, a pan pot, that is, distributing a mono signal in stereo works just the same only the other way around.

Basic Audio in Max/MSP

Conventional mixing

To get away from many additions, the [live.gain] objects all over the place, and crude [send~] [receive~] spaghetti networks, we can just implement our own fully modular, fully customizable mixing desk! Of course, we still have to keep things tidy, but this will make a lot of things a lot easier. Refer to the following screenshot:

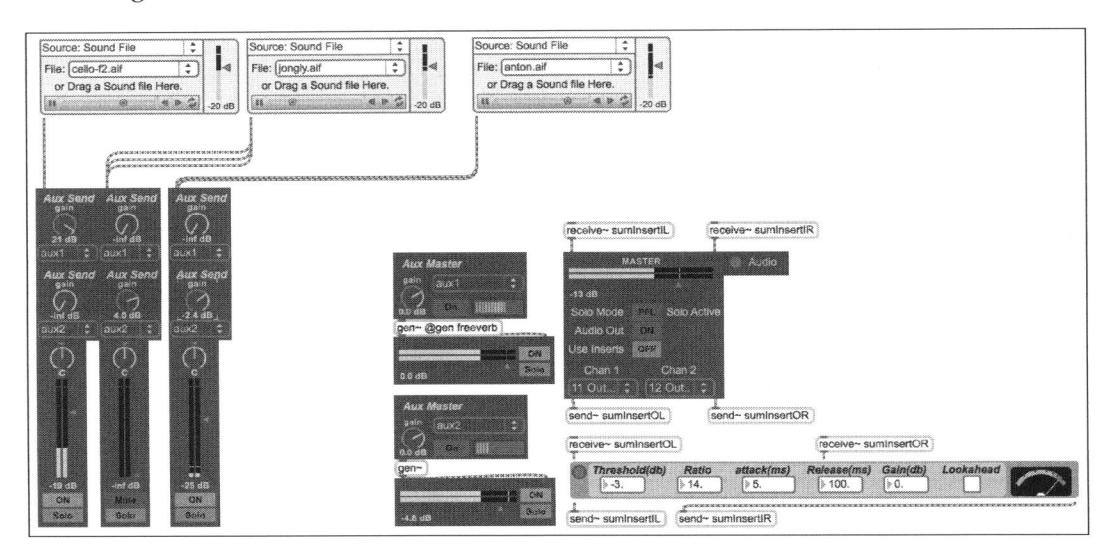

It's actually a very simple task to come up with a mixing desk in Max. We just need to establish some [send~] and [receive~] structures and design some little bpatchers objects. The only thing that might be a little tricky is getting **solo** to work properly, both **After Fader Listening (AFL)** and **Pre Fader Listening (PFL)**. This really is one of the most useful features a mixer offers.

Since it really is quite easy to do this, I'd recommend that you just take a look at this example, which is also located inside MixingAndRouting.maxpat. Also, think about using these as clippings, so you can always come up with an adhoc mixing desk, or build a mixing desk in a patcher that's located in your extras folder, so you can always open it and send some signals to it again via send/receive. For now, ignore the compressor that's inside the example here; we'll come to compression soon; it's just there to demonstrate that we have master inserts also.

Summary

In this chapter, we finally got to talking about audio. We introduced some very common techniques and thought about refining them and getting things done properly and efficiently (think about `poly~`). By now, you should feel quite comfortable building synths that mix techniques such as FM, subtractive synthesis, and feature modulation, as well as using matrices to rout both audio and modulation signals where you need them.

We'll now move on to the next chapter, essentially doing the same but going into more detail, covering some FX, FFT, compression, and lots more. We'll seek to slowly move away from the big picture to look at some more concrete examples and (re)usable pieces of MSP code.

Advanced Audio in Max/MSP

We'll now go into more detail and cover some more advanced techniques in audio processing. We'll start off with some more sampling techniques, take a deeper look at working in the frequency domain, and lots more. This chapter will comprise a general overview of audio processing inside Max; most of what is shown is highly expandable and demonstrates the techniques at a minimum setup in order to simplify the example. So, they are made to be expanded by you, to get you experimenting and get a good starting point.

In this chapter, the topics we'll cover are as follows:

- Audio-processing techniques
- Granular sampling
- Stutter, dynamics, and reverberation
- Fast Fourier Transform
- Accurate sample sequencing

More sampling

So far, we have played samples only using [groove~] by providing speed and starting point/loop points. Often, we need more control than that; for example, sometimes, we need to play a specific position at a specific point in time, or we want to modulate the position somehow. A basic setup is shown in the following screenshot; using [play~] for instance, we access a buffer with a position in milliseconds:

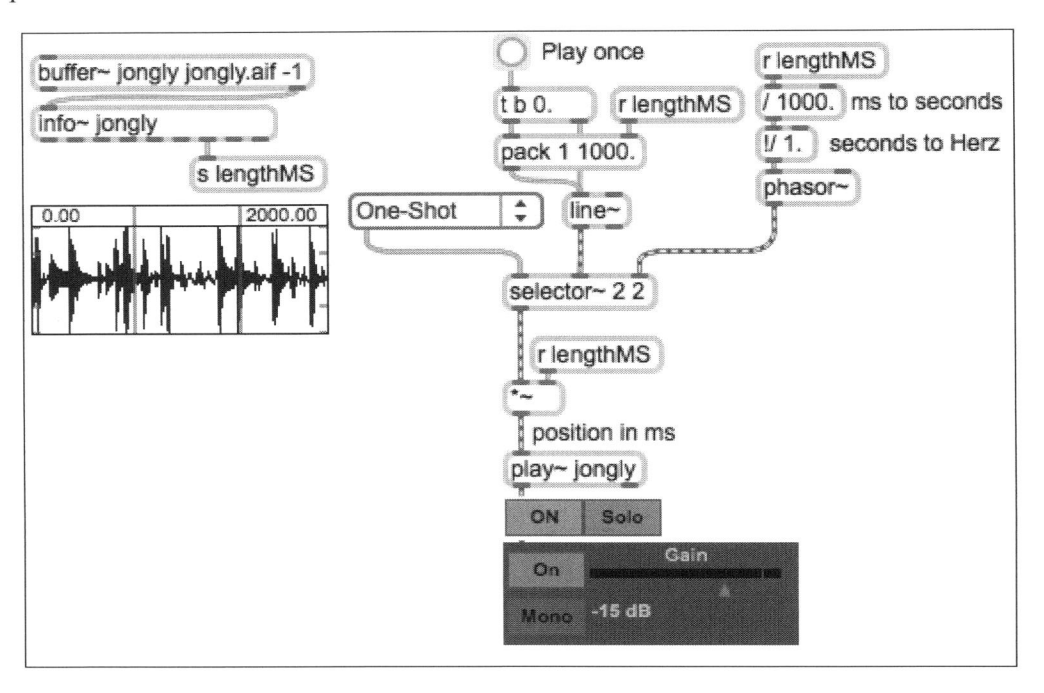

In the preceding screenshot, we implemented both a one-shot and a looping functionality using [play~]. This, of course, is more complicated than the use of groove, but we won some options. Besides having founded the basis for understanding granular sampling en passant, we can, for example, play a sample from one buffer and record it to the same position of another buffer very easily using this technique. As there is [play~] for position-based playback, there is poke~ for position-based writing. Transferring audio data from one buffer to another is easy; we can send a duplicate message to a [buffer~] object to duplicate the contents of another [buffer~] object. But what if we wish to put a lowpass on a sample? We'd need to play it, put that lowpass on the signal, and record again, and then probably use the duplicate message to get the result back into our original buffer. This principle can be quite handy if we want to process a sample once in real time and mute our FX afterwards using the recorded material.

Chapter 5

Other than that, this system is capable of reproducing a very old idea: degradation of material through repeated processing. Once we have duplicated the processed material back into our first [buffer~] object, we can just start all over again. If this is done often, the material can change very much in an iterative process that is hard to predict (depending on the applied FX of course). Refer to the following screenshot:

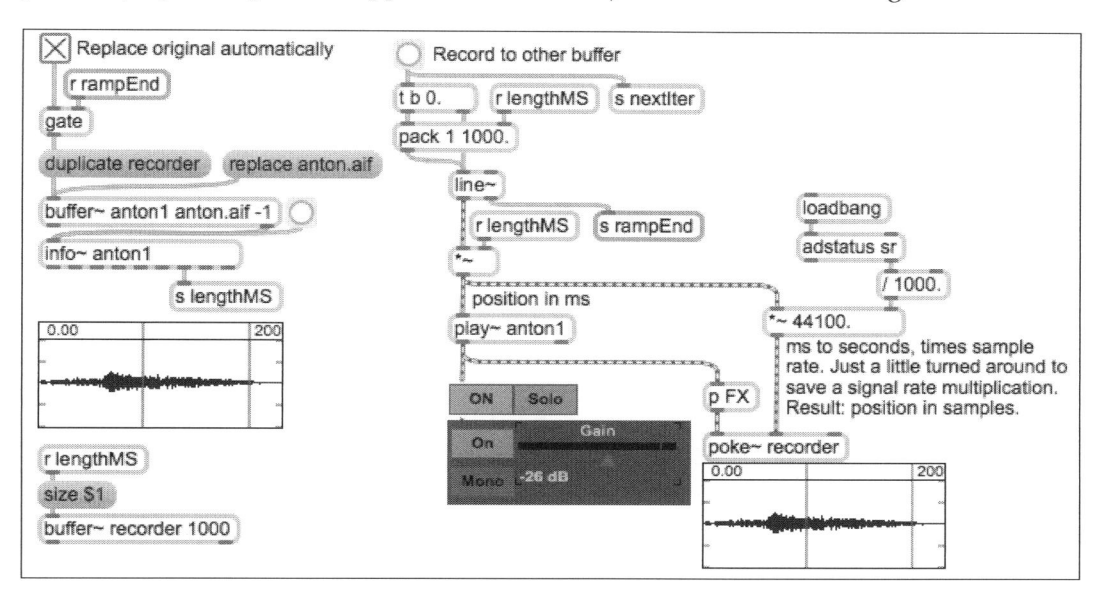

Sampling has a very close relationship to delays. Audio delays (such as the [tapin~] and [tapout~] combination) are nothing but buffers that are constantly written to and read from. Sometimes, buffers accessed this way are called ring buffers or circular buffers, and are used to illustrate the idea of writing to it again and again in a circular manner. So let's look at an implementation of a tape delay simulation using a buffer and position-based reading and writing.

Advanced Audio in Max/MSP

Note that this example was constructed for didactic reasons. There are only two advantages of making a tape delay this way (instead of using [tapin~]/[tapout~]); we always know the reading and writing position and have general access to the buffer in use. While this might be needed sometimes, the disadvantages of this implementation are numerous; [tapin~] and [tapout~] are made for us to be used as delays. Anyway, the advantage of knowing the position is used here to give us a nice visual representation of what's happening and hopefully give us a more clear idea of what's meant by ring buffer and how a delay works (for example, you might now see why we have to assign [tapin~] a maximum delay time / buffer length). Refer to the following screenshot:

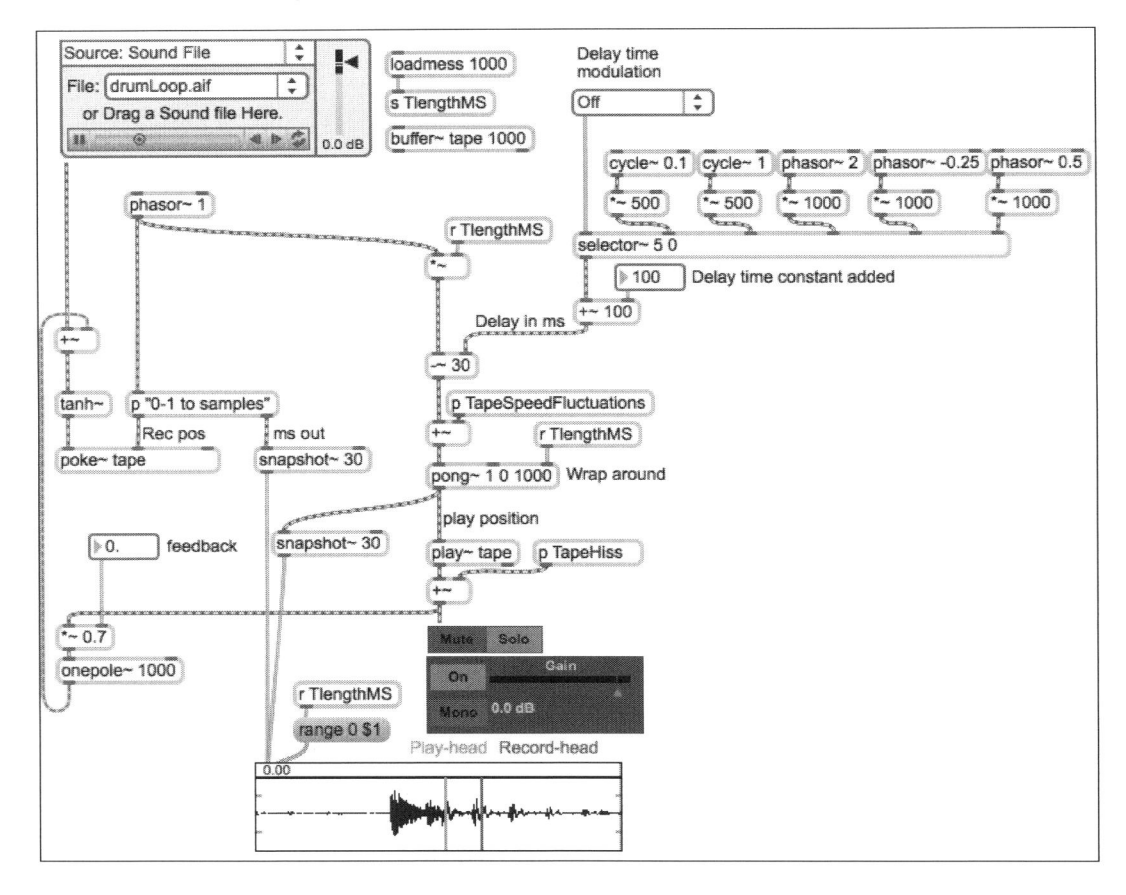

In the preceding screenshot, you can see the `Tape Delay` subpatcher inside `MoreSampling.maxpat`. The `[poke~]` object is used here to write to our buffer, and `play` is used to access it with an offset to the record position. This offset is the delay time. In addition, feedback has been added with a lowpass in the feedback path, which is quite common when trying to simulate a tape delay's behavior. Some saturation using `[tanh~]` has been added, and some filtered noise (inside the `TapeHiss` subpatcher) with a very low level is added to the output and the feedback path. Also, we added some modulation of the delay time, simulating fluctuating tape speed.

In addition, there is the possibility of modulating the delay time in some more extreme ways. This has been done since there are some pretty interesting effects we can achieve just by modulating a delay's time. We can make live input sound faster backwards, (including higher pitched and slower and lower pitched). Making something sound backwards this way definitely adds some latency. The idea of using a modulated delay to to make something sound backwards, faster, or slower is maybe a bit hard to understand without a visual representation of the `play` and `record` head. Take a close look at this constructed example.

While you do that, you may notice that though it's working quite nicely, we have a little problem. What if the play head crosses the record head? We will encounter a discontinuity.

Discontinuities, as you already know, add many high frequencies and sound like a click. When working with samples, we generally have to think a bit more about discontinuities than when synthesizing sound, since we often jump around in position. The simplest example of a jump is of course looping; jumping from the end of a sample to the beginning. If there is a big difference between the sample at the end and the one at the beginning, we'll hear a click.

This might also come up if we are just playing at any random point in a sample, or jump around wildly. In many cases, this click won't be very loud or we wouldn't hear it because the sample itself is probably a drum sample full of attacks and transients, or because the difference between the two points just isn't very large by coincidence. In the subpatcher discontinuities, we built an example of cello note looping, and the loop point has been chosen to be one where the clicking is especially prominent.

Advanced Audio in Max/MSP

In the following screenshot, you can see a way to avoid these click problems: a simple windowing method. We fade in at the beginning of the loop and fade out at the end, essentially attenuating the click. By taking loop start and end points, we calculate the loop length. This is multiplied with the [groove~] objects' sync outlet to obtain the position in the loop in ms. By clipping this value to, for example 0 and 44, we obtain a 44 ms ramp from 0 to 44 at the beginning of the loop with a value of 44 for the rest of the time. Dividing this by 44 normalizes it to 0 to 1. The same is done for the end of the loop; we just use a loop length minus loop position subtraction before the calculation. The two results are multiplied to obtain our window.

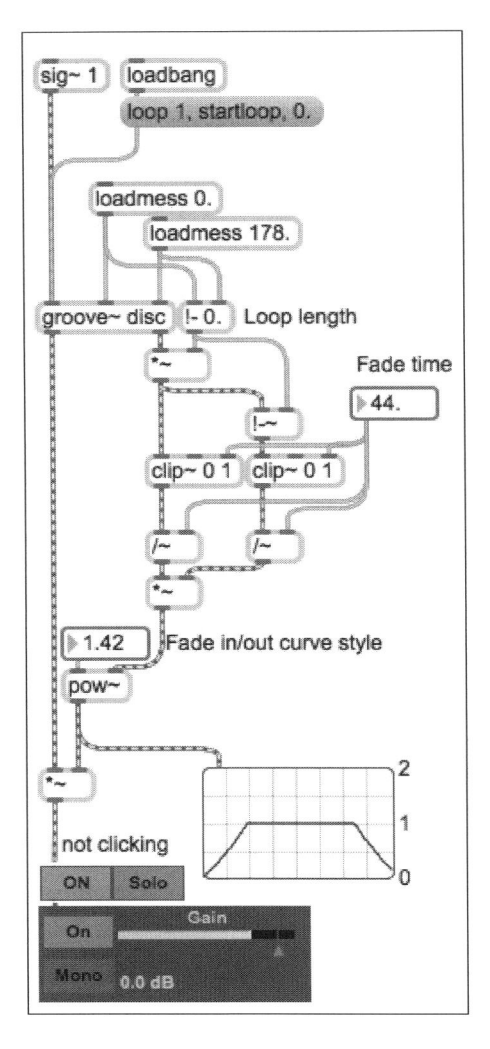

All this might sound a bit too complicated just for looping a sample without any artifacts or noises. However, we can put all this inside an abstraction, so we don't have to bother in the future. In fact, Max comes with an abstraction called [grooveduck] that does exactly the same. Also, we did this to introduce the idea of windows, which is going to be of great use both in granular synthesis and **Fast Fourier Transform (FFT)**.

Granular sampling

The idea of granular sampling is to take a piece of audio, a sample, and instead of simply playing it, play many short pieces (that is grains) of it. The aim is to create a mechanism that allows us to control playback speed and perceived pitch independently; the result is a lot more than that since it allows us to create really interesting timbres by tweaking the parameters. In order to get, for example, slowed-down playback but unchanged pitch, we will let all the grains play at a normal speed but shift their positions through the sample at a slower rate. The granular visualization subpatcher is shown in the following screenshot. This patcher has no audio functionality; it really just produces a moving image to visualize the idea for better understanding.

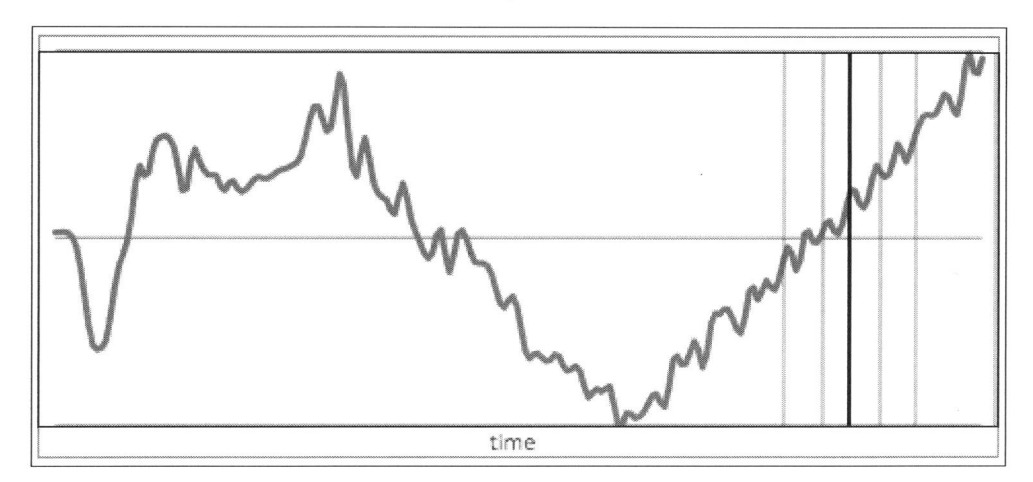

The background is supposed to be an audio waveform that we loaded. The dark vertical line is something like a master [phasor~] object or a master playback position. The slightly lighter vertical lines are the positions of the grains, which are scattered around the master position. As stated previously, the master position may have a different tempo than the grain playback rate. The grain playback rate influences the pitch, whereas the master speed controls the perceived speed.

Advanced Audio in Max/MSP

You can probably already imagine that once we get this basic setup going, we can start playing with many more parameters of the grains; for example, we can introduce random pitch variation for the grains, a random position in the stereo image, and so on. So, let's take a look at the basic setup in Max. The need for many simultaneous playback operations (the grains) should make you think immediately of one object: [poly~]!

Imagine us using a [play~] object inside [poly~] that plays a small portion of the audio file repeatedly, and whose position is shifted through the entire file via an external [phasor~] object. The small loop is also controlled via a [phasor~] object inside the [poly~] object. Now, the important thing is, if we have, say, fifty voices, so fifty little [play~] objects, each with their own [phasor~] objects, then all these are not playing synchronously. They play at the same time, all the time, but are out of phase starting at a different point in time and at a different position in the sample. So here is an example of the poly~ patch:

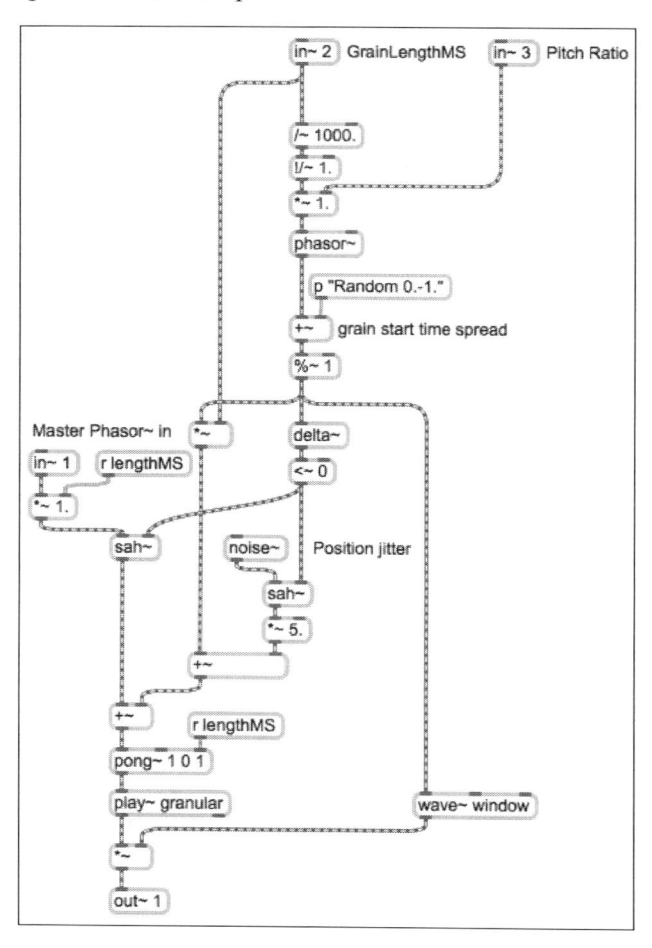

Let me break it down for you, since this setup might be a bit challenging.

The patch is loaded in a [poly~] object in an extra patcher called granular_1.maxpat. Let's assume that the master [phasor~] object that is coming in at [in~ 1] is shifting through the audio file at half speed and the grains are playing at a normal speed. As a result, the sample slows down, but its pitch remains unchanged. What you can see is that the [phasor~] object in this patch (let's call it grain phasor, to be more clear) is going to the [play~] object, added onto our master [phasor~]. Also, the [delta~] object in combination with [<~ 0] gives us an impulse if the phasor resets to zero (see the following information box), so at the beginning of a grain. We will need this pulse for a sample-and-hold section that only samples and holds the master [phasor~] object's position at the beginning of the grain. Otherwise, the speed of the master [phasor~] object would influence the resulting pitch.

> Why don't we simply check whether the phasor is 0 or 1? As you know, we are working with digital signals. Since a digital signal consists of samples that represent it, and these samples are typically in regular intervals of time, their position with respect to the waveform's phase might shift around. As a result, a wave might consist of different sample values per cycle. Sounds complicated? Look at the following screenshot that shows a 10 kHz phasor at 44,100 Hz sample rate:

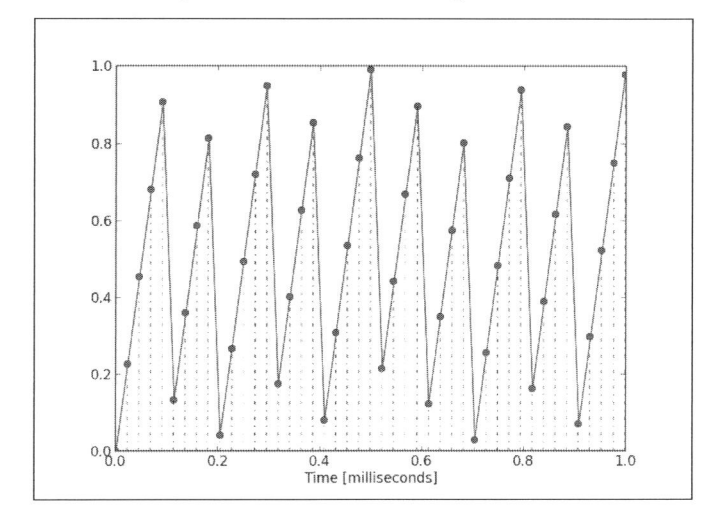

Obviously, we only have a couple of samples per cycle, and the exact maximum and minimum values per cycle vary over time. Note that the blue line that connects the dots is only here to make the sawtooth more visible; this line exists nowhere inside a digital system, only the samples (the dots) do. Everything between them is undefined.

Going back to the previous granular patch, you can see that we are introducing some randomness by adding sampled noise to the position and by adding a random offset to the phase of the [phasor~] grain.

Lastly, we use a [wave~] object that references a buffer in the parent patch to multiply our grain with a window function. In this case, we use a Hanning window (look at the parent patch to see how this can be generated easily). Different windows can have an effect on the noisiness, the overall amplitude, and spectrum of the result. In the following screenshot, you can see our Hanning window:

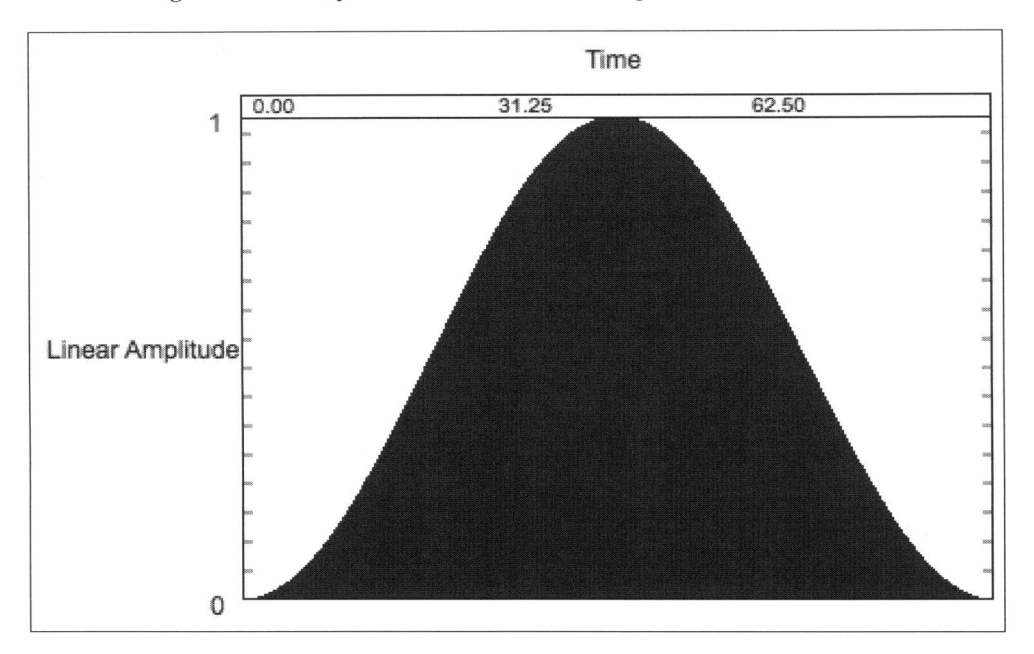

Starting with something that is sampling-based, let's turn to FX. Sampling, writing, and reading buffers will accompany us anyway; it's very useful in all kinds of contexts. Later, we will even write FFT data into buffers, so let's move on.

FX

We talked about filters and distortion (wave table lookups and transfer functions); we just made a delay and used [tapin~] and [tapout~]. So we got pretty much all the bread and butter of FX covered. What's still waiting for us is dynamics, reverbs, FFT-related algorithms, and some convolution-related ideas. Let's start with something easy and really funny: a simple stutter effect.

Stutter

We are going to construct a stutter effect here, so some device that has an input, a live signal that is continuously recorded and just fed through until we push a button activating the stutter. What happens then is that the recording stops, we loop what was last recorded, and feed that to the output. What sounds pretty simple here is in fact pretty simple but may look a bit complicated at first, as shown in the following screenshot:

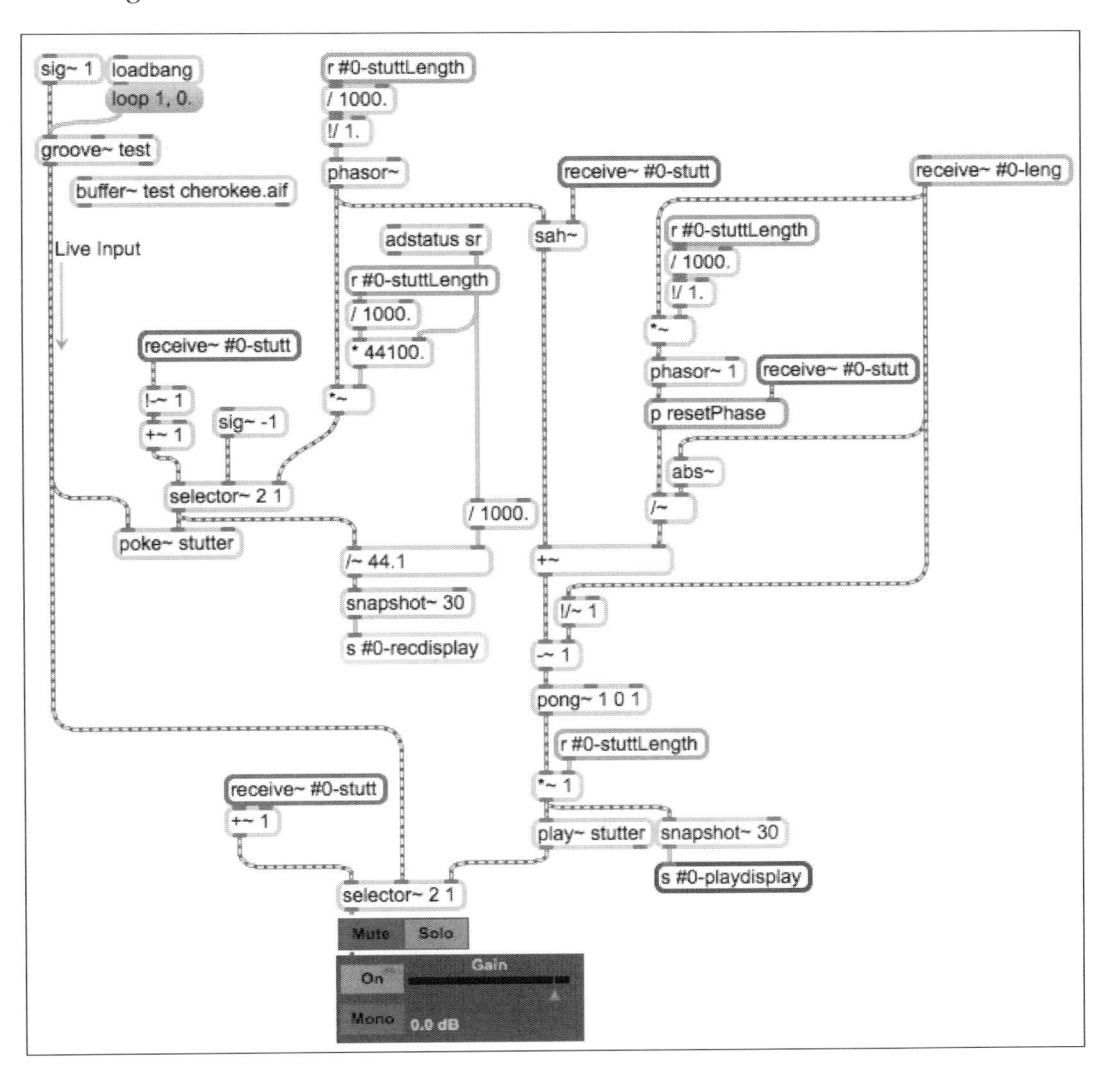

Advanced Audio in Max/MSP

This patch is inside `FX.maxpat`, the `stutter` subpatcher. Open it to see it fully, since some of it is not depicted as follows:

- A [toggle] object to switch the effect on and off. Its value is converted to a signal and reaches the mechanism via all the [receive #0-stutt] objects
- A [numbox] object to control the length of the loop, coming in at [receive #0-leng]
- A [buffer~] object named stutter, which is referenced by the [poke~] and [play~] objects that you see
- A small GUI to see where the record and playback heads are

The only really interesting part here is actually inside the resetPhase subpatcher. It's a neat little trick to reset a phasor at signal rate; this is also depicted in the following screenshot. It's important that we use a sample-and-hold circuit once again to get the recording position, add it to our playback phasor, and subtract the length from the result to place our playback phasor exactly at the position we just recorded. Nearly all the rest here is really just converting between units.

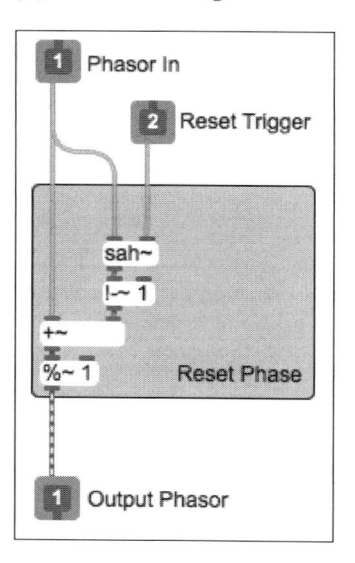

You already saw in the granular sampling patch that we can phase offset a phasor signal just by adding a value and taking a modulo of 1. Obviously, by looking at how much is missing from the value 1, and adding this value constantly, we get a phasor signal that is reset at that instant.

Here, a more or less basic structure is presented. What could be expanded here? What could be improved? For example, we could start windowing our loop, or rather, use the idea we implemented for smooth looping with [groove~]. On the other hand, since this stutter effect is often used in a very rhythmic way, some slight clicking might be aesthetically pleasing although technically not very correct. Another problem we have is that modulating the loop length will change the pitch during modulation. This is due to the fact that since we want our loop to always end at a certain position (the most recent record position), we are offsetting the phasor by changing the loop length. A sample and hold could be used to avoid this behavior, only updating the loop length on cycle completion.

Dynamics

We are now going to explore the world of limiters, compressors, noise gates, and expanders. Dynamic control is extremely important, for technical reasons (making sure a signal is never too loud, for example), for reasons of sound quality (gating the noise, or compressing a signal to increase speech intelligibility, for example), or as a matter of design. Using compression, we can often sculpt our transients and attack phases in a much more sophisticated way, and side chaining allows some interaction in a mix that very much changes its character.

Noise gate

Building a noise gate in Max is very straightforward. We have to check the input level, and if it's over a certain threshold, we let it through unattenuated; otherwise, we mute it. Since attenuation, [*~], and comparison, [>~], really are no challenge for us anymore, the only real problem here is what's called **envelope following**.

From an incoming signal, we need to somehow get a signal that represents the input's level most well. A basic envelope follower can be constructed by first taking the absolute value of a signal; after that, we typically smooth out the signal a bit. Ideally, to get a signal that depicts fast attacks well, we can use a filter such as [slide~] that allows us to configure the slopes for rising and falling signals independently. An example of this process is depicted in the following screenshot:

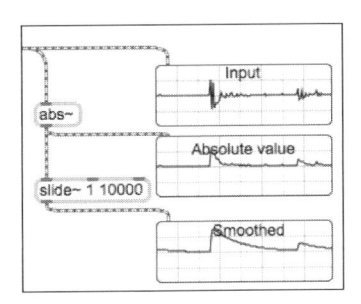

Advanced Audio in Max/MSP

If we don't use this smoothing filter, we might encounter problems due to very fast on/off toggling of our attenuation. A complete noise gate that also features a threshold in dB is depicted here and can be found in the `noise gate` subpatcher:

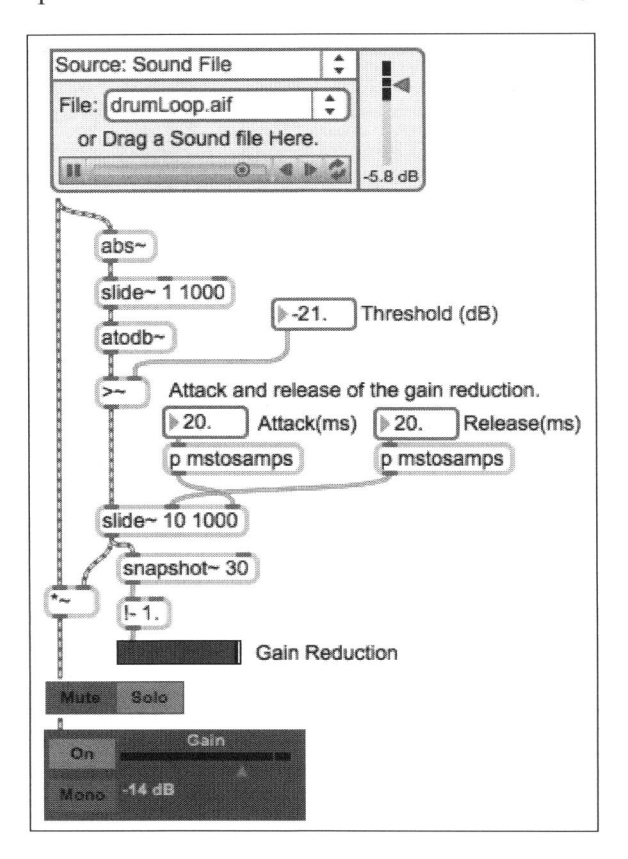

[Here, following the conventions, `attack` and `release`, are the attack and release of the gain reduction, not of the sounds coming through the gate. If you find this confusing, you can just swap the cords going from the controls to `[slide~]`.]

Now, what if we don't want to mute our signal completely but just attenuate it by some amount to make the result sound a bit more natural? We are going to need an expander.

Working with expanders

Expanders are great for adding some liveliness to a signal since we increase the dynamic range. If a signal is below the threshold, it won't get muted as a noise gate would, but it will be attenuated by a set ratio. For now, we will keep things really simple here and just expand (pun intended) our noise gate:

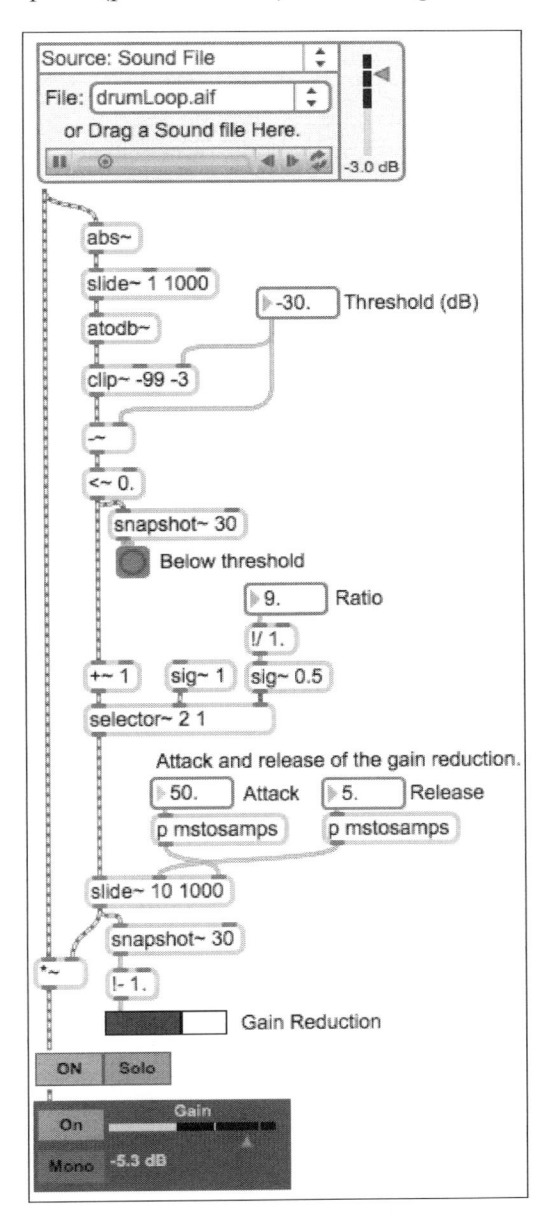

This is a very simple version of an expander. A more complex one can be found in the `examples` folder of the Max installation, but here we will also go into more detail. An expander is very similar to a compressor, so you can actually take the `compressor` patch that we are going to look at in a minute and use it as a more sophisticated expander if you use a negative ratio. First, let's talk about limiting.

Limiter

Limiting is often very important if we need to make sure a signal remains in a certain range. Along the way, we often used [tanh~] as a limiter/soft clipper. The problem here is that it adds harmonics pretty quickly, way before the input comes close to 0 or 1 dBFS.

Sometimes, this is nice to simulate analog saturation for example, but sometimes, we want our signal to stay as clean as possible but still be limited. Two very simple objects can do this for us, [overdrive~] and [clip~]. An audio signal going through [clip~ -1 1] will go through completely unaffected if it is in the range -1 to 1. If it exceeds this range, it will be clipped, that is, limited. The only problem here is that the extremely sudden attenuation (the clipping) adds a huge amount of overtones. The [overdrive~] object behaves similarly; the signal will be clean between -1 and 1, but outside this range, we'll get a lot of distortion. So all of these really limit the signal well, but often, we would want a limiter to prevent distortion, not to add it.

Summing up, we can say all of these three are really handy, but [tanh~] will add some overtones no matter what, but in comparison to overdrive and clip, it will behave more nicely if the input exceeds the -1 to 1 range. In the following screenshot, you can observe this behavior. Don't forget these objects; they are great for situations in which we know that our signal is somewhat in the ballpark, or if we don't care for or even want some saturation. Putting these on a final mix may not be the best idea if you want clean limiting.

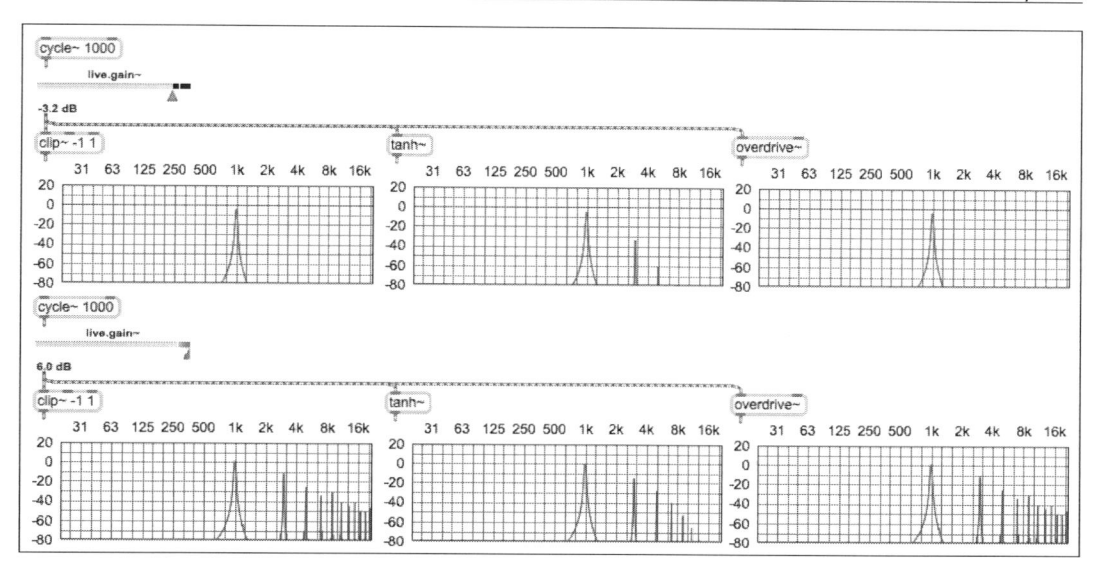

So, as a compromise between most secure limiting and least distortion, we will need to come up with a different solution. There is [omx.peaklim], a nice peak limiter coming with Max, but let's go ahead and build one ourselves! Why can't we just measure the incoming level and adjust the output level accordingly, as we just did with the noise gate and expander? Here a look at this screenshot:

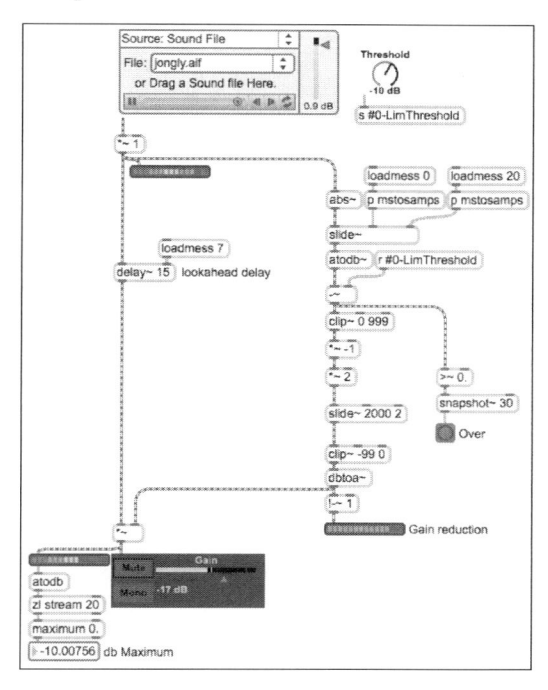

So, this is slightly different than what we had with the expander. We do some envelope following again, but this time, we do it really fast; we don't smooth rising edges at all and smooth the falling ones over 20 milliseconds.

Then, we go from linear amplitude to dB again to compare how much the input is over the threshold (the subtraction). To get rid of values below the threshold, we clip the result of the subtraction between 0 and practically infinity (we could have used `[maximum~ 0.]` here instead of `[clip~]`). So if our input signal is, say, at 5 dB, and our threshold is set to -10, at this point, we get 15 dB of attenuation. This is why we multiply it with -1 because we are going to need -15 dB.

Then, a multiplication follows with 2 compensating the loss of signal level caused by another lowpass after it; `[slide 2000 2]` is reducing distortion resulting from this quite fast amplitude modulation, and that's more or less it! But wait, what about the delay? This is what's called **lookahead**. Our gain reduction algorithm should ideally look in the future, and if a peak is going to come, it should start ramping down slowly to match the peak perfectly. In real-time signal processing, we can't look in the future, but we can pretend to. We just feed our input first to the algorithm that needs to know the future and delay everything else. This slight delay of a couple of samples shouldn't harm anybody in most cases and provide some extra safety.

This limiter is adjusted to be very safe; it's quite brutal though. On the other hand, truth be told, it will never sound very natural if we make heavy use of limiting. A nice feature of this implementation is that if you drive the signal into limitation very heavily and increase the attack time, for example `[slide~ 2000 10]`, and its preceding multiplication, we can shape attacks in such a dramatic way that incoming signals, especially drums, sound like they're being played backwards due to the heavy processing of the attack phases, shaping them to a slow exponential rise.

Compressor

Compressors are a great tool to shape sounds and to give a mix or a single signal more character. There are many ways to go about building a compressor, and since Cycling '74 provides a standard compressor (also in the `examples` folder), following the same idea of the expander, we will implement something only slightly different and add some functionality. Also, note that both the expander and the compressor provided in the `examples` folder are down-sampled for higher computational efficiency. We just don't do this here since it makes things a bit more difficult to look at for now.

> The important thing to note is the general structure and where the elements are that could be altered to give a more individual sound or to make the compressor work in a different way.

Chapter 5

If you take a look at the following screenshot, you can easily identify a couple of building blocks: the look-ahead section, a level detector, gain computer, and some coloring of the output. The coloring is just an additional feature that actually has nothing to do with compression of course. It does, though, provide a little analog feeling by boosting some low end and slightly distorting the high end.

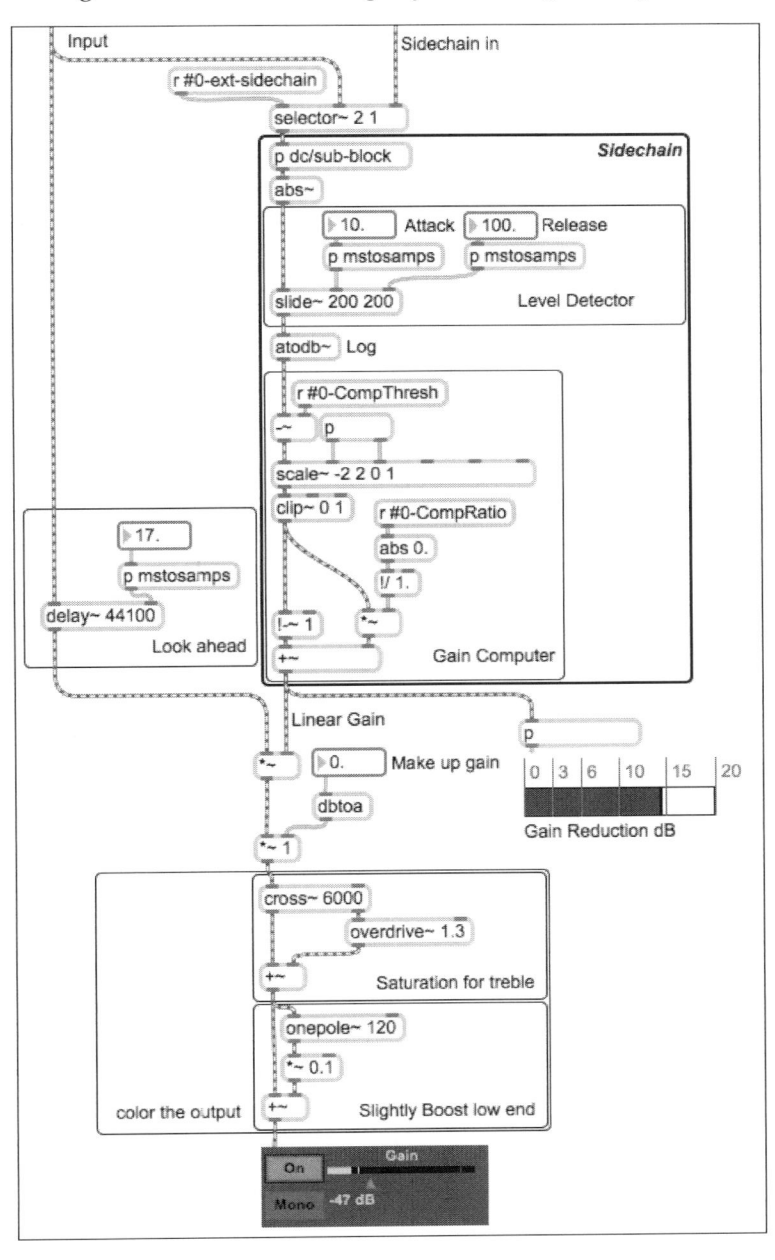

[155]

The really important parts are the gain computer and the level detector. Also, note that there is a conversion from log to linear and vice versa. The level detector is supposed to give us a good estimate of the input signals' level. What is implemented here is a peak detector, but by choosing long attack and release times, we can approach the RMS metering behavior.

Since this section is nothing but a low-pass filter, you can imagine that an arbitrary amount of complexity can be built here (how about a compressor that measures LUFS?). Using a unit step, we can take a look at the step response of that filter to see whether it reaches maximum in the right time, and we can start experimenting with different filters to shape the compressor's behavior in a more detailed way.

Also, remember that compressor design is not always about perfection; finding a filter that emulates old opto compressors will certainly make us look for rather slowly reacting ones, and non-linearities (as look-up tables for example) in the control signal can help to mimic analog behavior. As if the filter choice wasn't enough, what makes the compressor design a really wide field is that there are quite some design choices and a number of different topologies available.

For example, it makes quite a difference if we do the filtering in the linear or the logarithmic domain. Moreover, there are **feedforward** and **feedback** compressors. What is implemented here is a feedforward compressor, which is the more common one. A feedback compressor would instead compute the gain to be applied from the input gain and the gain it is already applying.

So you see, this is a really wide field, and if we dare to implement compressors that do not follow certain conventions, it can be an even wider one. I, for instance, like to use compressors that compute the gain in a very unorthodox way; anybody else would be very confused using it. What I meant to say here is, if you are interested in compression, start experimenting and researching!

> A good starting point for research is, for example, the paper titled *Digital Dynamic Range Compressor Design-a Tutorial and Analysis by Dimitrios Giannoulis, Michael Massberg, and Joshua D. Reiss*, available at http://www.eecs.qmul.ac.uk/~josh/documents/GiannoulisMassbergReiss-dynamicrangecompression-JAES2012.pdf.

Reverberation

While we just stated that there are many ways to go about building a compressor, here we can say that there are tons of ways to build a reverb. We have simply arrived at high-level FX and the possibilities are endless. Nevertheless, we'll talk about two different algorithms here, both based on proposals by Manfred R. Schroeder in his 1961 paper, *Natural Sounding Artificial Reverberation*.

Reverb, in real rooms, comes from the reflection of sound waves. Direct sound is heard first by a listener, since it travels the shortest path. After that, reflections arrive with increasing density and decreasing amplitude since these reflections might have been reflected increasingly often from different walls.

If we like to mimic this behavior, the most obvious idea is a lot of delays, maybe with feedback. We could probably use some filtering in the feedback paths, to mimic frequency dependent dissipation too. This is essentially it. The real problem is how to arrange the delays, how to control their parameters (reminded of additive synthesis?), and how to avoid fluttering and coloration. Luckily, there is a building block that is behaving so well in the last regard that we could call it a diffuser: a line of all-pass filters. All-pass filters are filters that have a flat magnitude response (so all frequencies have the same amplitude) but a potentially complicated phase response. If this sounds complicated, let's just bear in mind that it will not boost or cut any frequencies and look at its impulse response:

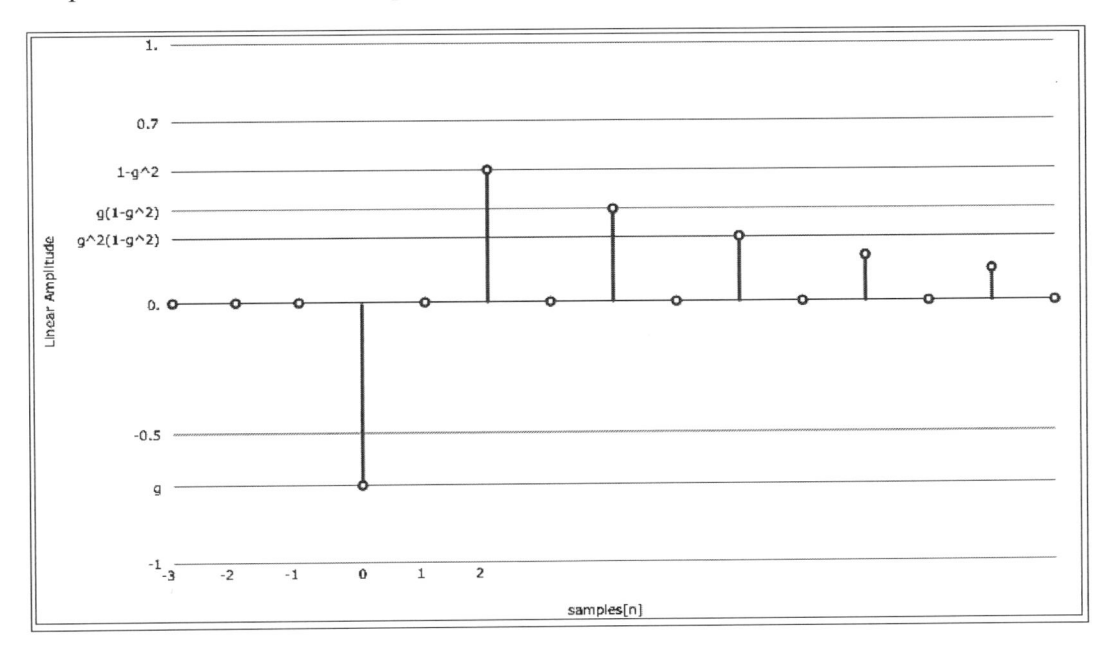

Advanced Audio in Max/MSP

We won't go into the details about how an all-pass filter works (it's worth looking at though!); just note that it is an IIR filter. In Max, we have the [allpass~] object that implements it. The previous graph shows the impulse response for an all-pass with gain, **g**, of 0.7 and a delay of 2 samples. So, all in all, this is perfect; we can achieve very small delay times with feedback without changing a system's magnitude response.

Let's consider something practical right away: the famous Schroeder reverb. It is usually built out of a couple of comb filters (typically about four) in parallel, summed, and sent into a couple of all-pass filters (typically about three) in series. A comb filter can serve as a crude simulation of two parallel walls, reflecting sound back and forth. If we'd like to simulate a cubical room, we'd therefore need three comb filters. Their result will suffer from fluttering or coloring, so we turn up their delay times to rather get flutter than color, and diffuse the result with a series of all-passes. Refer to the following screenshot:

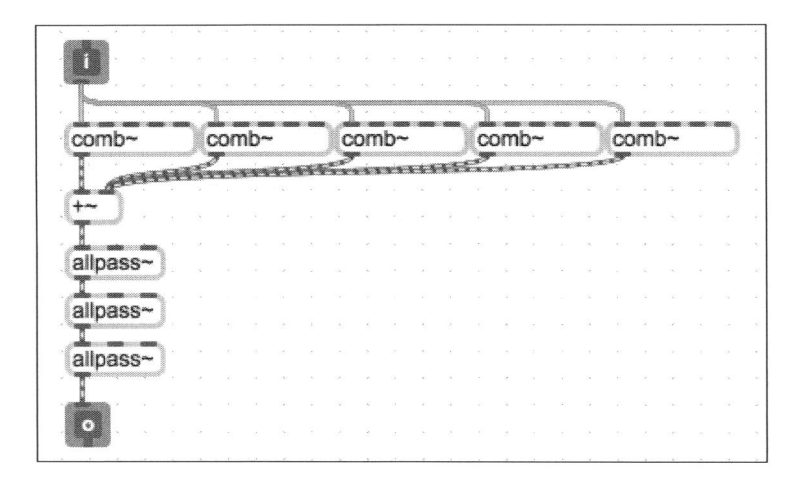

What is shown in the previous screenshot is the basic setup, just as an illustration of the circuit, but we didn't adjust any parameters here for now. What's the problem with the parameters? Let's consider the comb filters.

> Comb filters are just delays with feedback and some additional controls. Also, we will often find the delay time to be controllable in Hz instead of ms or samples. The important difference is that they mix the delayed signal with the original signal, essentially creating lots of phase cancellations and boosts by adding a signal with a delayed version of itself. The term comb filter comes from their property of creating comb-like magnitude spectra.

Let's assume that we set the first filter to a delay of 1 ms, the second one to a delay of 2 ms, the third one to 4ms, and the fourth one to 8 ms. What would the impulse response look like?

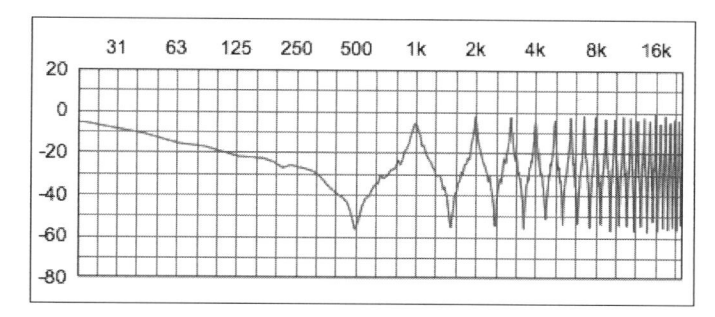

In the following screenshot, we see the approximate magnitude spectrum of a [comb~] object with 1 ms delay, gain equal to 1, feedforward equal to 1, and feedback equal to 0.9. Note the first peak at 1 kHz and the first trough at 500 Hz. The first peak will always be at 1/delay in seconds, that is, Hz, and the first trough at half of that.

Back to the impulse response of the previous comb filters; 8 ms after the impulse has occurred, all of the output would match up, resulting in a louder sum. Again, this would create a fluttering, since at all multiples of 8 ms we would get all four delays to match up; at all multiples of 4, the first three delays would also match up. This sounds highly unnatural and not at all like a reverb. It's just way too regular and correlated. Schroeder proposes to use delay times that are mutually prime, so don't have a common divisor (other than 1). Anyway, using values we like by their sound and adding some random floats mostly suffices here. Refer to the following screenshot:

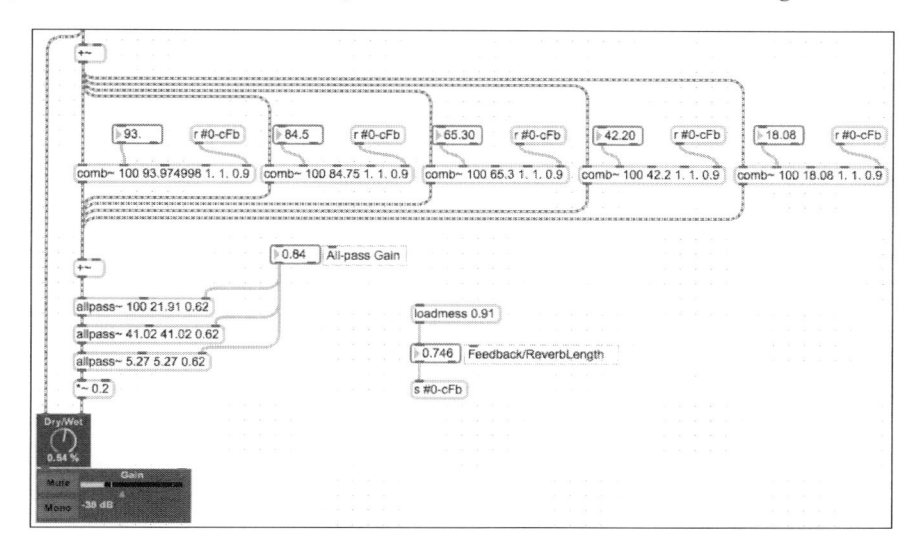

[159]

Advanced Audio in Max/MSP

Although this might not be the best reverb you ever heard, it is easy to understand and modify, which is a great advantage. Also, it demonstrates one of the many basic approaches of building a reverb. Another big advantage of this algorithm is that by flipping the whole structure (first passing through the all-passes and then into the comb filters), we can create different mixes of the comb filter outputs for two or more output channels. Obviously, this structure is scalable; we can just add more comb filters and all-passes to get a slightly higher quality.

However, Schroeder also proposes a different algorithm that is less known and sounds pretty interesting. It is basically built out of just one delay going into five all-pass filters in series and a feedback path back to the delay. This surprisingly simple algorithm creates a very interesting variety of reverb effects with quite intuitive controls and good quality. Although Schroeder proposes slightly different all-pass sections, the following screenshot shows the basic setup:

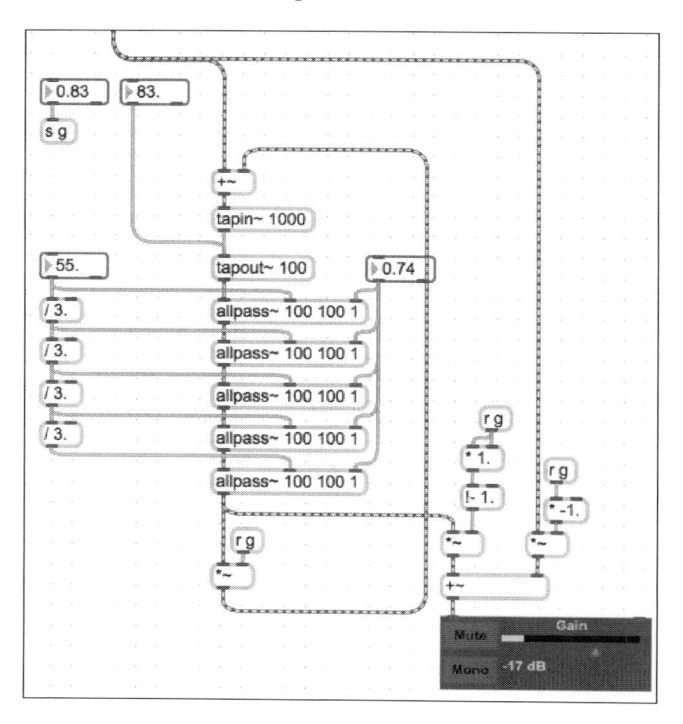

The construction uses the parameter **g** to not only fade between dry and wet, but also to control the amount of feedback chosen to guarantee that the output is still all-pass even when mixing. Also, it does provide an interesting control for reverb amount.

This sounds quite OK. However, if we look at a real room's impulse response for a moment, essentially at a reverb, we will see something like this:

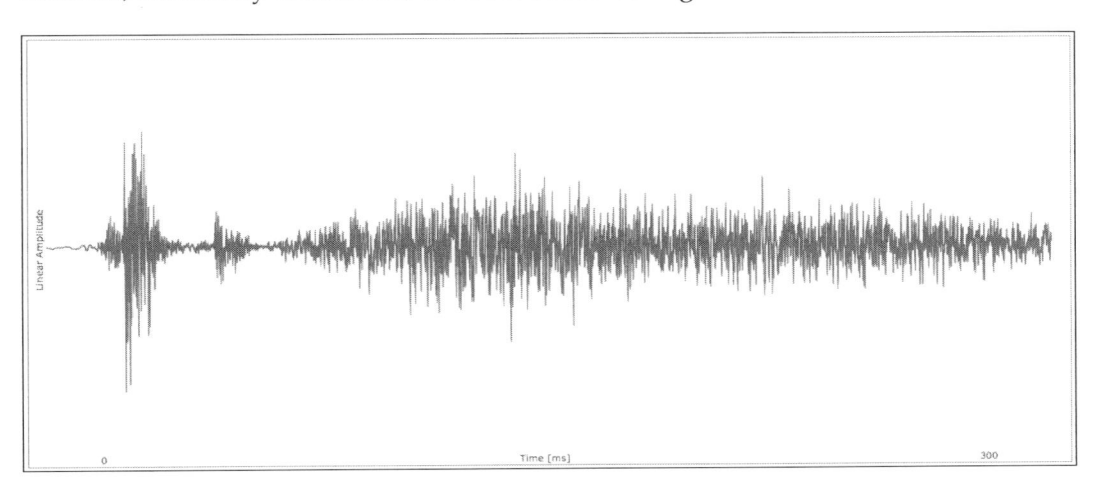

We can see that we have some pretty isolated pulses before the actual reverb tail. These are called early reflections. Obviously, some tapped delays that are diffused a little could generate something like this. After that, slightly later, we need to generate the actual reverb tail, which is a highly diffused, rather slowly rising noisy delay cloud.

So let's now create a more flexible diffuser that can be used as a building block for reverbs. Ideally, we will have a [poly~] object that contains just an [allpass~] object. Each instance will give slightly different parameters to the [allpass~] object, and they will run in series. This way, we could always decide how many all-pass filters we need, balancing efficiency versus density.

Also, we can come up with a bit of a more high-level control. However, [poly~], by default, doesn't allow us to connect the instances in series; they are in parallel. So let's attack this problem first; having an abstraction that allows us to use [poly~] to produce cascades will be handy anyway.

Poly as a cascade

We'd like to create an abstraction that sits inside a poly~ object. In this poly object, we'd like to have an effect, [allpass~] for example. The output of this effect should connect to our abstraction as well as its input. Our abstraction also connects to the [poly~] object's audio in and out.

Advanced Audio in Max/MSP

Given these connections to our abstraction, using a dynamically constructed send and receive network that spans over the [poly~] instances inside the abstraction will manage everything to build up our cascade. It will use the poly~ object's input, feed it through all instances, and send the last instance's output to the [poly~] object's output. Refer to the following screenshot:

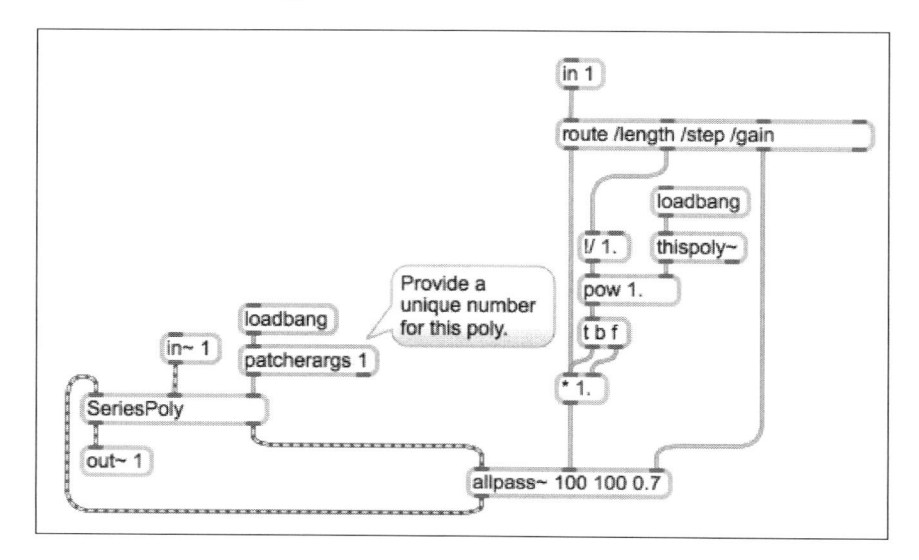

The previous screenshot shows how our abstraction is going to be used, along with the contents of a [poly~] object. There is one problem that makes the construction of the abstraction seemingly very complicated. Our send and receive network should work, even if we decide we want two or more of these cascaded [poly~] objects. The poly~ object's instances need to communicate, but the two [poly~] objects must not interfere. We cannot use the #0 trick inside [poly~] as it would disconnect everything.

Therefore, we provide a unique ID to the network from one level above, that is, as an argument to [poly~]. If we then put the [poly~] object inside an abstraction again, we can use the #0 trick to provide that unique ID. Alternatively, we could just generate a random number inside [poly~] ourselves to provide a unique context. Refer to the following screenshot:

Chapter 5

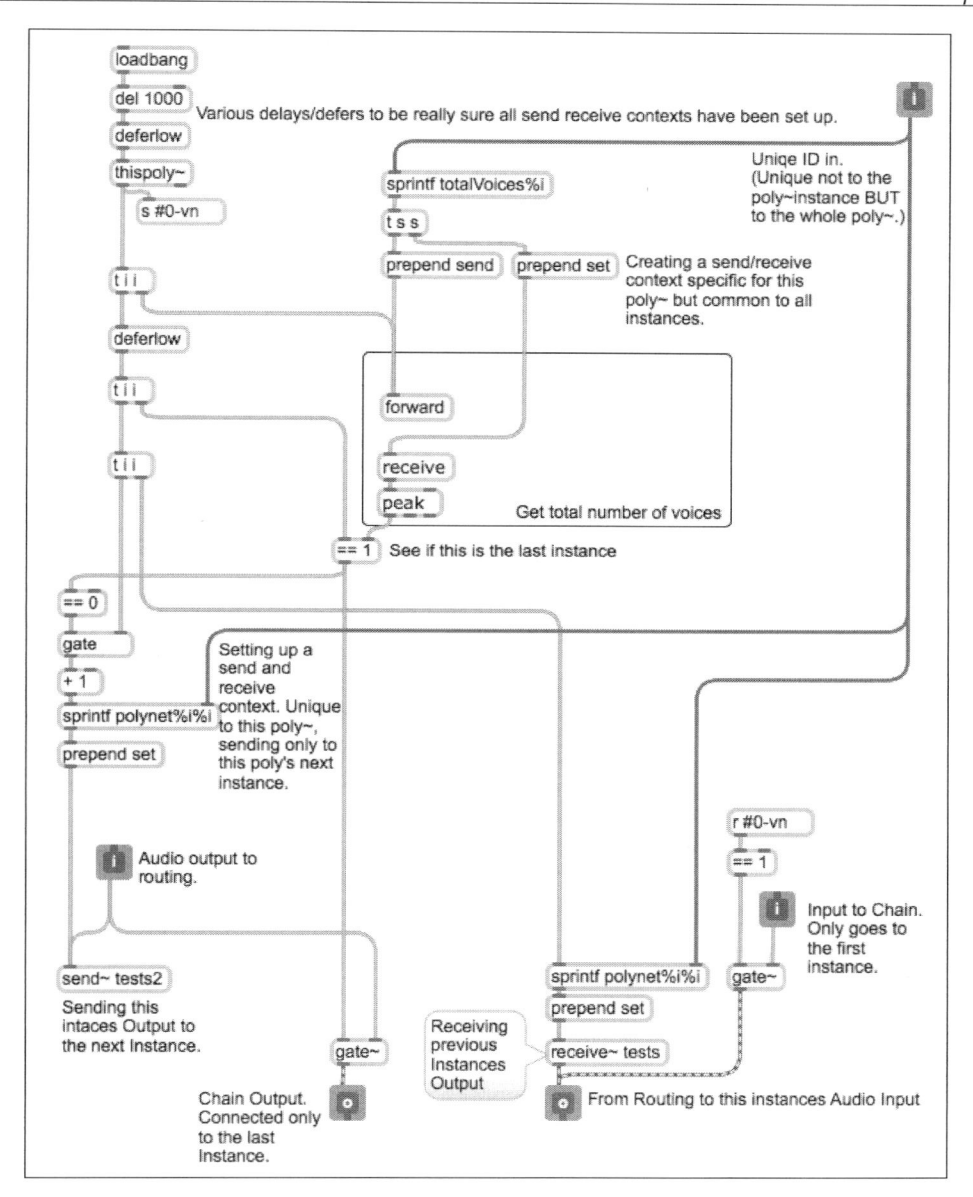

[Figure: Pure Data patch showing poly~ cascade abstraction with loadbang, del 1000, deferlow, thispoly~, s #0-vn, various t i i objects, sprintf totalVoices%i, forward, receive, peak objects, == 1 (See if this is the last instance), == 0, gate, +1, sprintf polynet%i%i, prepend set, send~ tests2, gate~, r #0-vn, receive~ tests, and associated annotations describing the send/receive contexts, audio routing, and chain connections.]

In the previous screenshot, you can see our finished abstraction, which enables us to use `poly~` as the cascade. It might look a bit complicated, but it really isn't; just go through the patch slowly, and you will see there isn't a lot of magic at work.

Advanced Audio in Max/MSP

As soon as we have achieved this, we quickly arrive at a generic diffuser patch, which is a bit performance-hungry but very customizable and handy to build a variety of reverbs. If we stick it into a clipping with some more or less meaningful controls, a nice modular reverb building workflow is at hand. That's the point where we can come up with heuristic approaches, building either reverbs that sound very natural through intelligent placement and adjustment of delays, diffusers, filters, and feedback paths, or building completely abstract, artistic, spatial, and room-ish-sounding FX, as shown in the following screenshot:

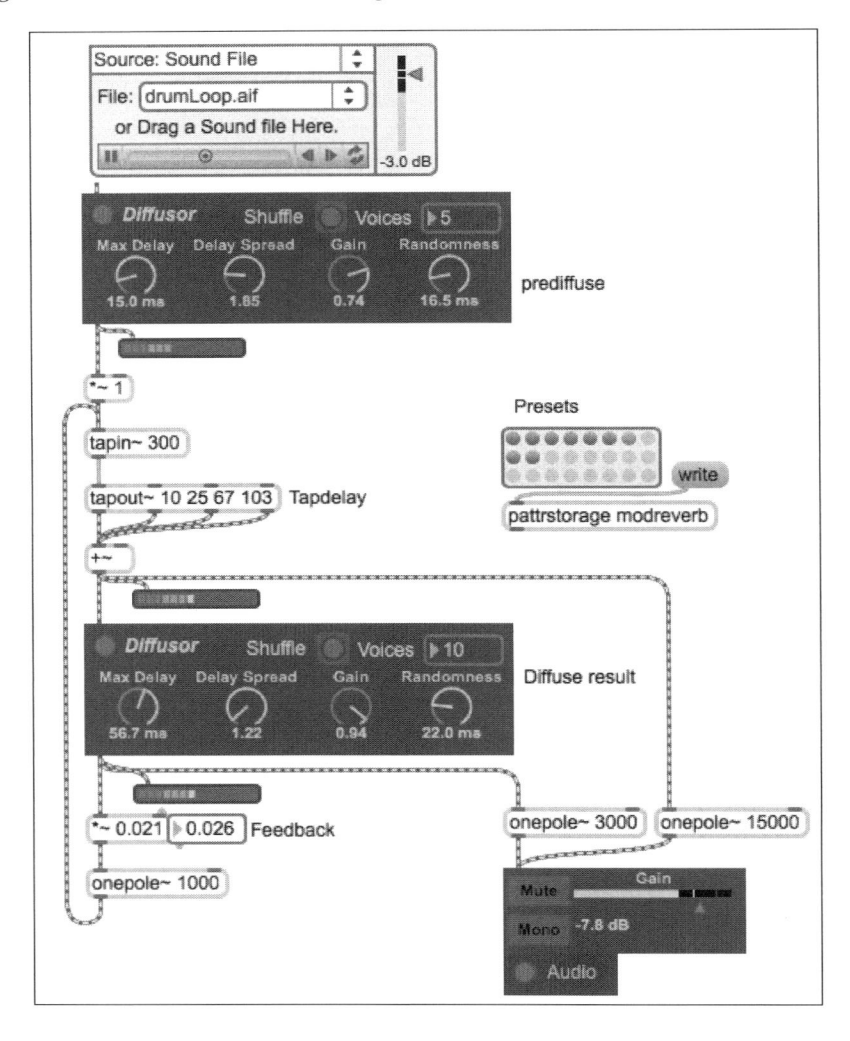

Chapter 5

We just learned two things: how to use `poly` to create custom networks of audio processing and we refreshed our knowledge about clippings and their use to build high-level FX. Using this information and what we just discussed on reverbs, come up with a building block that contains a variable number of delays, using feedback, but each delay has a different band-pass filter on its output to mimic reflection from different materials and distances!

Convolution

Convolution is a great way to generate natural-sounding reverberation. We have seen saw a convolution reverb in the section on filters, since convolution and FIR filtering are the same thing. An efficient way to do convolution in Max is by using the [multiconvolve~] external provided in the HIRT library.

We have already talked about FIR filters, so you should be able to get a basic understanding of convolution by the difference equation. We also saw a convolution reverb in which section, using a randomly generated impulse response. Again, we have talked about convolution as an IIR filter and as a difference equation.

Let's now take a look at a graphical representation of what's happening in the time domain, to look at the process from a more reverb-related perspective:

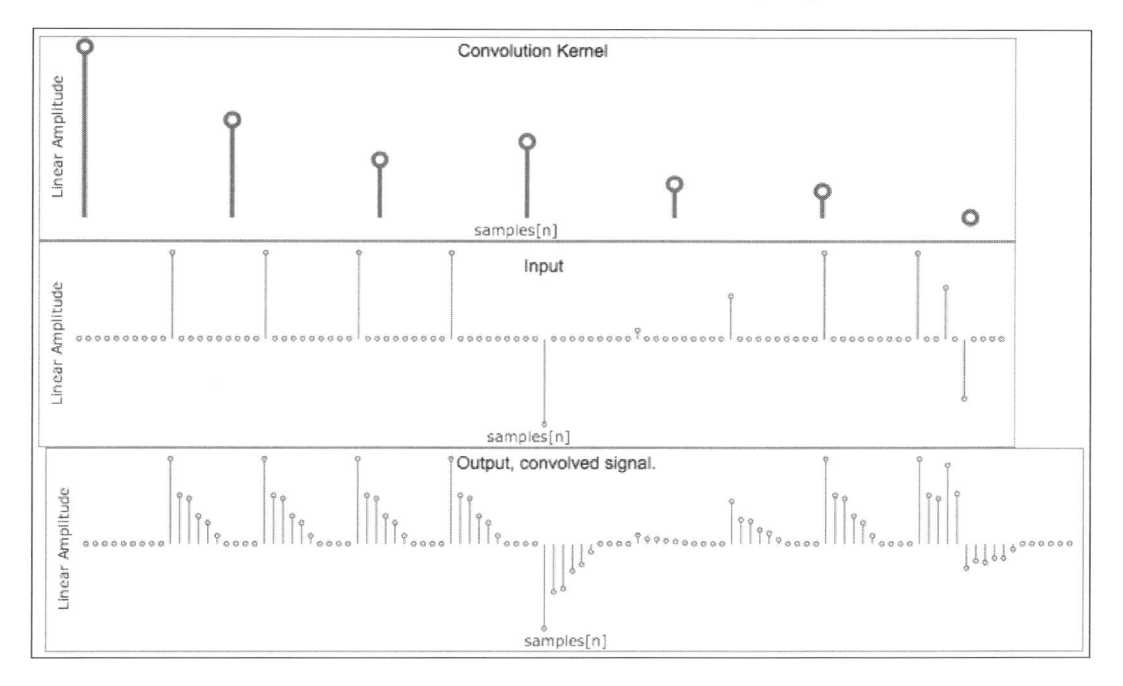

You can see the convolution kernel on the top, the input signal in the middle, and the result at the bottom of the previous screenshot. Obviously, it is like each sample of the input is scaling the kernel and adding this scaled version to the output. Feeding in an impulse train (as the beginning of the input) therefore results just in a few copies of the kernel, whereas when the signal becomes more complicated, the scaling and overlapping of the copied kernels becomes obvious. Take a close look at the ending of the input and its convolved pendant.

Also, note that the length of the resulting signal can be computed as input length plus kernel length. So you see, convolution can be used to give every input sample a little tail, which is perfect for reverbs. If our kernel is the impulse response of a real room, we can make any signal sound as if it is played in that room using convolution. Even more than that, if we have the impulse response of any system, convolution can be used to imitate that system in general, although without any further techniques, it is only able to recreate that system's linear features and cannot depict any nonlinear features (as distortion and so on).

What does convolution mean in the frequency domain? Convolution in the time domain is the same as multiplication in the frequency domain and vice versa. This is a very beautiful, simple, and deep fact; think about it for some time and try to view some time-domain multiplications as frequency-domain convolutions. Also, don't hesitate to go back to the section about AM in *Chapter 4*, *Basic Audio in Max/MSP*, and think about it once again with your knowledge about convolution.

Taking a room's impulse response

We know that a randomly generated IR can be a pretty nice reverb, but how do we actually capture a system's impulse response? The following figure shows how to measure a room; we just need a speaker and a microphone:

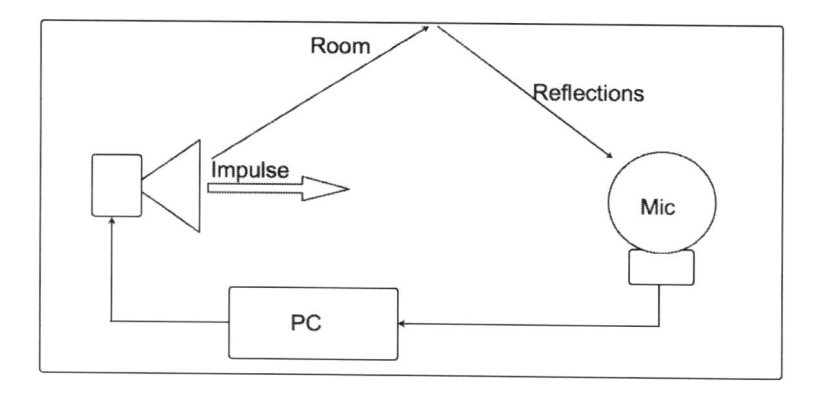

We send an impulse into the room and record the response. In Praxis, measuring an IR only rarely is done by using an impulse. Sometimes, you will hear that you don't need a speaker to generate an impulse, but you can use a gun to fire a shot, or you can pop a balloon.

The most common way to do it though is to use an **Exponentially Swept Sine** (**ESS**). Another way is to send noise into the system. In theory, all of these methods, the impulse, noise, and a swept sine, contain all frequencies, which is exactly what we need. The problem with the exponentially swept sine and the noise is that we obviously don't record an impulse response but a response to an exponentially swept sine, for example. This will, as it is, not yield expected results if used as a kernel. Some math will be necessary to compute the actual IR from that. Luckily, if we would like to rather use an ESS than our trusted old guns or balloons, the HIRT library contains an object called [irmeasure~].

Since this object really does it all for us, just take a look at its help file. Something to bear in mind is that by using a speaker, a room, and a microphone, we actually measure the whole system, the frequency response of the microphone, the speaker, and the anti-aliasing filters of our audio interface. Of course, these elements should therefore have a very linear frequency and phase response.

FFT

FFT stands for **Fast Fourier Transform**. It is the only one of several Fourier Transforms we will use here, but let's drop the "fast" for a moment and talk about the Fourier Transform first. We have talked a lot about spectra and frequencies, but have mainly stayed in the time domain. The Fourier Transform (or Fourier analysis) is a way to switch into the frequency domain. The Inverse Fourier Transform (or Fourier synthesis) is a way to go back again to the time domain. The Fourier Transform is converting a continuous signal, a function of time $x(t)$ to a continuous signal, a function of frequency $X(f)$.

How will this be done? Fourier (among others) proved that any continuous signal can be represented as a sum of sinusoids. Now, I could present a fancy formula here, and I will, but let's first think about it a bit. What helped me most in understanding the Fourier Transform is this; what if we want to see how much of anything is contained in anything else in math? Right, we divide; to see how much of three is contained in nine, we divide nine by three and see; three is three times contained in nine. So, can we just divide a time domain signal by sinusoids to see how much of each frequency/each sinusoid is contained? Yes, and that's what we do! It's really that simple, with a bit of fancy math around it.

Let's look at the formula first and then see how to smuggle in our division idea:

$$X(f) = F\{x(t)\} = \int_{-\infty}^{\infty} x(t) e^{-j2\pi ft} dt$$

What the previous formula says is that a function X of a variable f and a frequency in Hz is defined. It is equal to the Fourier Transform of the original time-domain signal, x(t), that's $F\{x(t)\}$. Now comes the fun part; $e^{j2\pi ft}$ is equal to $\cos(2\pi ft) + j\sin(2\pi ft)$. This identity is called Euler's formula. So these are just two sinusoids, one multiplied with **j**, the imaginary number. Now, to really shorten and simplify the whole thing, let's not care too much about complex numbers for now, but rather note that the exponent of **e** is negative. This again is the same as follows:

$$\frac{1}{e^{j2\pi ft}}$$

Therefore, we really just divide the time-domain signal by a sinusoid as follows:

$$\frac{x(t)}{e^{j2\pi ft}}$$

Integrating here just means that we accumulate the appearance of a certain frequency over the whole infinite signal, and we do this for each frequency. Lastly, we arrive at a signal that describes our original time-domain signal using sines. Now, as you know, to fully describe a sinusoid, we need to state its frequency, amplitude, and phase. Since the function we arrive at is a function of frequency, we need to state the amplitude and phase with that signal. This is where complex numbers come into play, and this is what we really need to know in a practical sense.

Let's assume our time domain signal is just one sinusoid. How can we describe its frequency with a single number? Well, complex numbers really are number pairs; we have a real part and an imaginary part. We can therefore view a complex number as a point in the complex plane; typically, we use the real part of it as the *x* axis, and its imaginary part as the *y* axis. The only problem we now face is how to get amplitude and phase out of these coordinates. This is just done by converting the Cartesian coordinates to polar coordinates, since the angle of the point represents the frequency's phase and the radius represents its amplitude. Refer to the following screenshot:

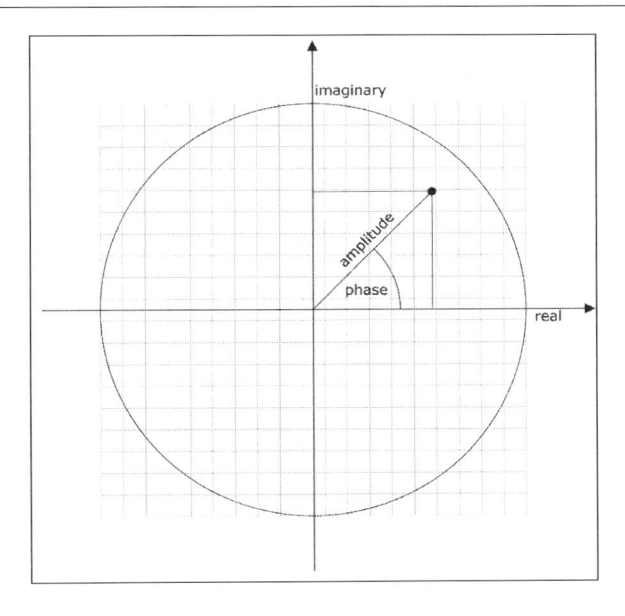

Before we come to a practical application, let's quickly get an overview of some of the different transforms. We have been talking about continuous signals for now as it makes things a bit easier, but in Max, we will deal with an optimized form of the discrete case (FFT), so if you ever get confused about all the different transforms, have a look at this:

	Continuous Time Domain	Discrete Time Domain (periodic spectrum)
Continuous Frequency Domain	Fourier Transform	Discrete Time Fourier Transform
Discrete Frequency Domain (periodic time domain)	Fourier Series	Discrete Fourier Transform

In the previous table, the top row is the source signal and the left column is the result of the transforms. Let's finally come to applying what we just learned in Max.

Drawing a signal's spectrum

Throughout this book, we have used the [spectrumdraw~] external to look at a signal's spectrum because it's just very convenient. However, let's roll our own primitive version of this just to get familiar with Max's FFT capabilities. Also, it's always good to graph data we are working with; now it's about frequency data, so let's look at how to get it and how to graph it manually.

Advanced Audio in Max/MSP

In Max, there are a couple of objects that deal with FFT: [fft~], [ifft~], [pfft~], [fftin~], [fftout~], and a couple more. Real-time FFT requires us to always compute the transform on a chunk of audio or a vector of samples. We can neither compute the FFT on the complete signal (it's real time) nor can we do the FFT sample by sample (what does the spectrum of a single value mean?). These chunks are called frames. Let's look at the patch doing the analysis and come back to the frame size in a moment:

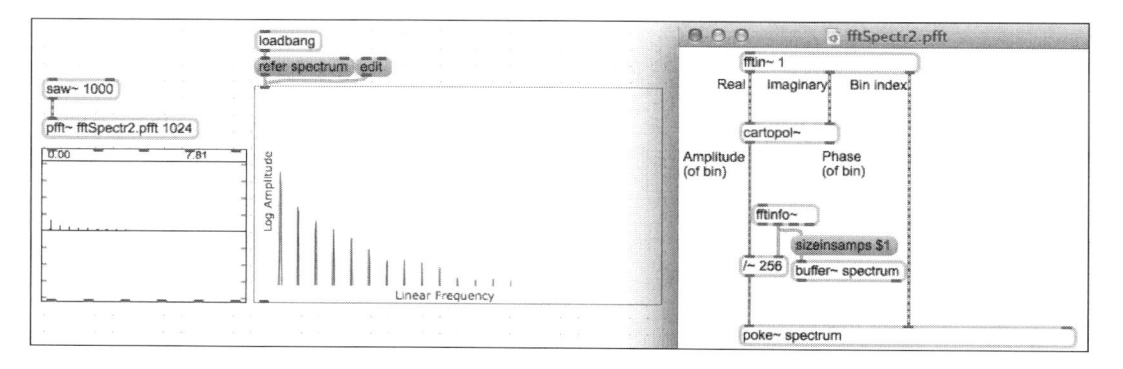

What you see in the previous screenshot are the contents of a [pfft~] object. The [pfft~] object, similar to [poly~], loads a patcher we made. Inside, we can work in the frequency domain, since its inlets, [fftin~] objects, by default perform an FFT, and its outlets, [fftout~] objects, perform an inverse FFT. So, the actual transform is nothing we have to care about at all in Max.

As you can see, we end up with three results of this transform:

- A real number
- An imaginary number
- A bin index

Real and imaginary numbers should ring a bell, but what's a bin index? Since real and imaginary numbers come out as a stream, we need some way to map these numbers to a specific frequency. This is done using the bin index, or to say it differently, per sampling period. We get three values: amplitude and phase values by means of real and imaginary numbers, and a bin index that translates to frequency.

We just discussed the frame size. If we decide to use a frame size of, for example 1,024, we would analyze 1,024 samples as a chunk and would also get 1,024 value pairs out of the FFT. Since the FFT analyses' frequencies up to the sampling rate, we actually only get half of that, that is, 512 useful values (we are only interested in frequencies up to the Nyquist frequency). So we end up with 512 analyzed frequencies.

The frame size controls both the length of the chunk of audio we analyze and the number of frequencies that get analyzed. But there is more to it; imagine we are using a frame size of 1,024 again, so we analyze 1,024 samples. Are there any low frequencies that do not fit inside 1,024 samples? Of course, right? We always analyze 0 Hz, so DC offset, but what's the next frequency to be analyzed (the so-called fundamental frequency of the FFT)? Refer to the following formula:

$$f_0 = \frac{sr}{fs}$$

The fundamental frequency (FFT) is equal to the sampling rate over the frame size. Guess which highest frequency is being analyzed. It is the Nyquist frequency, so the sampling rate is divided by two. Obviously, the greater the frame size, the deeper the fundamental frequency. But there is a tradeoff; by analyzing a greater chunk of audio, we lose timing accuracy because we analyze the time-domain signal a few times per second. So when doing an FFT, we always have to decide what's more important: timing accuracy or frequency resolution.

Let's get back to our previous patch. By using the bin index, we write the computed amplitude of each frequency into a [buffer~] object whose contents we can display using [plot~] or the waveform. What else happens in that patch? We get the amplitude out of the complex number by converting Cartesian to polar coordinates and using the radius outlet. Also, we need to normalize the amplitude by half of the frame size. The [fftin~] object allows us to access this number directly, which is also used to set the buffer size in samples.

There are more intelligent ways to do this, but I found this way the most instructive one. In the patcher fft_playground1.maxpat object, you'll find the DrawSpectrum1 subpatcher, which is shown previously, and DrawSpectrum2, which demonstrates a different approach.

Simple convolution

We have encountered convolution a number of times now. We looked at it as a FIR filter, as a method of reverberation, and now, we'll take a look at it in the frequency domain. Multiplying in the frequency domain means convolution in the time domain and vice versa.

The whole topic of FFT is a bit too dense to be presented here in a more or less complete way. Therefore, please take a look at the MSP tutorial on FFT and it would also be useful to pick up a book on DSP to fill in the gaps. Keeping things rather practical, we create a patch that is close to convolution and this allows us to understand things a bit better, but it's not quite convolution. For a couple of correct approaches, please look at the tutorial.

So, a correct approach would really multiply the two complex numbers; here, we are happy with just multiplying the amplitudes of two signals to create a spectral mixture of two sources:

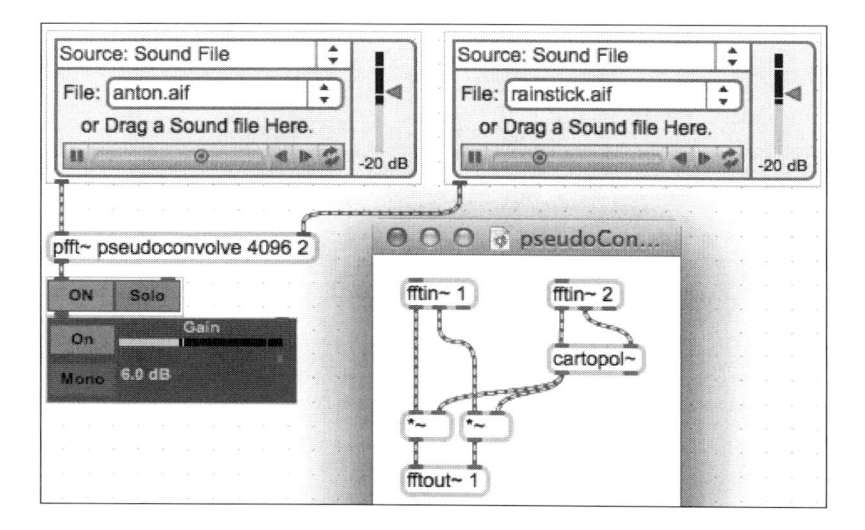

So what happens here is that we use the phase of the first inlet for the output. We extract the amplitudes of the second inlet and scale both coordinates by that value, thereby scaling the radius (amplitude), leaving the phase alone.

An FFT filter

We just modulated the amplitudes of a signal by another signal's amplitudes. So, of course, we can also multiply them by predefined values. A very typical application would be to store the amplitudes for all frequencies in a buffer and use a lookup to get the gain for each frequency. The following result is very similar to filtering:

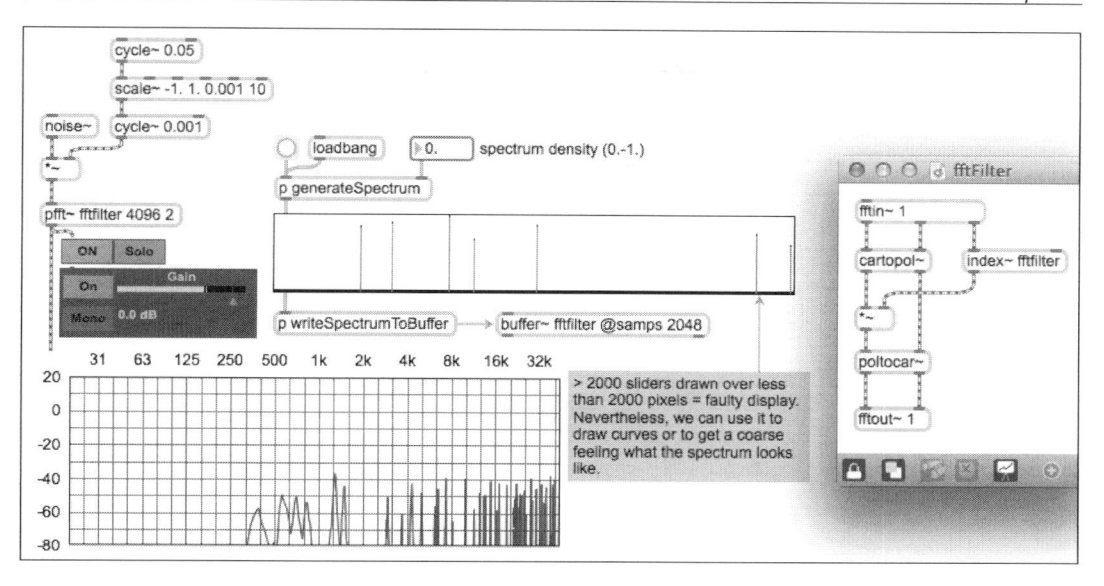

Although this is a very simple patch, it is able to produce a broad variety of sparse, glass-like textures and sounds. It's a good example of how very simplistic approaches inside the frequency domain can yield quite impressive results.

Spectral reverb and freezing

Now, all that we have seen here was pretty simple as it was just multiplication in the frequency domain. If we wish to actually do some more processing in the frequency domain, we will face the problem of all the data being packed in vectors. For example, if we wish to smooth out amplitude data in time, we would need to have an individual low-pass filter on each sample in a signal vector. Luckily, the [vectral~] object offers this functionality and more.

Advanced Audio in Max/MSP

Of course, this object needs to know both the signal vector size and what bin we are working on at every instant. On the other hand, we probably want to smooth out amplitude values within one frame, so if we have a peak at 1 kHz, we also have some positive values around that. This filter should not bleed into the next frame though. The [framesmooth~] object is made for this purpose. In the following patcher, we use both of them and a short buffer to reverberate, smear, and freeze the spectrum:

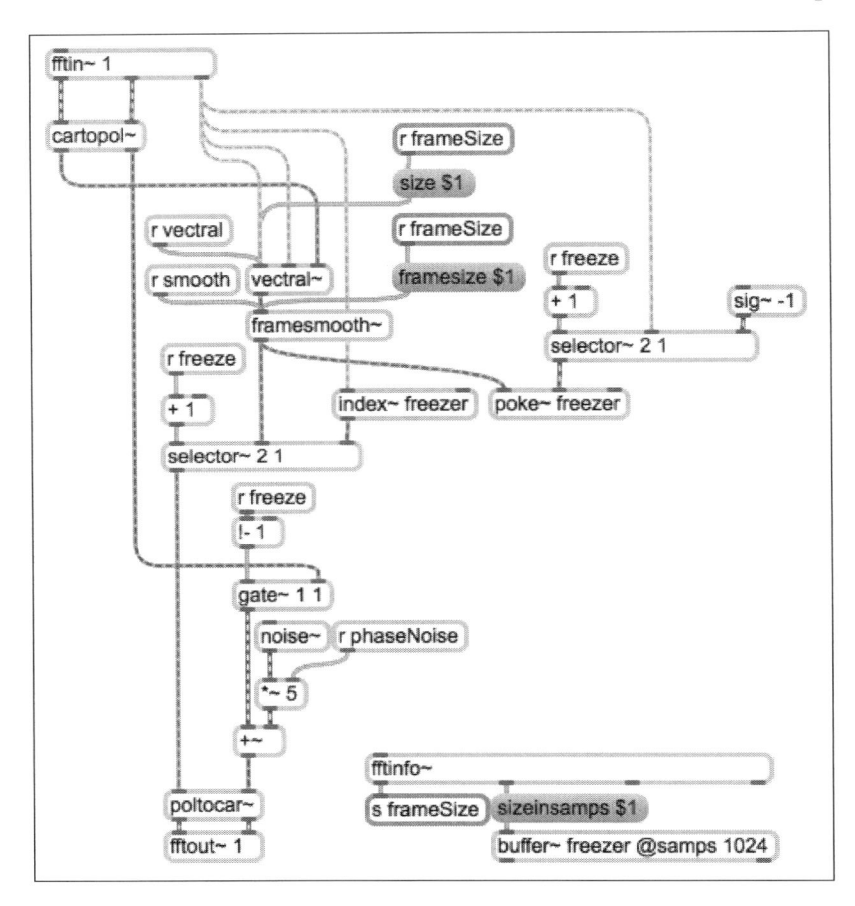

Since by doing a slow envelope following on the input amplitudes, we are introducing frequencies that are not present in the momentary input (but have been), we need to give them some phase. If we don't, they will just have the same phase, which doesn't sound very pleasing. So in this patch, we simply add noise to the phase of the resynthesized sound. As you will surely notice, this patch allows for very long reverbs and a very easy control of rise and fall times. Don't hesitate to make a clipping out of it to add it to our reverb building blocks!

Recording and playback of FFT data

A very nice feature of FFT data is that we can resynthesize the data at any playback rate without affecting the pitch, essentially performing time stretching/compression. All we need to do is analyze sound once, write all the data to a file, and resynthesize the data. Here is an example of how to achieve this:

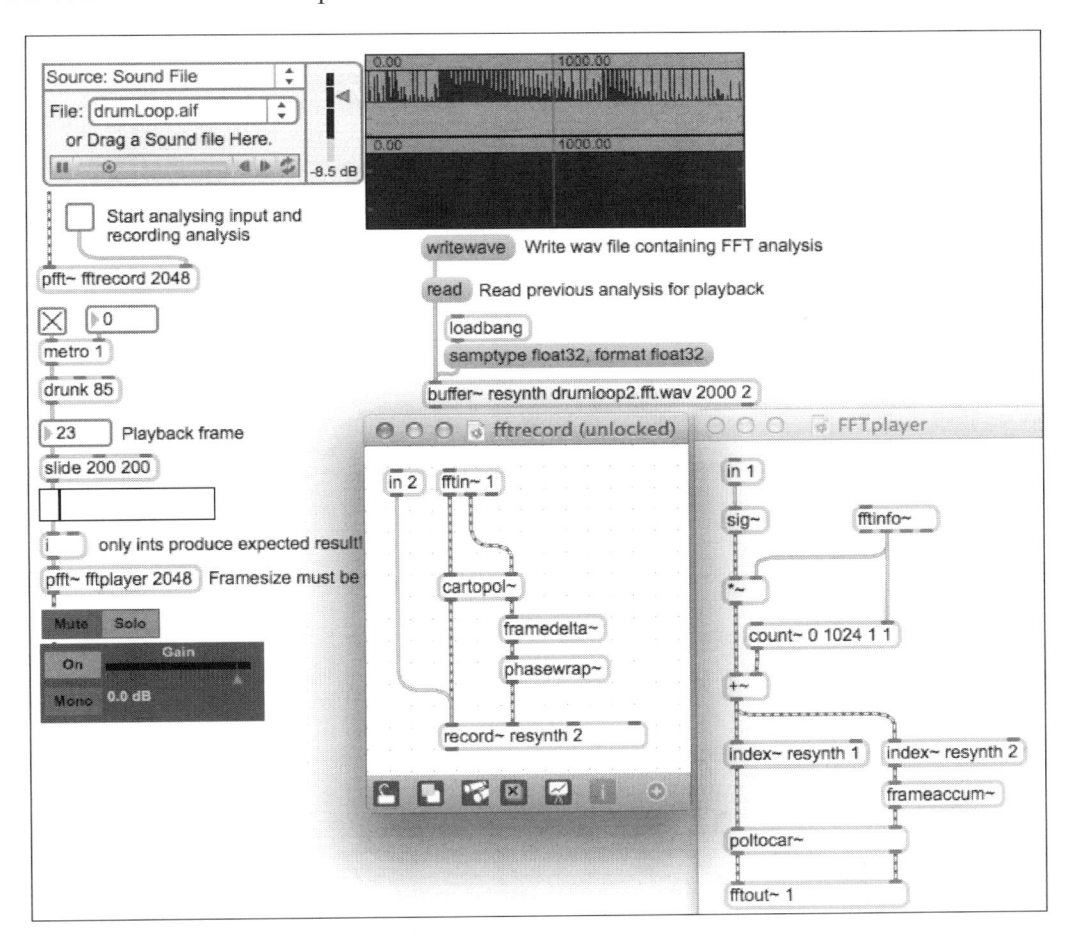

The only part of this patch that might be a bit surprising is that we do some processing on the phase of the original signal before recording it. The [framedelta~] object computes the delta of successive frames, resulting in the derivative of all the phases. When we play back the recording, we use [frameaccum~] to reconstruct the running phase. This needs to be done since we want to play back at arbitrary speeds.

Also, note that the format of the buffer/file we write to is of importance. Compressed or low bit-depth formats might compromise our data slightly, which might lead to distorted output.

Transient detection

In all sorts of occasions, especially when visualizing music, it can be handy to be able to detect beats or transients. While the usage of both, envelope following to extract a signal that represents amplitude, and a greater than operation, might lead to usable results, there are other techniques that are also able to detect greater subtlety.

The next step could be to look at and ensure that the amplitude's derivative is greater than some value instead of the amplitude itself. This way, we should be able to see whether there is a sudden rise in amplitude; therefore, we should be detecting beats. This is shown in the following screenshot:

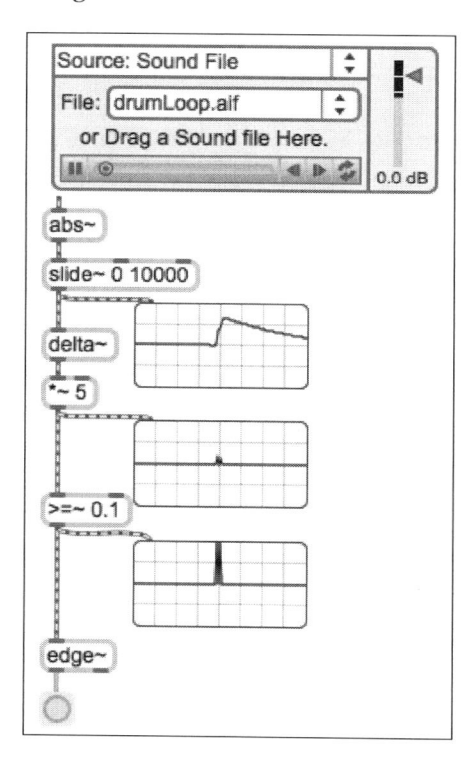

Well, this works more or less okay. We could implement an adaptive threshold instead of the constant **0.1** used here. This could be done by doing very slow envelope following, which gives us a rough estimate of the signal's average level. We could start comparing to that value instead of a fixed one.

Although we are now going to take another route, this approach is promising and might be added to what we are going to explore next. What we are going to use is called **spectral flux**. We are doing more or less the same thing we just looked at, but inside a [pfft~] patcher, looking at the delta of the amplitudes of successive FFT frames. This gives us a signal that represents an opportunity in frequency content, which in turn is a very good indicator for transients. Refer to the following screenshot:

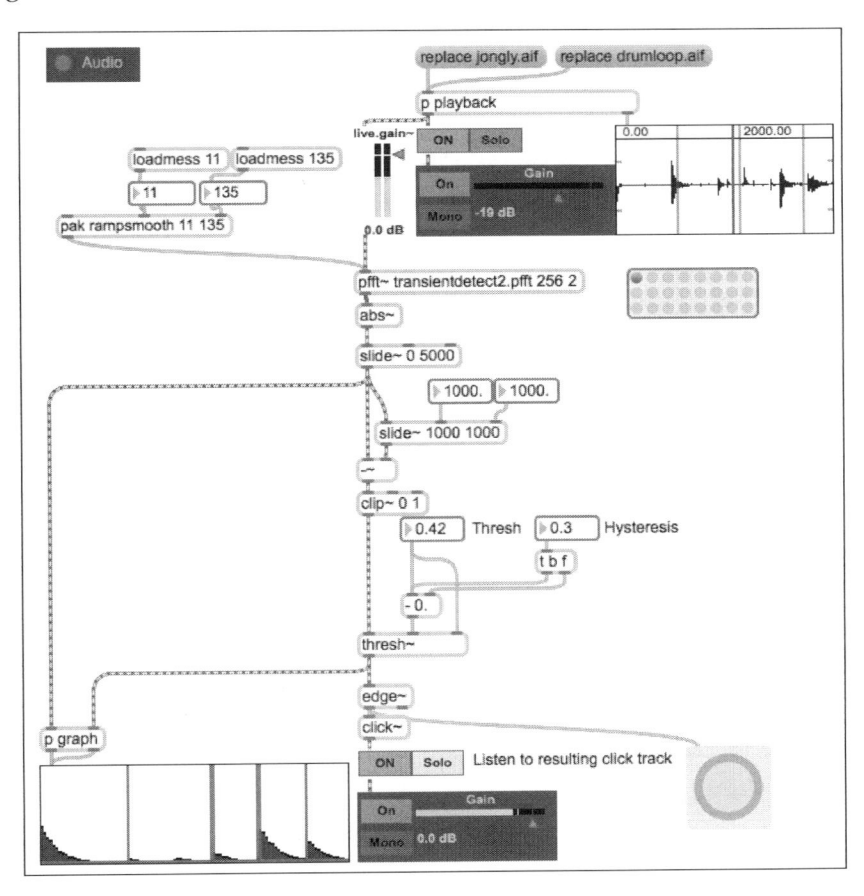

Advanced Audio in Max/MSP

Inside the [pfft~] object, we don't do a lot. We use [vectral~] to construct a more versatile per-frame highpass than [framedelta~], and use the square root to approximate a logarithmic behavior, as shown in the following screenshot:

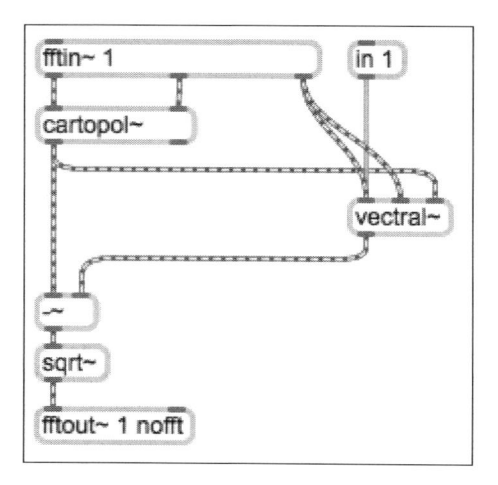

Some more filtering and envelope following give us a signal that is quite reliable as an indicator for transients. The [thresh~] object is used instead of a simple comparison, since it allows us to use **hysteresis**. It has two thresholds: a high one and a low one. The [thresh~] object's output goes high if the high threshold is exceeded, but it does not reset to zero until its input is lower than the low threshold again. This is a very effective method to avoid double triggering.

Sample-accurate sequencing

As you know, the Max scheduler does not compute at the sample rate. Also, we know that we have to be careful when adjusting certain parameters (vector size, overdrive, scheduler in audio interrupt, and so on) that affect the timing accuracy of our sequencing. However, there is a different way to ensure timing accuracy: doing all the computations at the signal rate. So the whole chain from timing generation to sequencing up to the audio synthesis/playback should be at the signal rate. As soon as we go back to the Max domain, we lose the increased accuracy we ensured by working in the signal domain.

Let's look at a very simple example:

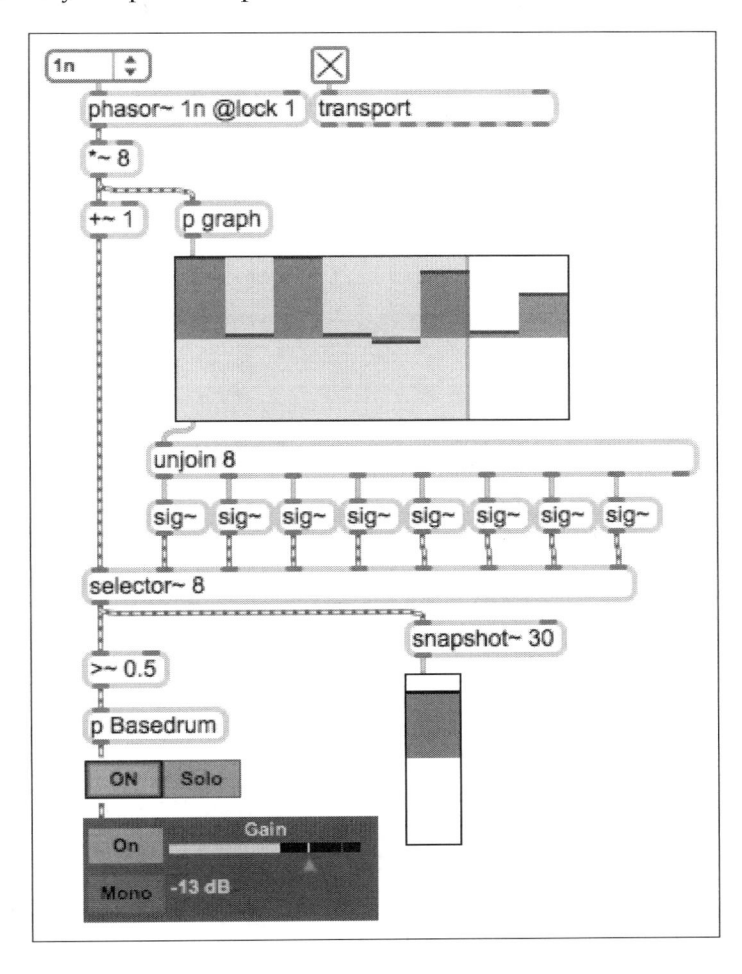

Advanced Audio in Max/MSP

As you see, we are making a phasor signal, controlling a selector, and going directly into our synthesis algorithm (which is completely in the signal domain too). Of course, we can generate or even modulate the values to be sequenced in the Max domain, and of course we can use the Max domain to display the current output. Now, this is nice and simple, but it's not scalable. What if we'd like to have 16 steps? So what did we actually do? We created an array of values we could access at the signal rate; this sounds a lot like [buffer~], right? So let's just use a [multislider] object to adjust our values, store them inside a [buffer~] object, and retrieve the values via [index~]. Refer to the following screenshot:

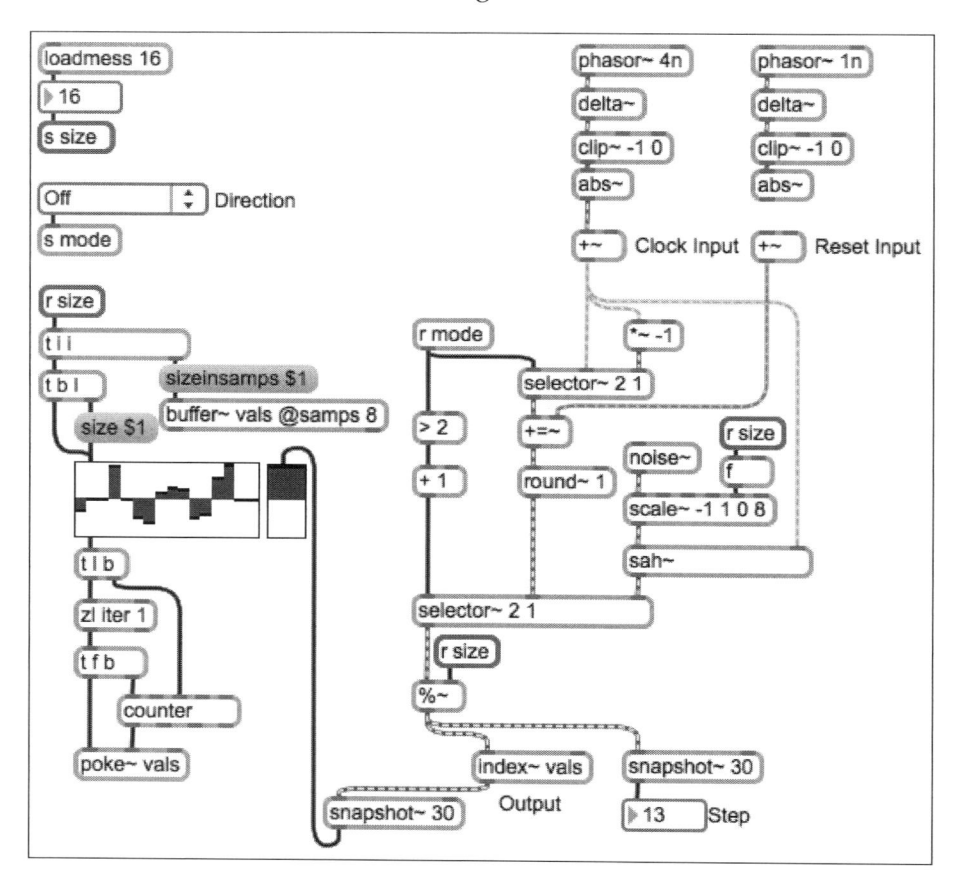

So the generation of our values can happen at message rate, and we can do things like our iterative sequencer just as before. We'll have to start thinking when it comes to different play modes of our signal rate sequencer, and when it comes to processing its output (how to build a signal rate pitch quantizer?).

The previous object implements some very basic alternative play modes as reverse and random. What might surprise you is that here, we have switched from using a phasor as a pointer for the values to using an accumulated value that is controlled by a pulse clock. I personally find it more convenient to work with pulses than with a phasor; also, it's nearer to the logic of analog CV sequencers. However, using a phasor directly works equally well.

Summary

This concludes our overview of some more advanced techniques of audio processing. Everything we discussed was meant to get you started, though there are tons of possibilities of going beyond what we did. We discussed dynamic range control and how you can build a system dedicated for transient shaping. We talked about reverberation and how you can go about building a more physically-based one. We talked about FFT and how you can build a pitch shifter (take a look at [gizmo~]). The possibilities are endless.

We are going to talk a bit more about audio processing in the next chapter, and then, quite soon, start creating visualizations. Remember what we learned in the previous sections about analyzing signals. This will help you understand how to visualize the data, be it amplitude, average power, or transients.

6
Low-level Patching in Gen

We are now going to dive into the world of Gen. By the end of this chapter, we will be able to create very efficient external-like objects that can be reused and exported to other kinds of code such as GLSL and C++. In fact, Gen patches are like regular patches, but they get converted to text-based code and compile right away to more efficient code. We could say that Gen patches are some strange objects that are somewhere between a subpatch, an abstraction, and an external written in C++. However, besides the advantages regarding performance, there is another big advantage on the audio side of Gen. We can use single sample delays that feature feedback, which is a problem in the MSP domain. Therefore, in this chapter, we will concentrate on examples that require short delays that feature feedback such as filters and physical modeling. Since this book proposes to use Max/MSP for audio and TouchDesigner for video generation, we will emphasize on the audio side of Gen here. In this chapter, we will cover the following topics:

- Introducing Gen
- The Gen workspace
- Exploring the differences between Max and Gen
- Examples

Introducing Gen

Gen can offer us the following features:

- Performance improvements over regular patches
- Single sample feedback
- Text-based coding inside a visual environment

Low-level Patching in Gen

On the other hand, we are constrained to a limited set of objects, which is one of the reasons we don't do everything inside Gen. Also, there are four versions of Gen, which are as follows:

- **gen~**: For audio/signal processing
- **jit.gen**: For general Jitter matrix processing on the CPU
- **jit.pix**: For the four-plane image matrix processing on the CPU
- **jit.gl.pix**: For image/texture processing on the GPU (shader programming)

Another reason for not using Gen all the time is that gen~, for example, can't deal with Jitter matrices; it can only deal with audio. So we can imagine each of them living in their own little domain, processing only audio, matrices, or textures. Also, it might be wise to not reinvent the wheel all the time. If we need a low-passed phasor~ object, let's just use [phasor~] and [onepole] instead of building a phasor and a pole inside [gen~].

As soon as we start using [gen~], we really arrive at digital signal processing in a more narrow sense. So, if you ever have problems understanding or building a complex network, it can help to pick up a book about DSP and apply the techniques presented in there, such as the transfer function calculation and the Z-transform. Let's get to know the environment a bit more before actually doing something with it.

The Gen workspace

Let's now take a look at an actual Gen patcher. If we create a new Max patch, then create a new Gen object, [gen~] as an audio example, and double-click on it; we can edit the contents of the Gen patcher. Something similar to the following screenshot will pop up:

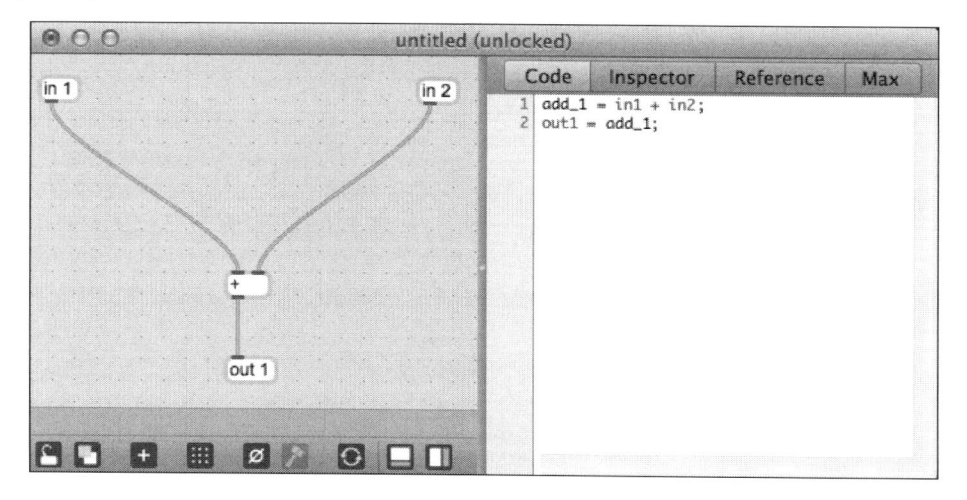

First of all, let's cover the GUI. You should be familiar with most of it, since it's the same for a regular Max patcher. In the toolbar at the bottom, we find the following three new symbols:

- The reset button
- The compile button
- The auto-compile button

The reset button is particularly handy if we deal with feedback. Digital systems that feature feedback need some kind of delay, and feedback systems can blow up. Resetting means we zero all delay buffers, so any circulating infinities or **Not a Number (NaN)** values are eliminated. Also, all parameters are reset to their default values (we'll come to parameters in a second).

The compile button is only available if we changed something about the Gen patch and had auto-compile turned off. That is to say, it's only available if there is something to compile. That's right! Gen patches compile. Since auto-compile is turned on by default, and the compile process is very fast, we won't notice this fact in many cases. We do notice it though if we create an error somewhere in the Gen patch that keeps Gen from recompiling. As a result, we will still hear the version that compiled successfully before. Therefore, we should always watch the Max window for errors or the code that results from the patch, which is displayed on the right of the previous screenshot. If recompiling is successful, the code also changes.

Exploring the differences between Max and Gen

Gen works just like Max; if you can patch in Max, you can do it in Gen too. The set of objects is a little different, but that shouldn't be much of a problem. However, there are still some differences one should be aware of. First of all, how do we communicate with the processing inside a Gen patcher?

Parameters through param

You've already seen that there are [in] and [out] objects, and they do exactly what you assume they do. They create inlets and outlets and we can feed signals through our Gen patches that way. This would be audio signals (MSP signals) for gen~ and Jitter matrices for jit.pix, jit.gen, and jit.gl.pix (jit.gl pix is special in this regard; we feed in matrices or textures and get out textures). However, there is a Gen object called [param] that allows us to communicate with the Gen patcher through messages too.

If you take a look at the following screenshot, you can see that as soon as we put down a [param] object with a name, we can use that name as if it were an attribute of our Gen object:

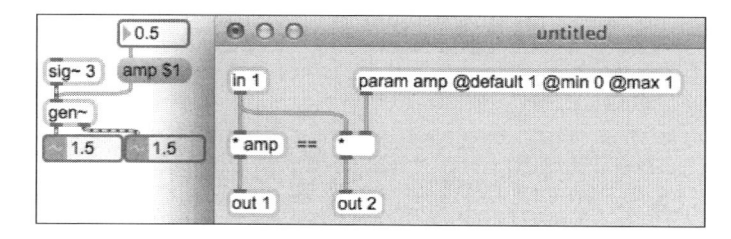

Inside the Gen patcher, we can use the value of that parameter directly or access it through the name. In order to use the named parameter (as it's done in the left multiplication), we have to declare the variable though, so a param object with that name has to be somewhere in the patcher. Also, note that we get rid of the tilde in gen~ although we are dealing with audio signals. Why? Simply because there is no message domain inside Gen.

Buffers and data

Inside [gen~], we will often need to store and retrieve values as we do it with buffers in the MSP domain. Inside [gen~], there is the data object to temporarily write and read sample data. We need to give it a name, and the resulting array can be accessed via the [poke] or [peek] object. However, we can also reference buffers that reside outside a gen~ patcher. If you look at the following screenshot, you'll see the syntax is quite obvious:

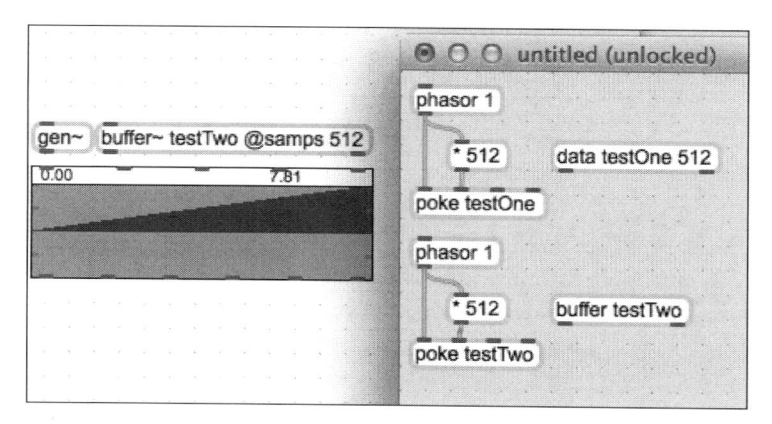

If we'd like to reference a [buffer~] object, we need to put down a [buffer] object inside Gen as well; only then will the Gen environment find it.

Subpatchers and abstraction inside Gen

Subpatchers and abstraction work pretty much straightforward inside Gen, although there are some points to note about it. In Max, we first use the `[patcher]` object, or `[p]`, to create a subpatcher; inside Gen, it's `[gen]`. Abstractions are just the same as in Max, a saved Gen patcher must be somewhere in the search path. In the following screenshot, you can see an example for both a subpatcher and an abstraction (rpole):

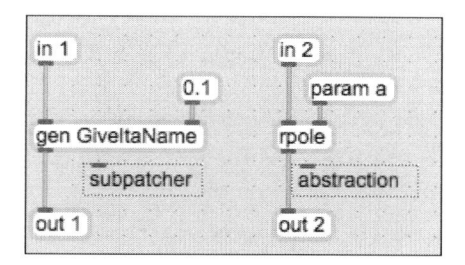

We can save a Gen patcher just by double-clicking on it to view it and choosing **Save as** under the **File** option. Depending on if the opened Gen patcher resides inside `gen~` or a Jitter Gen object, we can save it as an `*.gendsp` or `*genjit` file.

> For now, once we save a Gen patcher in this way, we can't simply open it by locating it in a file browser or opening it via the Max application directly. However, we can open it in a text editor and copy-and-paste the whole text/XML code into a new Gen patcher. We will be presented with our Gen patch and can inspect our patch that way or overwrite the original.

You can probably try to use a `param` object inside an abstraction/subpatcher. You'll quickly notice that this doesn't work. We need to use the `[setparam]` object to access the `param` objects inside subpatchers, as shown in the following screenshot:

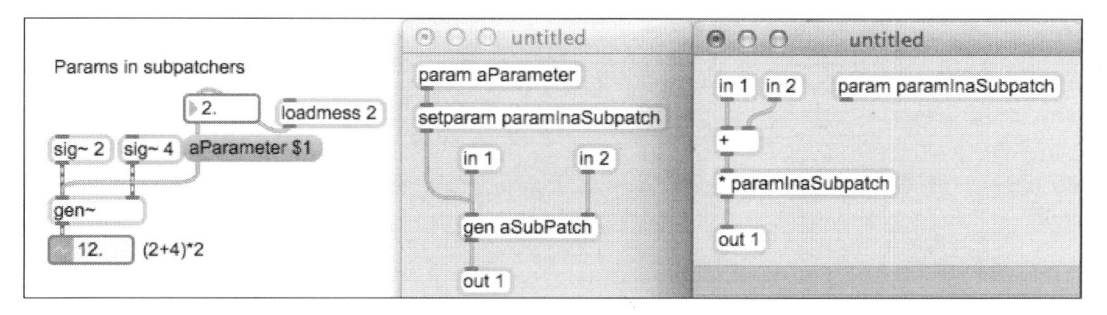

Low-level Patching in Gen

Besides using the saved `*.gendsp` or `*.genjit` files inside Gen, we can also load them from outside using the `@gen` attribute, as shown in the following screenshot:

gen~ @gen rpole

So there are the `*.gendsp` and `*.genjit` files. However, there is a third one we can use for abstraction: `*.genexpr`. This file type is reserved for written text-based code to be called inside Gen. So let's now take a look at Gen's powerful text-based coding capabilities.

Genexpr and the CodeBox

Inside Gen, we can use our visual programming paradigm as we are used to, but we can also go for text-based coding. The beauty lies in the fact that there is no performance difference whatsoever between the different methods, since Gen compiles and optimizes what we do anyway. So we can switch between graphical programming and code all the time, always using what's more convenient. In the following screenshot, you can see three versions of doing a power of two operation. So they all do exactly the same thing:

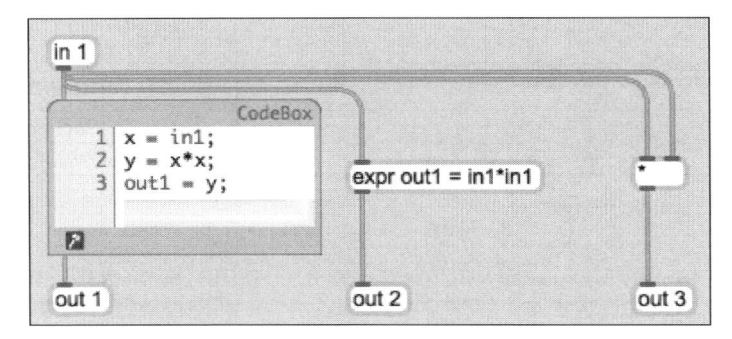

```
in 1

CodeBox
1  x = in1;
2  y = x*x;
3  out1 = y;

expr out1 = in1*in1

*

out 1       out 2       out 3
```

In the preceding screenshot, the CodeBox on the left is of course created by just making a new object and typing `codebox`. In there, a code similar to C/JavaScript can be entered.

> While it is convenient to code inside a CodeBox directly, there is another option. We can, of course, use our favorite text/code editor to write the code and paste it in there. For Sublime Text, snippets and syntax highlighting are available, so it can be a lot easier to write the code outside Max.

Although we cannot go through the whole syntax of genexpr here, let's at least look at how to define functions and how to reference the *.genexpr files. If you look at the following screenshot, you'll see that in the first CodeBox, the one sent to [out 1], we generated a sine wave via the cycle function. In the second one, we defined a function inside the CodeBox and called it inside the same CodeBox. The third CodeBox just used the require command to load a *.genexpr file that contains just our function definition. After that, we called our function. Obviously, all three versions lead to the same result.

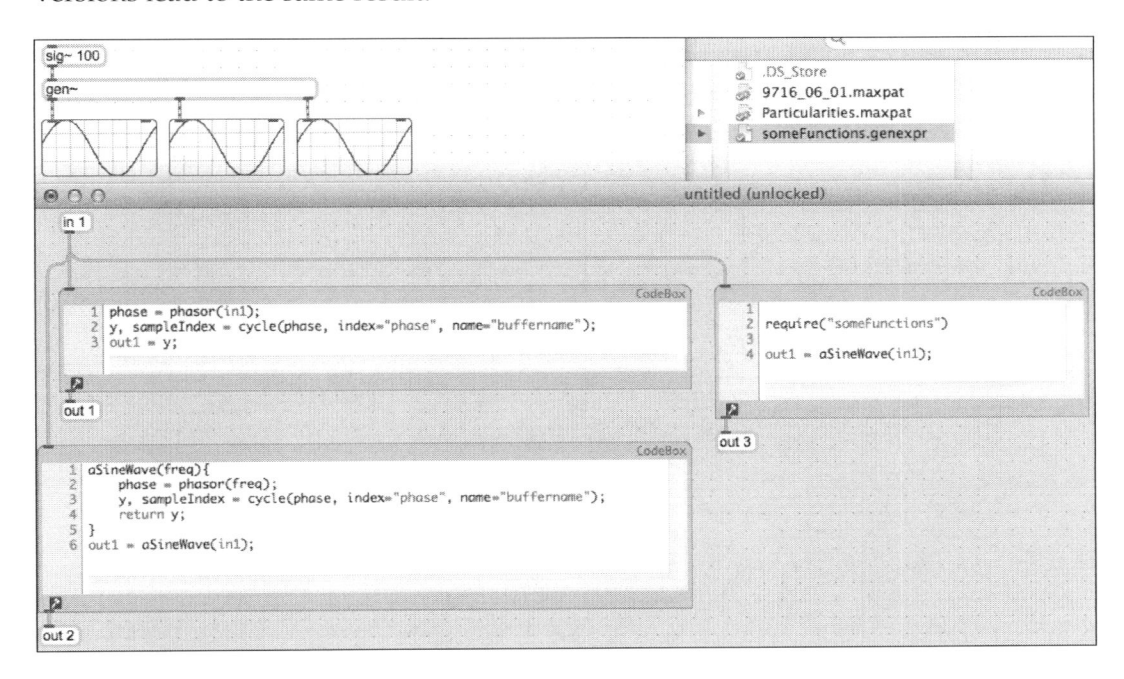

```
phase = phasor(in1);
y, sampleIndex = cycle(phase, index="phase", name="buffername");
out1 = y;
```

```
require("someFunctions")

out1 = aSineWave(in1);
```

```
aSineWave(freq){
    phase = phasor(freq);
    y, sampleIndex = cycle(phase, index="phase", name="buffername");
    return y;
}
out1 = aSineWave(in1);
```

To learn the genexpr language, it is useful to watch the code window on the right while patching. For example, if we'd like to find out the genexpr syntax for a delay, we can just patch one together and take a look at the following resulting code:

```
Delay delay_1(1000);
tap_2 = delay_1.read(1000);
out1 = tap_2;
delay_1.write(in1);
```

The Sublime Text snippets make writing a delay a matter of a couple of keystrokes. You can find the Sublime Text package at http://cycling74.com/forums/topic/genexpr-for-sublimetext/.

Efficiency

In general, networks inside gen~ will be more efficient than native MSP networks. Gen does add some overhead, so having, for example, just an addition inside a gen~ object will likely be more inefficient than an MSP [+~]. The bigger the Gen network, the more sense it will make efficiency-wise. The jit.gl.pix object is an exception here since it actually creates a shader that runs on the GPU. Processing a texture on the GPU is generally faster than processing a matrix on the CPU. Since most Jitter-native operations are computed on the CPU, even simple things can be a lot faster inside jit.gl.pix (or jit.gl.shader/jit.gl.slab).

Additionally, there is the possibility to measure the CPU consumption of a Gen patcher using the dump-outlet object, which has to be enabled via an attribute as follows:

```
qmetro 30 @active 1
getcpu
gen~ @dumpoutlet 1 @cpumeasure 1
                        cpu 0.000328
```

Using this technique, the view CPU usage feature, and the [poly~] techniques, we learned to compare CPU consumption more accurately. We can find out whether a gen~ object makes sense for a particular task, if the performance is very crucial.

Examples

As mentioned previously, we will mainly go through examples that require short delay feedback inside gen~. This still is a vast field, and we will try to narrow it down further by exploring physical modeling at this point since gen~ is an exceptionally well-suited tool for it.

Physical modeling means observing physical phenomena and trying to simulate it using digital systems with the aim of synthesizing their sound. Obviously, this is quite a difficult task, and also, often a very CPU-consuming one. Physical modeling, therefore, often deals with simplifications. Also, it might be a hard task to describe real physical systems as differential equations in the first place, so in practice, we'd rather translate differential equations to digital systems or try to find digital algorithms right away and modify them.

The Karplus-Strong synthesis

The Karplus-Strong algorithm is another technique to synthesize a plucked string. For now, we'll not go into details about its possible correlation with physical forces, since it is a great simplification, which also makes it very efficient. The basic idea is shown in the following screenshot:

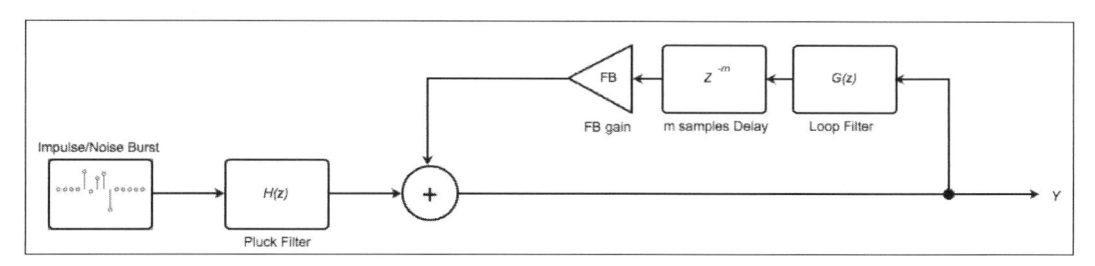

We simulate the string using a delay with feedback. The loop filter is a low-pass filter that simulates losses at the terminations of the string; the delay length determines the pitch of the algorithm. The resulting frequency will simply be the inverse of the delay time in seconds. We excite the resonator (the delay/string) using an impulse or a short burst of noise.

> An impulse will always be the same; a short burst of noise will always be a bit different. So an impulse is good to build/test resonators since it makes the results more comparable. A short burst of noise will bring in variety and might sound a bit more natural, which is often desirable for a finished instrument.

Low-level Patching in Gen

Optionally, we might filter this burst before feeding it to the resonator to vary the simulated material of the striking object, as shown in the following screenshot:

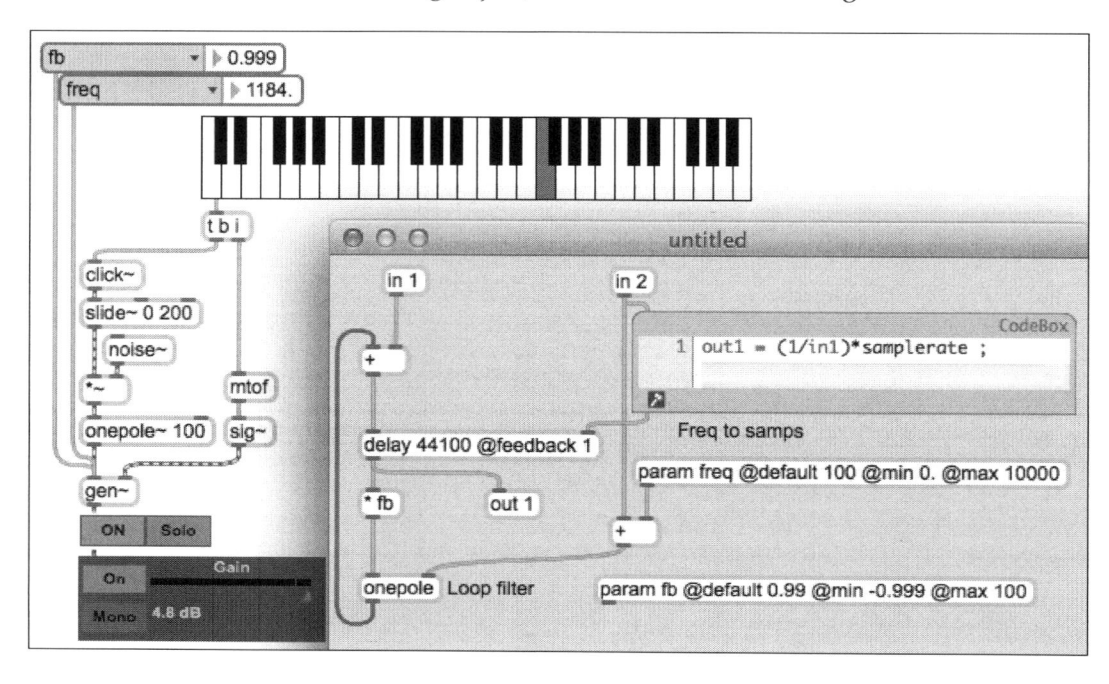

So you see, Gen implementation is quite straightforward. There is some conversion necessary to get a MIDI note converted to delay time in samples; the frequency input has also been used to offset the cutoff of the low-pass filter (which doesn't have any physical analogy). The low-pass filter is an abstraction, a simple one-pole low-pass filter.

> In physical modeling and derived techniques, we often divide a model of sound into the exciter and resonator. This has the big advantage that once we are happy with a resonator, we can feed in any exciter. How would you go about creating a simple bowed string synthesizer?

Since gen~ is such a great environment for creating filters, let's take a break here to look at the one-pole abstraction for a moment. It is just another low-pass, IIR filter. We already know the simple recursive circuit. However, what about its coefficient generation, and how do we get to two gain coefficients from a cutoff in Hertz? The different solutions that you could adopt are shown in the following screenshot:

```
in 2  freq, Hz
                                        CodeBox
1  //from Freq to radians per sample
2  w = 2*pi*in1*(1/samplerate);
3
4  out1 = sin(w);
5  out2 = 1-exp(-w);
6  out3 = w;
```

in 1 freq, Hz

param approxSelect 1
selector 3

out 2

!-1

*

+

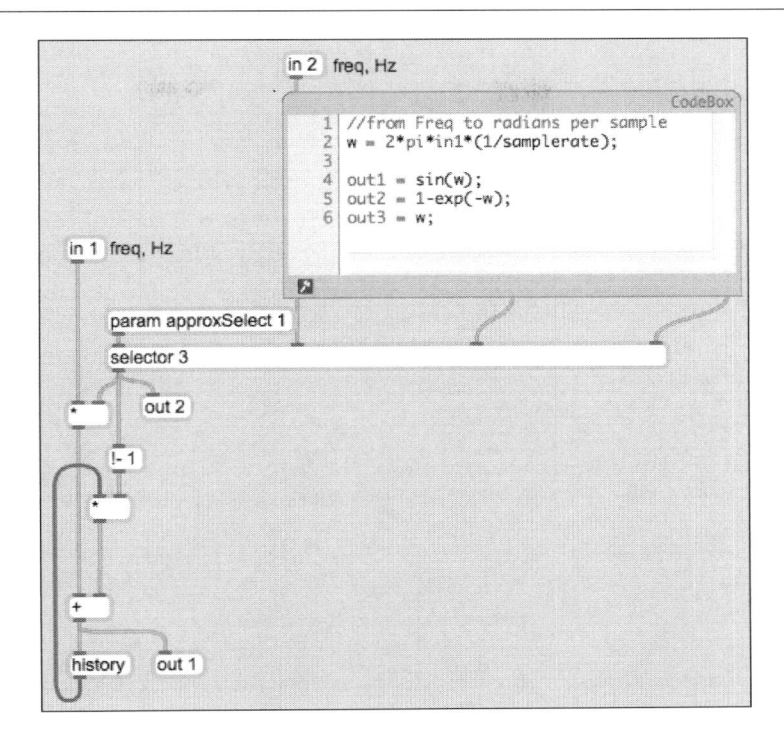

history   out 1

In the preceding screenshot, you see three different solutions to the problem. Sadly, we don't have the time here to go through all the details since it would require us to dive into the z-plane. However, let's put things in a simple way:

1. First, we calculate the cutoff frequency in radians per sample from the given cutoff in cycles per second or Hertz.
2. Then, we use that value as follows:
    - Directly, as an approximation; this works well if the cutoff is way under sample rate/4.
    - Using $1 = e^{-\omega}$; we'll explain this later.
    - Using the sine of omega. The circuit we have previously is like a portion of a bi-quad, and using the sine is like extracting the a1 coefficient.

As you can see, we are controlling two multiplications with the resulting value, one inside the loop and the other before the loop. This is because our one-pole low-pass actually boosts low frequencies instead of attenuating high frequencies. We are compensating this by attenuating the input, the multiplication before the loop. What about the solution using Euler's number now? First of all, we can drop the **1-** for our explanation since you can see that we are always using a number for one multiplication and **1** minus that number for the other one. The solution using **e** is pretty handy:

$$e^{\frac{-1}{d}}$$

This can be used, *d* being the time constant of the filter. This means that it will take the filter *d* samples to decay to 36.8 percent. So this is pretty useful if we use a filter to smooth values or create envelope followers. On the other hand:

$$e^{-\omega}$$

This will allow us to determine its cutoff frequency with omega being the following:

$$\omega = 2\pi f_c \frac{1}{sr}$$

Let's get back to our string. As the next step, we can go ahead and use our plucked string algorithm to model a violin. In the second Karplus-Strong patch, you'll see a very simple approach using a sawtooth in combination with noise to model a bow. Note that here, we completely ignore that there is an interaction between the string and the bow. The generated string sound is then sent into a couple of resonant bandpass filters that model the body of a violin. Refer to the following screenshot:

Chapter 6

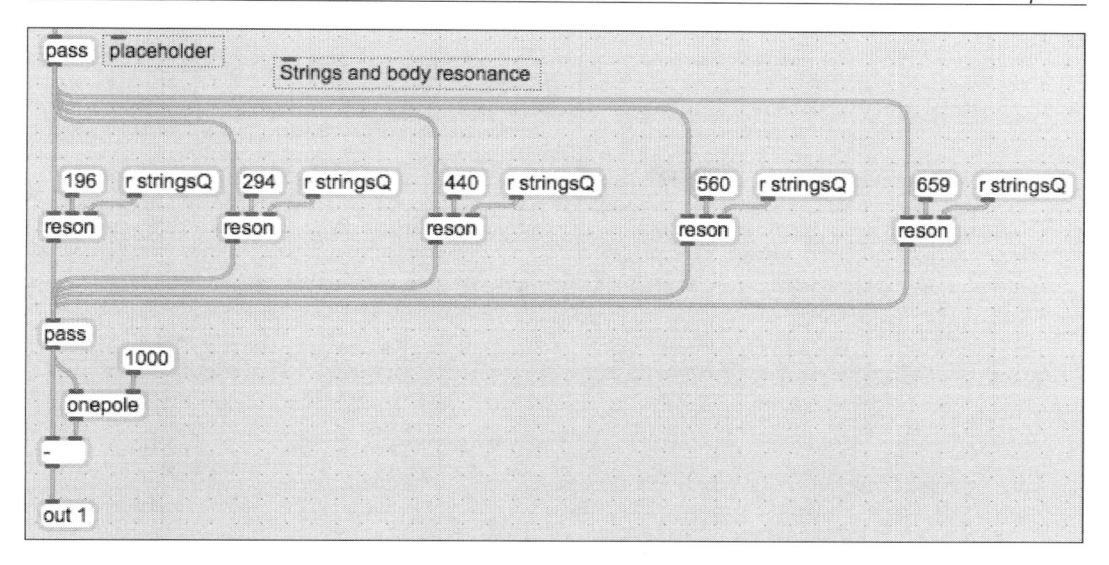

[Diagram: Pd patch showing "Strings and body resonance" with pass placeholder, five reson filters at frequencies 196, 294, 440, 560, 659 each with r stringsQ, followed by pass, onepole 1000, and out 1]

This is just an example, so don't take the frequencies of the bandpass filters too seriously. If we'd like to model a resonating body, we tend to use bandpass filters and need to know their correct parameters: the amplitude, decay rate (related to Q), and frequency. For a given body, in general, there are a number of options to find out these parameters, and they are as follows:

- We can calculate them, which grows very complicated, unless the body is not an ideal string, tube, plate, and so on. On the other hand, many bodies can be simplified to a combination of basic shapes.
- We can measure them, recording the impulse response of the body and analyzing the sample. In practice, this means we hit the body, trying to get as little room reflections into the mic as possible. After that, we can take a look at the most important resonances and estimate the parameters.

> A very handy piece of software to analyze the sample is Praat, which can be found at http://www.fon.hum.uva.nl/praat/.

- We can also use professional simulation software for the task. Very conveniently, construction engineers and product designers also need to know resonance frequencies of the parts they design. Therefore, many big CAD software packages offer the simulation of what we just talked about: hitting the body and measuring the modes. So this approach requires us to build our body in 3D, in the correct scale, and assign the correct materials inside CAD software to get a list of resonance frequencies.

A mass-spring system

We just used the Karplus-Strong algorithm to arrive at a more or less useable result; let's now pause for a moment and look at really simulating a physical system. Probably, the most important system for our wave-related tinkering is the mass-spring system. Here, we will use the differential equation of the mass-spring system to arrive at a very meaningful but slightly naive and inefficient digital simulation. A more efficient version would feature a scattering junction, which we will explore later.

An ideal mass-spring system is governed by the following equation:

$$F = -kx$$

The force is always equal to the position multiplied by a constant k. This means that a spring always wants to go to its equilibrium position. Where does the mass come into play?

$$F = ma$$

So force equals to mass multiplied by acceleration. This is a famous formula and we can just put it in there to arrive at the following equation:

$$ma = -kx$$

Since acceleration is the second derivative of the position x, we can simplify this differential equation:

$$\frac{d^2x}{dt^2}m = -kx$$

Chapter 6

There are a number of methods to discretize differential equations, for example, the binomial transform, which is often used to discretize analogue filters. Another very common one is the Euler's method, which is very handy because of its simplicity. Here, we are not going to differentiate at all but need a discrete method for integration, since what we want is to build a system that takes a force as an input and outputs the position of our spring. Leaky integrators are going to do the following for us:

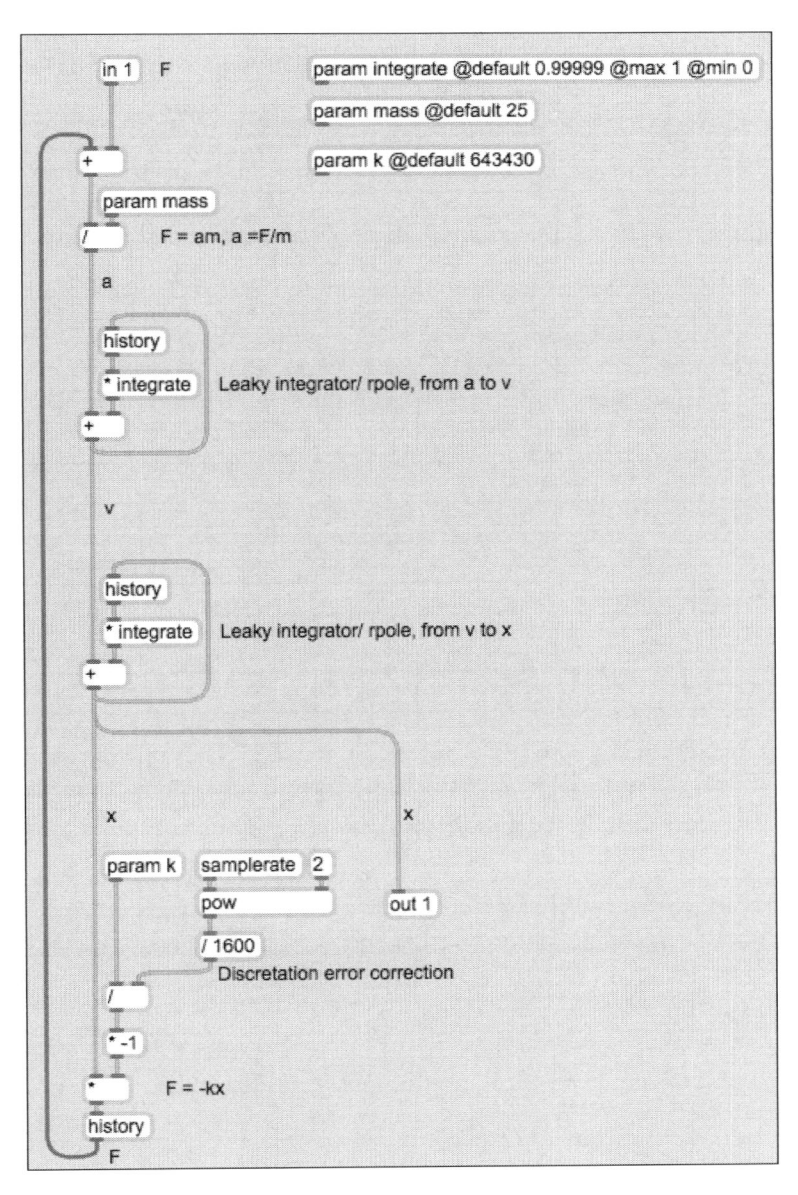

[197]

We end up with quite a complicated system that takes an impulse and outputs an exponentially decaying sine wave. You might say "But we already got that; it's called a bandpass filter!"; well yes, but physical models like this have the advantage of offering the possibility to apply physically meaningful manipulations. Also, they take physically meaningful parameters: what are the coefficients for a bandpass if we like to simulate a spring with *k* equals to 25 and a mass of 3 kg? So you see, our model indeed has some use if it's about simulation instead of production, and simulation is an excellent tool to understand systems or phenomena in general.

If you have looked at the `gen~` abstractions we already used, you have already seen the **history** operator. It is used extensively in the previous screenshot since it is an enormously important object when it comes to building filters (the whole mass-spring system can be considered a filter). It applies a single sample of delay and allows feedback connections.

> Now, try to come up with a physical model yourself! A good one is a leaky tank. Given a tank filled with water and a hole in the bottom, try to simulate water running out, outputting the height of the water inside the tank at every instant. The tricky thing is that the water runs out more quickly if there is more water in the tank. Search for the differential equation online or try to find it out yourself; draw a block diagram for a continuous system, one for a discrete system, and then implement it in Gen~!

Let's get back to our string and we are going to use a more sophisticated technique now: a **waveguide**.

Waveguides and scattering junctions

A digital waveguide implements the idea that at any position on an ideal elastic medium (such as an ideal string, plate, or tube) at any point in time (we have two variables here, space and time), we can sample the waveform digitally. We can follow the geometry of the body and build up a simulation model out of delay lines, filters, and nonlinear operations.

A basic waveguide is made up of two delay lines, if we think about a plucked string; one delay contains a wave traveling to the right, and the other one to the left along the string. At both ends of the string, the wave gets reflected, so it is sent into the other delay. Also, the reflection causes an inversion of the wave, so it gets multiplied by **-1**. To not end up with an infinitely vibrating system, we simply reduce the absolute value of one of the multiplications, introducing a loss of energy as shown in the following figure:

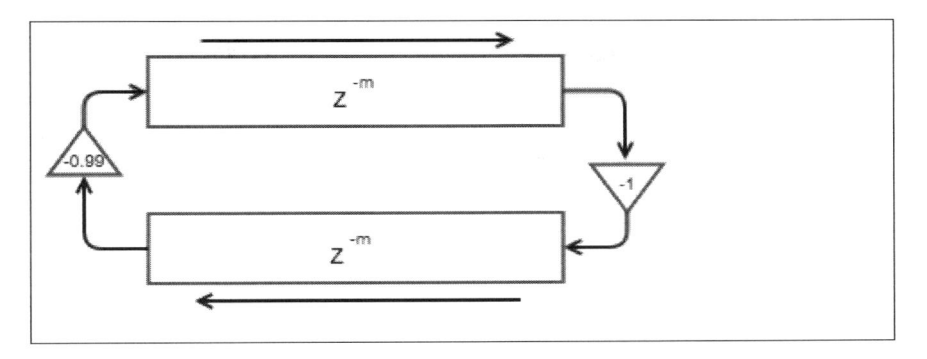

"Alright, where is the input? Where is the output?", I'm hearing you. If you do a little research about waveguides, you will find quite many of these no input no output systems. The reason for this is that depending on where we make the output, we get a signal with a different physical meaning or no physical signal at all. The idea here is to sample the string spatially too, so we can construct the two delays out of many smaller delays, each representing a part of the string. Depending on which of these small delays we excite, we decide where to pluck the string, and depending on which delays we feed out, we decide where to listen to the string. The reflection coefficients, **-0.99** and **-1** in the previous figure, can be combined with a filter to mimic frequency-dependent reflection properties. Let's do something about our input-output problem, going into Max right away, as shown in the following screenshot:

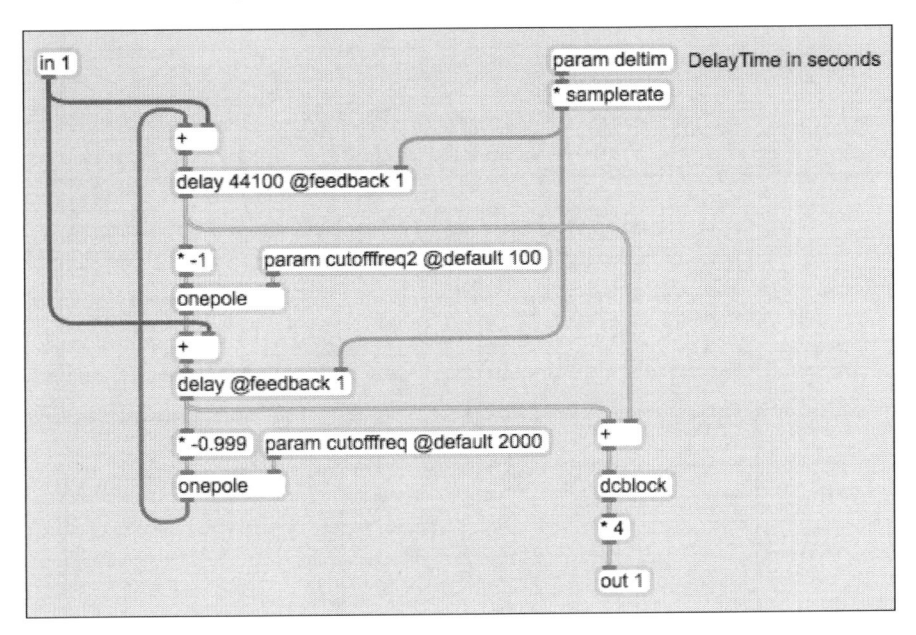

Low-level Patching in Gen

You can see that we excite the string by feeding a signal into both the delays and we get our output from both. Two low-pass filters simulate two different materials at the string's termination. A common method to simulate different pluck positions is feeding our exciter through a comb filter. Now that's pretty simple and leaves our waveguide untouched, which is nice because we'll now modify it to get different listening positions. We just imagined that we have many small delays; let's just divide each of our two delays into two, resulting in four delays. Now, let's put our listening position in the middle of both the delays. We end up with something like this:

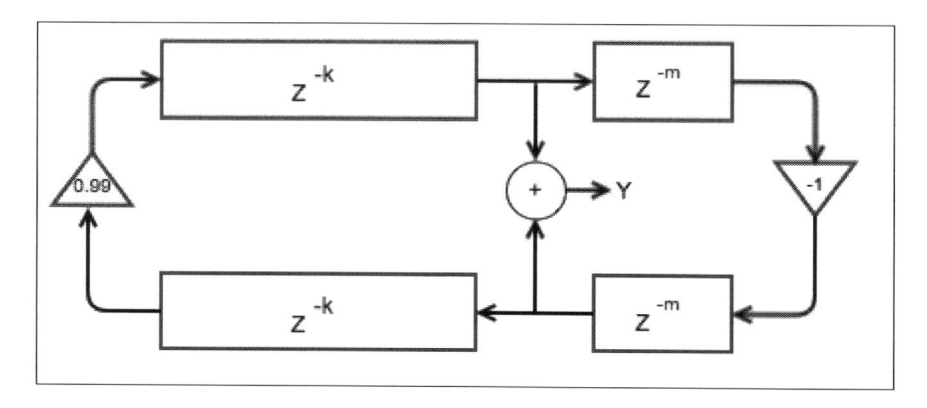

Here, $k + m$ is always equals to half the total delay time. By changing the ratio between **k** and **m**, we can vary the listening position. A Max implementation could look like this:

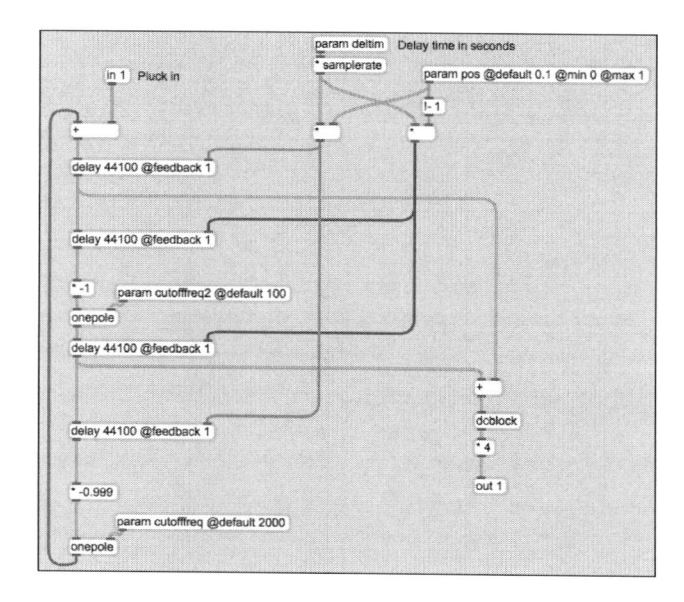

Let's now turn to a blown tube. The beautiful thing is that we simulate a tube in the same way as a string, using a waveguide. If you find a long tube and tap on one of its ends, you will hear that it sounds very similar to a plucked string. You can imagine that for a simple blown tube, we would therefore just send filtered noise into our existing waveguide. However, we are going to move on at this point and simulate two tubes that are connected but have a different diameter. This introduces the concept of a scattering junction.

A scattering junction is a construction that allows us to simulate changes in media, changes in bore size in the case of two tubes, and so on. It is a way to connect two waveguides and simulate these parts of the wave so that they get reflected and other parts get through. Its parameters are determined by relating the impedance of the two elements to each other. In the following screenshot, you can see a scattering junction as a block diagram, since it's a bit tidier than a Max patch:

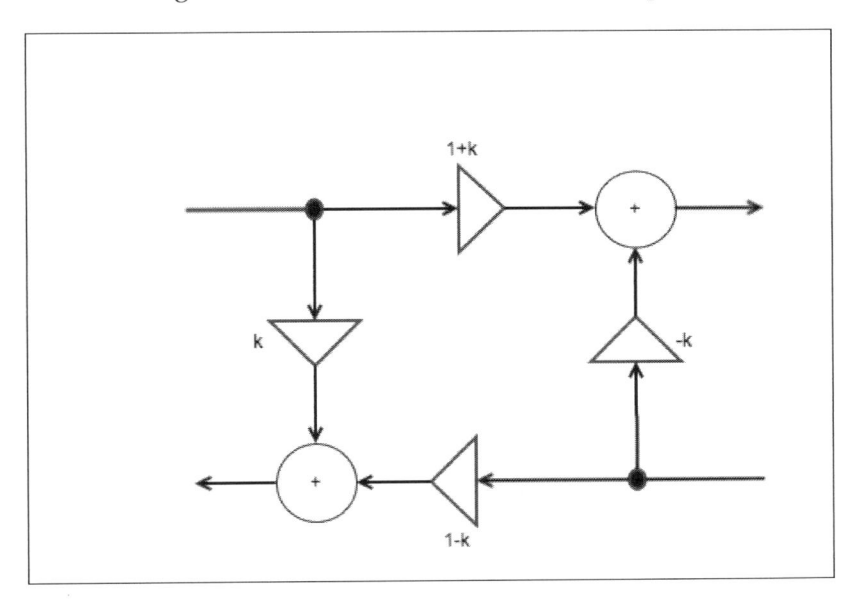

When connecting two tubes, the value *k* can be calculated by relating the two cross sections of the tubes *A1* and *A2*:

$$k = \frac{A_1 - A_2}{A_1 + A_2}$$

In the previous tube example, each of the four *k*-dependent coefficients had a meaning of its own too:

- *k* was the reflection coefficient of the traveling pressure wave
- (1+*k*) was the transmission coefficient of the traveling pressure wave
- -*k* was the reflection coefficient of volume velocity
- (1-*k*) was the transmission coefficient of volume velocity

For the string, you can exchange the term volume velocity with the string velocity, and the traveling pressure wave with the string displacement. So we arrive at a `gen~` patch that features two waveguides interconnected with a scattering junction. Beware, this is a very basic model that is ready to be extended. As mentioned, it could also be used to simulate a string, so feel free to experiment, as shown in the following screenshot:

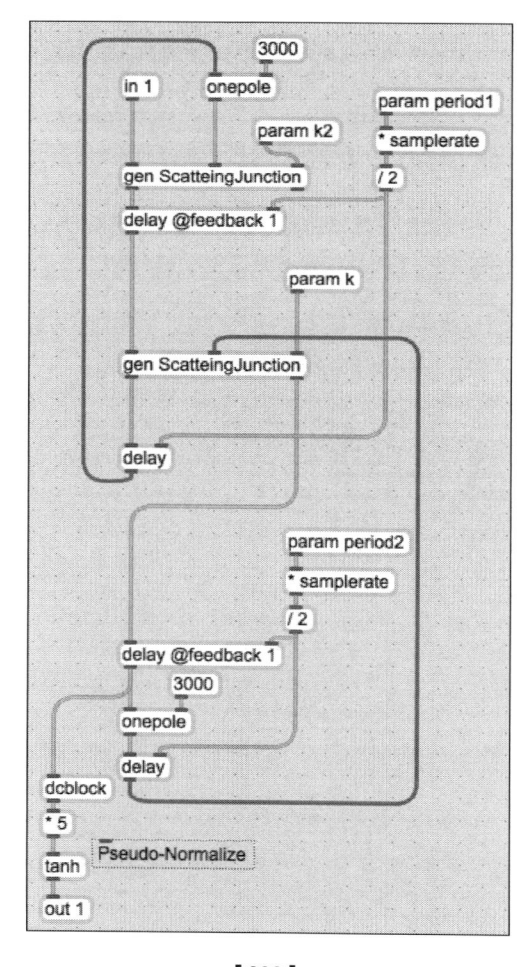

Obviously, we have two scattering junctions here, one at the entrance of our tubes and one that connects the two tubes. This model is directly derived from the so-called Kelly-Lochbaum Vocal tract model, which tries to model the human vocal tract by piece-wise approximation. In reality, since tubes are often slightly conical, we approximate the conical shape via several ideal tubes that have different diameters. The original model, therefore, has more delay stages, but you can hopefully see the bigger picture.

Further reading

- Miller Puckette:
    - `http://msp.ucsd.edu/techniques/v0.11/book-html/book.html`
    - `http://msp.ucsd.edu/techniques/v0.11/book-html/node4.html`
- Julius O. Smith III:
    - `https://ccrma.stanford.edu/~jos/filters/filters.html`
- Stephen W. Smith:
    - `http://www.dspguide.com/`
- Perry R. Cook:
    - *Real Sound Synthesis for Interactive Applications*, CRC Press

Summary

This concludes our journey through the world of `gen~`. With `gen~`, we can export code by just using the `exportcode` message, which produces C++ code that is ready to use. In this chapter, we unfortunately couldn't explain the whole huge topic of signal processing, and therefore, you might feel a little lost in trying to come up with custom filters inside `gen~`. However, you now have all the knowledge about the tool you will need, so pick up a book about signal processing, and you can start off by building filters. Some very good material is presented later, and there is a wealth of design and analysis methods waiting for you.

7
Video in Max/Jitter

We already talked a bit about the format Jitter uses in the very first chapter: the Jitter matrix. Now, we'll take a look at Jitter and video/matrix processing in Max, and probably take a second look at what we talked about in the first chapter; don't get scared of planes, cells, and data formats. It's really logical and we will quickly revisit the concepts to get accustomed with them. But first of all, we'll try to get some input and output techniques going in order to get some tools to analyze what we are building.

In this chapter, we will cover the following topics:

- Inputting and outputting Jitter data
- Matrix processing and feedback/delay
- Geometry manipulation and shaders

Inputting and outputting Jitter data

First and foremost, we'd like to get video input going, both to get an image from a camera into Max and to load prerecorded movies. As the next step, we'd like to display these images. The `jit.qt.grab` object allows us to grab a camera input and the `jit.qt.movie` object allows us to play back a movie. All Jitter objects start with `jit`, and to save us some typing, if we create a new Jitter object, we can just type `j` instead of `n` to create a new object with the text `jit.` in it. The `qt` term in `jit.qt.grab` and other objects stands for quick time, so an up-to-date quick time version is required.

Video in Max/Jitter

In the following screenshot, you can see we used `jit.qt.grab` to feed in a live camera image. In the case of multiple available cameras, the help file of `jit.qt.grab` tells us how to query available devices and how to choose which one to use. The `jit.qt.grab` object is a good example of how Jitter works; we need to send in bangs to make something happen, and it outputs a Jitter matrix, which is also illustrated by the greenish patch cords. So the frame rate of a Jitter network is typically determined by a `metro` (or `qmetro`) object. Right beneath `jit.qt.grab`, we have an in-patcher display, a very handy object called `jit.pwindow`. So this in-patcher display actually is one of our most used debugging tools when dealing with Jitter. We can put them everywhere to always know what's happening at every point of our network. Although putting these everywhere really drains our CPU quite a bit, and we will therefore look at more useful ways to always be aware of our signals, it's still a very useful technique.

Another very useful object to inspect signals is `jit.fpsgui`. In the following screenshot, it is located right next to our **jit.pwindow** that shows us the current frame rate. However, it can also show us the resolution or the number of planes. By clicking on **fps**, we can choose what it should tell us about its input signal.

As you see in the following screenshot, we have some more options to inspect the data; there is also **jit.window**, which opens an additional window that we can render to and put to fullscreen. Also, there is **jit.scope**, which is capable of drawing basic image/color analysis graphs, and there is **jit.cellblock** to look at the numerical values directly.

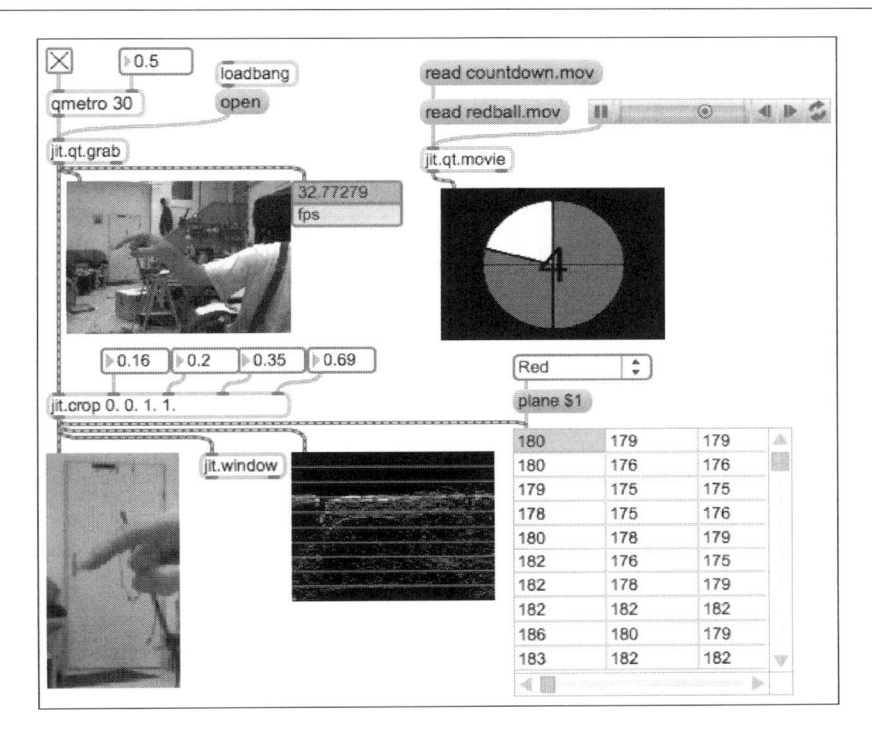

We'll use `jit.cellblock` in a second to have a look at the different data formats that Jitter offers, but first, let's stay in this patcher and have a look at Matrix probing. Think of MSP; if we hover over a connection and have probing enabled, we see both the numerical value and a little meter that indicates the signal level, and there is something similar that comes handy for Jitter signals. If you activate **Matrix Probe** found under **Debug**, a little floating window pops up:

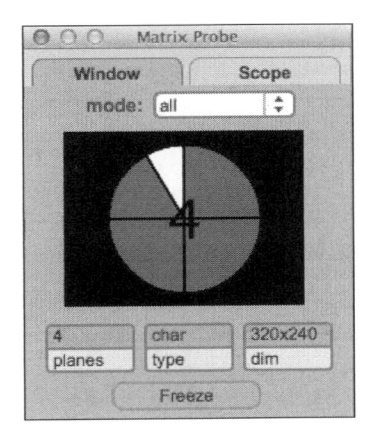

Video in Max/Jitter

In there, we will always see the signal that is sent through the connection we last hovered over. Obviously, it also shows us the plane count, resolution, and data type and has some more features. Having this window open so that we can see it while working with Jitter is very handy and is highly recommended.

Getting started with the Jitter matrix

So let's revise. Do you still remember what the plane count is and what dim means? It's probably a bit strange, but in Max, we talk about resolution as the dimensions of the matrix, and color channels as planes. Since a `jit.matrix` object is reserved memory space, we also have to tell Max what the format should be. So now, let's generate some matrices with different formats, dimensions, and plane counts to get more comfortable with the whole system, as shown in the following screenshot:

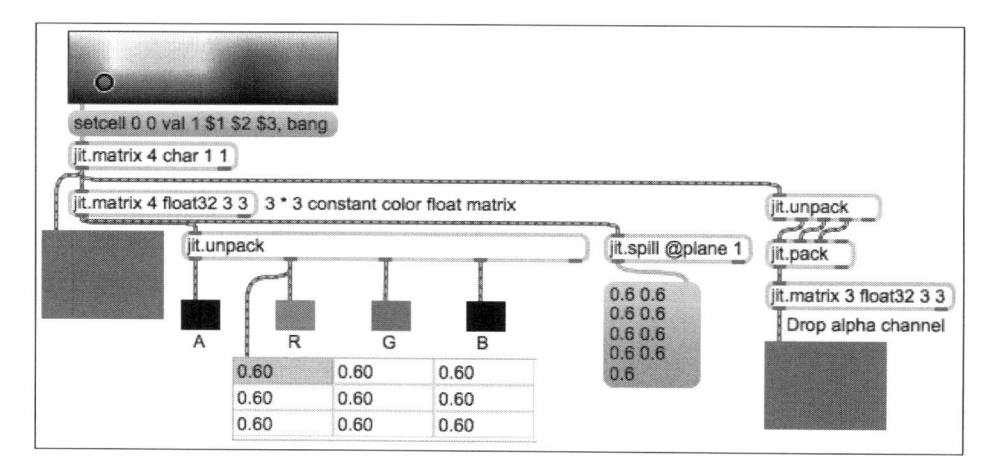

In the previous screenshot, you can see how we first make a matrix with 4 planes, **ARGB** (Alpha, Red, Green, and Blue), in the character format, with a resolution of 1*1 cells or pixels. We use the [swatch] object to set the values of our single pixel and then convert the matrix to a 4-plane, float 32, 3 x 3 pixel matrix. After that, we use [jit.unpack] to access the individual planes, look at the values via [jit.cellblock], and use [jit.spill] to get a list of values from one of the planes into the Max domain.

To the right of the previous screenshot, you also see how we can unpack and pack planes to access different channels, or to get rid of the alpha channel in this case.

> While this example is easy to understand, we can also use a single [jit.matrix] object to achieve the same result using its @planemap attribute.

Also, to further stress the point that [jit.matrix] is a very versatile object, take a look at jit.crop, the abstraction used inside the patcher depicted first in this chapter, basics.maxpat. In there, we achieve cropping only using jit.matrix and some coordinate generation out of float values.

Matrix processing

So what can we do with a matrix once we have it? Where are all the FX? The really cool and efficient stuff will have to wait a bit until we arrive at OpenGL (open graphics Library, a standard API used to program 2D and 3D graphics), since all the spectacular FX should be done on the **Graphics Processing Unit (GPU)** (the processor on our graphics cards); otherwise, we will run out of CPU cycles quickly. There is jit.qt.effect, which will apply quick time FX, but honestly, this won't make us happy for more than a couple of minutes. So let's look at more low-level tools for matrix processing; jit.op used to be our Swiss army knife for matrix operations before the arrival of Gen, and is still very important. In the following screenshot, several modes of [jit.op] are demonstrated:

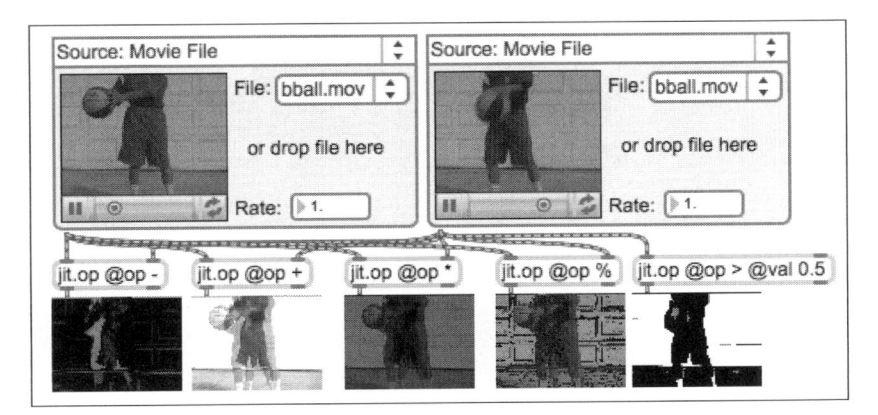

As you can see, a lot of math operations can be realized with [jit.op], and we can therefore use it for basic compositing as well.

Feedback and delay

Feedback cannot be achieved directly but is simply done using named matrices. We can name matrices to make two matrices share the same data, just like how the [coll] objects work, as shown in the following screenshot:

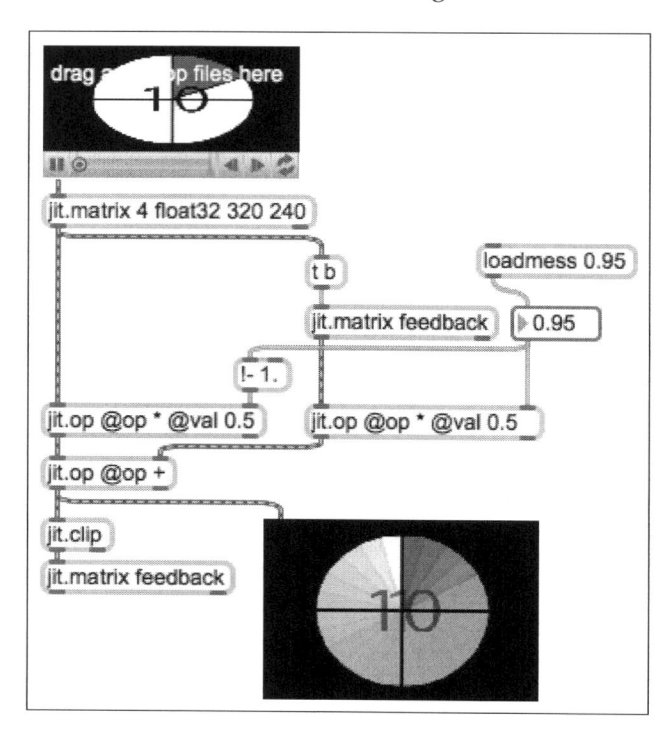

As you can see from the previous screenshot, we created a little feedback network, a one-pole filter if you will. We assigned a name to two matrices and used this to get the output back to the input. The input also makes the feedback matrix output by triggering it with a bang. As you can see, before we enter our feedback network, we perform a data-format conversion. In general, it is wise to use high resolution in feedback networks as we just get more beautiful gradients.

Let's now look at a delay. As [jit.matrix] stores a matrix, there is also an object to store and retrieve multiple matrices: the [jit.matrixset] object. It works in a simple way; we can send in Jitter matrices and tell it at which index to store that incoming matrix. This way, we fill its internal buffer. On the other hand, we can always get it to output any matrix in its storage by use of the outputmatrix message. This way, we can easily build a delay by just generating series of numbers for storage and read positions, as shown in the following screenshot:

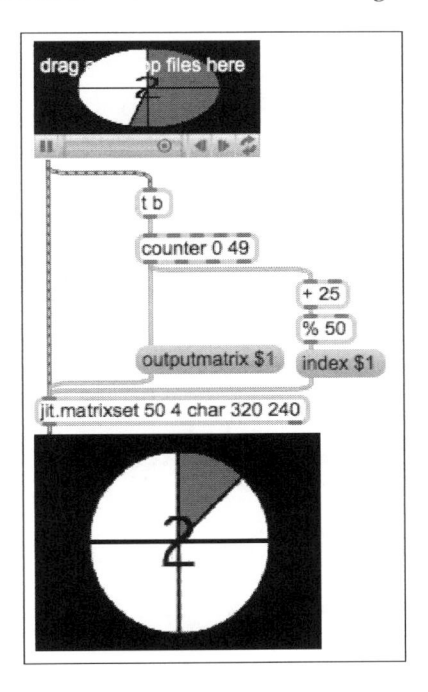

In the previous screenshot, you can see an example of a video delay.

> Go ahead and build a delay with feedback! Max is waiting for your custom jit.delay abstraction!

So we have seen some basic matrix operations; let's leave it like that to now dig into the wonderfully efficient world of OpenGL!

Using OpenGL in Jitter

OpenGL is a great framework for hardware-accelerated rendering. Before losing any more word about it, let's consider a more basic rendering setup to draw a 3D sphere to a floating window, as shown in the following screenshot:

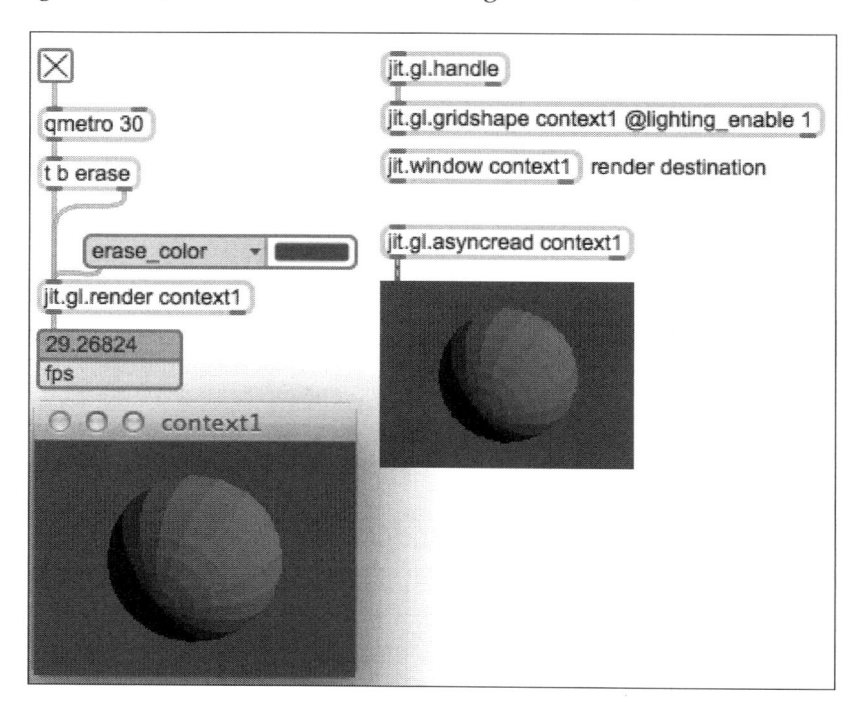

So what we have here are as follows:

- A `jit.window` object that provides us with rendering destination or rendering context. Its name is referenced by the other OpenGL objects.
- A `jit.gl.render` object that controls and drives our rendering. We need to send a bang to it to draw the next frame. But before that, we send it the message erase, so the last frame is overwritten with the background color. An `erase_color` message with 4 numbers sets up a new background color. If this color has an alpha value smaller than 1, the last frame will still be partly visible, causing feedback-like effects. Play around with it to get a better understanding of the erase message and the process of drawing a frame!
- A `jit.gl.gridshape` object that contains the data for a spherical model and that draws this model to our rendering context. At the moment, we have just one attribute set, but you will see that attributes are very important in the world of Jitter.

- A `Jit.gl.handle` object, which lets us interact with a model by dragging the object around in the window. We can rotate by dragging, use *Alt* + dragging up and down to dolly, and use *command/Ctrl* + dragging to move around.
- A `jit.gl.asyncread` object that allows us to read the OpenGL frame buffer in an asynchronous (very fast) way. By doing this, we can actually get a matrix out of our rendering if we need it (notice that until this point, no matrices have been involved).

This certainly isn't very impressive yet, so let's expand on what we have. In the next version, we will be making extensive use of attributes. Many objects in Jitter just have so many parameters that it makes sense to just type them in there; many of them won't be very interesting to interact with too. For example, the `smooth_shading` attribute gets us **Phong** shading, so we don't see each individual polygon, and the model will look smooth. This is something we will just want to activate regularly using an attribute, as shown in the following screenshot:

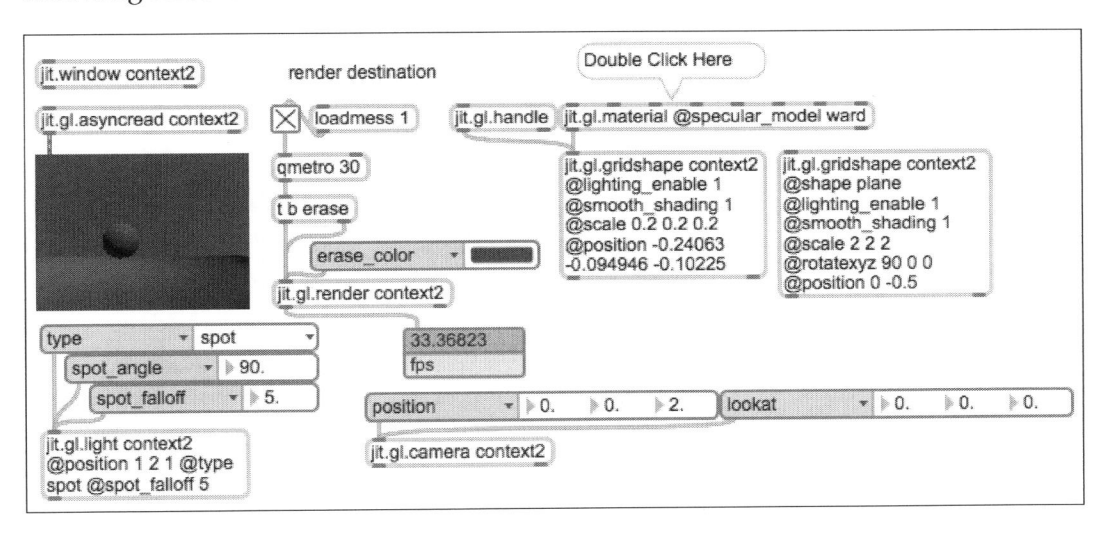

Here, we also added a camera to have some control over perspective and a `[jit.gl.light]` object that is set up to be a spotlight to give the scene a bit more character. Note that we also added a material here. The `[jit.gl.material]` object offers some very sophisticated shaders and even allows us to design and experiment with materials with an interactive editor. Just double-click on it to open a material editor window. Materials are the key to getting interesting renderings; take some time to play around with them!

Video in Max/Jitter

> You might find that the renderings somehow don't look very pretty. A big difference can be achieved by turning on **fsaa** for the window we render to, which stands for full scene anti-aliasing. The edges will become a lot less jagged, and the overall result will look a lot more beautiful and smooth. We will talk a bit more about aliasing in the TouchDesigner section of this book. In the screenshots here, we didn't use [jit.window name @fsaa 1] because [jit.gl.asyncread] does not support fsaa. There are workarounds though, using [jit.gl.sketch].

Before we come to putting FX on the results of our renderings, that is, how to use shaders to finish up what we render, let's quickly look at how geometry can be manipulated.

Geometry manipulation

After all, geometry data is just numbers, and since we have some pretty neat tools inside Jitter to look at multidimensional data, don't hesitate to look at these numbers. However, somehow, by default, we can't access the data that a jit.gl.gridshape object produces. That's because the @matrixoutout attribute is off by default. If we activate it, the geometry won't be rendered, but instead, a matrix will be outputted, which we can process in all ways we can think of. Luckily, there is also the [jit.gl.mesh] object, which we can then use to render a matrix that contains point positions, as shown in the following screenshot:

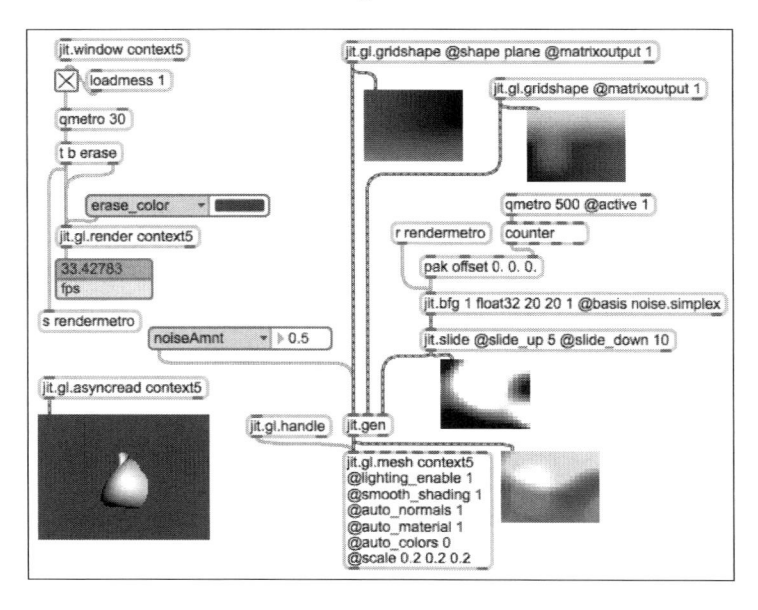

In the previous screenshot, you can see that we can just look at geometry data using a [jit.pwindow] object to get a feeling of what the geometry might look like. For example, the picture that comes out of the plane doesn't have any green in it, why? Because the **y** values are all zero. The [jit.gen] object only adds up all its input in this case, so you see, we can simply start mixing shapes, in this case, by increasing the noiseAmnt parameter. We also mix in the very mighty [jit.bfg] noise generator to end up with a morphing organic shape.

Shaders and FX

So there are jit.gl.shader, jit.gl.slab, and jit.gl.pix, all for hardware-accelerated FX and data/image processing. The jit.gl.pix object might be the easiest one to get into, unless you are already capable of writing shader programs. Before we can use a shader, which is a program that runs on the GPU, we have to get our picture, our matrix, on the GPU, where it will be stored as a texture. There, a shader can work on it, output another texture, and we can render the result. In the following screenshot, you can see how a shader might be used to apply FX to a regular movie:

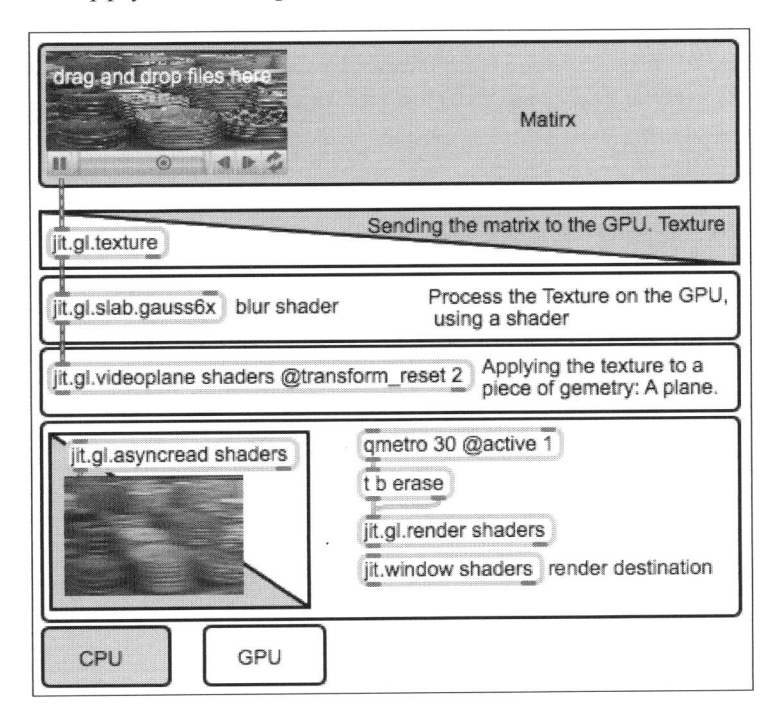

The previous screenshot depicts what happens on the GPU and what on the CPU isn't hundred percent accurate (for example, a metro certainly does not process on the GPU), so take it with a grain of salt. It should, however, show you the bigger picture and demonstrate that we can switch back and forth, and how it is done. Beware that this switching back and forth takes quite some time, and therefore shouldn't happen too often in our chain. Ideally, we just send commands and images to the GPU and let it do all the work. Note how we get our texture to be drawn to the window (which is not visible in the screenshot). Finally, we apply the resulting texture to a piece of geometry, a plane. This plane, [jit.gl.videoplane], is special since it has the ability to always be positioned so that it fills the camera view. That is why we just make our texture fill the entire screen, and can't see that actually we are rendering a plane in 3D space. Cumbersome (but logical) as it might seem, it is a very widely used technique and an efficient way to get our results out to the display.

Now, we know that switching back and forth is not very efficient if we do a rendering of 3D shapes and want to apply FX; the rendered result must be somewhere on the GPU already. Can we put FX on that without going to the CPU and rendering again and so on? Yes, it just needs some careful timing with regards to what to render at what point. We would need to first render our scene into a texture, process that texture, then put that texture onto a video plane, put that video plane on stage, and render again, and all this is done in one frame. Take a close look at the following screenshot; here, we managed to get that setup running. The [jit.gl.render] object knows the message to_texture texturename, so this is how we render to a named texture. All geometry objects have an attribute @automatic, which controls whether the object is drawn automatically, or we need to send it a bang for it to be handed over to the renderer. If we switch off that attribute, we gain full control over the order in which objects are drawn.

Chapter 7

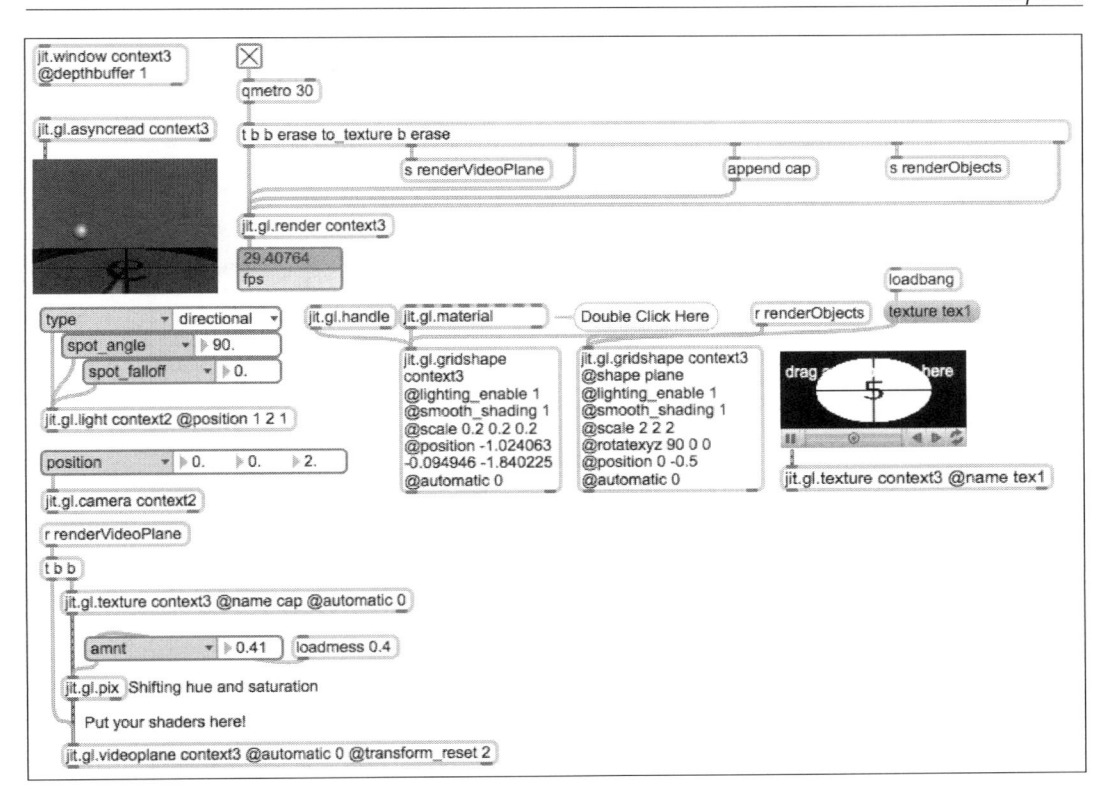

So you see, once we set up the order of events, we can just process the whole scene. Here, we applied a simple hue and saturation processing using `jit.gl.pix`, but more advanced shaders can easily be implemented here. Also note that we could have split up the rendering further to apply our effect just to the floor or just to the ball.

Summary

This concludes our short overview of Jitter. Although we concentrate on using TouchDesigner in this book for 3D real-time graphics, don't underestimate Jitter. Also, think about it in this way that both Jitter and TouchDesigner send commands to OpenGL, so in essence, they are capable of the same thing. Also, don't forget that Jitter is great for processing lists or higher dimensional arrays, such as matrices. The data doesn't have to be visually meaningful. Some great examples are the famous FFT Jitter patches by Jean-Francois Charles that accompanied his article *A Tutorial on Spectral Sound Processing Using Max/MSP and Jitter* in the MIT Computer Music Journal. Find both the patches and the article on his website at `http://www.jeanfrancoischarles.com/`.

In the upcoming chapter, we will get to know Max4Live. We are going to get an overview of how to implement our patches into Live, which will give us a powerful tool for sequencing, composition, and more.

8
Max for Live

Max for Live allows us to use Max/MSP/Jitter inside Ableton Live. Plugin design could hardly be any easier than the **Max for Live** (**M4L**) system. We can easily build custom audio FX, instruments, MIDI FX, or sequencers, or even control the Live application using a custom Max patch. The lack of a full-featured timeline/sequencer inside Max is resolved by porting our Max patches to Live, and if we ever need something inside Live that isn't there, chances are that we can quickly patch it together. As in every complex piece of software, there are a couple of pitfalls for the beginner and general particularities inside the Max for Live environment. So here, we'll try to shed some light on how to use it and what the differences between regular Max patching and the creation of a Max4Live device are. In this chapter, we are going to cover the following topics:

- Introducing the fundamentals of Max for Live
- Parameters and saving
- The Live API
- An example device – a parameter modulator

Introducing the fundamentals of Max for Live

When we want to make use of Max inside Ableton Live, we will need to add a Max for Live device. We have three options for doing this:

- Using a Max instrument
- Using a Max audio effect
- Using a Max MIDI effect

This just reflects Live's architecture. There are audio and MIDI tracks. An audio track can just contain audio; therefore, we can only use an audio effect in it. MIDI tracks, on the other hand, can contain all three different devices, or to put it differently, the following:

- A Max instrument takes MIDI input and outputs audio
- A Max audio effect takes audio input and outputs audio
- A Max MIDI effect takes MIDI input and outputs MIDI

This actually forces us to think about what comes in and what goes out of our Max patch before building it, which is a good design strategy anyway. We can of course also change our opinion later on by just copy-and-pasting what we built into a different device type.

If we now choose to drop in a new Max instrument, we are presented with a window, as shown in the following screenshot:

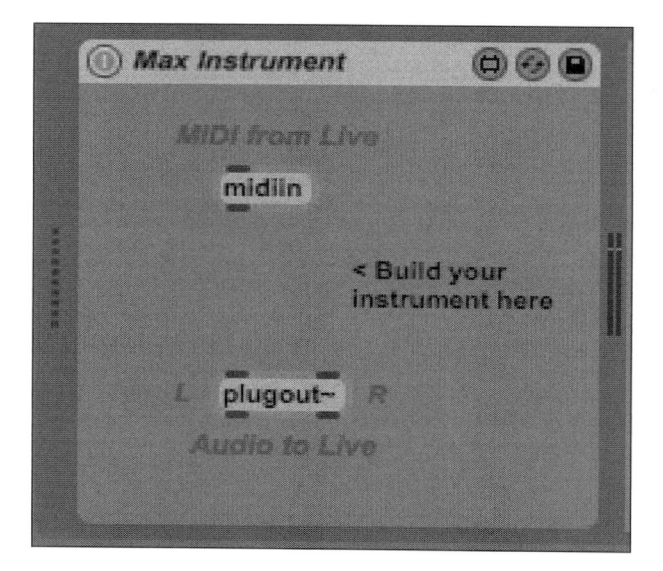

The device has the same buttons as any other Live instrument in addition to the **Edit** button. The device's interface just shows us our patch, which means that the patcher loaded by default has **Presentation** switched off in its patcher inspector (*Shift + command + I*). This is something I would personally change first since the device's vertical limit line, which you can see in the following screenshot, is also a bit distracting while patching. Also, we just typically want to see the patcher's presentation mode inside Live. If we push the **Edit** button, we can actually start patching, but let's take a close look at what's different in Max here:

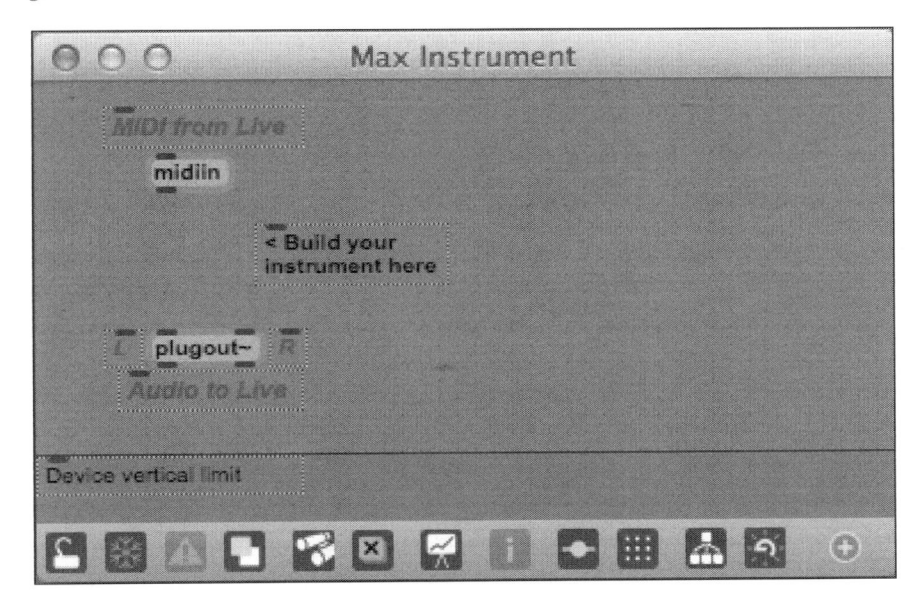

Let's first explore the icons that are added to the toolbar compared to a regular Max patch.

The second icon from the right, **Preview On/Off**, switches between the saved version of the device and the version with any edits we may have made. Essentially, it means switching between Max and Live, since during editing, both of them are actually active.

To the left of the preview button, we find the **show containing project** button, which we know from regular Max patches. It tells us that every Live device is utilizing Max's project feature.

Max for Live

Second and third from the left, we find two more new icons: the **Freeze Device** button and the **Conflicts** button. Both of them, like the project feature, have to do with dependency and conflict checking. When distributing a device, we can freeze it, which means it collects all dependencies and stores them with the device. These features really matter if we plan to distribute our devices; it's not rocket science, but you should have a good read about freezing before distribution or migration at the following links:

- `http://cycling74.com/docs/max6/dynamic/c74_docs.html#live_freezing`
- `http://cycling74.com/docs/max6/dynamic/c74_docs.html#live_resolveconflicts`

So the new buttons yield some pretty neat features, but they don't matter too much when we have just started using M4L.

MIDI in/out

As the comments suggest in the default patch, we can get MIDI into our patch using the [midiin] object. The [midiin] object is pretty cumbersome to use in many cases, for example, if we are just interested in the arriving MIDI notes or CCs. Just because the [midiin] object is the only one in the default patch, don't think that we have to use it; the familiar [notein] and [ctrlin] objects work just fine, and so do their output pendants in the case of a Max MIDI effect.

Of course, the functionality of these objects is a little different inside Live. By using them, we receive the MIDI signals that go into the Live device; we cannot access different MIDI ports or channels directly.

Audio in/out

We send and receive audio signals to and from Live using [plugin~] and [plugout~]. Both of them have the additional feature of just forwarding their inputs to their outputs when we are working with them inside Max. This doesn't happen in Max for Live. Sometimes, it's very convenient to develop something inside Max and switch to M4L later, so in this case, it might be handy to use [plugin~] and [plugout~] this way, as follows:

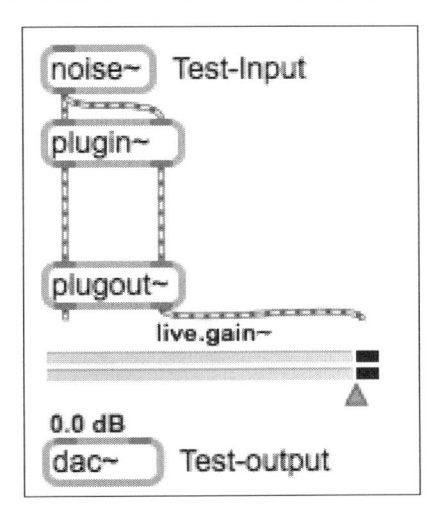

Synchronization

All our familiar tempo notations work inside Max for Live, so a [metro 4n @ quantize 4n] object will sync perfectly with Live's transport.

> It is often useful to use a metro with the @autostart attribute set to 1, which will just turn it on or off depending on Live's transport play/stop state.

Since we can't change the vector size inside Max for Live (it's fixed to 64 samples), and therefore we can't obtain control over timing accuracy, we might consider going for sample-accurate timing. In order to do this, we'd use [plugphasor~] to get a phasor that is synced to Live's transport. The [dspstate~] object will still get us a sample rate and so on, and [plugsync~] can be used to retrieve information about transport settings such as BPM.

We can have a signal sent and received between individual devices using [plugsend~] and [plugreceive~]. The [Send] and [receive] objects work just fine, although there might be some latency involved. Sometimes, it's nicer to do inter-device communication via UDP/localhost.

> When using [udpsend] and [udpreceive], beware that only one application can bind to a specific port to receive a signal, and if Max is using a certain port, Live can't bind to that port. What this means is that during development, it might be necessary to turn off Max for Live and reload the device to make the port available for our device inside Live.

Parameters and saving

From dealing with normal Live devices, we know we can automate dials or other parameters, we can MIDI-assign them with just a few clicks, and just have Live be aware of the parameters. But how do we do this with our Max for Live devices? How do we tell Live which parameters are important and should be embedded in Live's management of parameters?

Let's build a really simple audio effect, one that can attenuate its input and invert the left and right signal. We'll use a live.dial object to control the amplitude and use two [toggle] objects for signal inversion from left and right. We'll arrive at something like this:

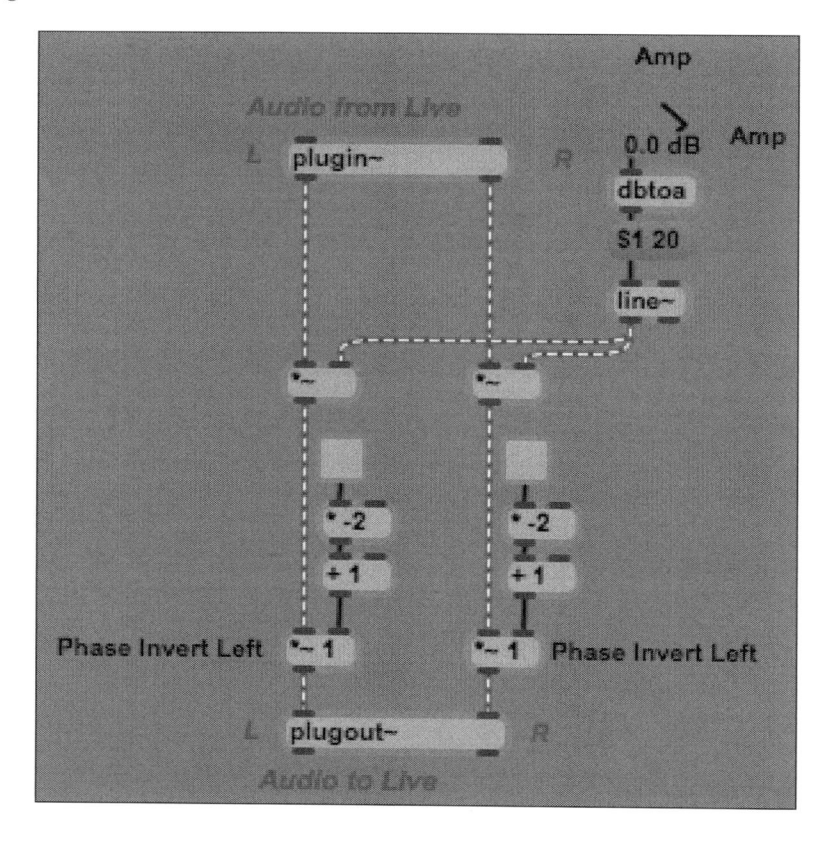

As you can see, the patch itself is extremely simple, and all we did with the parameters is we configured the [live.dial] object's Short Name attribute to give it a nice **Amp** heading, and switched its Unit Style and Range/Enum attributes to make it read reasonable dB values. The [Live.dial] object is one of the Max for Live GUI objects, and therefore, it is set up to be integrated into the Live system by default.

This means we can automate and assign MIDI controls in it right away. If we want to expose our two toggles to the system, we can (and in praxis, we probably would) exchange them with the [live.toggle] or [live.text] object. However, what if we really like our regular toggles or if we need some other object like a [multislider] object that doesn't have a Live pendant? We need to set the `enable` attribute of the object's parameter mode to 1. After this, many additional attributes appear in **Inspector**, as you can see in the following screenshot:

▼ Parameter	
Order	0
Parameter Mode Enable	✓
Link to Scripting Name	☐
Long Name	PhaseInvertLeft
Short Name	PhaseInvertLeft
Type	⇕ Int (0-255)
Range/Enum	0 1
Modulation Mode	⇕ None
Modulation Range	0. 127.
Initial Enable	☐
Initial	
Unit Style	⇕ Native
Custom Units	
Exponent	1.
Steps	0
Update Limit (ms)	1.
Defer Automation Output	☐
Parameter Visibility	⇕ Automated and Stored
Automapping Index	0

Some of the attributes may be grayed out. We need to assign our object a certain `Type` attribute, so Live knows whether this item stores a list, a single integer, a float, and so on. If, for example, we had a [multislider] object, its values could be a list. How would Live be able to show an automation of a list? Or think of a [textedit] object; what's the modulation of a string? In these cases, the type would be `Blob`. So Live would be able to save the state of whatever the actual type of the values is, but we wouldn't be able to do much with the value inside Live (modulation, automation, and MIDI assignment wouldn't make sense). So in the case of our toggle, via its attributes, we just tell Live that it's an integer that ranges from 0 to 1, and voila, we can use presets, automation, and all the other comfortable features of Live's parameter system.

Most of the other newly appeared attributes depicted previously are pretty self-explanatory, but if you have trouble understanding one of them, don't forget the **clue** window.

The Live API

With our combined knowledge about Max and about the objects that interface with Live, we can now create all kinds of audio FX, instruments, and MIDI FX. However, one of the points that makes Max for Live way more powerful than any **Virtual Studio Technology (VST)** plugin is that we can actually control the host application and get information about the host into our device. Live's **Application Programming Interface (API)** is the way to access Live through Max for Live. However, in order to control Ableton Live from within a device, we have to tell Max exactly what we want to query/control, and since the Live API is not a chaotic pool of parameters but a hierarchical system, we need to understand how to maneuver to a certain parameter of Live. This is what the **Live Object Model (LOM)** looks like:

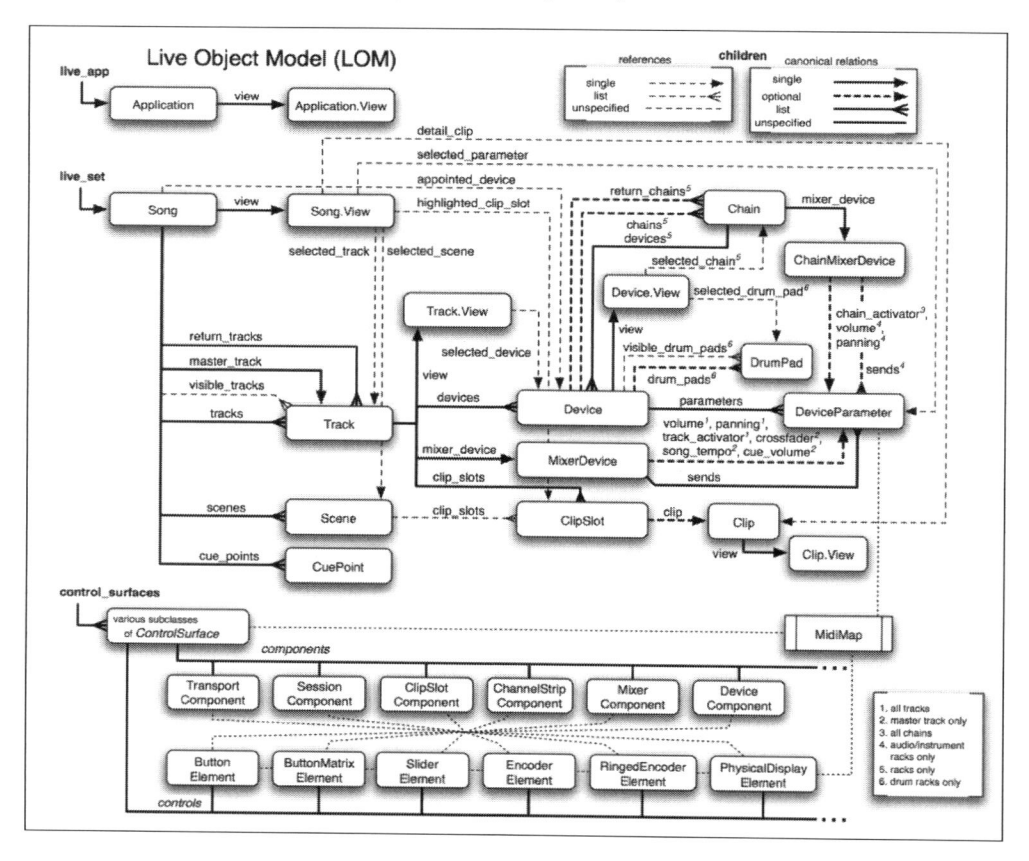

Chapter 8

The LOM looks really complicated, but note that first of all, if you look up the LOM in the Max help system, this picture is interactive and meaningful. You can click on the boxes to get to a specific object's reference. Secondly, we don't need to know the whole LOM; we rather use this to look up the path of an object that we'd like to use. Let's look at how to use these paths and the objects responsible for access to the Live API:

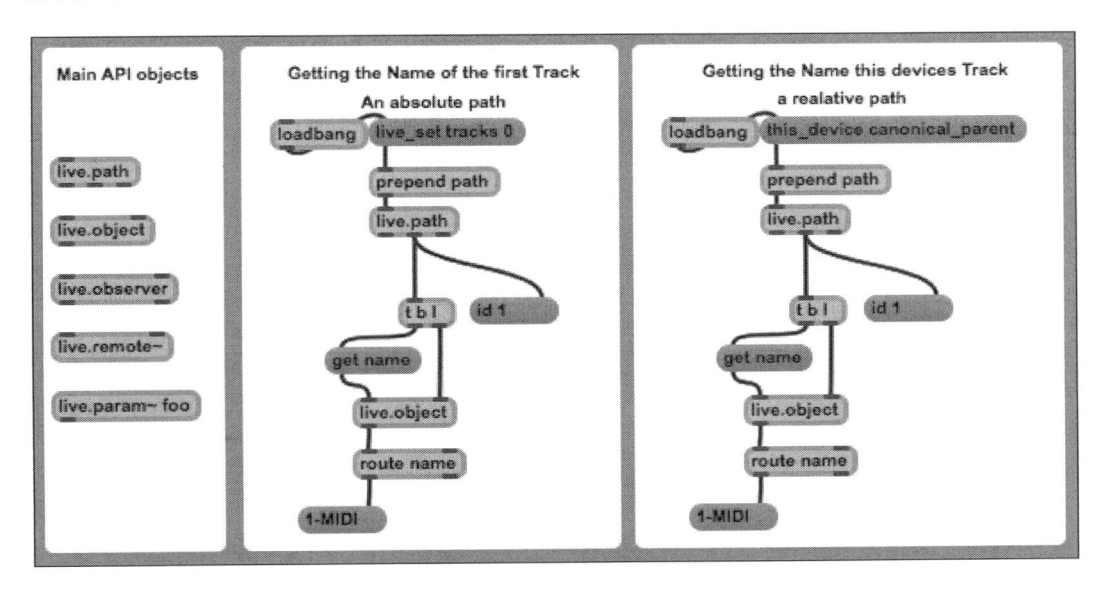

In the preceding screenshot, to the left, you can see all the main objects that can be used to access Live. The [live.path] object is used to translate a path from the LOM to an ID number, which can be used by [live.object] for example. When [live.object] receives an ID, it can be thought of as representing one of the boxes in the LOM. Each box, such as a track, for instance, has individual **functions** and **properties**. A property of a track would, for example, be its name. Using the get message in [live.object], we can query its name. Using the set message, we can set its name. All the paths and objects, their functions and attributes, and which attributes can be written or read are documented in the LOM. You will see that each property of an object has an individual set of possible access methods: set, get, and observe. Some objects only support a read operation, such as the get object. Others can also be set. The observe method can't be used with [live.object], but this is what happens when we hand over an ID to [live.observer]. It's similar to reading (get) the object all the time and outputting a value if it changes.

An example for a function of the `track` object is the `stop_all_clips` function. Obviously, it will stop all fired or playing clips. The function can be called by sending the message `call stop_all_clips` to `[live.object]` that is assigned to a track.

In the previous screenshot, you saw how an absolute path, using `live_set tracks 0`, can be used (we got that from the routes in the LOM picture) to make `[live.path]` generate an ID for the first track. We assign that ID to `[live.object]` and are then able to control that object. Here, we just query the track's name.

To the right of the previous screenshot, you see that since the LOM's objects are organized in a hierarchy, we can also use relative paths. Starting from `this_device`, which represents an object that is the device this patch is in, we can access its parent, such as the track the device sits in. In what track does the device sit in? Of course, it's the first track, so in this case, both methods lead to the same target.

An example device – a parameter modulator

Let's put to use what we just learned. We won't talk about the devices that you will probably build most often, such as simple synths, samplers, FX, MIDI FX, and so on. Why? Because it's just Max/MSP with the addition of using `[plugphasor~]`, `[plugin~]`, and `[plugout~]`.

> Go ahead and build a simple Max for Live synth on your own at this point!

Here, in order to get accustomed to using the Live API, we will take a look at a device that really interacts with Live instead. We are going to make a simple LFO, which is able to modulate parameters of Live. This way, we can add noise to a selected effect parameter, or if you expand the effect, start using arbitrarily complex sequencers to start expanding Live's capabilities of non-linear composing.

Our device should be simple to use; when we want to click on a parameter, click on a button in our device, and it should memorize that parameter. After this, it should start modulating right away. Our modulation signals will be standard LFO waveforms; the important thing here is to get the concept going. After that, we can start building more complex control signals.

Later, you see a section of the finished device that excludes the LFO, which is coming in on the bottom left. To observe which parameter is selected, we will use [live.observer]. We get an ID, but this ID is not usable right away. The [live.path] object outputs two IDs on reception of a path: one that follows the path and one that follows the object. What's the difference? The one that follows the path will point to a different object if we move the track of the modulated object or if we insert an effect before that device (changing its path). Therefore, we need the ID that follows the object, which will always be the same in these cases.

So having the ID from [live.observer], we resolve its path and use live.path to get the object ID.

As you know, Live will store parameters of GUI objects, so we can use [live.number] to make Live remember what parameter we modulate. The [live.number] object is an object whose value can be modulated by default. Its parameter visibility attribute by default is switched to Automated and Stored. We don't want to modulate that parameter, and we really don't want to think about what chaos could occur if we do, so let's just switch that to Stored only.

Max for Live

After that, we use [live.remote~] to control the parameter at the signal rate. We could have also used [live.object] with a message like set value 0.5. However, since this is an LFO, we use [life.remote~] as follows:

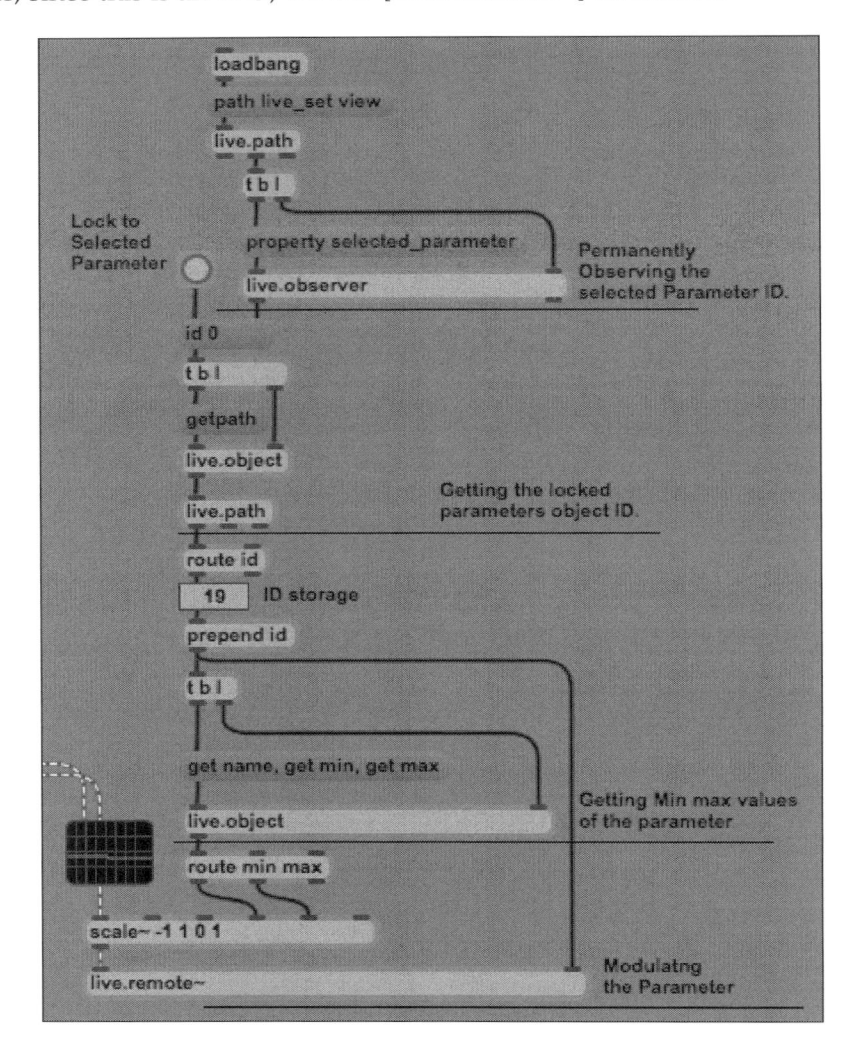

Summary

First and foremost, we learned that if we are good at Max/MSP, we are quite capable of building lots of things in Max for Live. We didn't go into building audio FX and spectacular synths since these are just straightforward Max/MSP tasks. Rather, we concentrated on how the Live API works, how to access Live, and how to control it. Although we haven't explored Max for Live a lot, it should be obvious that the possibilities are huge. At this point, switching around freely between detailed linear composition in Live or complex non-linear experiments in Max for Live should be easy. Any small utility you imagine inside Live should be at your fingertips, opening up the whole Ableton Live system.

In the next chapter, we are going to explore visualization and start to learn about TouchDesigner, which will enable us to easily realize our visual ideas and experiments.

9
Basic Visualization Using TouchDesigner

Let's finally explore how to visualize our analyzed data. We're going to choose **TouchDesigner (TD)** as a tool for this task. This chapter should give us both an overview of the software and introduce some practical techniques that will help us to work with TouchDesigner. It seems to be a really easy and intuitive piece of software at first, and well it is, but it also is very deep. There are lots of little hidden gems, some of which will be revealed here to give us a jump start. In this chapter, whenever you feel comfortable with the interface, you can probably take a break and try to set up a UDP connection between Max and TD to motivate yourself, and start visualizing sound analysis data. Remember that the OSC in CHOP will come in handy, but we will soon see what this means. In this chapter, we will cover the following topics:

- The need for TouchDesigner
- Getting help
- TD basics and its user interface
- The components and structuring a project

Basic Visualization Using TouchDesigner

The need for TouchDesigner

TouchDesigner is a software that allows us to build very efficient tools for real-time video processing, 3D rendering, procedural visual work, multi-touch interfaces, and much more in a very easy visual way. Its flexibility has been used in numerous large-scale commercial projects, so, in general, we can be sure it's rock solid. As with Max, it's a very open system that can be expanded upon easily with custom additions. Added to it is the fact that we can use Python within TD, which makes it an even more powerful system. However, why don't we just stick with Jitter? Jitter is great for many things, and certainly everything we see in the TD-related chapters can somehow also be done in Max/Jitter. However, some things would require us to write a good amount of **OpenGL Shading Language (GLSL)** code while working solely inside Jitter and trying to achieve these same things. Max came from algorithmic composition and moved towards audio processing. TD, in contrast, genuinely comes from graphics. Naturally, it has some advantages over Max's Jitter, which I won't list here since software is an ever-changing development. Even still, there are other languages such as **vvvv** and **Processing**. Let's just say I personally think TD is the most intuitive one, without being less powerful; on the contrary, it is very powerful. Also, besides its bare capabilities, TD encourages experimenting, artistic expression, and technical development in a nearly optimal balance. So let's get started.

How to get help

There are several resources that offer help in TouchDesigner. First and foremost, there is the Wiki, which can be accessed from within TouchDesigner, along with the forum and the tutorials. There are lots of video tutorials online too. Finally, there are the operator snippets. Accessible via the **Help** menu in TD, we can find examples of how different operators work and start using these right away. If you are lost while finding help on 3D or procedural modeling, look into other environments' tutorials too, or look for more general information about 3D, OpenGL, or modeling techniques. Since we are modeling procedurally in TD, and TouchDesigner is a derivative of a SideFX software called Houdini, you might also look at Houdini's video tutorials on modeling. Houdini and TouchDesigner don't work exactly the same, but they have many things in common, and we can adopt many techniques documented rather for Houdini users.

Basics and UI of TouchDesigner

After you have downloaded, installed, and opened TD, you will find something like this:

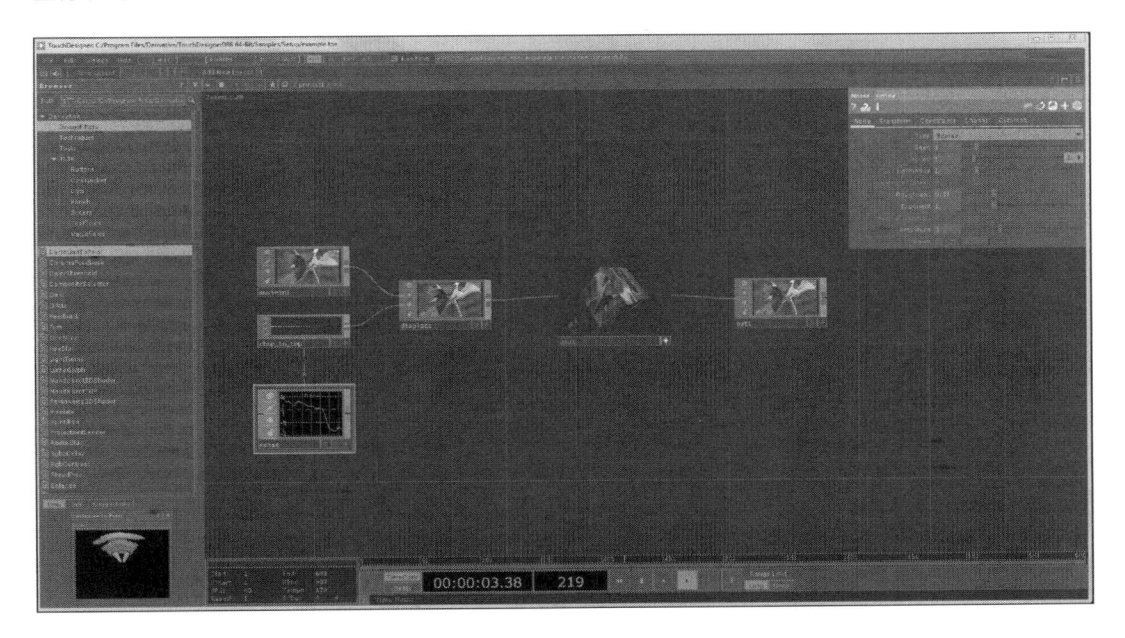

What you see is a default network that consists of a couple of operators or OPs wired together. Just as in Max, we create things by wiring up boxes or nodes; in TD, the boxes are called operators instead of objects, and what you end up with is called a network instead of a patch. The signal flow is also slightly different as you can see. In Max, inlets were at the top of an object while outlets were at its bottom; this encouraged a top-to-bottom signal flow. In TouchDesigner, the flow is from left to right since inputs are at the left of an OP and outlets are at the right. Now, press *F1* to get to what's called performance mode, and press *Escape* to get back into editing mode. In performance mode, we can essentially output our creation to a screen without having the editor rendered, so obviously, this is more efficient for performance. Let's now delete everything we found in this network and create our very first one from scratch. After we learn about scripting in TD, we will create our obligatory **Hello World** network, going though the UI a bit at the same time.

A scripting prologue

We won't go too deep into scripting and expressions right at the start, but there are some things that you should know about before we begin. Scripts and expressions can be very short and powerful, so don't be afraid of them. The most important thing to know is that in TouchDesigner, there are actually two languages: Tscript and Python. Why is this so important right at the start? We probably need an expression to do something for us, but we aren't able to code it ourselves. So we find something on the Internet and try to put it in our network, but it doesn't work. Why? This is probably because it's the wrong language. Since TouchDesigner 088, Python has been the default scripting language. If we try to enter a Tscript expression, we have to tell TouchDesigner that this particular expression is not Python code; otherwise, we'll just get an error. Switching between languages is done in the parameter dialog, as we will see shortly. Since all this wasn't the case in earlier versions, you might have to do that extra step of switching to Tscript if you are watching a video tutorial made with an older version of Touch for instance, or you'll have to look up the corresponding Python expression.

So, when should we use each language? Usually, you should always strive to use Python. However, we don't have all the functionality of Tscript yet, and Tscript sometimes has the advantage of being much shorter, since it's written for TouchDesigner. For example, to get the frame number at an instance, we use $F in Tscript and me.time.frame in Python. In general, don't be afraid of scripting; it's extremely powerful, and mostly, our scripts can be very short. Also, TouchDesigner helps us a lot when we enter expressions into parameters; Python expressions are often structured in a hierarchical manner. Take the previous example where we have a class called me, which stands for the operator that expression is located in the Op class. This class has a member called time. This again has a member called frame. Now, TouchDesigner helps us by evaluating what we select with the cursor if it's only a part of the expression we entered. So if we entered 3 + 4 and selected this, the tooltip will show 7. This is an incredibly helpful debugging tool since it allows us to see what part of what we entered might be a mistake. Refer to the following screenshot:

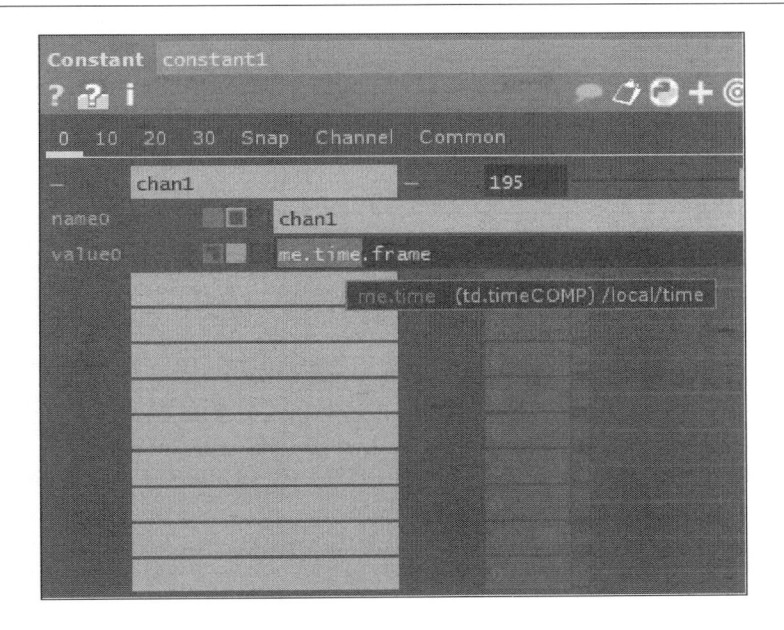

I said that we wouldn't go into scripting too deep but we will still start using them pretty soon, since it makes things a lot more easy and tidy.

> One can use TouchDesigner without any scripting for years and be quite happy with it. In many cases, you could get the same results without scripting; it just takes more time. Sometimes, we simply don't have that time, especially if it's 5 minutes before a show.

Hello World

You'll quickly notice we can navigate around in the network with the left mouse button and zoom using the mouse wheel. Holding the middle mouse button and dragging up and down also zooms in and out. This is true for most of TouchDesigner's interface, be it zooming in to data (CHOPS), video (TOPS), or geometry in 3D space (SOPs). It is highly recommended that you use a three-button mouse or a mouse with a mouse wheel when working with TouchDesigner. In order to create operators, we just double-click on the network or press *Tab* to bring up the **OP create** dialog, as shown in the following screenshot. Notice that for all categories except the COMPs', we find a slight difference in color that seems to be randomly distributed over all the OPs; some are light and some are a bit darker. The darker ones generate or read back data (such as noise, oscillators, and movie players), and the lighter ones process data (filters, effects, and so on). Also, think about switching on **Expose All** to really see all the operators in the **OP create** dialog.

Basic Visualization Using TouchDesigner

There are some possibilities to speed up the creation of OPs. If we press *Ctrl* while selecting an OP, the dialog will not disappear, so we can create multiple OPs at once. If we do the same with *Shift* pressed, they will even be connected in series automatically. Also, we can just start typing the beginning of the name of an OP when the dialog is open and press *Enter* to create the OP.

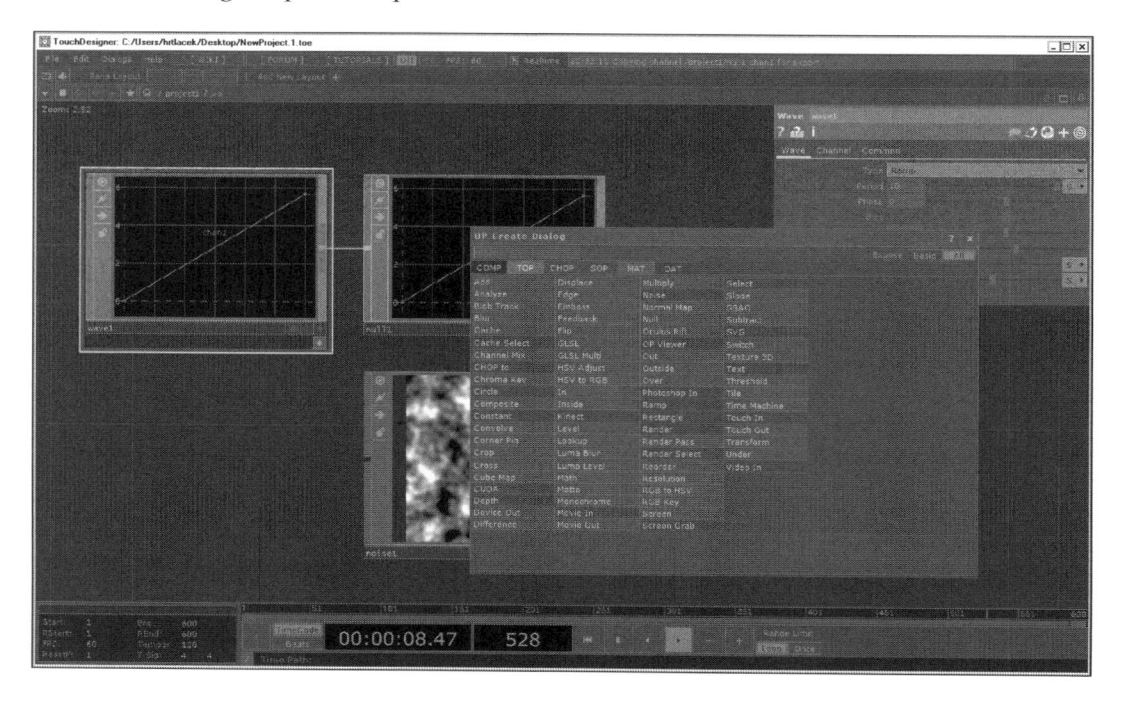

From all the available operators, this dialog allows us to choose which ones are ordered into categories or operator families.

COMPs

The official documentation on Components can be found at `https://www.derivative.ca/wiki088/index.php?title=Component`. Components are divided into subcategories, 3D panels, and other. We will revisit Components later, but for now, let's just say components are a bit like special subpatchers in Max; they can contain networks and have different features. A Geometry COMP has 3D translate parameters to move the contained geometry around, whereas a Slider COMP doesn't have these parameters but rather a parameter for its color, for example.

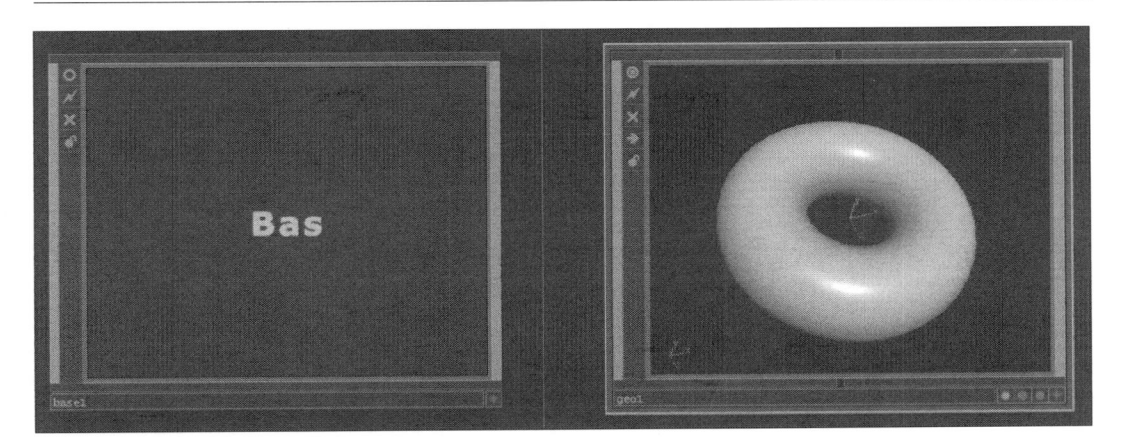

TOPs

Texture Operators are operating on textures. TD comes from 3D rendering; therefore, all images (stills or movies) are transported to the GPU. We find effects for image processing in this category. All of the Texture Operators are GPU accelerated, but some things such as movie decoding are done by the CPU, and therefore can be very efficient. Don't forget that images are just data; if we want to use TOPs in order to work on data other than images, that's fine too; just the format has to be right. We will talk about moving between OP families later. More information can be found at `https://www.derivative.ca/wiki088/index.php?title=TOP`. Refer to the following screenshot:

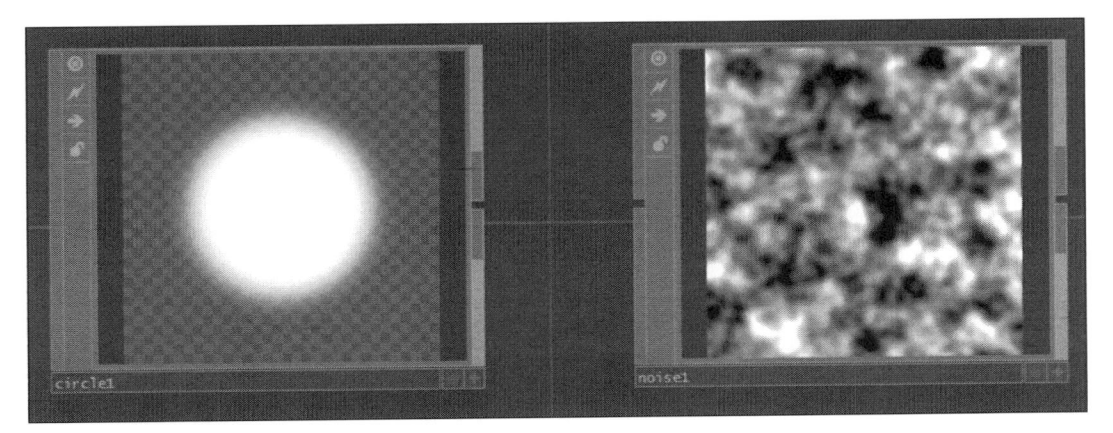

CHOPs

Channel Operators (CHOP) are there for control signals. For example, an audio file can be loaded using the audio file in CHOP; an LFO can be created with an LFO CHOP. However, more generally speaking, we could say that CHOPS are there for movement, animation, control of parameters, and control signals. CHOPs can contain any number of samples and channels. Also, there are CHOPS for OSC in/output, Audio in/output, DMX, and many other interfaces. Refer to the following screenshot:

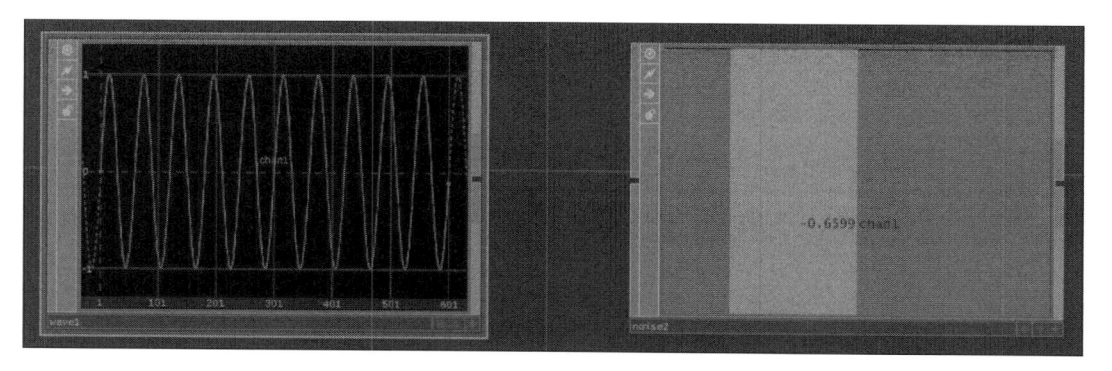

More information on CHOP can be found at https://www.derivative.ca/wiki088/index.php?title=CHOP.

SOPs

The official documentation on **Surface Operators (SOPs)** can be found at https://www.derivative.ca/wiki088/index.php?title=SOP.

Surface Operators are operators that act in 3D space. They allow us to model in a procedural way, transform, scale extrude, twist, and edit geometry procedurally. Refer to the following screenshot:

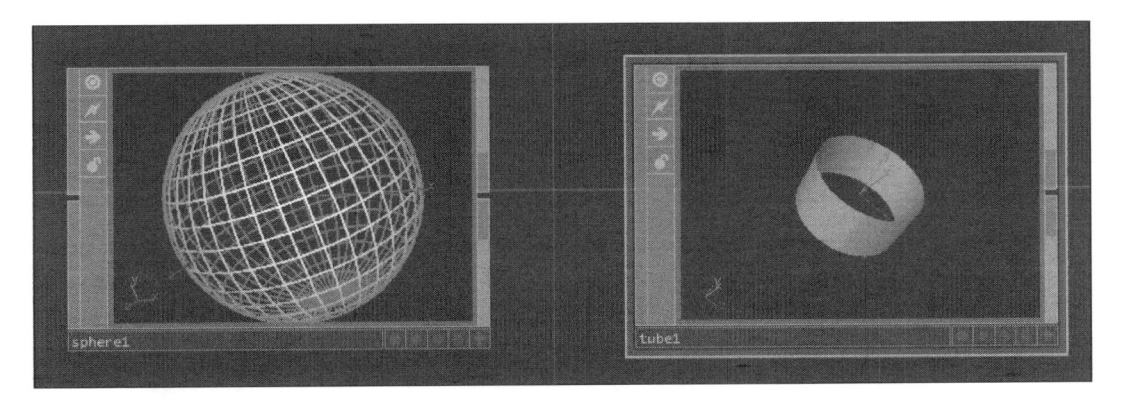

Chapter 9

SOPs are processed on the CPU and then sent to a render TOP to be rendered to an image. Their CPU consumption heavily depends on the number of points they are dealing with. Also, SOPs can contain different types of data, such as polygons, NURBS, meshes, primitives, and bezier.

MATs

The official documentation on **Materials (MATs)** can be found at `https://www.derivative.ca/wiki088/index.php?title=MAT`.

Materials are used to shade geometry, so this determines the look of our 3D objects. We can adjust the color, achieve different reactions to light, and more. Refer to the following screenshot:

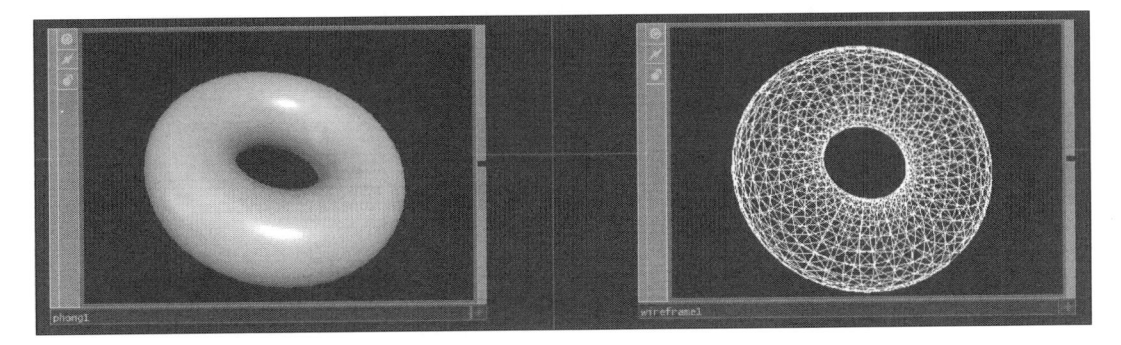

We are going to visit them later.

DATs

The official documentation on **Data Operators** (**DAT**) can be found at `https://www.derivative.ca/wiki088/index.php?title=DAT`.

Data Operators allow us to enter, edit, and process text, code, and tables, and they handle incoming data as OSC, UDP, TCP/IP, MIDI, and so on, as well as output data using these protocols/interfaces. These powerful operators can help us visualize data in yet another fashion; they can process data in many ways, and their code can be triggered by events. Refer to the following screenshot:

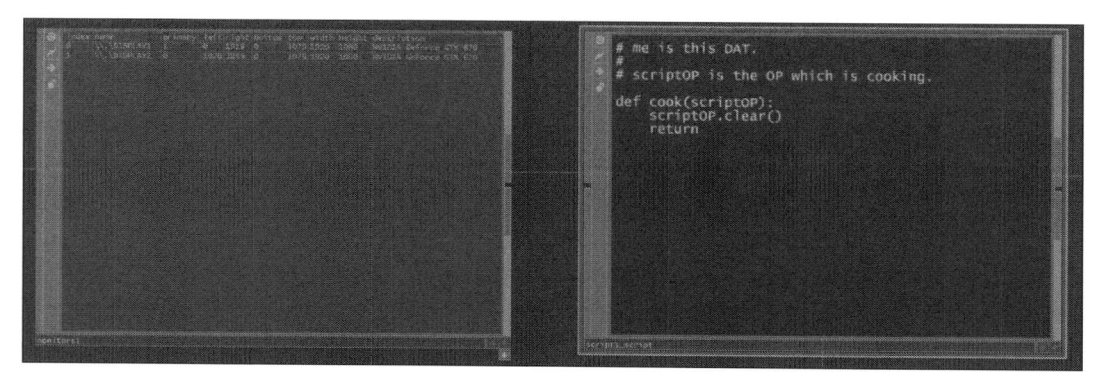

Now that you have a feeling of the material to play around with, let's select a couple of OPs for our first network; let's put down a Noise TOP and a Movieout TOP. Now, just hook the noise TOP's output up to the inlet of the Movieout TOP. What are these TOPs doing? The Noise TOP generates noise and the Movieout TOP records an image or video on the disk. However, we can always find out how a specific OP works if we select it and click on the little question mark in its parameter dialog, which is also depicted in the following screenshot. To hide or show the parameters window, use the shortcut *P*.

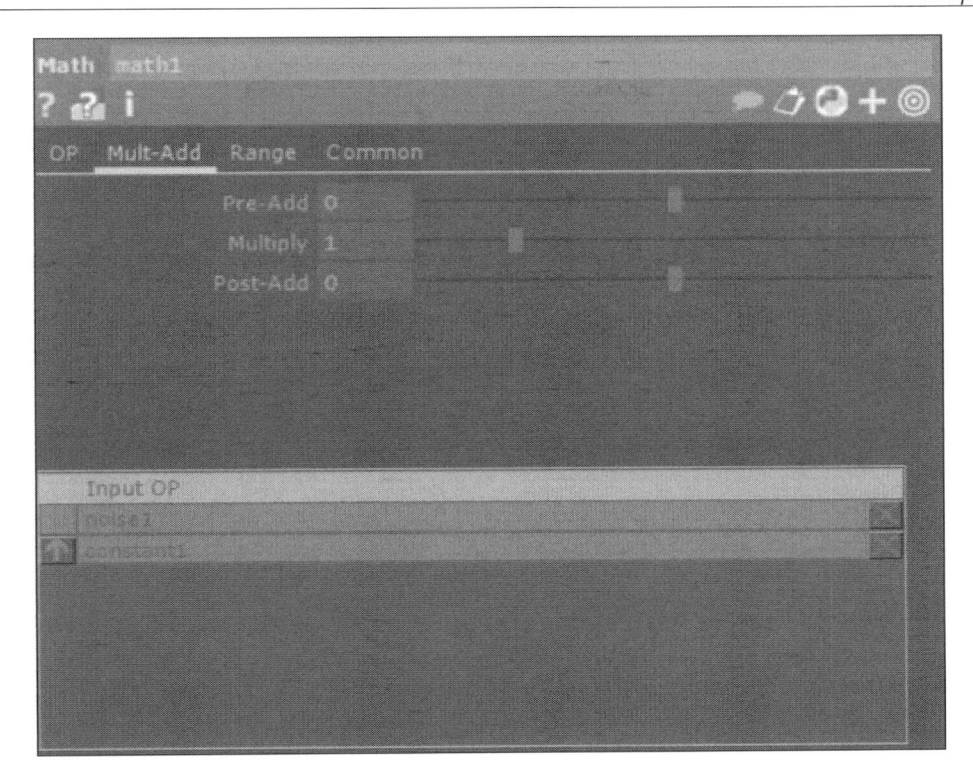

Operators in TouchDesigner are typically more powerful than objects in Max. For example, in Max, we have the [+], [-], and [*] objects; in TouchDesigner, we just have the Math CHOP, which does it all. It's just two different concepts: fewer more powerful things or more less powerful ones. It's more or less the same. This should illustrate the importance of the parameter dialog since this is the place where we actually define an operator's behavior.

Basic Visualization Using TouchDesigner

Now, this is what you should see:

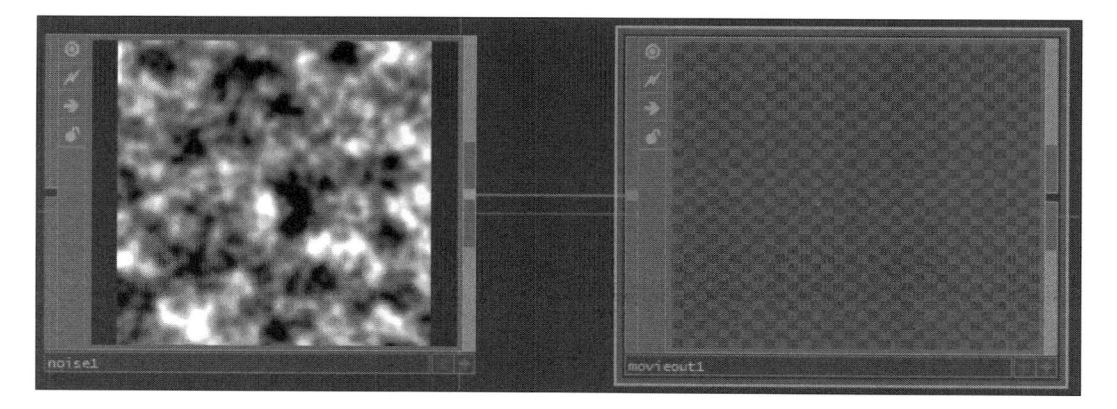

Let's bring in some movements right away. We want to animate the noise, so let's use a CHOP to do that, although, truth be told, the best way to do it in this case is using an expression. So we'd like to do what's called **exporting** a CHOP's channel to a parameter, which means we are simply controlling a parameter with a channel of samples. In order to do this, we'll put down two other operators: a wave CHOP and a null CHOP.

> The null CHOP will be referenced by another operator. We could have used the wave CHOP right away, but what if we decide that we want to multiply it before exporting, or putting other CHOPs in between before the value goes out? It's a good practice to use null operators at the end of the connected OPs to be referenced if we want to process the value further at a later point. It makes things a bit easier and tidier.

Hook up the output of the wave to the input of the null CHOP. After that, press and hold *Alt + A* and click on the name of the channel we want to export, in this case `chan1`, inside the null CHOP and drag it onto the noise TOP. A long list appears; choose **Export to: Translate Z**, which is one of the noise CHOP's parameters. We could also have dragged the channel on the desired parameter in the parameter window directly. Voila, the noise is moving! Since the default wave in the wave CHOP is a sine wave, the noise is moving back and forth, so go to the wave CHOP's parameters and change it to a ramp. Also, increase the period of the wave to 10 seconds. This corresponds to the length of the timeline and therefore, we get our noise to move constantly with the propagation of the timeline.

Since the animated noise goes to the Movieout TOP, if you wish, you can now take stills of a noise or record a movie using the Movieout TOP's parameter dialog. So now, if you create something awesome in the future, you know how to record it immediately and in real time if you choose so. Refer to the following screenshot:

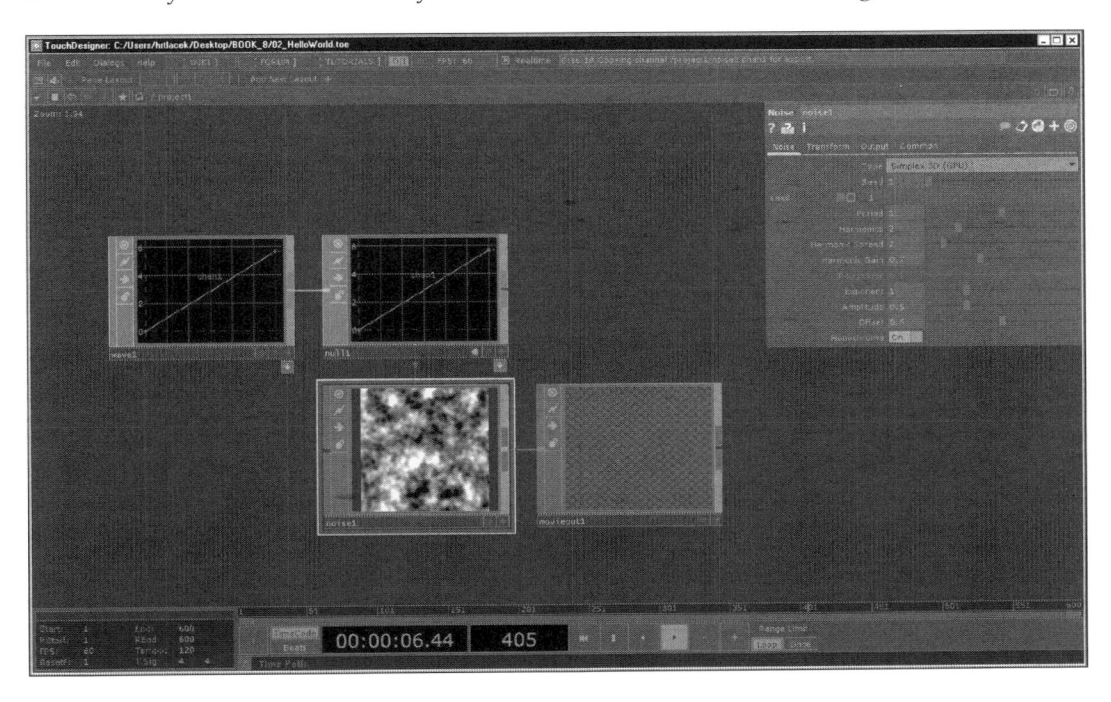

Let's look at what we have just done in a bit more depth. We used the parameter dialog and operators, both of which have a lot of hidden features, which, if we know, make our lives a lot easier.

The operators

Depending on the family an operator belongs to, its GUI looks slightly different, but let's first look at what's common to them all. All nodes have a name and a viewer, can have input and output, have a **middle mouse-click** info box, and have certain flags. Inputs are at the left of an operator and outputs are on the right side, as you surely have already noticed. The **middle mouse button** info is a very powerful tool to see what's going on with a specific OP.

Try it and find out how much time our noise TOP needs in order to cook a frame! Flags are not parameters, but they configure the OP's behavior and appearance. Let's take a look at the flags all OPs have, in the order from top to bottom, as you can see in the following screenshot on a COMP:

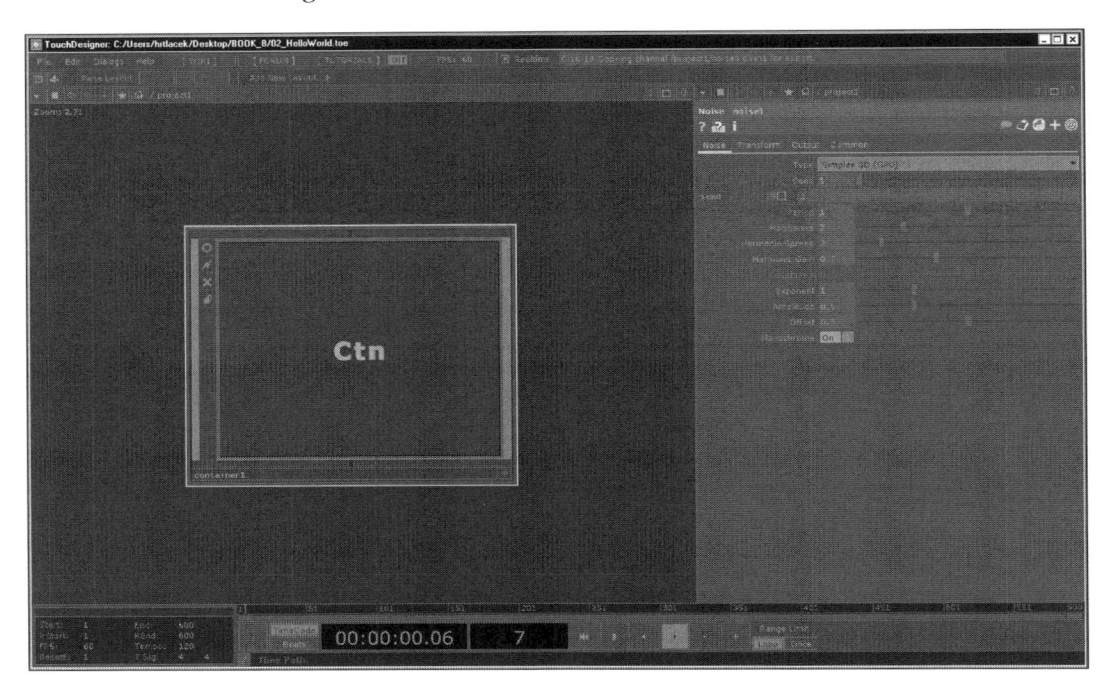

The viewer flag

The viewer flag toggles the Viewer, so the central window shows an OP's data as on/off.

The clone immune flag

We'll come to cloning later, but you can imagine it as a technique used to replicate parts of networks with a master network/node. If we turn on the clone immune flag, the connection to the master gets loose, and the instances can be edited.

The cooking flag

Cooking is a synonym for processing. If the cooking flag is turned off, we force TD to not cook this operator. TD cares about what is necessary to be cooked in a very intelligent and efficient way, so an operator might not be cooking although this flag is on. If its input/parameters are not changing, a new output is not needed to be computed and therefore it won't cook.

The bypass flag

Obviously, The bypass flag the first input or simply deactivates cooking if it has no input.

The lock flag

This flag is used to protect the data that the node holds from any change. It won't cook and won't react to the changing of input or parameters.

The viewer active flag

The viewer active flag is the little plus sign at the bottom right of the window. This flag is probably the most often used of the ones we mentioned until now. You can toggle it on/off with the shortcut *A* for the selected operator, *Alt + A*, to activate it momentarily for all operators, and press *Shift + A* to toggle the **Always active** option for all operators. Instead of just showing the viewer, which the viewer flag does, it activates it and makes it interactive. Interactive means we can, for example, inspect our 3D geometry, inspect the individual channels of a video, or zoom in. Try it out with the network we already have; with the viewer of our noise TOP active, click in the viewer and drag it to move or use the middle mouse button to zoom in. Use *H* to go to the home of the viewer if you are lost. Notice that the shortcut *H* also works for homing our network view. The viewer active flag opens up a lot of possibilities depending on the OP type. For example, we can use the shortcuts *A*, *R*, *G*, and *B* to view just the specific alpha/color channel of a TOP. Try checking the right-click menu for all the options that come up when the viewer active flag is set.

Basic Visualization Using TouchDesigner

CHOPs and SOPs have a very rich set of options and possibilities when the viewer active flag is set to on. With its viewer active flag on and field guide enabled, you can see a Moviein TOP only showing its blue channel and displaying pixel values in the following screenshot:

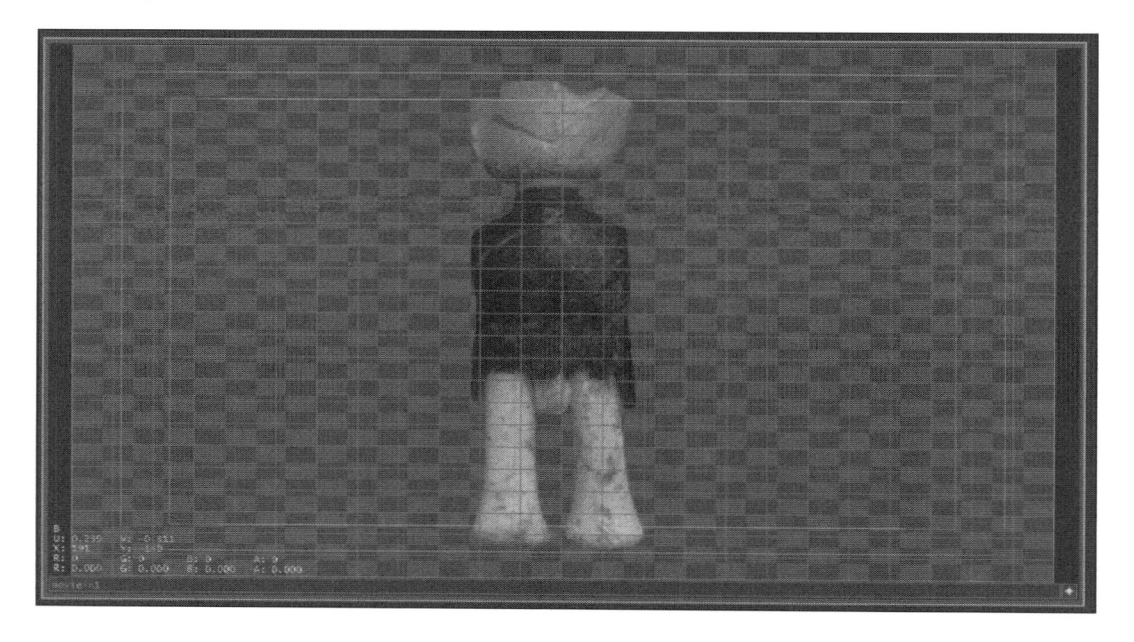

Another example of the possibilities of the viewer active flag is shown in the following screenshot. It's a wave CHOP that has been configured to show all kinds of things: a time bar, editing tools, and interactive handles, so we can adjust the parameters as the phase of the wave, for example, just by dragging around a handle displayed directly on the wave.

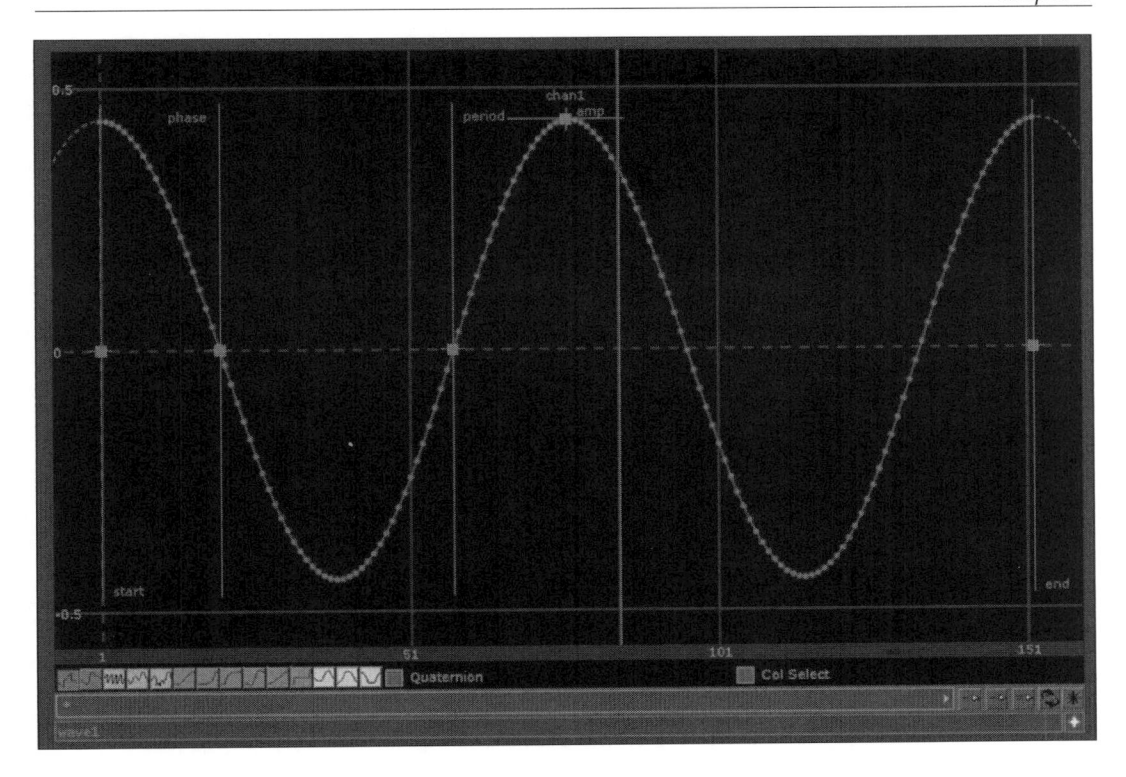

Specific to the different operators, there are other flags and features we will get to know in the course of this chapter.

The parameter dialog

The official documentation guide on the parameter dialog can be found at `https://www.derivative.ca/wiki088/index.php?title=Parameter_Dialog`.

The parameter dialog holds all the parameters of the corresponding operator. It is split up into pages and can be viewed/hidden with the shortcut *P*. Also, it can be viewed in a floating window by right-clicking on a certain operator's **Parameters**, or a pane can display it.

Probably the most important thing to know about the parameter viewer is that if we want to adjust a numerical value, we can use the middle mouse button to open what's called the ladder menu. This menu behaves like a horizontal slider, which allows us to adjust the value interactively, but even more, we can choose the step size out of some different powers of ten.

Every parameter that's actually available has a little + sign next to it if we hover over its name. Clicking on it expands the parameter to give us some information of what's actually going on with it, and allows us to edit the parameter in a more sophisticated way. If we expand the translate parameter of our noise TOP, we will see something like this:

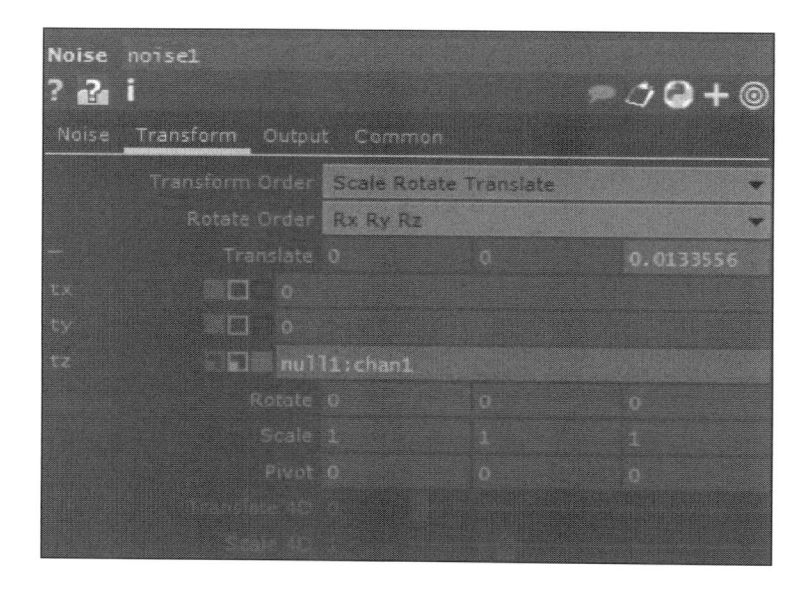

This expansion revealed a different name, `tz`, three little boxes, and a **null1:chan1** string. The name `tz` is the parameter's actual scripting name, and we will come to a little scripting later on. The string displays the path to the operator and the channel we used to modulate this parameter, that is, the null CHOP's channel 1. The three little boxes allow us to choose whether we want to use a constant, an expression, or a CHOP export to adjust the parameter. For example, you could press the bluish button to switch to expression mode for that parameter and enter `me.time.frame/600` to achieve the same result for this parameter.

At the top of the parameter editor, we find a couple of very helpful buttons; let's go through them one by one:

- **Operator Help**: This leads us to the corresponding Wiki page of the OP.
- **Python Help**: This takes us to the Python Wiki page of the OP or rather to one of the classes that belong to that OP and its members and methods.
- **Operator Info**: When this is clicked, the information about the OP is shown, such as the number of channels for a CHOP or the CPU cook time. The same information can be accessed via a middle mouse click on the OP itself.
- **Comment**: This allows us to place a comment on the OP that is visible in the middle mouse button information box.
- **Copied Values/Clipboard**: This allows us to inspect what values we have copied and are therefore present on the clipboard.
- **Switch Language**: This allows us to switch to which language we wish to use in this operator's parameter dialog, that is, between Python and Tscript. Also, this button will try to convert any present expressions to the language we switched to.
- **Expand/collapse parameters**: This shows us all the expanded or collapsed parameters.
- **Show non-default parameters only**: This is an extremely helpful feature, especially if we try to find out what's going on in a network we didn't build ourselves or don't know very well. As it says, this button will only show parameters that have actually been changed.

Wires and links

The official documentation guide on **wires** and **links** can be found at https://www.derivative.ca/wiki088/index.php?title=Wire and https://www.derivative.ca/wiki088/index.php?title=Link.

Basic Visualization Using TouchDesigner

We have already made a small network using wires and hooked up operators. We can only wire operators of the same family, but links, indicated by gray arrows, can go between OP families. In the following screenshot, you can see both wires and links; the wires are on top and links are beneath:

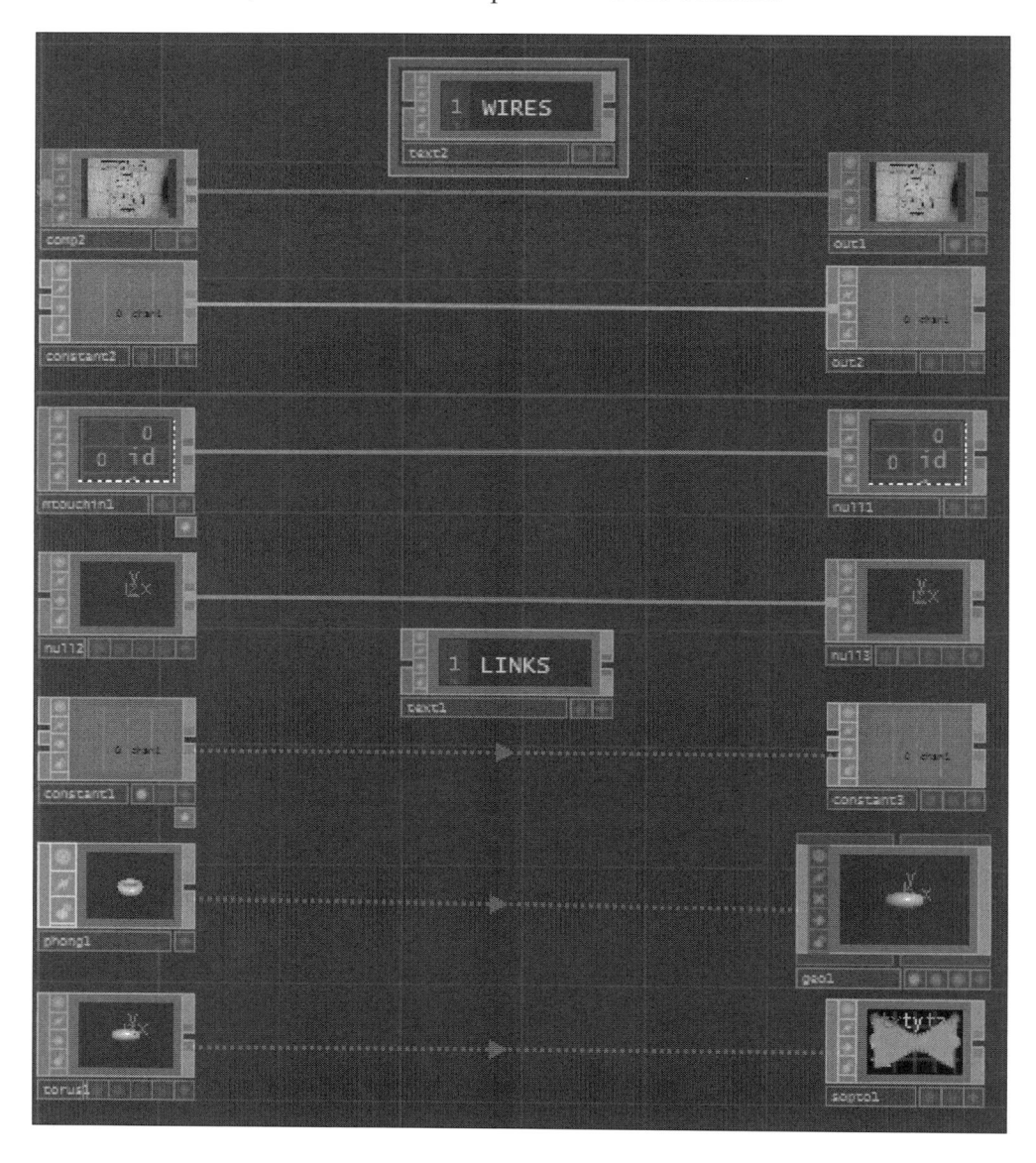

The most common example of a link is exporting CHOP. A CHOP actually feeds its data into any operator type. In general, we can think of links as a kind of reference; for example, if we put down an info CHOP and type `noise1` into its operator parameter (or simply drag-and-drop the noise TOP, not the channel this time, on the parameter), we reference the noise TOP in the info CHOP, which results in a link. We'll learn more about moving between OP families, which is a tremendously powerful tool, but first, let's take another look at linking OPs: parameter referencing. Suppose you have two noise TOPs and want to layer them. We probably don't know what resolution we need yet, but for sure, we want the resolution of each OP to be the same. What we can do is right-click on, for example, the *x* resolution parameter in one noise CHOP, choose **copy parameter**, go to the other TOP's *x* resolution, right-click on it, and choose **paste reference**. Now, these two are linked, which will also be indicated with the familiar arrow. If we expand the parameter now, we will see an expression pasted in there: `op("noise2").par.resolution1`. Again, without going into too much detail about the code, be aware that you could edit this expression to, for example, make one noise TOP always half the resolution of the other. Go ahead and try!

> **Exercise**
>
> Finally, we want to put our Noise on top of an incoming movie. Actually, let's multiply them all together. However, we want one noise to have the same resolution as the movie, and the other one half of it. Also, we'd like both noises to move around a bit. Remember the script from the scripting prologue? If not, use a CHOP export again. To get the resolution of the movie, we can use an info CHOP, and for multiplication, let's use a composite TOP. The solution is in the `03_Hello_world_links` component.

The select OP

The select OP plays a special role among the connections. It enables us to get the contents of any OP in our network at any time. You can think of it as Max/MSP's send and receive system, but if you do, you might wonder why it's so complicated. We always need to know the path of the sending operator, which seems to be a bit cumbersome at first. What we achieve is that, like every node in our network, it has an imaginary `send` operator attached only if needed. If you take a look inside the select OP COMP inside the `03_Hello_world_links` component, you can see a couple of examples on how to use the select OPs. We can hardcode its source to just have a wireless connection, we can choose to retrieve only individual channels of a CHOP, and we can even change the source via scripting.

Without going into too much detail about the actual expressions, you should notice the power of this routing system. To make this even more attractive, assume that our sources (the Moviein TOPs in this case) are created by some heavy processing. Cooking, that is, processing of data is only done if it's really needed; therefore, if we don't display them, they won't cook. So, using a select OP, or also a switch OP for that matter, can dynamically manage what is actually processed.

Take the use of the select OPs in this example with a grain of salt though. They work just fine as they are configured, but one problem might be that their paths are relative. So, if we decide to, for example, put them somewhere else into our network, say, we just want to throw them into the **exercise_solution** COMP for some reason, we will break the connection and change the path. This issue will be addressed in a later chapter and can be dealt with using modules for example.

A closer look at timeslicing, CHOPs, and exporting

We have already seen that CHOPs can come in two flavors: sometimes we see a graph in their viewer and sometimes it's just one value. So, they can simply hold one or multiple samples. Fair enough, but what does it mean when we say a CHOP holds multiple values? We have already exported CHOPs that hold a graph and have many values; did they all influence the parameter at the same time or get messed up somehow? No, of course not. If we just export a graph, so to speak, a CHOP holding many samples, then the individual samples of this CHOP are played in sequence, and looked up by the progression of the timeline at the bottom of our interface. We can, on the other hand, also look up the values of a CHOP ourselves. Look at the first example in the `05_CHOP_examples/timeSlicing` COMP. Here, we used a time slice CHOP to get one value out of many, but we will come to time slicing in a second; it has more to offer than just that. In the second example, the time slicing parameter in the noise CHOP has been activated, which results in only one value at a time. In our first example, notice that constraints have been used to create noise only from frame 200 to 400; this is not possible if we turn on timeslicing. Also, notice that the values are not the same although the parameters are equal. The first method is great for linear/deterministic work. If we need noise (but it should always be the same no matter how often we play back a sequence), the first method is the way to go. The second method, on the other hand, is ideal for nonlinear work; a noise CHOP adjusted this way won't care about the momentary frame number, and since it doesn't reset at frame one, we don't have a possible discontinuity there.

In the third example, we used a wave CHOP instead of noise. We use a lookup
CHOP to query the value from the wave CHOP, and a constant CHOP to generate
the index to look up in the wave. Works fine, right? So should we not use that
technique simply because it's more complicated? No, the real point here is to
understand what time slicing really does for us. It not only reduces a bigger number
of samples to a single one in time, but also makes sure everything runs smoothly. If
we are doing some heavy processing, we might skip some frames sometimes. Time
slicing computes all samples, regardless of the frames being skipped. This makes
sure our animations are accurate and smooth, or to put it differently, a Time Slice
or timeslice is the time between the last cook frame and the current cook frame. In
CHOPs, it is a set of short channels that only contain the CHOP channels' samples
between the last and the current cook frame.

Most CHOPs cook a timeslice of channels to assure that curves are smooth and
pulses are accurate, even if the TouchDesigner process is skipping frames. We can
see the effects if we turn off the bypass flag of the Hog CHOP in the third example.
The Hog CHOP simulates heavy processing and we can therefore observe the
steepness of our lookup method. One important thing to notice is that if we only
see one value in a CHOPS viewer, it doesn't automatically mean that CHOP is
time sliced. We'll have to inspect that CHOP using the middle mouse info box
to see whether it has been time sliced.

Some CHOPs are designed to be always time sliced, for example the LFO CHOP,
which you can compare with the wave CHOP in the third example. Notice the
discontinuity at the wave CHOP's trails in frame 1, whereas the LFO CHOP runs
through the shifting phase in regard to the frame number at each cycle of
the timeline.

For some more examples and further explanation, please refer to
`http://www.derivative.ca/wiki088/index.php?title=Time_Slicing_Vid`.

Last but not least, consider the bottom part of the time slicing component.
The different time slicing methods are displayed here, and you can see their
behavior in a trail CHOP as in the other examples.

> The most important example here is probably the use of the trail CHOP
> to inspect our results. Don't forget that you can always pause the timeline
> to more deeply inspect the trail. This way, we can always find out a lot
> about our signals or an operator's behavior. A record CHOP can also be
> used for this.

Basic Visualization Using TouchDesigner

Now that we have a basic understanding of what the data presented in a CHOP's viewer means and how data might be time sliced, that is, interpolated, let's look at different export methods. In the `05/_CHOP_examples/exportMethods` COMP, we can see different methods being applied. On a CHOP's common page, we can choose what method we'd like to use. Typically, these won't matter too much for us, but in some cases, it can be very handy to be aware of this. In general, if we don't care for the method, the default is used: the DAT table by index, which is shown in the uppermost null CHOP and is also depicted in the following screenshot:

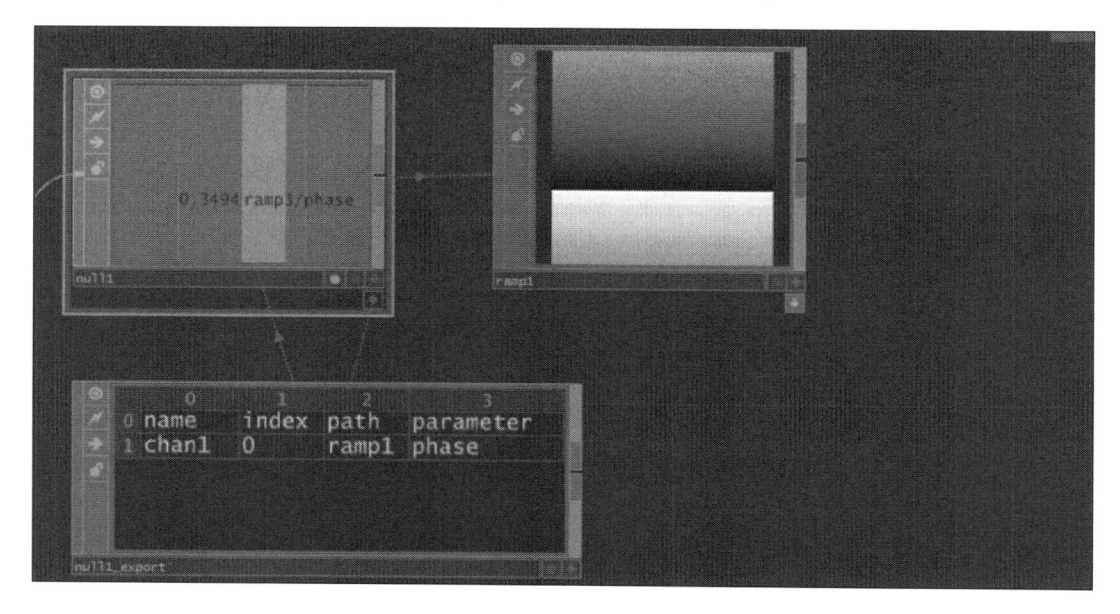

By exporting a CHOP using our drag-and-drop technique, automatically, a table DAT is created, docked to that CHOP, and referenced in the CHOP's **Export table** parameter, and the CHOP's export flag is turned on. The export flag is the little green button at the bottom of CHOPS and DATs and allows us to turn the exporting option on or off.

Docking is quite handy sometimes, and we can also dock OPs together simply by right-clicking on an OP and choosing **Dock to**. This will cause the docked OP to always have a location in the network that is relative to the OP it's docked to; and it can be hidden/shown by clicking on the little docking arrow. In the preceding screenshot, you can see a DAT that is docked to the CHOP and it's exposed. The ramp TOP, by default, also has a DAT docked to it, which contains some of the ramp's parameters. But in this image, the docked DAT is hidden and only indicated by the little docking icon.

Now, why should we use a different method? It's all about creating/changing CHOP channels dynamically. By adjusting the index value in the switch CHOP in our example, we can choose which of the noise CHOPs to forward to the three exports. You will see that the exports react differently on the change of the channel name. Suppose we are using an **OSC In** CHOP as our source. If we use the **by index** method, no matter what address or channel name is present, the first channel will be used. This sounds like something we wouldn't want. To avoid this behavior, we can, for example, use a select CHOP to isolate the specific channel or use the **by name** method directly. On the other hand, sometimes, we don't really care what the name of a channel is; we just want to export what's present. Yet another case might be that we just want to determine where a CHOP is exporting to by giving the channel a certain name, probably dynamically. Experiment with the different methods for a bit and see how they react.

Panes

The official documentation guide on the panes can be found at `http://www.derivative.ca/wiki088/index.php?title=Pane`.

If we look at TouchDesigner's interface, we could say it is divided into the following three parts:

- The toolbar, including menus, buttons, and so on
- One or more panes
- The Timeline/Playback controls

Most of the top part of the preceding points is pretty self-explanatory; we will talk about timing at a later moment, so let's dedicate our attention to the pane for now. The pane, by default, holds the network editor, in which we can connect operators, and is switched to full screen (meaning we only have one pane). At the top of a pane, there is always the **pane bar** option, which allows us to configure what a pane displays. A pane can be split up horizontally or vertically, and it can be made floating and so on using the rightmost button in the pane bar. Also, it can hold information about the network editor and also about the geometry viewer, a panel viewer, a TOP viewer, and more. The type of display of a pane can be chosen using the leftmost button in the pane bar. What it actually displays (what TOP displays in the TOP viewer) is determined by switching on the display flag of the chosen operator(s).

Basic Visualization Using TouchDesigner

In the following screenshot, the blue little display flags have been activated and therefore the contents of the TOPs are displayed as a backdrop of the pane:

Exercise

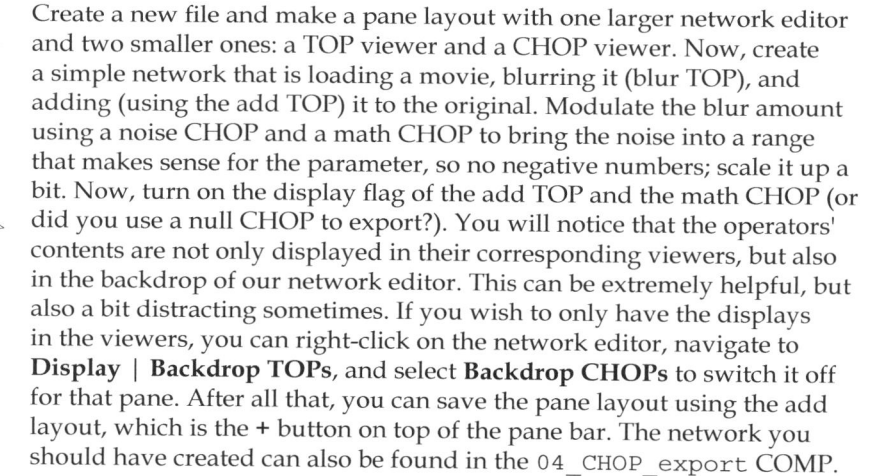

Create a new file and make a pane layout with one larger network editor and two smaller ones: a TOP viewer and a CHOP viewer. Now, create a simple network that is loading a movie, blurring it (blur TOP), and adding (using the add TOP) it to the original. Modulate the blur amount using a noise CHOP and a math CHOP to bring the noise into a range that makes sense for the parameter, so no negative numbers; scale it up a bit. Now, turn on the display flag of the add TOP and the math CHOP (or did you use a null CHOP to export?). You will notice that the operators' contents are not only displayed in their corresponding viewers, but also in the backdrop of our network editor. This can be extremely helpful, but also a bit distracting sometimes. If you wish to only have the displays in the viewers, you can right-click on the network editor, navigate to **Display | Backdrop TOPs**, and select **Backdrop CHOPs** to switch it off for that pane. After all that, you can save the pane layout using the add layout, which is the **+** button on top of the pane bar. The network you should have created can also be found in the `04_CHOP_export` COMP.

After the exercise, you should have something that looks like this:

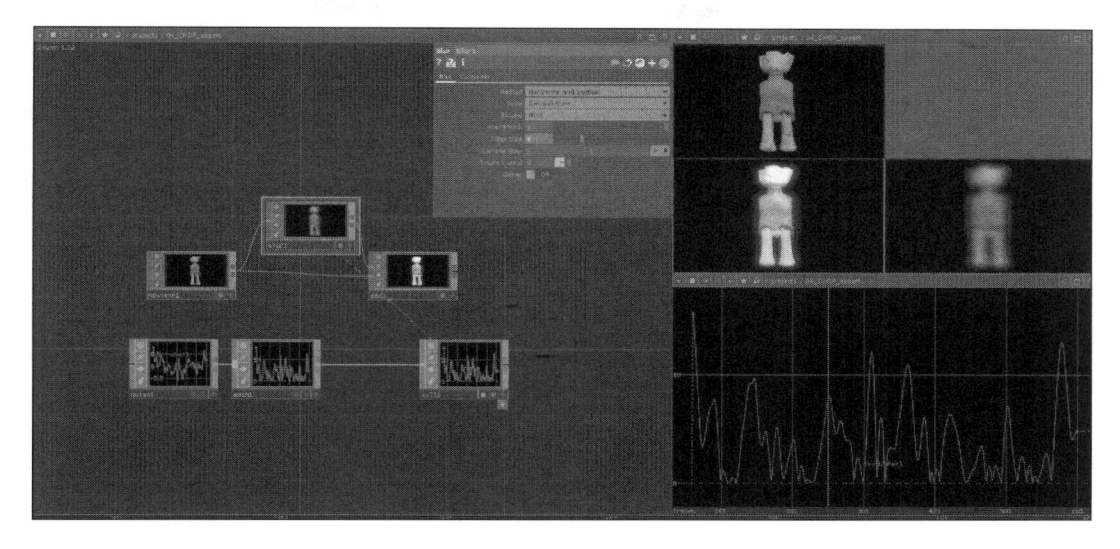

Notice that each individual pane's path has to be configured correctly; we have seen that we can go levels up and down, so these panes need to know where the operators are and where it should display. We can point it to the path of a selected COMP by pressing the **>>** button in a pane's path. So since we are talking about paths now, let's take a closer look at how our networks are structured, and let's talk a bit about COMPs or components.

Components – structuring a project

Components, or COMPs, are not only a powerful way to structure our networks but they can also do lots of other things for us. They are, to start with a comparison, Max's subpatcher, abstraction, and bpatcher, all in one and more.

Where am I?

You might have noticed that we are always shown a path like `/project1/` >> in the pane bar. In any TouchDesigner file, if we press the little house icon at the left of that path, we can go to **root**, so /. As we used subpatchers in Max, we can have a tree-like topology in TouchDesigner. By default, in root, there are a couple of components and one that's called **project1** in which we usually start to build things. We can move up and down by just zooming in to a COMP with the mouse wheel to go in or down and by zooming out to go one level up. Also, the shortcuts *U* and *I*, for up and in, allow us to move vertically through our files. Double-clicking on a COMP or pressing *Enter* when a COMP is selected also allows us to go inside.

> To get a good overview of what's happening on the level that we are in at the moment, we can use the shortcut *O* to get a little overview window, or even better, the shortcut *T* to get a table view of all the operators of the component we are in.

So COMPS are used to encapsulate things, but which one should we choose for a certain part of a network that should be encapsulated? Well, first of all, not all COMPs are just there to encapsulate things for us. Some of them fulfill a special functionality, as the camera COMP acts as a camera in our 3D renderings, or the animation COMP will hold our animation curves. We can get in there to see what's happening in them, but typically, we won't do a lot in there. The camera COMP, for example, only holds a 3D model of a camera for display reasons. The real all-round encapsulation COMPs are the **Base** COMP and the **Container** COMP. However, the container already adds some functionality, which we might not need; it's able to create a GUI. Since we quite often will want a GUI for an encapsulated network, it's very common to use a container COMP for everything, but the base COMP is what we should think about first, when it's just about encapsulating. Then, we might think about what is supposed to be in that capsule. Will it have a GUI? Will it be 3D? Depending on these thoughts, we might change our choice to probably use a container for instance. Take the Max analogy again; the base COMP is a subpatcher, and the container COMP is equivalent to the bpatcher. Don't be tempted to use a bpatcher just for everything. The OP creates **Dialog also Groups** COMPS in the following three different columns:

- 3D
- Panels
- Other

Most of the components in the example files are base COMPS. If you also create one and take a look at its parameters, you will see that we can't do a lot there. It basically has all the parameters that we find on the common page of all the other COMPS. So let's see what we have.

The **Node view** and **Operator viewer** options allow us to configure what the COMP's viewer shows us. A base COMP can only display another OP's viewer; that's why we can't choose a lot there. The OP that will be displayed is of course configured by the **Operator viewer** parameter. The default here is `/out1`. There is some subtlety in this little string. The `.` parameter means me, so `/` means inside of me, and `out1` is the name of the operator. The nice thing is that this operator doesn't yet exist when we create the COMP. However, as soon as we create an output of our COMP, it will, by default, have the name **out1**. Also, it doesn't matter if we create an `out` CHOP, `out` SOP, or TOP; they all will, by default, have the name `out` and a number, so the first one we create will automatically be displayed. If you look at the `06_comps` component, you will find that the `out1` TOP is what's displayed in the viewer. Its image is created by the line COMP, which is a base component with a CHOP input and a TOP output. In there is a little TOP feedback network I invite you to examine. One interesting point to notice is how the CHOP input works. Noise is connected to the line COMP, but if we disconnect it, the internal LFO's component is used. Input in TouchDesigner have the ability to have a default source, which is overridden if we connect something to that inlet.

We are still at the Base COMP `6_comps` parameter window. We'll skip the clone parameter to address it later and take a quick stop at the path variable. The path variable allows us to assign a variable to the component's path. Remember we said there are problems while using the select OP? This is one way to overcome these problems. Inside the `selectOP_using_pathVariable` component, the path of the select OP has been set to `var('compsVar')+'/moviein1'`, which evaluates as `/project1/06_comps/moviein1`, since we assigned the `06_comps` component's path to the `compsVar` variable by use of the path's variable parameter. In Python, we can get the value of such a variable using `var()`; in Tscript, we can just use `$` to access a variable, for example `$compsVar`. All this is pretty handy, and you see that our expressions can be very short and useful. The + sign in the expression just means the concatenation of two strings, in this case, the `'/project1/06_comps'` string and the `'/moviein1'` string. Notice that if we try to enter an expression into a parameter, we have to expand the parameter and click on the little bluish button to indicate that we are entering an expression. If we encounter an error, the middle mouse info box can give us hints of what's wrong. Also, as you can see, an evaluate DAT can help us see what the result of an expression is. We just have to configure its output parameter to expressions.

Creating our first UI

The previous section might have been a bit theoretical, so let's get some more fun stuff going; let's create a really simple GUI. You'll find an example of this at `07_UI`, but try to build this yourself first. I guess you have played around with TOPs or even SOPs already along the way, so try to think of something you'd like to control with a GUI, or maybe you want to control one of our Max patches with TouchDesigner? The **OSC out** CHOP is your friend in this case. Otherwise, just copy the `07_UI/basic/processing` COMP and only create the GUI for it. The processing COMP is just a container COMP whose background TOP parameter has been adjusted to show our output.

To build a really basic UI, we just put down a container COMP. In there, we put down a couple of slider components. While we are inside the container, we can press *V* to view its panel in a floating window. If we've done that, we'll see only one slider because they are all stacked upon each other. We can now offset each slider individually using their x and y parameters, or we just go to our container's parameters and set **Align** to, for example, **Layout Vertical Top to Bottom**. This way, they will be aligned automatically. The individual slider's **Align order** parameter decides whether a slider is on top or at the bottom in this case, or how they are ordered. Now, our sliders don't seem to fill the whole container's panel. So let's reduce its width and height parameters to fit the content. Finally, let's use a merge CHOP to combine all the outputs of our sliders and send them to an out CHOP for processing. This was easy, wasn't it? So let's introduce some expressions to make this a bit slicker. First of all, don't hesitate to look inside the slider's components. We can do lots of things in there; for example, we'd like to name our sliders and also probably see their values. So for the next GUI, let's create a good slider.

We are going to make use of a neat little trick; if you put down a slider, select it and press *F11*, you are able to switch around what you wish to see in the slider's viewer. Actually, we thereby adjust the component's **Node View** and **Operator Viewer** parameter. If we do that switching around, the COMP displays either its panel, the `out1` node in it, or a node called `define`, which is not present by default. If you go into `07_UI/aNiceSlider/container1` and try the *F11* trick, you can see and edit a table where you can redefine some values such as the name and range.

The network inside the actual slider may seem a little scary at first, but it's actually quite simple. The **nullDisplay** TOP is used as a background TOP for the slider COMP. The name has been retrieved from the table using a select DAT. This might be an easier way than doing it with an expression. In the panel CHOP, which is grabbing our mouse position if we move the slider, an expression has been used to directly get the name from `define`. In the Math CHOP, the table is referenced to rescale the channel correctly. Here, we are using an expression, `op('define')['lowerRange', 1]`, to directly access DAT's range values for the lower range limit for example. The `Op()` part indicates that we want to access an operator; `op('define')` indicates we are looking for an operator called `define`. The notation with the square brackets simply is a way to access cells in a DAT table, which we can always look up at http://www.derivative.ca/wiki088/index.php?title=Working_with_DATs_in_Python.

Hierarchy

Quite a lot of scripting has been used in this example to make the sliders always fit the width of the container in which they are. For this, the expression `me.parent().par.w` has been used. This again is an expression to remember; it's very handy but also easy to remember if we understand it. The `me` part indicates the operator in which the expression is located. This operator has a parent in hierarchy, in the path. So in our example, slider2's parent is the `container1` component. Inside the parenthesis, we can decide how many levels we wish to go up. If we don't pick a number for this value, or don't give the method an argument, the default is used: we go one level up. So `me.parent()` is the same as `me.parent(1)`.

At this point, we arrived at `me.parent(1)`, an operator again. The expression stands for the `container1` component in this case. It references it in a relative way of course. Now, we can start querying this operator's parameters using the `.par` notation and choose which one by again putting a dot and a name after this. That's how we arrive at `me.parent().par.w`, where `w` stands for the width parameter, and we can find that out by just hovering the mouse over any parameter's name. All of this just returns a number that defines our slider's width.

Basic Visualization Using TouchDesigner

There is another notion of hierarchy in TouchDesigner. Some component types can be put in parent-child relationships without the need of putting one inside the other but by merely using a connection. Look at the **08_hierarchy** COMP in the provided file. Again, a very primitive UI is built, but notice that it is structured via the top and bottom connectors of the container COMPs, as depicted in the following screenshot. This is going to be particularly useful when we deal with 3D geometry since geometry COMPS inherit their transform parameters this way.

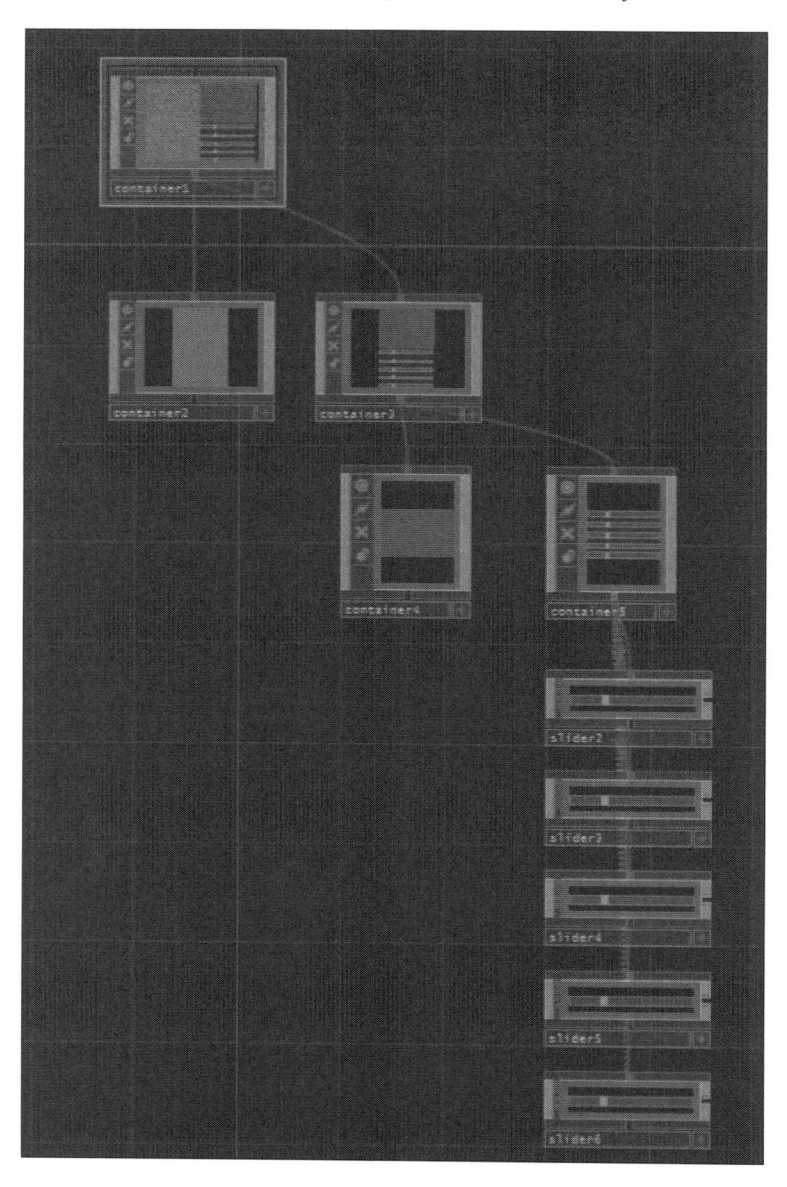

If you wish, check out the width and height parameters of the individual components in there. You will see that if you change the parameters of the topmost container, all others will scale correctly since some simple expressions have been used. Don't forget the **Non-default parameters only** button in the parameter's dialog to quickly see what has been changed. Making a UI easily scalable saves a lot of time.

Abstraction

Let's forget about all the fancy scripting again for now and think about what we can do if we have achieved something with or without it. Let's go back to the common page of the parameter dialog of our base COMP. What we also find there is the external .tox parameter. TouchDesigner files are saved as .toe files, so where can we get a .tox file from? We can right-click on any component and choose **Save component** from the context menu to save out a tox of that file. This file can now be referenced in any component's external tox parameter. This, of course, is a very helpful tool if one works with lots of custom tools or also in collaborative work, but we have discussed the advantages of abstraction in the Max section already. One interesting expression in this context might be project.folder. Project is a class that references our project file, and it has a member named folder. This returns the folder in which our .toe file is located.

So if we build a bigger project, we might end up with a project folder that contains subfolders such as audio, image, and so on. TouchDesigner is able to do this for us automatically via **File | Create Project Folder**. One of the subfolders might contain all our abstractions, that is, .tox files. These might be referenced in components via project.folder+'/tox/myAbstraction.tox'. This way, if we move the whole project folder, it will still be working and self-contained. As you see, keeping a tidy file structure is quite important here, but before migrating a project, you should always try the opfiles command. Open a textport or switch an open pane into the textport mode, switch its language to Tscript, and type opfiles. This will cause TouchDesigner to print all the used files, and you can see whether there are any references to things outside your project folder or whether absolute paths are used somewhere that could break due to migration. An example of an external tox referenced in a relative manner is the **05_CHOP_examples** COMP. Its source file lies in a folder called tox that in turn lies right next to the actual TOE file.

After doing all of this, having made sliders ourselves, exported, and imported components, let's take a look at what TouchDesigner offers us natively without us having to do all that we have just done; let's have a look at the palette.

Palette

The palette can be opened and closed via the **Open palette** button that is to the left of the pane layout buttons. Refer to the following screenshot:

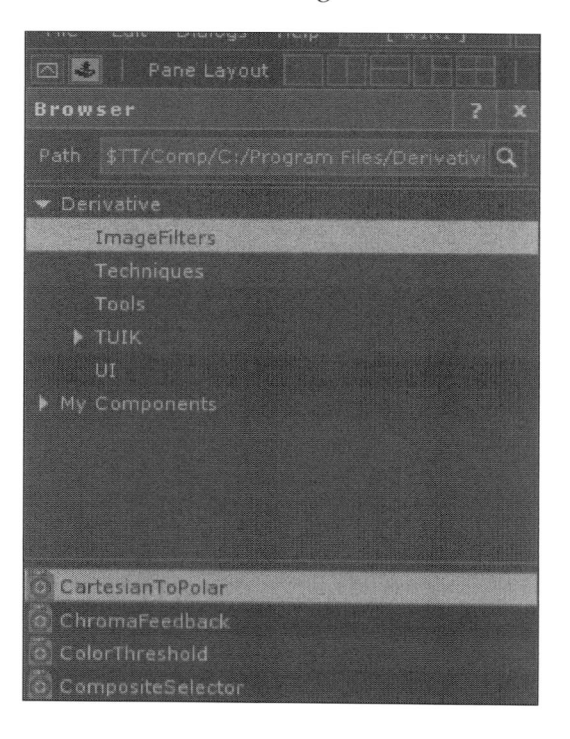

The palette is a collection of pre-made, ready-to-use components. They have a different functionality, such as 3D modeling, UI elements, and image processing. Also, they are a great source for learning, so take a look inside some of these! The nice thing is that we can add our own ones simply by dragging them onto the palette. Also, we can create new folders via a right-click. In fact, the palette is simply a file browser. Our custom components lie at C:/Users/username/Derivative/Touchdesigner088/. If you are annoyed by the fact that we have gone through a rather hard way of building a UI and afterwards discover the palette where lots of great UI elements are ready to use, you should know that it's good to at least know the fundamentals of these. The time, we'd like to modify what's there will come soon enough.

Local

Components form a local context for variables and inherit these through the hierarchy. A classic use case for these variables is resolution. TOPs, in general, use their input's resolution, aspect ratio, and bit depth/pixel format. However, some TOPs won't have an input in our network, such as noise TOPs, ramps, and so on. So if we decide to change the resolution at the last moment before our show or the minute we want to leave our installation, we just have to change a variable in a central place. So that's how we do it; in our network, we just put down a base COMP we call `local`. In there, we create a table DAT, call it `variables`, give it two columns, one for the variable name and one for the value, and voila, we created a neat place to store our variables. Refer to the following screenshot:

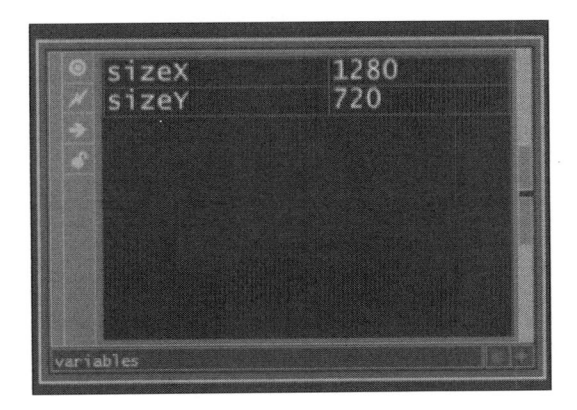

Look into the **09_local** COMP; you'll see this construction and you'll see a noise TOP that uses the variables in its parameters. Now, there is another base COMP in there. This one has its own local COMP again, which can override the inherited variables. This inherit-and-override behavior and the notion of local can do a lot more than just store variables.

For example, we can easily add a local time to a component. This is done by right-clicking on the network and choosing **Add Component Time**. When this is done, we get a (possibly) independent new timeline, and all OPs inside that component will reference this new timeline. Also, we can define our own reusable scripts inside modules inside the local COMP. Obviously, the local COMP is a very special place and we will use it a lot in the upcoming chapters.

Clones

We have learned a little about clones already since we have a clone immune flag on every OP. Cloning is a powerful technique that is related to abstraction. The idea is that we have a master component somewhere in our network, for example, a slider we created or a 3D modeling network. Changing the master changes the clones, but each individual OP within a clone can be excluded from being identical to the master's corresponding OPs. In the example, the slider from the UI component has been used as a master. We still want to configure the names independently though, right? So we just turn on the clone immune flag of our define table DAT, and the slider is ready to be cloned. Cloning is simply done by creating a component of the same type as the master. On the common tab in its parameter dialog, we provide the path to the master and end up with a clone. Later on, we will see how this, in combination with the replicator COMP, can be a very quick method to create big complex networks.

What's happening in root?

We saw that, by default, there is a component called Project1 in which we build our stuff. But why can we actually go one level up then? Well, while it's still recommended to put everything we need into our **project1** COMP, outside are some things that are important to us. First of all, the two components, ui and sys, are not saved with the .toe file, so it doesn't make a whole lot of sense to do things in there. The local component is, as usual, defining variables and so on. Partly, its contents are defined by dialogs as the MIDI mapping, for example. What really matters to us right away is the perform COMP. It actually is a window COMP that is opened when we enter perform mode using *F1*. So its placement, resolution, and what operator it displays are all things that are of great interest to us. For further information, please visit http://www.derivative.ca/wiki088/index.php?title=Root.

Assign a text editor to TouchDesigner

We have briefly talked about preparing a system for installation/performance work. There is one helpful thing left that should probably be mentioned when thinking about preparing a system for TouchDesigner work. As you have seen, we are dealing with expressions a bit, and sometimes, we might miss a full-featured code editor with syntax highlighting and so on. If we are editing an expression in a parameter or a DAT, we can right-click on it and choose **Edit parameter/edit contents**. This causes an external editor to be opened. The editor that's used is configured with an **environment variable** option. An environment variable option is set in the OS, and Windows provides a dialog for setting these so-called environment variables. It's useful to either do a quick web search or refer to the Microsoft support to learn how to set environment variables. Anyhow, to tell TouchDesigner what editor we want to use, we will set up a variable called `TOUCH_EDITOR` and assign the full path to our favorite editor (for example, Notepad++ or Sublime Text) as a value. After doing this, working with expressions will become a charm.

Summary

We started this chapter by claiming that TouchDesigner is both intuitive and deep, and by now, I hope understand what was meant by that. We saw how to get some movement in TOPs using CHOP exports; we have arrived at a basic understanding about what the UI is showing us and what it is capable of. Also, we saw how to enter performance mode and how to record movies, how to build a simple UI, and how to inspect what's actually happening using the viewer active flag, the display flag, the evaluate DAT, the trail CHOP, and other techniques.

Now, we'll put all of what we've learned to some use! We're going to first connect Max and TouchDesigner to get some basic audiovisual experience going!

10
Advanced Visualization Using TouchDesigner

Let's get started with generating some basic audio-reactive video. After this, we'll move over to connecting Max and TD over UDP/OSC in order to be able to use the ease and sophistication of Max's audio analysis capabilities for TD. Also, we'll think a bit about timing, synchronization, and the problem of getting event-based data into a stream-based system (TD). Along the way, we'll meet some more scripting techniques, and try to discover some ways to structure our networks.

In this chapter, we will cover the following topics:

- Replicator COMP
- Connecting Max and TouchDesigner
- Dealing with time
- Introducing 3D rendering

The basic audio-reactive video

Let's dive right into the `01_AudioReactiveBasic` network, which is depicted in the following screenshot:

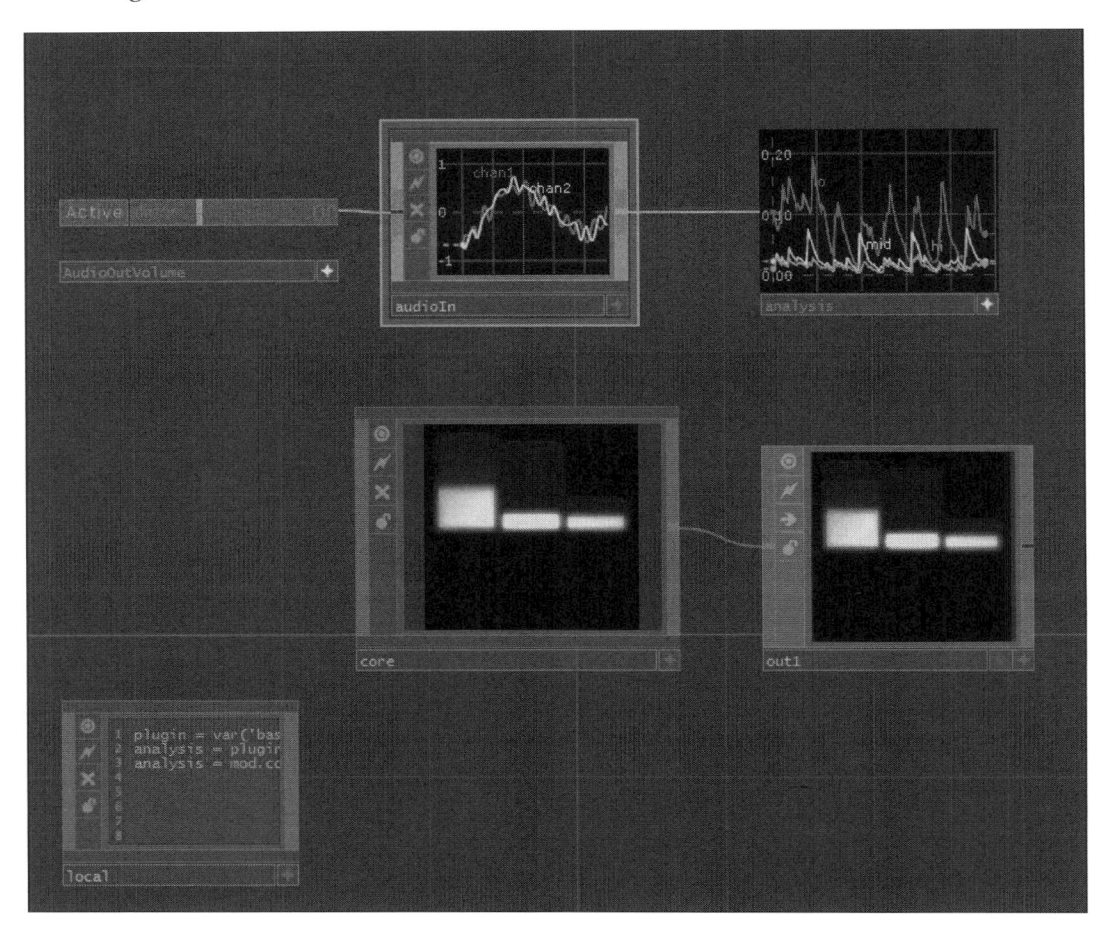

In this network, as shown in the preceding screenshot, we'll see only six things:

- A slider that controls audio output amplitude.
- Base COMP for audio in; you might have to go in there to configure Audio Out CHOP correctly in order to hear something, especially if you want to hear the sound over an external sound card, or anything but the default. Also, if you want to use live audio input, go in there, Audio Device In CHOP is already there for this purpose.

- There is another Base COMP for audio analysis. It first combines the two stereo channels to a mono channel, and then applies three filters to split up the incoming sound into low, mid, and high frequencies. Afterwards, Analyze CHOP is used to get the RMS of each band. Again, Trail CHOP is used to get a nice display of what's happening outside COMP.
- Also, we have Core COMP, which is another Base COMP, and Local COMP and Out TOP.

If you imagine all these in the `/project1/` `level` folder, this will be a typical structure for a project. Before we look a bit deeper at what Local COMP does for us, let's look at the more fun part of this network, which is Core COMP. Refer to the following screenshot:

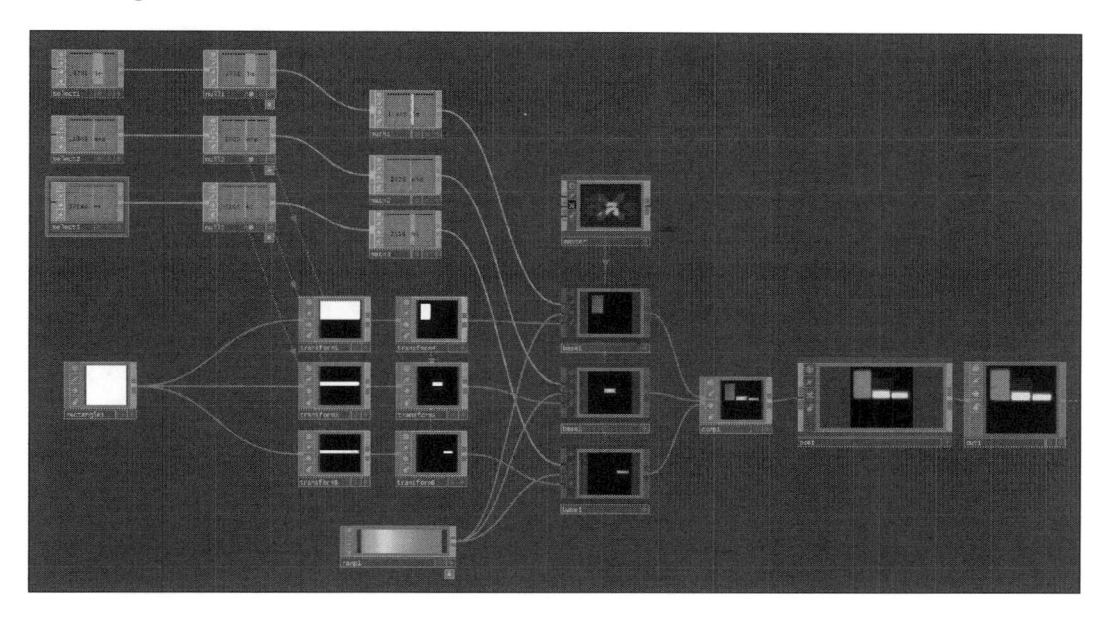

We retrieve the individual envelopes using Select CHOPs that point to the output of the analysis COMP. Again, how they point to this has to do with our Local COMP, and we'll come to how this is done in a moment. Of course, we can use In CHOP instead. These values are then used to drive the `scale y` parameter of some Transform TOPs. Therefore, the square coming into Transform TOPs is scaled if you look at the **transform3** TOP, for example; but wait a moment, does it take too much time to look for this node?

Advanced Visualization Using TouchDesigner

> Whenever you look for an OP by name, or you look for the one OP whose display flag is switched on in a huge network, press *T* to get a table view of the network.

In the following screenshot, the table view of the same network is shown:

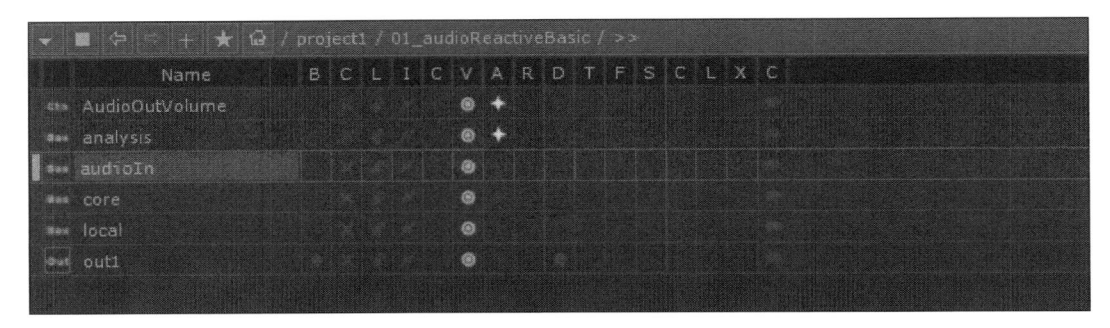

Alright, so if you look at the `transform3` TOP for a moment, you'll see that it's translated into *y* using an expression:

```
me.par.sy/2
```

This expression looks at the same node's `scale y` parameter and divides this value by 2. This is necessary to give our rectangle a stable base; otherwise, the rectangle will look like it's growing towards the top and bottom of the screen. Try it out; you can always press the constant button of a parameter to bypass an expression.

So, we have three bars growing and shrinking to the grooves; let's color them a bit and composite them. First, they are shrunk to make some space, but then they all go into COMP that is a bit grayed out. We know already that these gray COMPs are clones of the master COMP we mentioned previously. Also, note that the `scale x` parameter of the uppermost Transform TOP, `transform4`, controls the same parameter of the other two Transform TOPs, so they all have the same width, and their width can be centrally controlled. This is also why this node was colored.

> It's a good idea to develop a color code for yourself. You can color OPs by just pressing *C* to bring up the color palette. For example, you can decide to color the nodes that are referenced by a select OP in orange, or an OP exporting its parameters to other OPs in yellow, and stick them to this pattern; this way you can always see more quickly what happens in your networks.

[274]

Inside the cloned components and their master, we find that the incoming CHOP (accessed via In CHOP) is converted to TOP (using CHOP to TOP). What this does in this case is that since this particular CHOP contains only one sample, we get out one pixel that has the **rgba** values of the incoming value. This pixel is then used to look up a color from the ramp, which is also fed into COMP, using Look Up TOP. The result is then just multiplied by the incoming white bar. What we get is, as you see in the following screenshot, a dynamically colored bar. After compositing the three bars, the effects inside the `post` component are applied. In there is just some blurring and a feedback network.

Since feedback inside TouchDesigner might seem slightly confusing at first, let's look at this a bit more closely for a second:

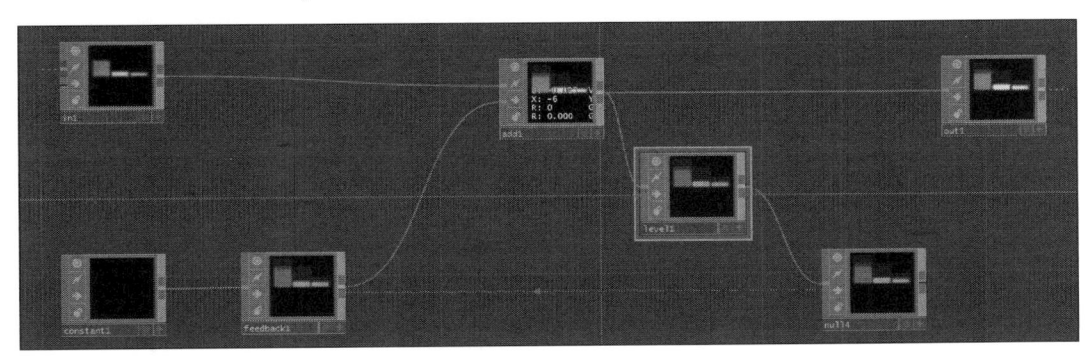

To isolate the feedback loop, in order to make this a bit more easy to talk about and look at, it has been kept inside another Base COMP, `core/post/feedback`. If we look at it, we see that the loop is closed via a link rather than a wire. The feedback TOP has a Target TOP parameter, which has been given the **null4** TOP as a value. This parameter is actually the source; don't let yourself be confused, think of it as the feedback TOP's input. Now what's this constant TOP doing on its actual input? It is just what output is if the feedback is bypassed. What might be confusing is that it is obligatory to have something connected here, be it the input to our loop (that makes a lot of sense in many cases, but does not break the recursion), a constant, or anything you wish; it doesn't matter at all if we don't plan to bypass the feedback.

> If we use a constant TOP, it is a good idea to configure its resolution to what we wish our loop to have as resolution. It is important to note that Add TOP's `Fixed Layer` parameter has been switched to input 1 to the image entering our loop. The `Fixed Layer` parameter determines, besides other things, which input's resolution and aspect ratio are used for the output image of the corresponding node (and therefore, the resolution of our loop, in this case). If the resolution of our loop determines the resolution of our loop, we will have a problem.

Advanced Visualization Using TouchDesigner

Of course, as in any other feedback, there is the danger of blowing up the circuit. In TD, we typically attenuate the loop using Level TOP. On the **Post** page in Level TOP's **Parameter** dialog, we find an `Opacity` parameter. Also, the `gamma` and `black level` parameter help us to avoid ghosting effects since they help to attenuate low levels. So, Level TOP is a nice way to attenuate the circular amplification. Try it out, what does it mean to blow up a thing in TD? Turn up the opacity, inspect the pixel values, and check if they clip or are infinitely large.

To our great convenience, they are clipped.

> **Another exercise**:
> Try to forget about an image being processed and two dimensional (+time), draw a block diagram of what you see, and think about what this will do to an audio signal, assuming the feedback TOP also adds one sample of delay! From the block diagram, it should be obvious, but if it isn't, implement the thing in Max's `gen~` and listen to the result.

Let's get out of our core component to finally look at our local COMP. Local COMP, in this case, is there for us to navigate through our project. Here, there are a couple of things to notice. The viewer of the Local COMP has been adjusted, so it shows us the **modules COMP** inside. This in turn is adjusted to display **Merge1 DAT**. So, we can view all Text DATs from two levels up. Also, until now we have just seen that we can define variables in the Local COMP using Table DAT, so what is this modules COMP? As we created the local COMP, we can also create Base COMP and call it `modules`, so all Text DATs in there will serve as **modules**. In the following screenshot, you can see two modules being merged within the modules COMP:

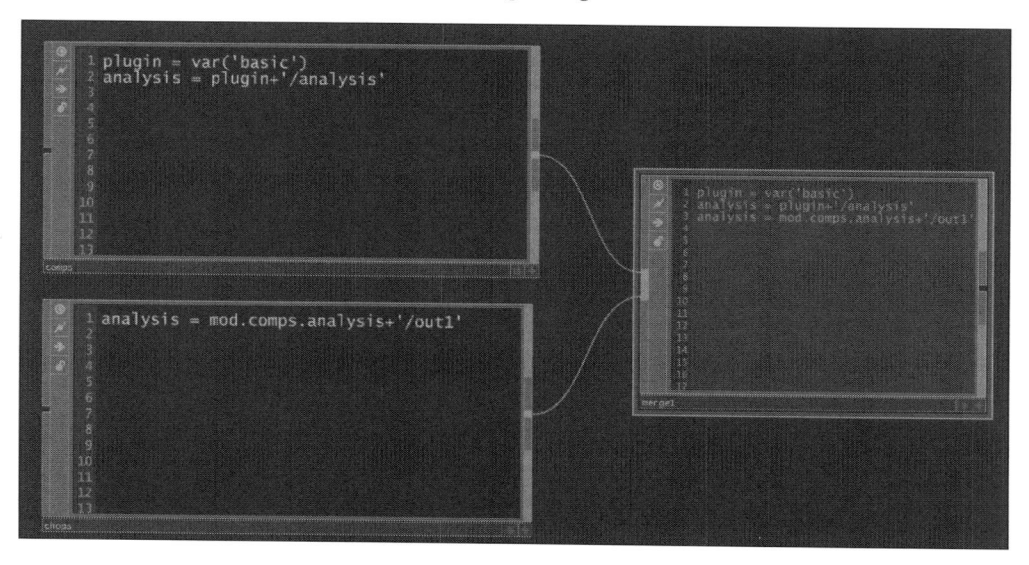

A module is simply a named collection of variables, functions, and classes. In this case, our modules contain just variables. So, there are two modules present: COMPS and CHOPS. These modules contain variables that give us smooth access to the most important OPs in our network. The advantage of using modules, instead of simply variables, is that we can structure our variables better. For example, if we need to reference the output of our analysis COMP, which we also did inside Core COMP (the select CHOPs, remember?), we can just write `mod.chops.analysis`. Here, `mod` says we want to access a module, `chops` is the name of the module, and `analysis` is the member we want to access, which is the last node inside of analysis COMP, (or broken down further as `basic/analysis/out1`). You can now see that analysis in the CHOPs module is defined using the analysis variable in the COMP's module. However, how is a plugin defined? A plugin is defined by querying the variable basic, and basic is just what is written in the path variable of the `01_audioReactiveBasic` COMP. So, you can see that we can keep a nice list of important OPs here, which can be highly relative, and thus, the whole thing is self-contained, moveable, tidy, and easy to modify.

> Any Text DAT can be module-independent wherever it is; it doesn't need to be inside COMP modules, it just needs to be found and correctly written. If we call a module, TouchDesigner first checks if there is DAT in the current COMP that matches the name, it then looks at the current COMP's modules COMP, and then tries the same for all COMPs up the tree until it reaches root. If it still doesn't find anything, it will perform the regular Python disk search.
>
> So, it makes sense to have COMP-called modules in a network where you can use certain mods. This can be done at different levels; the most common is inside the `local` folder at the root of a large project. For self-contained containers, they will have their own Local COMP inside.

This technique will be used extensively further on, but as I already said, you can simply wire up things and not care about this if you don't like the system. This might also be unnecessary for smaller projects, and wires might be perfectly fine.

> If you want to know more about ways to access modules, visit http://www.derivative.ca/wiki088/index.php?title=MOD_Class"http://www.derivative.ca/wiki088/index.php?title=MOD_Class and http://www.derivative.ca/wiki088/index.php?title=Introduction_to_Python_Tutorial#Importing_Modules.

Advanced Visualization Using TouchDesigner

A 2D composting example

We have now used TOPs quite a bit, but before we come to 3D, it might be a good idea to do some more extensive 2D work to have a more solid base. Have a look at the `02_AudioReactive_two` component. I know, what a kitsch sunset! However, it's a good example of how much of a complex scene we can achieve just with some Noise TOPs, Ramp TOPs, and a Circle TOP as a source, using some FX, and compositing everything together. This is really something to remember; real-time 3D rendering is more about clever faking to keep the performance drain low.

As you can see in the example COMP's top layer, we have the same structure as we just saw at `/project1/02_AudioReactive_two`. There is audio in, audio analysis, local, and so on (we are repeating the concepts; ring a bell?). The only thing that's different is what's inside the local and core COMPs. If you look inside the core, you'll find a pretty small-looking network, but really, it is not that small:

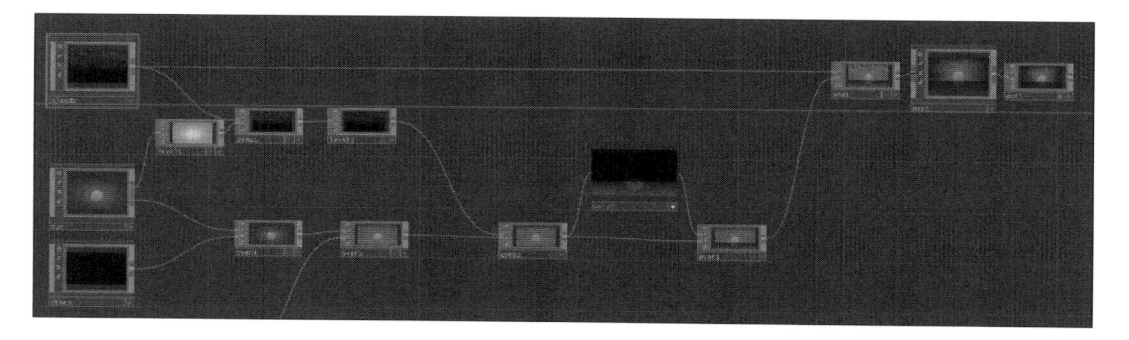

As you can see in this image, it is divided into sun, clouds, stars, water, and some post-processing. We won't go over everything here; feel free to explore it yourself, or even better, look at the result and try to come up with something replicating it, though the motivation to produce beautiful sunsets might be mild, I presume. So, let's have a look at the sun first. By now, you should be able to see what's happening in there quite quickly. There is a colored circle that is translated, or moved, by our low frequency envelope. First, Ramp TOP is used to color the sun, then it's translated, and finally multiplied by another Ramp TOP to make the sun darker as it sets and brighter as it comes up. After this, there is just some standard blurring and a little bit of feedback to give it some glow.

So, let's look at the stars next. It might look complicated at first, so let's start with defining the objective here: a black image with some sparse dots, appearing and disappearing, varying in color a bit between white, yellow, blue, and red. These are our stars. Also, we would like to have a shooting star or meteor on every hit of the snare drum of our example track. This meteor, a white dot, should always appear at one random position, move to another, and fade out during its course. As you can see, the actual TOP network is pretty simple; what makes it a bit complicated is the control of our meteor. This is a network with many links, so it's important to mention this.

> If you hover over a link, a little info box appears, telling us the source and target of the link.

So, to get the hit of our snare, we just take our mid-frequency envelopes and use Trigger CHOP, which has a `threshold` parameter, so we can adjust the parameter when the envelope that it generates shoots. The rest of the idea is simple. Now, we proceed with the following steps:

1. Generate four random values at each trigger and use them to scale and offset the envelope. Math CHOP provides us with the neat feature of defining output ranges from a given input range, so we can just modulate this with an envelope at its input. Hold CHOP does the job of a standard sample-and-hold function, so our random values don't fluctuate during the course of our meteor.

2. Notice that our Noise CHOP generates four streams of noise at the same time, and Hold CHOP processes them at the same time too. This makes our network a lot tidier.

3. After having a quick look at Noise CHOP's **Channel** page in its **Parameter** dialog, you will find that **chan[1-4]** is written in the **Channel Name** parameter. This is the shorthand to write *chan1 chan2 chan3 chan4*, and this in turn makes the noise CHOP generates for four channels.

4. Going over the TOP network, we see that the meteor itself should be clear, and the **starsBG** COMP generates our colored stars, of course. We do this by using noise as a source and gating it using Threshold TOP. The result is an image that is black; only the brightest pixels of the source image appear as white.

5. By increasing the `Soften` parameter of Threshold TOP, we can allow very bright pixels, or those close to the threshold, shine through a bit. This will give our sky a bit more depth and variation with regards to the brightness of the stars.

6. To color our stars, we just multiply the result with noise that looks up colors from Ramp TOP.
7. Next, let's inspect the water. Since the water should reflect the sky/sun, we have this as an input.
8. We just put Ramp over it to cut some of it away, then flip the image and move it in place, both using Translate TOP. Other Ramp/Noise TOP combinations give us some water that we can composite the refection on. Displace TOP is used to give the whole ocean some waves.
9. Lastly, another Ramp allows us to cut a sharp edge of the otherwise displaced horizon. Since all this will be kept over the rest, a Null TOP called `ViewAlphaChannel` has been added to observe what exactly we do with the alpha channel (pressing the right mouse button on TOP, with its viewer active, allows us to select Alpha only, or just hit *A*). Now, only one thing is left: the clouds.

The clouds have been made using a lot of noise. You will notice that the noise is displaced both in the *z* and *x* axes to give our clouds some, admittedly fast, sideways movement (*tx*), and also to have them transform a bit (*tz*). Also, Noise TOP has a scaling parameter, so some of it has been stretched a bit in *x*. Of course, the expression `me.time.absFrame` (instead of `me.time.frame`) has been used to prevent discontinuity at loopback. To understand the parameters of Noise TOP a little better, have a look at **FractalNoise** COMP. Simplex noise, the default noise generator of Noise TOP, is similar to **Perlin** noise, which implements the idea of layering noise with different frequencies and amplitudes, a typical fractal idea. This COMP has been set up to be able to explore these different layers. In it, we layer these noises ourselves, giving us more flexibility for the cost in a way that's not as efficient as implementation.

However, there is more to learn about this COMP. Here, we first use **Replicator** COMP, so let's pause here a moment.

Replicator COMP

The official documentation of Replicator COMP can be found at `http://www.derivative.ca/wiki088/index.php?title=Replicator_COMP`.

Let's consider some more simple examples, and then come back to the noises. Lastly, we'll consider an example using a replicator in combination with cloning.

The first example we will talk about is `/project1/03_ReplicatorComp/simple`. Here, we find the basic setup of a replication: Replicator COMP, Table DAT, and some other OPs to be replicated. Replicator COMP takes a so-called master operator, in this case `slider1`, and creates a copy of it for every row in the table referenced in the **Template Table** parameter. Create or delete some rows in DAT (right-click on it and select **add/delete row**, or use its `rows` parameter). You will see sliders appear and disappear immediately. Can we modulate this behavior? Sure, have a look at `project1/03ReplicatorComp/DynamicExample`. When you get all this, the rest of Replicator COMP's parameters should be quite straightforward to understand. One of them should be mentioned though, the **Script** parameter. Here, we even have a drop-down menu that gives us some often-used expressions right away. One of them, for example, is `me.curItem.par.paneldisplay = 1`. Can you imagine what this does? If we use replication to create multiple UI elements, we often don't want the master to display only the replicants. If we turn off the master's `display` parameter (which makes it display on a panel; not to be confused with the display flag) and recreate the replicants, their `display` parameter will also be turned off. The given expression just turns them on. The `me` expression, in this case, is the Replicator COMP, `curItem` which is a member of it and represents each replicant that is created. The rest should be clear; we can just access OP's parameters via `par`. Refer to the following screenshot:

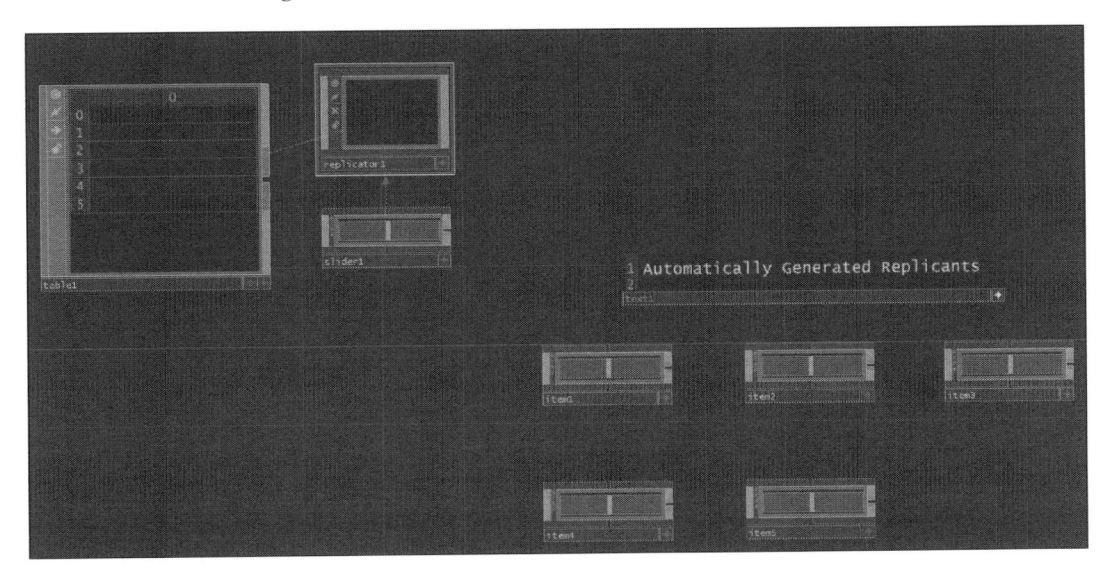

As in the preceding screenshot, our Table DAT looks so empty in these examples; we sure can do something with it. Let's look at **FractalNoise** COMP now, which has simply been copied to /project1/03_ReplicatorComp for your convenience. So, here Noise TOP is being replicated, and the DAT null2 is our Template Table. This time, it is filled, and it is filled using CHOPS. We will take a closer look at converting between OP families soon, so let's not think about this too much right now. If you look at the Noise TOP that is being replicated, which is noise1, its parameters are full of expressions. This might look scary, but it's really simple, and we'll take some time at this point.

So, most of the noise1 Noise TOP's parameters are simply linked to the noise2 Noise TOP's parameters. Why? Well, all replicant parameters are linked to just one noise TOP, right? Replicating does not mean that the parameters are the same as the master's parameters all the time. They are just initially the same, and then they are independent. So, this is just to control all of the Noise TOPs all the time from a central point.

The me.digits expression as a way to individualize replicants

There are three other expressions: the **Seed** option is set to me.digits+0.33, the **Period** option is set to op('null2')[me.digits, 'period'], and the **Amplitude** option is set to op('null2')[me.digits, 'period']. The me.digits expression accesses the integer that OPs have at the end of their names by default. So, for example, we get 1 if we enter me.digits into one of the parameters of the TOP noise1. If we do the same thing to the TOP noise2, we will get a return of 2. We use this to give each noise a different seed. Also, we add a float, which is just a good habit to prevent the unlikely event of similarities for different integer seeds.

> A seed for a random generator is an initial value. Noise generators or pseudo-random number generators produce sequences of values, most often in a recursive manner. The seed is the initial value (not at the output) of this process. For any particular given seed, the random sequence will always be identical and entirely predetermined, but seemingly random, and thus, pseudo-random.

Also, `me.digits` is quite handy since replicants are numbered, so we can use this number, for example, to look up a different value for each replicant from a table. This is exactly what we are doing. If we enter `op('null2 ')[me.digits, 'period']` in OP with the digit 3, for instance `item3`, we will look up what's in the cell in the third row (starting at 0) and the column named `period` of the OP called `null2`. So, each replicant looks up the amplitude and period from the table, which actually contains values generated using wave CHOPs.

Above all, this is a tiny script to connect the OPs to Composite TOP. So, if you change something in the master or want more Noise TOPs, you can just push the button to connect them again, or, of course, just select them all and drag them from one outlet to Composite TOP, and they all get connected. This might not seem very handy, but there are many cases where we don't really need to connect OPs, especially in UI design, creating lots of **Movie In** TOPs to access them using Select TOP or 3D, as we will later see in this chapter.

So, let's now take a look at one of the most handy ways to use replication, which is in combination with cloning. In the `COMP /Project1/03_Replicator/ReplicatorAndCloning` folder, you'll find a basic setup that is also depicted in the following screenshot:

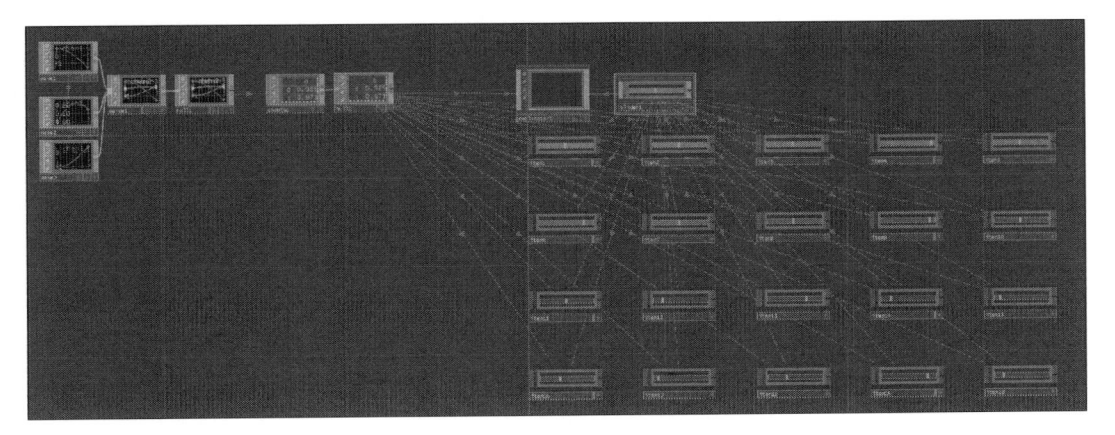

The idea is to put the master COMP in its own `Clone` parameter, so all the replicants will be clones of the master. If we now start using expressions in the master referencing CHOP channels, or more commonly, DAT cells, we can build very flexible big networks. We'll use these techniques along the way anyway, so let's leave this topic and come back to our initial aim, audio-reactive video. So, let's connect Max and TD now.

Connecting Max and TD

We can use Max to analyze audio to send the data to TD, or even better, if we generate audio in Max, we can just send the data generating the audio to TouchDesigner. There is no need to do FFT on a stereo sum if we can just get the parameters of a synth directly. Things such as BPM detection or fundamental pitch estimation are possible if we don't have the data directly, but they are, of course, a bit unreliable and unstable.

First, let's look at how Max and Touch can communicate. The weapon of choice here is UDP/OSC. **User Datagram Protocol** (**UDP**) is a protocol that is part of the transport layer of the OSI model. Compared to **Transport Control Protocol** (**TCP**), it has the advantage of being faster and the disadvantage of being more unreliable, which is not an issue for our purposes most of the time. OSC is, as you probably know, a very widespread protocol, that somewhat became the commonly accepted MIDI successor. We won't go very deep into the structure of OSC, so, for further information, refer to `http://opensoundcontrol.org/`.

A nice thing about OSC is that our messages can be composed in a hierarchical way, so, for example, we can send `/synthesizer1/filter/cutoff 1000`. Here, 1000 is, of course, the value, and everything else is the address. Values can also be lists or strings, but we will use floats most of the time. This is nearly everything we will learn about OSC, although we'll have to confront ourselves with queue sizes a bit. OSC has many more features, such as time tags and so on. Consider downloading the Max MSP externals by CNMAT to access these, which can be found at `http://cnmat.berkeley.edu/`.

Look at the component in `/project1/04_UDP`. Also, open the Max patcher UDP. All this is a bit overloaded; it's not only a simple OSC connection, there are also some tools to look at the performance of our connection. Let me strip it down a bit: what we really need for a working OSC communication between Max and TD is a `[udpsend]` object that gets a properly formatted message and has been given the right port and host address. On the TD side, we just need to put down an OSC in CHOP. So, what's all this? Refer to the following screenshot:

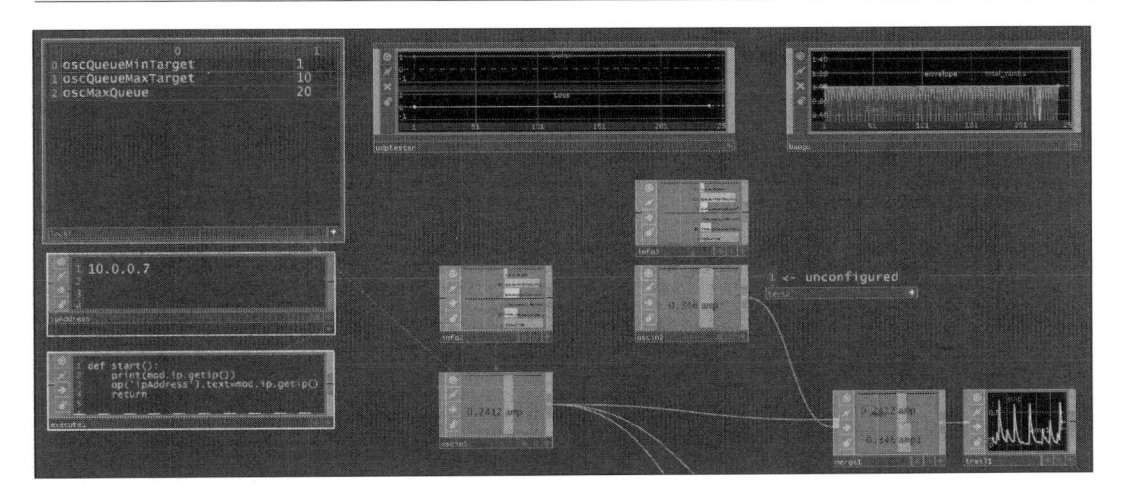

On the Max side, we do some simple envelope following and use [prepend] to compose a message that reads /amp 0 if there is nothing coming in. This message is sent to the IP address 127.0.0.1, so localhost, since we provided this as an argument and to the port 10000, the default port of the **OSC In** CHOP.

On the TouchDesigner side, we can see that there are two OSC In CHOPs, where the oscin1 parameters are partly configured using variables, and oscin2 is just as the default values. If you look at Trail CHOP, you can see that these aren't quite aligned, or more specifically, the one with the default values has a significant delay. Something to bear in mind in order to understand the parameters of OSC In CHOP and its behavior is that it outputs a stream. If we don't send something at some point in time, it will still output the last values received at the global sample rate/FPS of typically 60 Hz, by default. Therefore, it will repeat values if we send our messages too slow or drop messages if we send them too fast.

This is also the reason to have one central [metro] in Max, which triggers the audio-to-message rate conversion, and therefore, the message outputs at 60 Hz. Refer to the following screenshot:

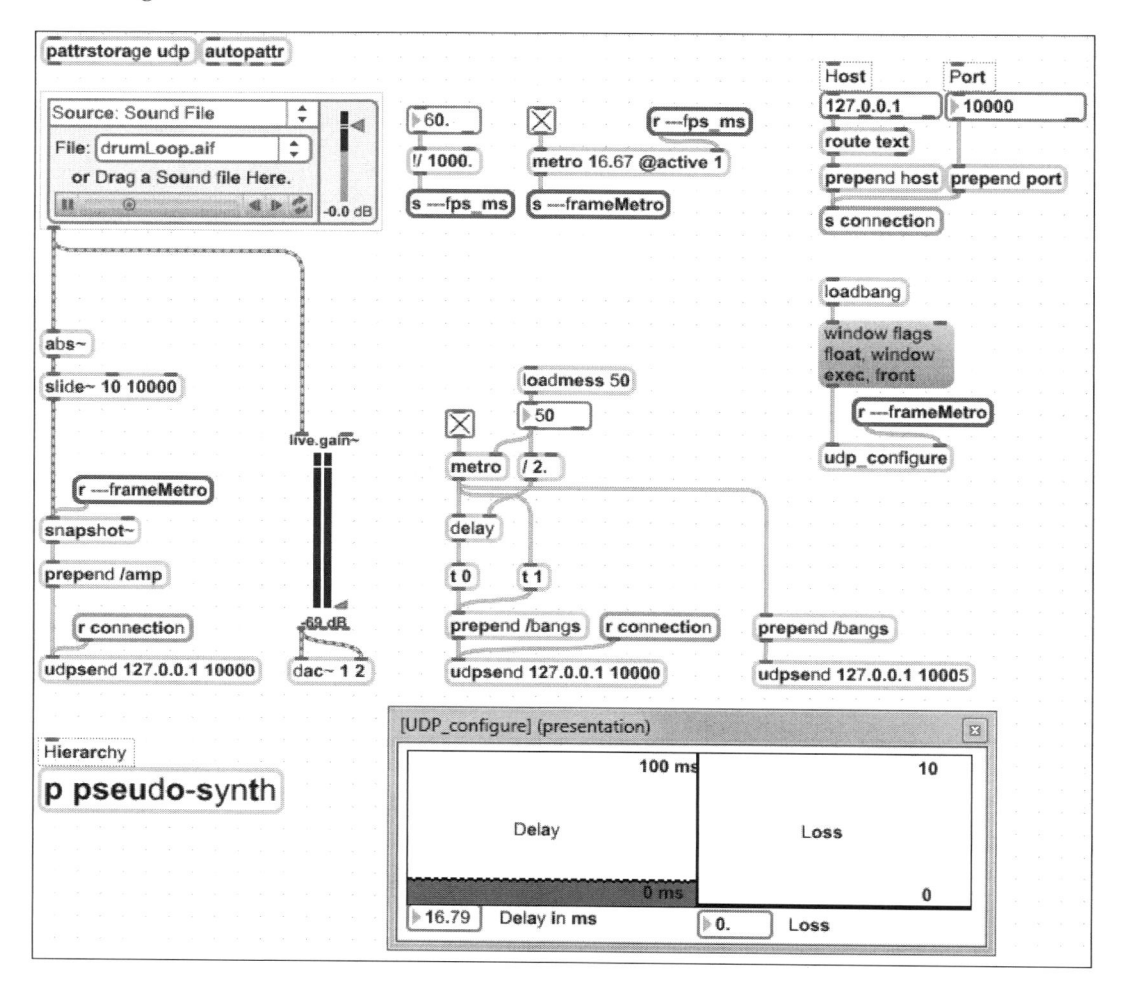

You might wonder what the queue might be or what it affects. We can compare it to audio buffers or Max's IO vector size. A long queue will cause a big latency, but, on the other hand, it will ensure a smooth output and help avoid repeated values and discontinuities. Keep in mind that often we don't necessarily need minimal latency; constant latency is required since we can delay the other side to line things up again, as shown in the following screenshot:

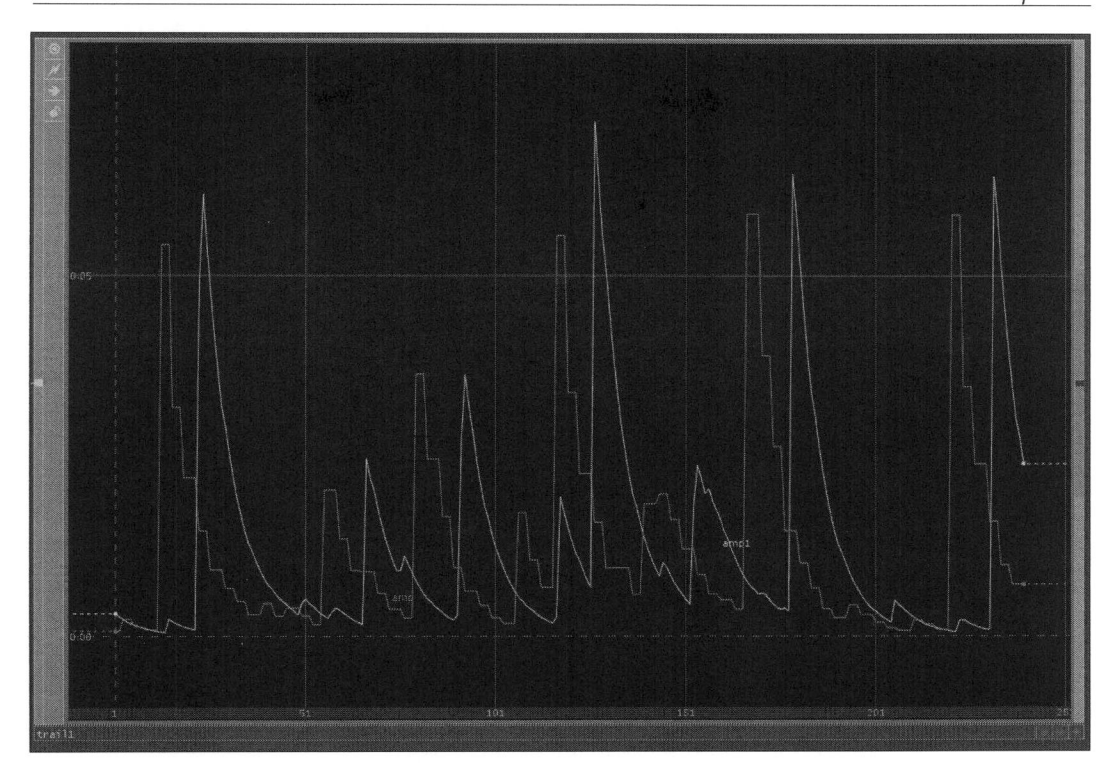

The **Max/Min Queue Target** parameters configure this balance between latency and reliability, and since it is a balance, there are obviously no values for them that will result in optimal performance in every situation. Therefore, the `udptester` container is set up to show us how our settings perform. All OSC In CHOPS in there get their parameters from the corresponding variables that were set up, of course. Go in there, and you will see the graphs it draws are made by sending values out of TD and receiving them in TD again. The `oscin1` and `oscin2` parameters are in there to form a loop generating the graphs in Max, which also show us information about how our connection performs. Try out some values for Max/Min Queue Target, and use Hog CHOP to see how the settings behave if your system is a bit stressed. Notice that the `oscin1` CHOP's parameter, **OSC Address Scope**, is set to **/amp**, so we only receive these messages. Often, we'd like to take advantage of OSC's hierarchical possibilities. On the TD side, this is easy; have a look at the **hierarchicalDispatch** COMP. The important thing is what pattern matching is. We encountered some of this already when we created three channels of noise by setting Noise CHOP's **Channel Name** parameter to `t[xyz]`, resulting in `tx ty tz`. Here we use `*` to match any sequence of characters inside Select CHOPs. For some more pattern matching, refer to http://www.derivative.ca/wiki088/index.php?title=Pattern_Matching.

Advanced Visualization Using TouchDesigner

On the Max side, we need some externals to pack our OSC packages efficiently and correctly. There are ways around this; the first and foremost is the [sprintf] object, but I'd recommend that you use the CNMAT externals and have a look at the subpatcher pseudo-synth.

As I said, the basic OSC setup is very simple, so don't be scared about all of these problems and special cases being addressed here; however, there are two more things we should briefly talk about. The first is how to get our beloved bang into Touch. We probably want to create a CHOP channel from this bang very often, so receive a single event and create a signal. Since we already stated that UDP can have loss, although it's not very probable, this isn't a very good idea. Also, CHOPs can't handle string values, so sending the OSC message, /ourbangs "bang", will be ignored by CHOP. OSC In DAT can handle these, and you can see an example in /project1/04_UDP/bangs. It is in contrast a better idea to convert our bangs into a stream of floats/ints on the Max side and send it out. You'll find examples of both.

> Note that we use a Python function to find out our IP address within TD. The Text DAT ipAddress is set by an execute DAT that is docked to it and executed at startup. This in turn calls a Python function that is stored in a module at local/modules and was found by a quick web search. Getting an IP address inside Python doesn't have a lot to do with TouchDesigner, and is a pretty standard task. This is a typical case for lots of Python programmers who rely on the Internet.

Now, let's finally examine the fun part of the little network. Noise TOP moves through the noises spaced by the integration of the amplitude coming in. Speed CHOP does the integration for us. This noise is then used to displace/distort the incoming image, but not all of the image's channels. On TOP's common page (Displace TOP, in this case) in the **Parameter** dialog, we can deactivate the processing per channel (configure the **Channel Mask** parameter), and here, we only distort the green and blue channels.

A component for lots of movies

Finally, take a look at the image that is fed into our chain. A component, which is also depicted in the following screenshot, has been set up to let us access all image files that come with the TD installation:

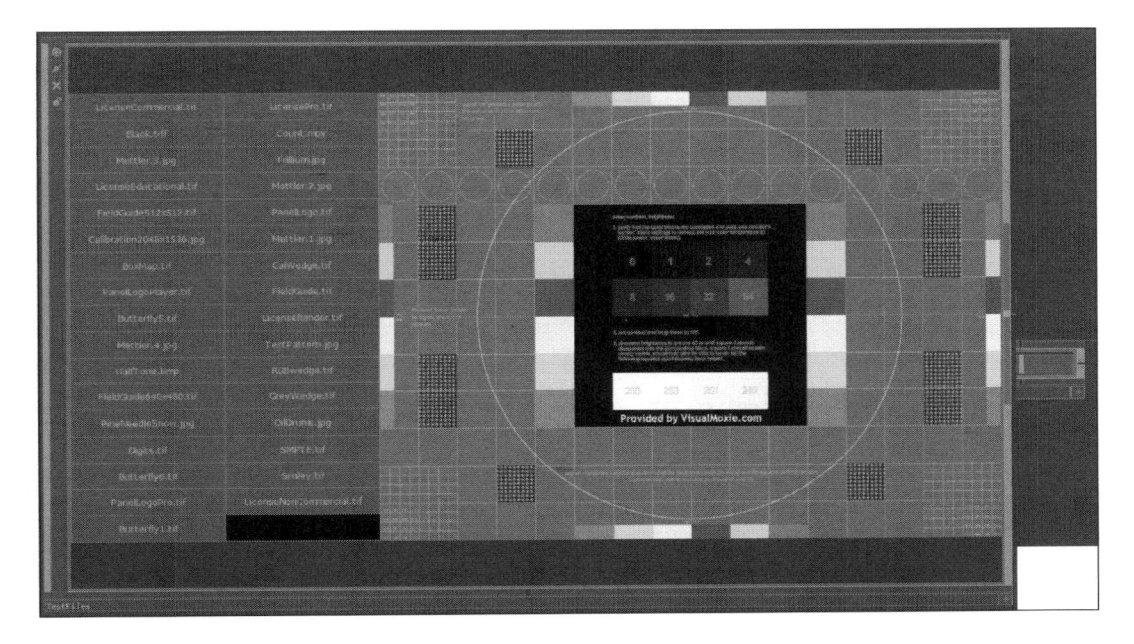

Here, we again use Replicator COMP to produce all Movie In TOPs. The paths to the files as well as the container's Template Table are the `null1` DAT, which are filled by a folder DAT that points to the directory. Field COMP accesses the filenames, and we place a panel CHOP in it to get out the number of the button we click on. Our friend Select TOP does the rest. This structure is something to bear in mind if there is a need to use lots of movies. If we want to have this COMP in our palette, we can just drag it there; the OP Viewer TOP called **icon** allows a nice little picture of COMP to appear in the palette; the text DAT called **help** allows us to have some description in the palette.

Converting between OP families

Switching between OP families is a very powerful tool, but it can sometimes be a very resource-consuming process (especially a TOP-to-CHOP conversion if **Download Type** is switched to **immediate (slow)**). Of course, it's important to be aware of the possibilities of conversion since certain operations on data are often difficult in one domain and straightforward in another; therefore, even switching back and forth can sometimes make a lot of sense. You'll find COMP at /project1/05_OPconversion if there are a couple of example conversions. Sometimes, data needs to be prepared in a certain way for the conversion to work. For example, CHOP data needs to be in the range of 0 to 1 for a conversion to TOP, and DAT needs to have certain titles in its first row to tell DAT and SOP which column means what. You'll find two OP family full cycles, so go through all the families until we arrive at the family we started at. One of them is depicted in the following screenshot:

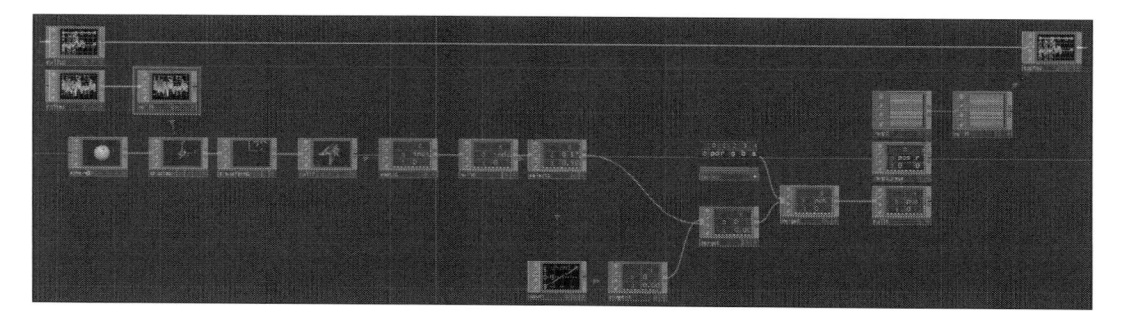

Since these cycles are somewhat theoretical, you'll find some more practical examples in COMP useful. Here, we see how to create visual patterns using CHOPS, make a smooth curve out of a table with defined values, get some glitchy sound directly out of an image, make a beautiful-sounding oscillator out of a 3D circle, and some other 3D jazz. They are either quite straightforward or there is too much 3D involved to allow us to talk about it before we actually come to SOPs. However, no worries, we'll convert around a lot, so this will all get familiar anyway. Be sure to take a close look at these examples:

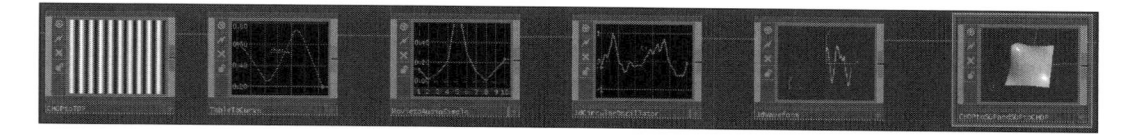

Dealing with time

As you have seen, most things in TD can be/are ignorant of time, frame number, and looping. Sometimes, we need to sequence things, coordinate more complex animations, and so on. You already know the timeline at the bottom of TD's interface. Refer to the following screenshot:

Nearly all the buttons should be pretty self explanatory. We have the usual transport control, the possibility to step ahead or back one frame using the big **+** and **-** buttons, and above this are handles to loop only certain regions of the timeline. By moving these handles, we adjust the **RStart** and **REnd** (range start and range end) values at the left of the timeline. Here, we can also change how many FPSes we like (it's highly recommended to do this at the beginning of a project and not later) and how long our timeline should be. Two things might be a bit mysterious though—the big **I** button and the time path at the very bottom. Both of these have to do with the fact that the timeline is actually controlling a component's time. Every component can have its own time. A component time can be created by just right-clicking in an empty area inside the component and choosing **Add Component Time...**. What we get is a local Base component and Time COMP inside. Also, we get a mini timeline at the bottom of our editor, sitting right on top of our regular one. Refer to the following screenshot:

This mini timeline again has the **I** and **S** buttons. The **I** symbol stands for run independent, so regardless whether the main timeline, or rather the next component time upwards in the network hierarchy, has stopped or is playing, it will play or stop as we tell it to. The **S** symbol stands for scope, which means that we want to control this mini timeline using the normal timeline controls. If we do so, the timeline turns into another color, indicating we are not controlling the main time anymore; the big **I** button will suddenly be available and do just the same as the small one, and the time path will show us the path of the component whose time we control. If we want to go back to our normal timeline control, we can just press the **/** button next to the time path. You might assume this already: the Time COMP we control with the default timeline is, of course the **/** button's, or the root component's, time that's always located at `/local/time`.

Advanced Visualization Using TouchDesigner

> A local time can never have a higher frame rate than the root timeline; it can only have lower ones. So, if the main timeline runs at 30 FPS, a local timeline can't have 60 FPS.

I'd recommend you to go ahead and make a component, give it a local time, and play around a bit to find out what things are dependent on time and what's not. However, of course, you can go right to /project1/06_time/aLocalTime. Here, you'll find some OPs that are bound to the timeline. Refer to the following screenshot:

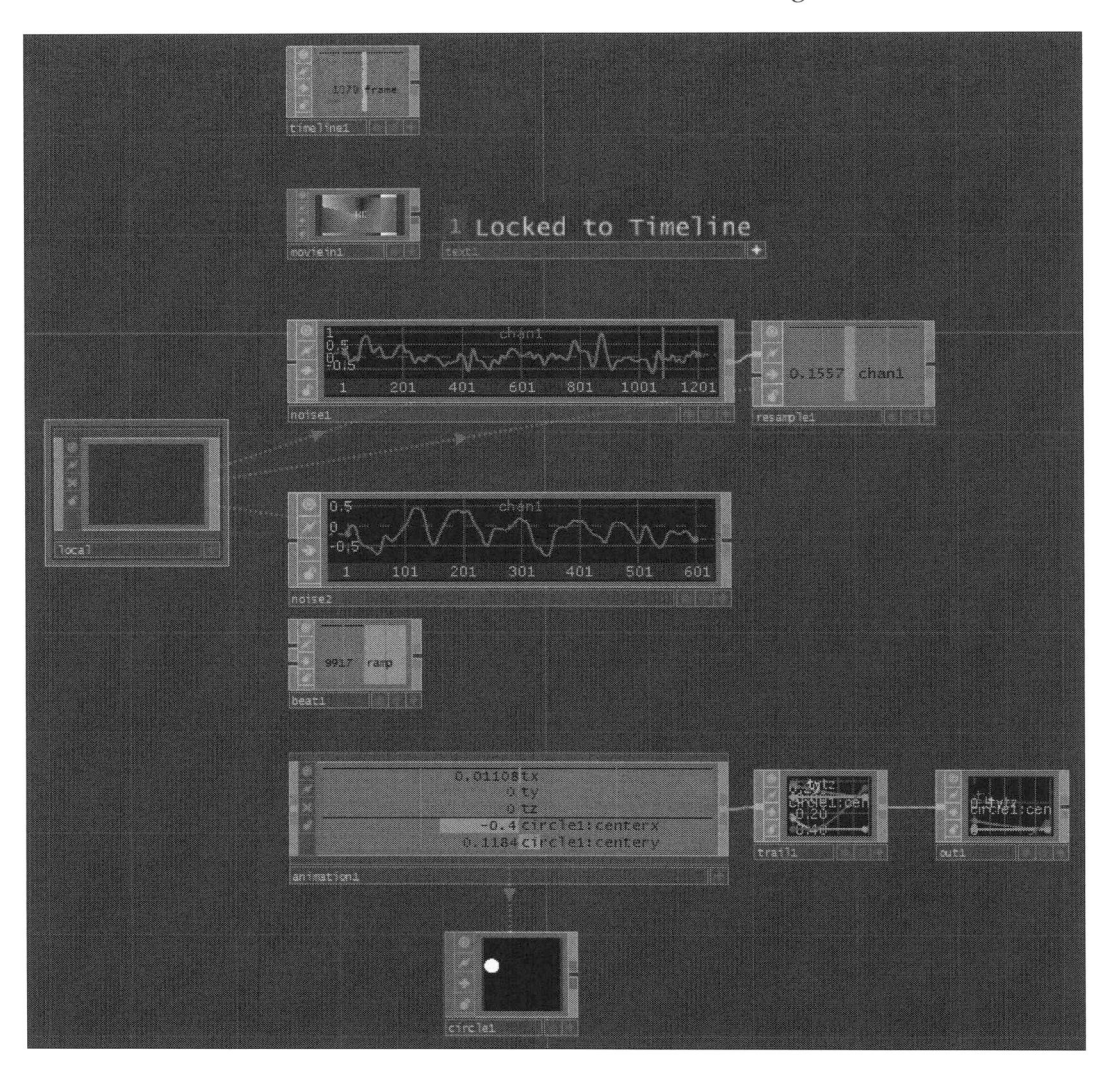

So, as examples of time dependent OPs, we have the following:

- A timeline CHOP that just outputs the current frame number
- Movie In TOP whose **Play Mode** parameter has been set to **Locked To Timeline**
- Noise CHOP that hasn't been changed at all, but which samples its values according to the timeline
- Noise CHOP that is transformed in z by the expression `me.time.frame/10`
- Beat CHOP
- An animation COMP

All of these are dependent on the timeline's state. Surely, the animation COMP has caught your attention, but before we think about this, we'll have a look at controlling time some more.

If you look at the **basicControl** COMP, you will find another COMP in there that has its own time. This time is controlled from the outside of COMP. This is important to avoid recursion errors. In general, it is not a very good idea to modulate the frame rate of a whole component since too many things, such as time slicing, depend on it. However, it is a fun thing to do, but just be warned. Also, there are other things we might like to control, such as starting or stopping a component's time, which works the same way. The key is to manipulate things from outside and activate clone immune, including children (press the clone immune flag twice), at Time COMP inside local. If we did this, we can start messing around in there, for example, overriding the frame number as it's done here:

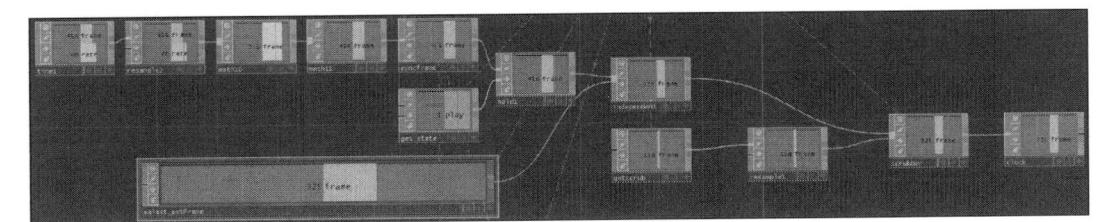

A more useful example is located at `/project1/time/twotimes`. What's done here is that we have two identical COMPs; the only difference is that one of them has a reddish output TOP. From outside, their times are controlled. At frame 1, the LocalTime COMP has been reset already, and it's time it started. At frame 198, a transition begins, the LocalTime1 COMP is started, and Cross TOP is animated. The transition will go on till Frame 278, then the first COMP will be stopped and reset. The second COMP will run until Frame 600, where it is reset and we have a hard cut to the beginning again. This can be pretty useful, but it seems a bit crowded and not very elegant.

> Is this really useful if we have many scenes? What about transitions? Try to come up with a more generic system!

This might be a hard task, but certainly, if you try it, you will learn a lot and put a lot of thought into structure. If you take a shot at it, look at `/project1/06_time/manyTimes`. We use cloning to create the infrastructure needed. If we have a couple of scenes, each sits inside a core COMP, which is inside COMP with a local time, which in turn is controlled via some logic, all of which sits inside a clone. The core here can be seen as a template featuring fetching the previous scene and managing a possibly individual transition. Since all the techniques used in this example have been talked about already, but are combined in a bit more complex way, we won't talk about it; but you should just take a look at it yourself.

The Animation component

The official documentation of the Animation component can be found at `http://www.derivative.ca/wiki088/index.php?title=Animation_COMP`.

The Animation component is a very handy tool, and you shouldn't think it's only useful for linear work. We can put down one of them, right-click on it, and choose **Edit Animation...** to open the **Animation Editor** window. Most of this editor will seem very familiar if you are used to editing cores or automations in DAW or animation programs such as After Effects, 3D Studio Max, Maya, and so on.

More information on Animation editors can be found at `http://www.derivative.ca/wiki088/index.php?title=Animation_Editor`. Refer to the following screenshot:

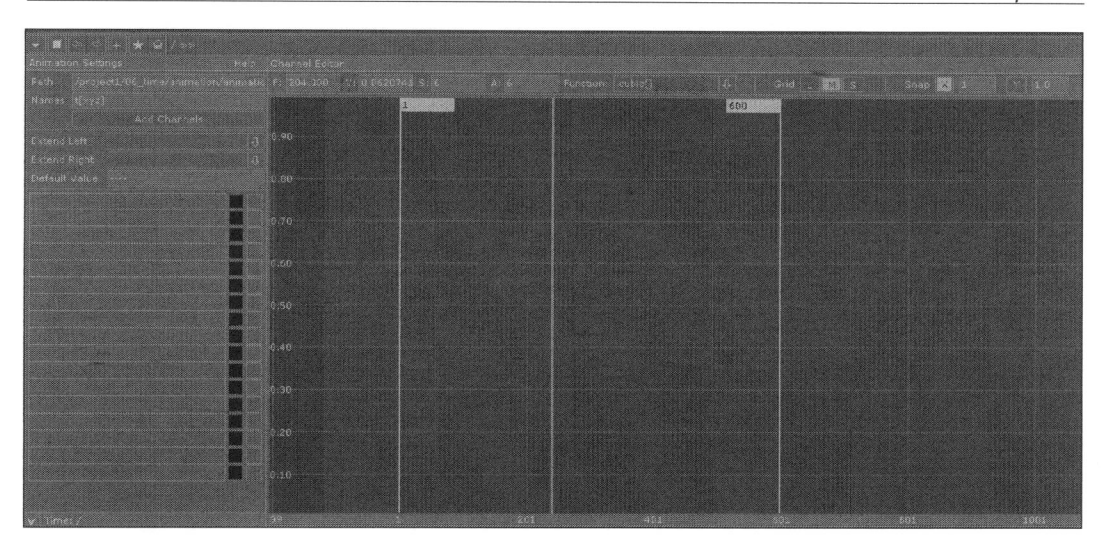

What we have here is the easiest way to create and edit curves in TD. We can add channels with the **Add Channels** button, of course, and we can give them names by editing the **Name** field before creating a channel. Note that this field allows pattern matching, so t[xyz] will give us three channels at once, which are called tx ty tz. Adding new keyframes is done by selecting a curve, *alt*, and clicking on the desired area. The navigation is coherent with the rest of TD's GUI, so we can zoom in/out with the middle mouse button, pan around clicking on the left mouse button, and select the box clicking on the right mouse button. In the topmost toolbar, we can specify the keyframe properties. We can set its exact frame number, value, interpolation coefficients (availability depends on chosen interpolation method), and interpolation algorithm. Also, we can adjust the grid and configure the snapping of keyframes here. Another thing to notice is that we can activate the little pink box next to a channel to activate its Template flag. The Template flag is something we will encounter again when we finally come to some serious 3D rendering; it basically enables us to compare things. A channel that is templated will be displayed dotted, but won't be editable.

To make use of the channels we created, we can, of course, reference Out CHOP of Animation COMP with an expression such as `op('animation1/out1')['chan1']`, we can just use regular CHOP exporting, or use Select CHOP anywhere where we need our curves, which might be the most useful variant. There is another way though. We can simply right-click on any parameter, select **Keyframe Parameter in...**, and choose the animation COMP we want to use. It's often convenient to do it this way, but then our handy null CHOP middleman isn't there for us to easily insert motion FX like Lag CHOP, Spring CHOP, or other Mathematics between the curve and parameter. One of the key concepts behind CHOPs, or TD in general, is procedural animation, so directly linking a parameter to a curve is again sometimes handy, but a bit cumbersome to revert, and we lose the convenience of combining OPs to shape a motion more procedurally.

Using the animation COMP for nonlinear purposes

I guess you are comfortable with Animation Editor, so let's talk about the animation COMP. We already talked about the idea of using the animation COMP for nonlinear work. This is mainly possible because of the following reasons:

- We can choose to drive our animation with an external source
- We can configure its **Play Mode** parameter to **Use Input Index** for an example to feed in any channel and essentially use our animation channels as an interpolating lookup table
- We might come up with a system that calls a random cue point if **Play Mode** is set to **Sequential**
- We configure its **Play Mode** to **Output Full Range**, essentially outputting the complete curve

Examples of these techniques can be found at `/project1/06_time/animation`. Having one animation COMP with many cues might seem a bit cumbersome. What we win using this technique is, of course, a central place to edit our curves; what we lose is flexibility. If you compare the **randomCue** COMP to the **manyAnimatios** COMP, you will see what I mean. However, there are many ways to achieve something like this. What's missing in the manyAnimations COMP, to be really equivalent, is just adding all the channels together, combining them to one.

Lastly, do not underestimate the **Play Mode Output Fullrange** option. It simply outputs the complete curve that is perfect for the many situations in which we might need to map some values to another range of values in a nonlinear way. In the following example COMP contrastCurve, it is used as an easily editable curve defining an image's contrast:

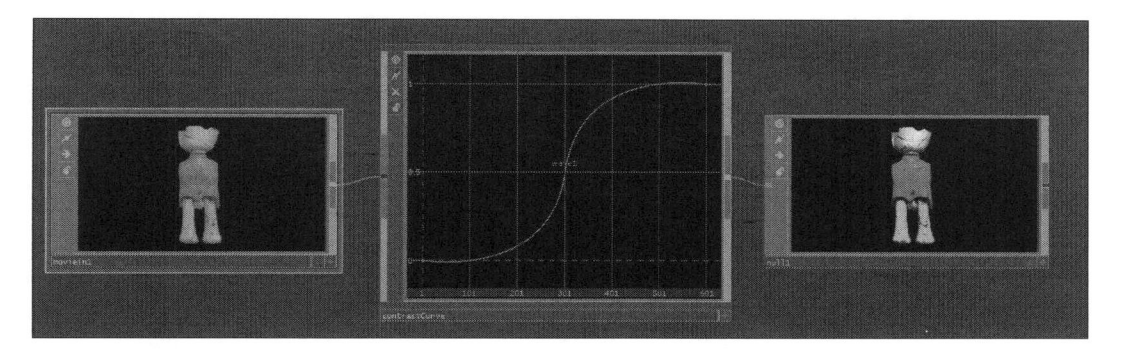

Synchronization

We have a couple of options to synchronize TD's time to an external master. Here, we will only talk about syncing to Ableton/Max/Max4Live. However, here we also have a couple of options: we can go with MIDI, OSC, or even audio as an interface. To add still more options, the question we have to ask is what we'd like to synchronize. We can, for example, only synchronize one or more animation COMPs, which might suffice in many cases, and it is a very straightforward thing to do. Do we want to have a beat ramp inside TD to just know the beat in there? We might not be interested in the playback position of Live's or Max transport. Do we really want to synchronize the time of a component, or just send some cues?

First of all, there is an official method to synchronize TD to Ableton Live. It is very powerful, has a lot of features, is well documented, and can be found at `http://www.derivative.ca/wiki088/index.php?title=Ableton`. However, we won't talk about this at all for two reasons: it is well documented and quite complex. We won't always need this complexity, and it's often preferable to thoroughly understand what we are working with. So, let's start with simply sending a synchronized ramp out of Max with the `sync1.maxpat` patcher, depicted in the following screenshot, and see where it gets us. Don't forget all the things we learned about timing accuracy in Max; otherwise, the patch won't do any good.

Advanced Visualization Using TouchDesigner

We really want a very stable signal in TD. Refer to the following screenshot:

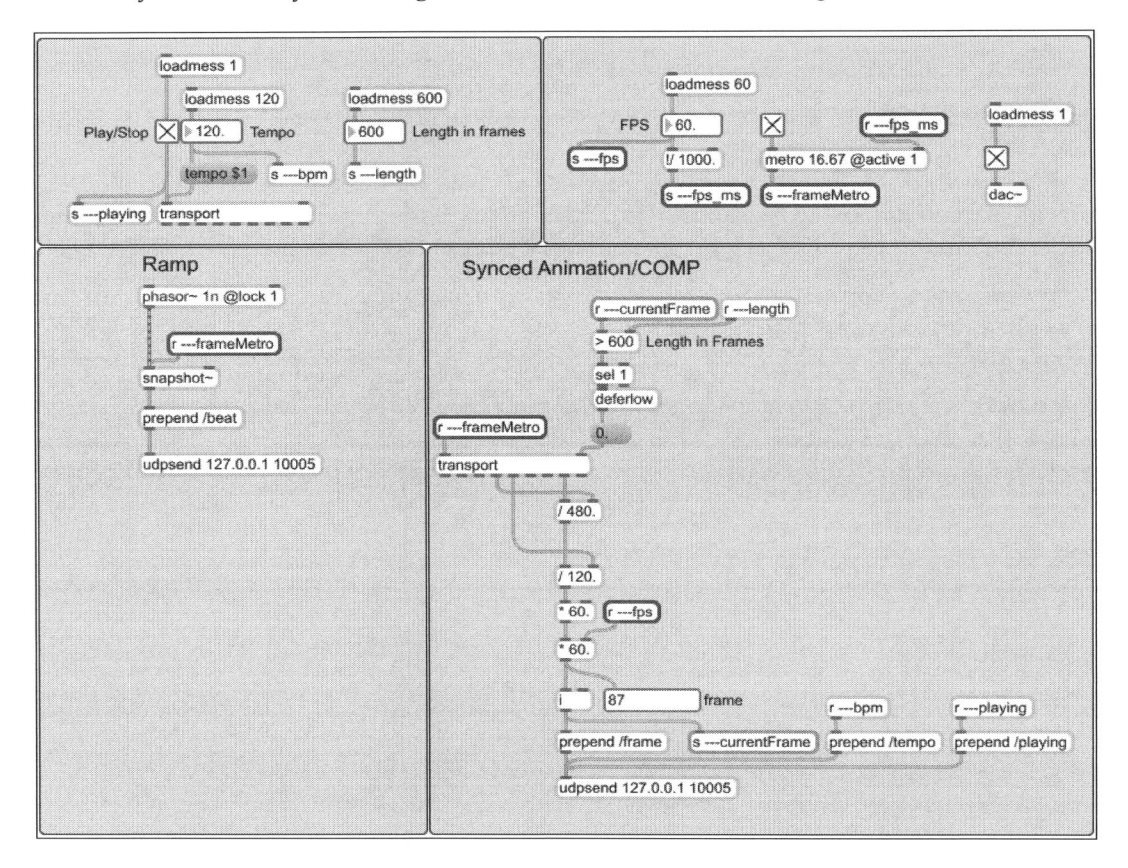

So, the COMP present at `/project1/06_time/synchronization/ramp` gets Max's [phasor~] sampled at 60Hz via UDP, in this case. This signal can then be used to sync up some Beat CHOPs to get any subdivision.

> With some clever resetting logic, I'm sure you can come up with some Beat CHOPs that are slower than the input, for example, two beats. Give it a shot!

Alright, so the whole beat thing is done pretty quickly. I guess the next one should also be easy for you—syncing up an animation COMP. We just calculate a frame number in Max from the transport and send out this number. Also, we make Max's transport loop. This frame number is then just fed into the animation COMP, which is, of course, in **Use Input Index Play Mode**. If we get this, syncing up a component's time is just one step further. You'll find examples of both in the synchronization COMP. Now, I also mentioned MIDI and audio as possible synchronization methods. Getting the MIDI input in general is simple; there is MIDI in CHOP and MIDI in DAT for this purpose. However, getting sync working isn't easy and not quite worth the trouble as we have better alternatives such as OSC. What about audio?

SMPTE LTC

Audio might be the wrong term; what I meant is to use a SMPTE timecode sent over audio drivers/devices. SMPTE and LTC stand for **Society of Motion Picture and Television Engineers** and **Linear** (or Longitudinal) **Time Code**, respectively. Refer to the following screenshot:

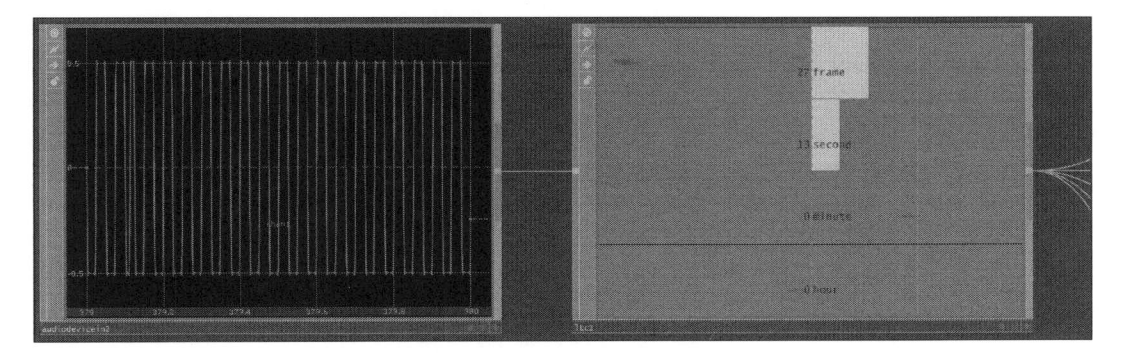

We'll quickly go over SMPTE usage, but the bad news is that SMPTE LTC officially only goes up to 30 FPS. If you are happy with this frame rate, SMPTE is the best choice. It's stable, has constant latency if sent over audio interfaces, and is a widely used standard. What we can do to get this working is simply download a SMPTE WAV file containing a suitable timecode, or generate one ourselves. To do this ourselves, we have many options, for example, the website `http://elteesee.pehrhovey.net/` offers us a timecode maker. Also, there is a Max external `[smpte~]` available at `http://cycling74.com/toolbox/smpte/`. If we get this, we can just put the WAV file in an audio track of any DAW, or play it back in Max, sending it to TouchDesigner.

The connection between DAW, for instance, and TD can either be made via Jack Audio (http://jackaudio.org/) or Soundflower (http://cycling74.com/soundflower-landing-page/) if DAW is running on the same computer as TD, or just via outputting the audio stream and getting it back into TD via Audio Device In CHOP. In COMP LTC, you'll find an example of syncing COMP to SMPTE LTC.

Audio ramp

Since audio rate synchronization is very appealing due to its constant latency and high sample rate, we'll make an attempt to create our own primitive protocol that features 60 FPS. We'll just come up with a ramp that indicates the time, create it at the audio rate, and send it into TD to down sample it, decode it, and use it to control time. Refer to the following screenshot:

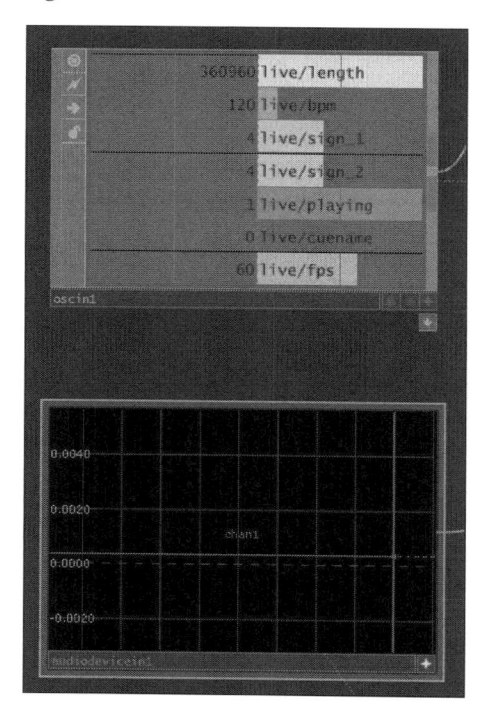

This has the advantage of giving us 60 FPS, which LTC won't, and have constant latency, which UDP won't. However it is, although working perfectly fine in most circumstances, it's a stupid idea since we lose the robustness of binary code. This simple ramp cannot be transmitted via analog audio output/input since it will most likely be messed up by gain mismatch, anti aliasing, anti imaging, and DC blocking filters. So, if you use this technique, use digital ins/outs such as ADAT, SPDIF, or stay in the box with Soundflower or Jack Audio.

The creation of this ramp and the accompanying Max4Live device is described in the Max4Live section of this book. Here, we will just look at COMP that receives the `/project1/06_time/synchronization/AbletonLiveAudioSync` ramp. We receive the ramp with Audio Device In CHOP and some data via UDP as the total length of our live set. Multiplying the ramp with the length in frames gives us the frame number; the rest is more or less the same as in the other time control examples. The Max4Live device generating the ramp is called `Tdsync_AudioRate_2.amxd` and is present in the folder of this chapter.

UDP

Finally, be aware that syncing Ableton Live or other sync masters via UDP is also an option, which is demonstrated in AbletonLiveUDPsync COMP and its pendant, the `Max4Live Device TimeSync_4.amxd` patcher. Refer to the following screenshot:

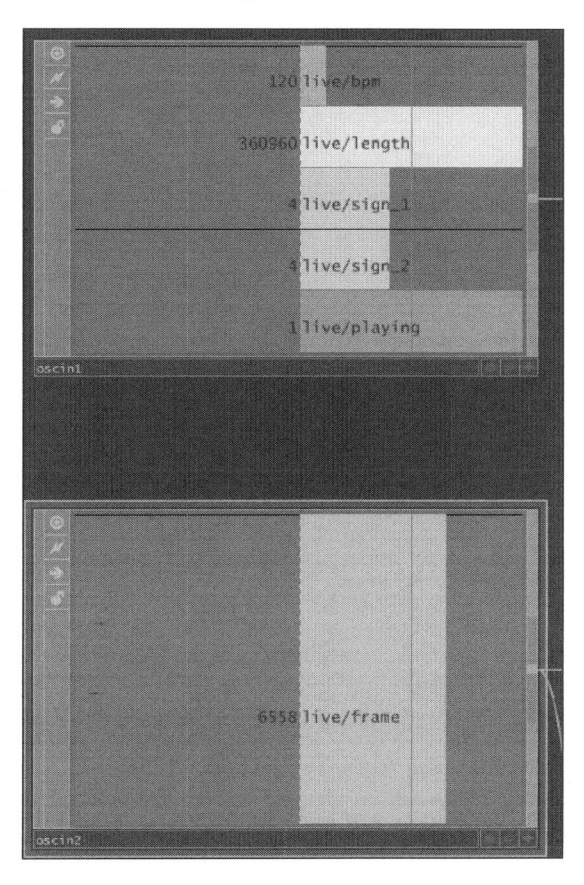

[301]

This might even be the most obvious way to do it; the problem is that if we sync a COMP's time, TD is quite sensitive to Jitter, and UDP doesn't guarantee constant latency. Nevertheless, try it, it's for sure the most convenient method if we don't hit its limits.

Introducing 3D rendering

We have actually met SOPs a lot already, but always kind of ignored them. Before we get to know them a bit better, let's start with the basics that will get us started rendering. Refer to the following screenshot:

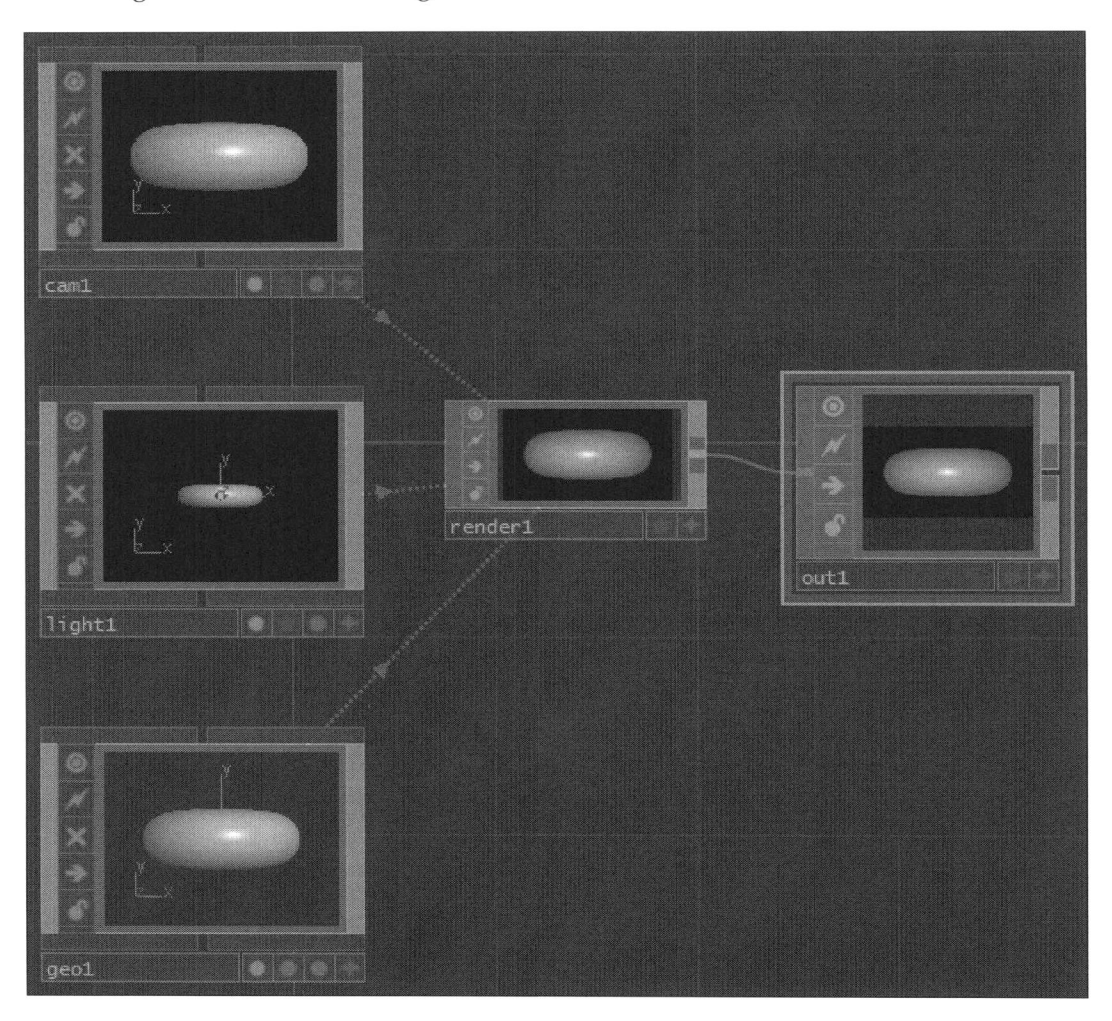

What you see in the preceding screenshot is a basic setup to render 3D content in TouchDesigner. We create Render TOP, the central point where our three-dimensional information gets converted into two-dimensional frames. To actually draw a (shaded) scene, we need at least the following:

- Geo COMP (to insert geometry to be drawn)
- Light COMP (to light up our scene and make shading possible)
- Camera COMP (to let us define how to look at our scene)
- Render TOP (to draw the scene)

Render TOP allows us to draw geometry, and what geometry is supposed to draw is configured on the **Render** page of its parameter dialog. Refer to the following screenshot:

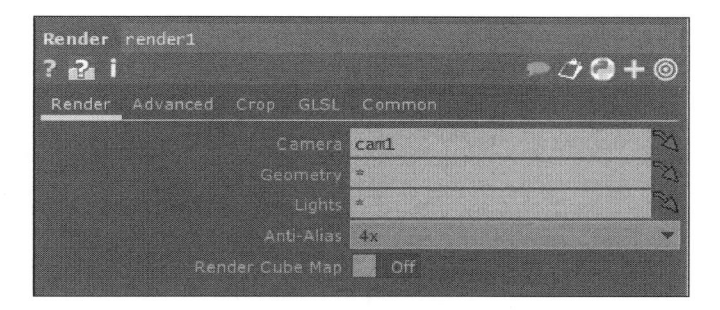

As you can see, by default, pattern matching is used to draw all **Geometry** COMPs that are found. The same is true for **Light** COMPs. As a camera, **Camera** COMP is used; it's called cam1, which is the default name of Camera COMP we put down in a network. Therefore, if you make a new network, just put down these nodes. They will automatically work; all will be referenced by default in Render TOP. Since we are at it, let's cover Anti-aliasing too. In general, rendering a 3D scene is done by sampling a three-dimensional space to a two-dimensional space. As we know from the audio realm, sampling is a process that works perfectly under some conditions. Here, we sample in space instead of in time, and aliasing appears in a spatial domain too, of course. If you look at the following picture, you will see a box being rendered twice:

Here, the left picture was created with Render TOP's anti-alias parameter set to **1x** with a setting of **32x**. You hopefully can see the jagged edges on the left; on the right, a lot more anti-aliasing has been used, so up sampling and interpolating essentially makes them disappear. If you can't see the edges properly, you can also go to the `/project1/rendering/antiAliasingPlayground` COMP. Here, you can play around with different settings. Don't be surprised, there are a lot of Light COMPs in there. This is to make our graphics card work a bit. Anti-aliasing happens on the GPU, and all the work that is done on the GPU is not visible in the cook time we see when we click on the middle mouse button on OP, for example. So, we can't simply inspect the performance drain of GPU intense tasks. We can, however, inspect the GPU memory used via Performance CHOP and see the frame rate going down if our GPU can't do what we ask. So, Light COMPs are there to challenge the GPU and make the drain caused by high anti-aliasing visible. Delete/add Light COMPs, according to your systems specs, and see that anti-aliasing can quickly eat up GPU memory and cycles.

SOPs

Surface Operators (SOPs) are operators containing information about points in three-dimensional space and are computed on the CPU. They have somewhat different flags, so let's look at these first:

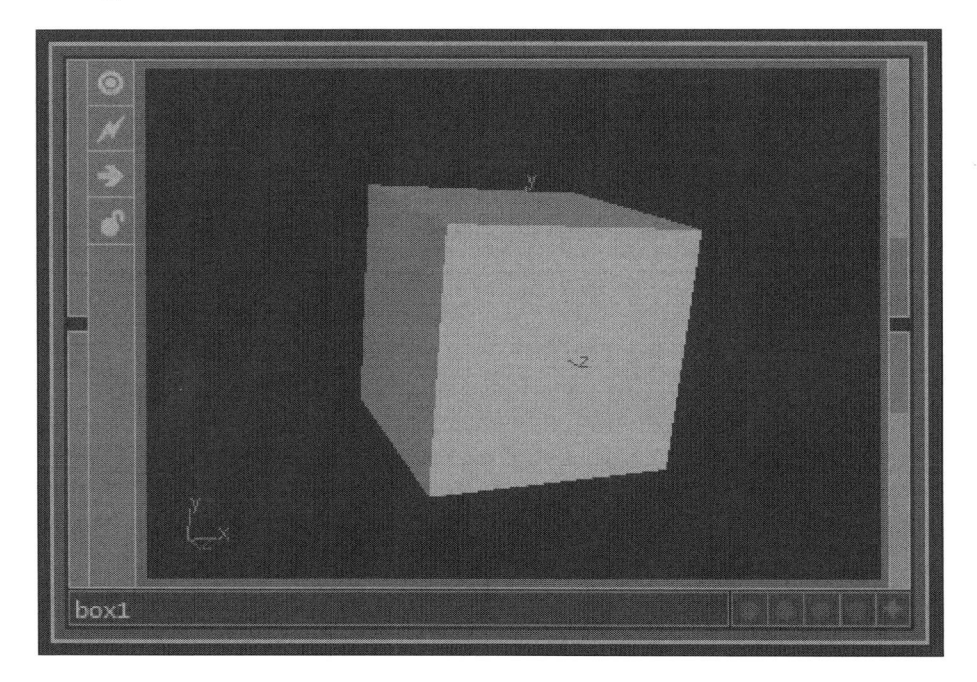

From left to right, we have the following flags:

- **Compare flag**: The compare flag allows us to see the OP's input in its viewer; therefore, we can compare what it does to its source OP easily. In the following screenshot, you can see a sphere that has been scaled down using Transform SOP whose compare flag is on:

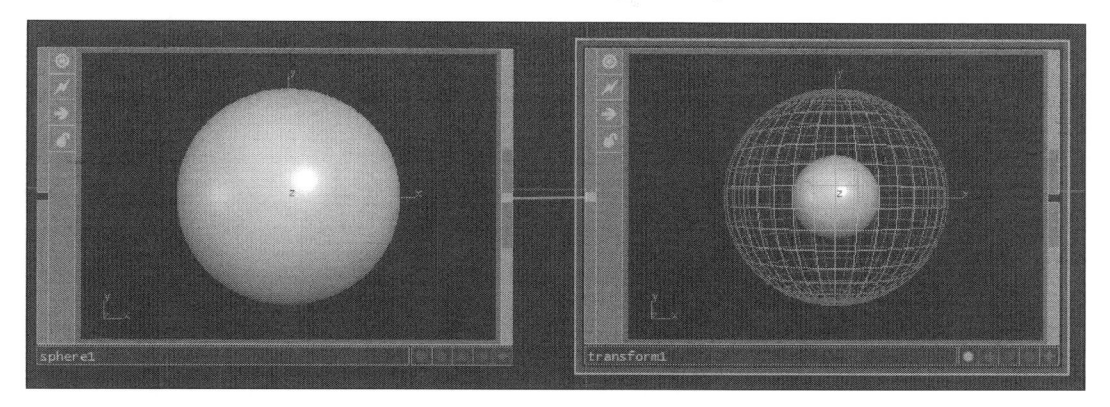

- **Template flag**: Remember we had the template flag in Animation Editor? This is basically the same. All the SOP flags decide where and how to show the containing geometry. The template flag shows us this piece of geometry in the **Geometry Viewer** window as a templated wireframe model with a pinkish color. We can make any pane to view the **Geometry Viewer** window. In the following screenshot, you can see a setup where the right pane is in **Geometry Viewer Mode**, the same network has been used again, and the bigger sphere has been templated to be visible in the viewer:

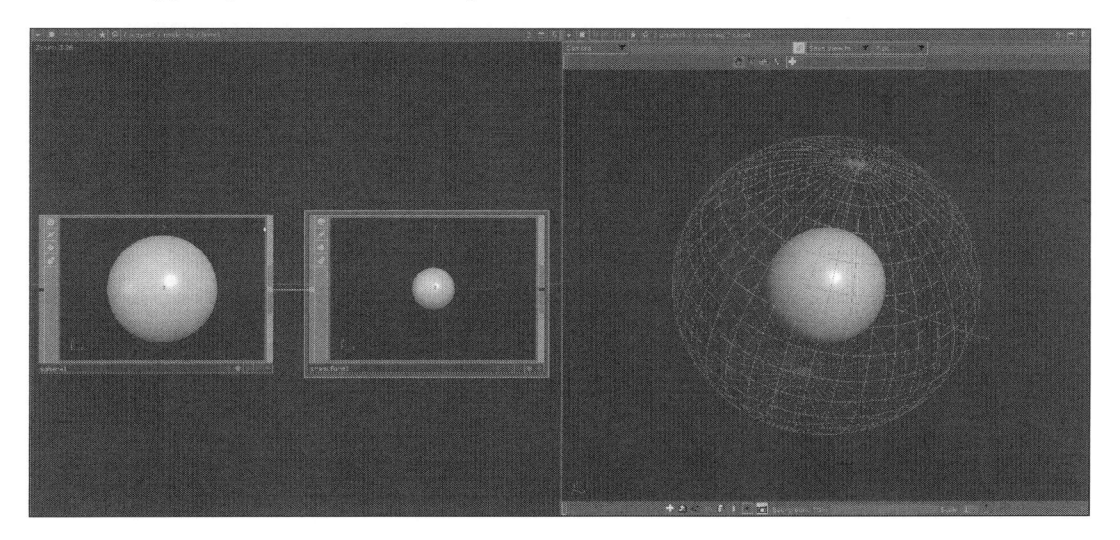

- **Render flag**: The render flag is like an output to the renderer. SOPs with their render flags set to on in Geometry COMPs that are referenced by Render TOPs will be drawn in this Render TOP. Often, a SOP network ends with Null SOP, with its render and display flags activated.
- **Display flag**: The display flag decides if SOP is visible in **Geometry Viewer** and the viewer of its parent COMP and if its Geometry COMP. Also, as TOP's or CHOP's display flag will do, it decides if the OP is displayed on the backdrop. By default, though, the display of SOPs on the backdrop is switched off. For any network viewer, you can change this by right-clicking and navigating to **Display | Backdrop Geometry**.

When we work with SOPs, it's a good idea to dedicate some of our workspace to **Geometry Viewer**, just to keep track of everything.

Assigning a material

Now, let's do something more motivating; a noisy reflective torus. The basic setup is like before, but we add **Material Operator (MAT)**, namely, Phong MAT and Movie In TOP. Also, we modify the SOP network inside Geometry COMP. Refer to the following screenshot:

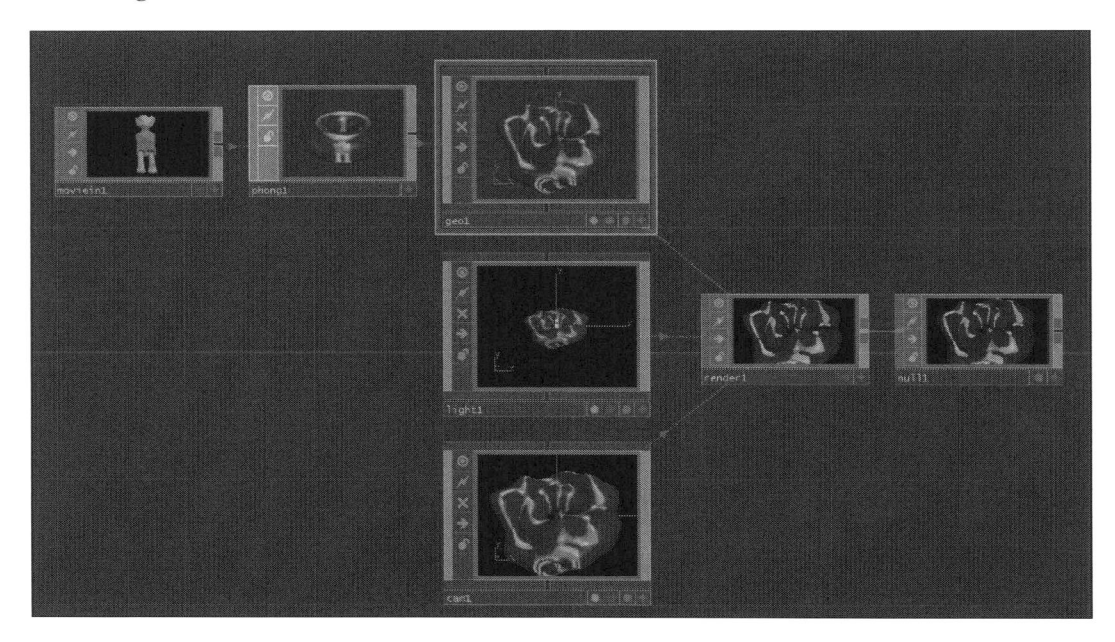

However, before talking about Phong MAT, let's visit the SOP network. Refer to the following screenshot:

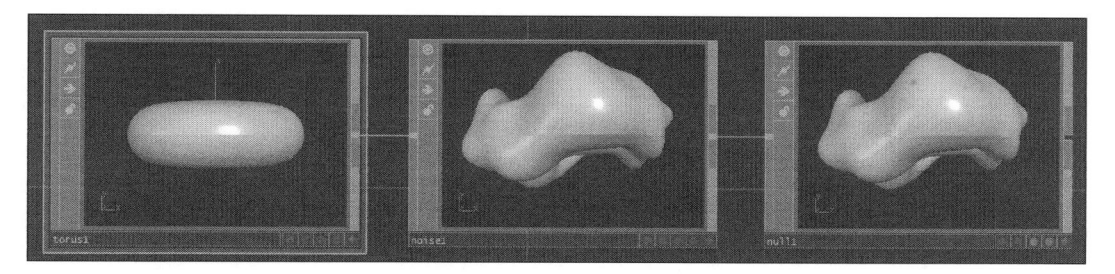

You can see the default torus has been left alone, Noise TOP has been added, and Null SOP is used as an output since its render and display flags are active. The torus has been adjusted though; its **Primitive Type** has been switched to **NURBS**, so we'll talk about primitive types soon. All this can be found at `/project1/rendering/basicRenderTwo`; go ahead and try out other primitives to get a feeling of what's happening for now. While you are there, can you find out why/how the noise is animated?

If we now go back up one level, you can see that our Phong MAT is referenced by Geometry COMP. As always, in TouchDesigner, we can establish this reference by just dragging and dropping MAT on COMP or manually entering the MAT name in the **Material** parameter of COMP. Phong MAT is probably the most commonly used material and is very flexible. We can obtain all kinds of looks just by configuring this material. In the case of this example, we give our noisy torus a reflective look by referencing Movie In TOP in its **Environment Map** parameter. Hopefully, this example motivated you a bit because now we'll have to visit a more theoretical topic to make ourselves ready for some more 3D work.

The data inside SOPs

If you go to `/project1/rendering/3dData`, you will see this:

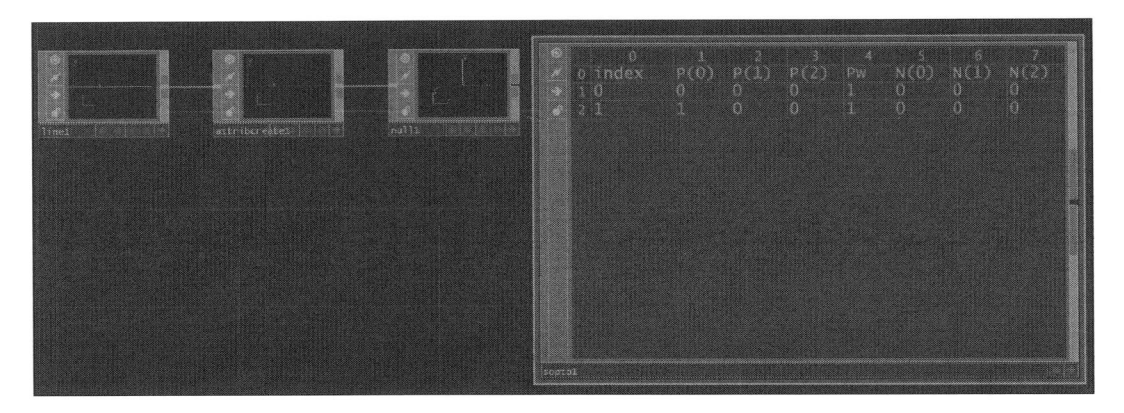

It's Line SOP that generates a **primitive**, which, in this case, is a **polygon** that looks like a line. If you click on the middle mouse button of any SOP, you can obtain information about what exactly it contains. However, by converting SOP to DAT, we can see even better what's in there. What we see in the table are the points of the geometry. In this case, the geometry is made up of two points, one with the index 0 and the other with the index 1. These two points have certain **point attributes**. Naturally, a point needs to have a feature, an attribute of its position in space. The P(0) attribute is a point's X coordinate, P(1) is its Y coordinate, and P(2) is its Z coordinate. The Pw attribute is another attribute, the point weight, which we will ignore for the moment. Lastly, we have N(0-2), which are the **normals**. Normals are vectors that ideally point away from a surface orthogonally. These vectors are used to determine the reaction of a surface to light. You can imagine that a point not only needs to have a position but also an orientation to properly compute its appearance if light is in the scene. This orientation is given to the renderer by a point's normal. Line SOP does not generate any normals (if you think about it, it would not make a lot of sense), so we created some for the sake of this explanation using **Attribute Create SOP**.

In the following screenshot, you can see the point normals of a piece of geometry consist of nine points. Not only do points have normals, but primitives can have these attributes too. Also, points can have many more attributes if we need them, for example, a point color attribute.

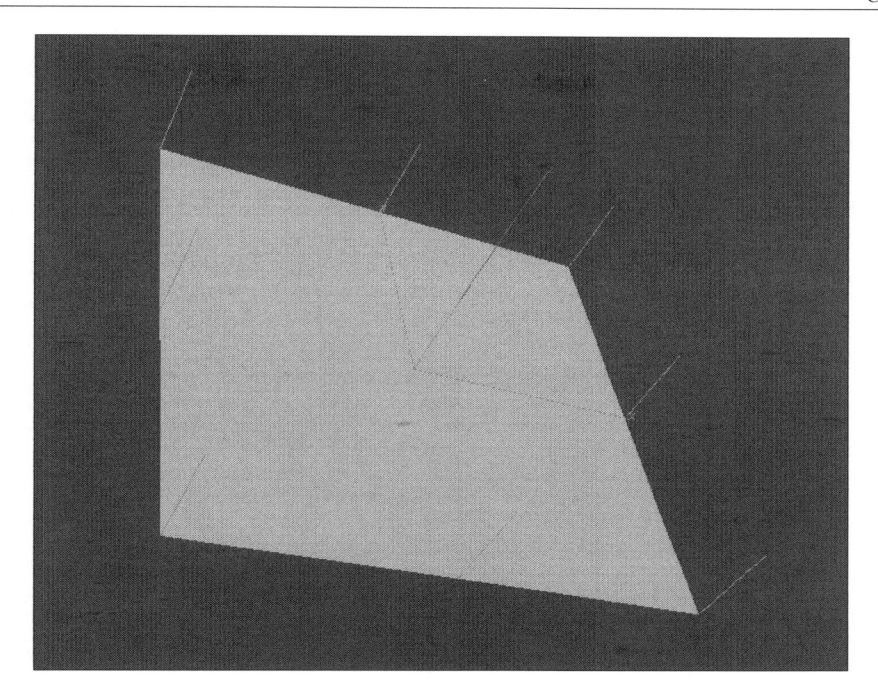

In the following screenshot, you can now see the primitive normals too, drawn as pink lines. It is the same geometry as shown in the preceding screenshot, it's just switched to view the wireframe and show the primitive normals.

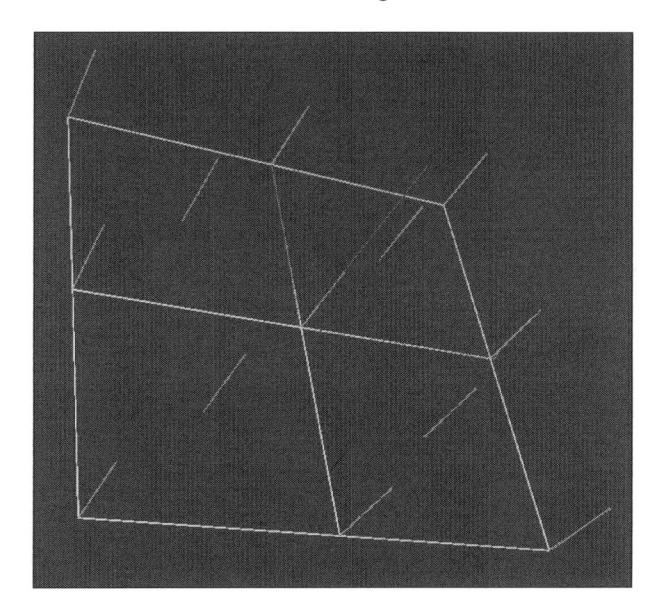

So, we already know we can gather information about what's happening by converting SOP to DAT (the conversion to CHOP can also reveal a lot) or by clicking on the middle mouse button on SOP. How can we see the normals or wireframes this way? SOP displays can be configured using the **Display Options** dialog, depicted in the following screenshot. This dialog can be brought up by pressing *P* while a SOP viewer is active, or by right-clicking on SOP's active viewer and choosing **Display Options**. This context menu also allows us to toggle between a wireframe and shaded mode, and it reveals a lot of other handy options and their shortcuts:

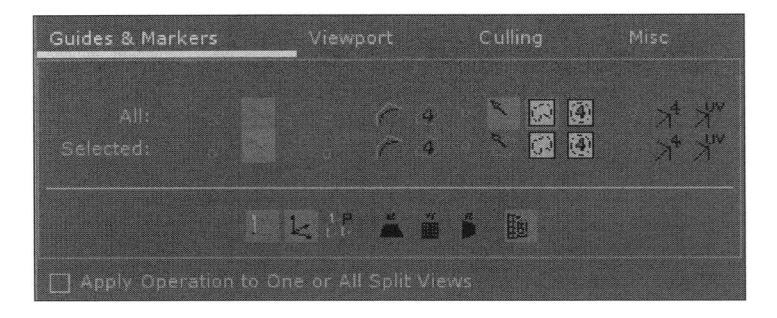

However, let's back up to Line SOP. Clicking on the middle mouse button reveals that Line SOP contains two points, one primitive, two vertices, and one polygon. Since these might all be new terms to you, let's bring some order to them.

You can imagine any geometry is made up of points in 3D space that are somehow connected and skinned; a surface might be drawn using these points. If and how these points are connected to form a surface is determined by the type of the primitive(s). The term primitive really just means a list of vertices, and this list is of a certain type, for example, polygon. The type tells the OpenGL engine what to do with these vertices and how to connect them. Now, if you have had any experience with 3D before, the term vertex or vertices might be familiar to you. If not, vertices are points, but are not the same as points in TD. To ease the confusion, let's look at a polygonal surface, Grid SOP. This grid or planar surface has been configured to be subdivided to a certain degree; we have nine points here, and therefore four primitives that are four polygons. However, we have 16 vertices. Now what's that supposed to mean? A vertex is a point, I said, so what's the difference to a point? A vertex is not really a point, it rather has a point. A point is merely data. It has a position, sometimes attributes, but it's nothing else. A vertex is a part of a primitive. You can imagine a single polygon having four points and four vertices, so it's a rectangle. This polygon is a primitive, as you know. If we now go ahead and create a plane consisting of four of these polygons, some of the corners of these four rectangular polygons will share the same point; they will be at the same position as another corner. For example, in the center, all four polygons meet, their corners are at the same position in space, and they share the same point.

However, each of them has its own vertex at the position, referencing this point. To visualize this idea, have a look at the following screenshot. Here we have our plane; the pink numbers (in the centers of the squares) are primitive numbers, and the blue ones (at the corners and line-crossing points) are point numbers.

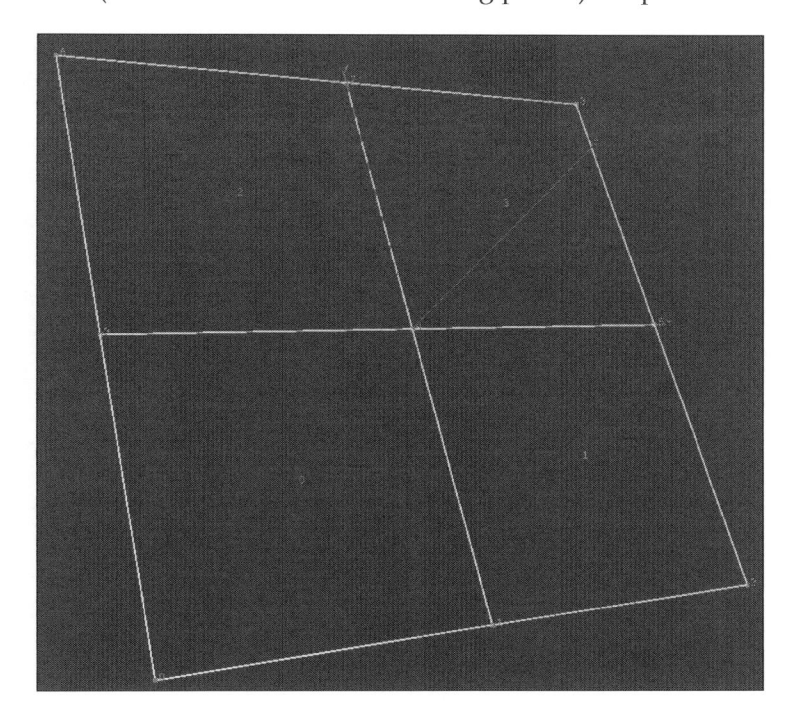

In the following screenshot, we can see SOP to DAT showing us the primitives, not the points as we saw before. What SOP to DAT shows is that it can be configured with its **Extract** parameter. In the vertices column, you can see each vertex mapped to a point number. Notice that the point number **4** is used by each primitive. Primitive 0's third vertex uses point **4** as well as primitive 1's fourth vertex. So, point **4** is in the center of our square.

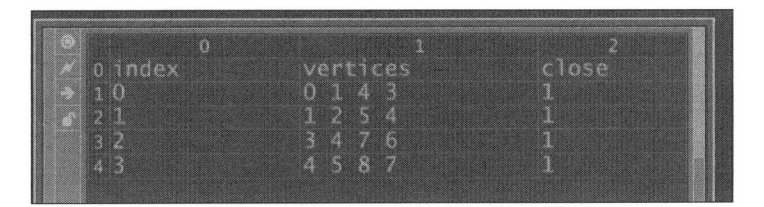

Close is just another attribute. It determines how a polygon is drawn; a closed polygon will have faces giving it a surface, a polygon that is not closed, won't.

Now what exactly is a polygon? Polygon is a word originating from ancient Greek, which means multiangle or multicorner. What's important is that a polygon's points are connected via straight **edges** and can be covered with planar faces. In the following screenshot, you can see three polygonal circles, the first with four points, the second with 10 points, and the third with 40 points:

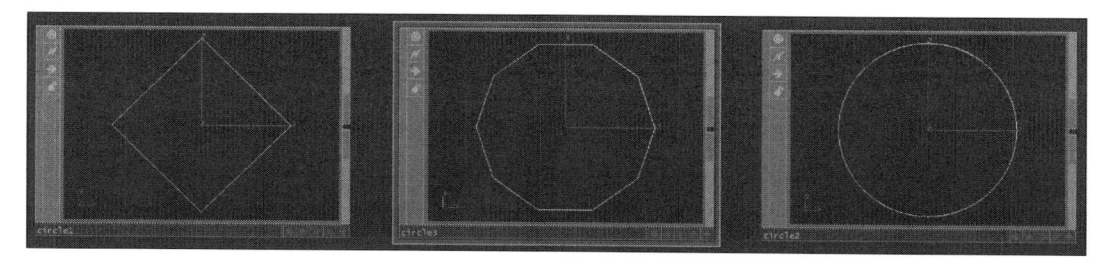

The first circle with four points sounds intuitive, but isn't actually true. In fact, it has five points. Imagine going around the rectangle, starting at the top, for example, and drawing a line from one point to the next. Count how many points you need! You will see that the first and last points are in the same position in space to close the square. These are Circle SOPs, and Circle SOP allows us to choose whether the result should be closed. If you play around with it, you'll notice that a closed circle, in the sense of having a surface, will not need this extra point.

Obviously, the first one doesn't look like a circle at all. The problem is that a high point count will often not be very handy to manipulate a model, will use a lot of CPU if the model is processed, and will take up a lot of GPU memory. Therefore, we have to balance things a bit. So, we can't use a point count that looks good all the time. After having told you another disillusioning message about not being able to do anything, we want to find ways around this limitation. So, to motivate you a bit, and to make you remember what we learned about normals, let's see another example.

Go to `/project1/rendering/normalMapping`; here, you will see this rendering:

Chapter 10

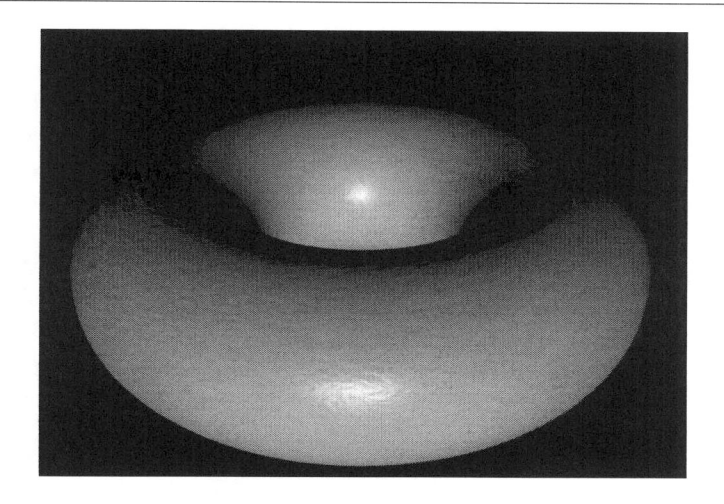

If you look at the highlights, you will see that this model seems to have some structure, some little wrinkles. A simple way to produce this, or a similar look, would be to have a geometry featuring a very high poly count. In this COMP, you will find a simple approach too, with a model containing about 10,000 polygons. The preceding screenshot is achieved by modulating a model's normals. A phong shader has the advantage of interpolating between normals. So, in order to determine the color of a pixel that was sampled from a piece of geometry, a face, it takes into account the point normals around it. If it doesn't do this, and only the actual primitive normals are used, we will not get such smooth-looking surfaces. Every point (pixel) sampled from a specific face will be considered facing in the same direction as the whole face. In the following screenshot, we can see one smooth sphere and another sphere that looks as if there is no such interpolation algorithm:

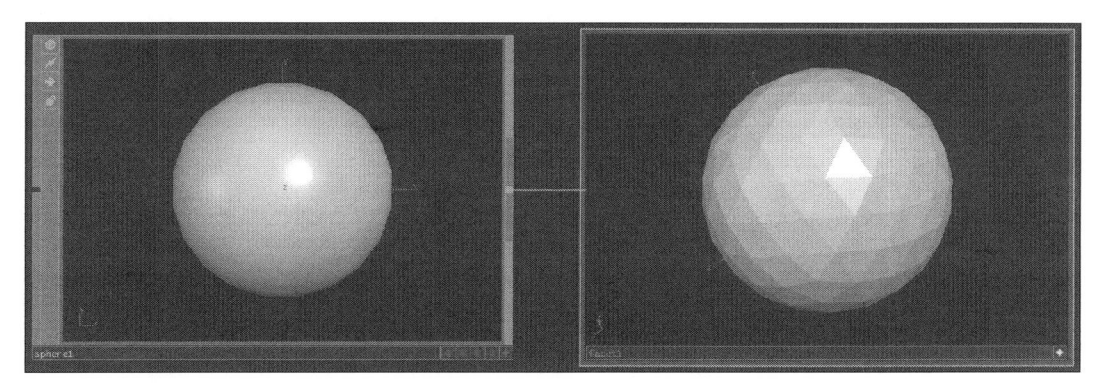

[313]

A normal map will allow us to influence this higher resolution map that emerged from the interpolation. Therefore, the shader acts as if the geometry has slight variations on its surface, which can have a very high level of detail for low cost. The technique of using normal maps for this purpose is very commonly used; however, note that this technique has limitations. If you go to `/project1/rendering/normalMapping/limits`, you will see this rendering:

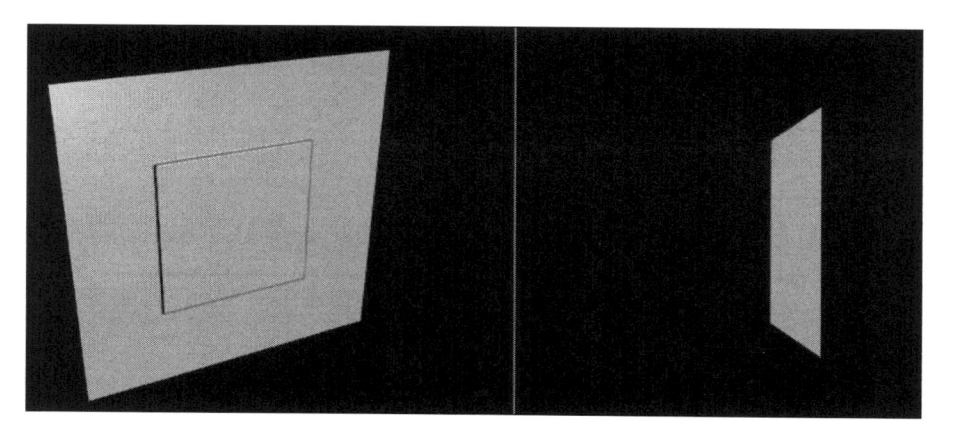

This is a simple Grid SOP, generating a plane via normal mapping. We make it appear as if there is a square coming out of it. It is rendered from two different angles using two Render TOPs and Camera COMPS. If you manipulate one of the cameras to look at the object more from the side, you will see our square become less convincing; we don't actually modify the model. In order to place our camera to a more sideways position, just manipulate its translate vector/parameters. Note that the camera will always look at our geometry because we set the camera's **Look At** parameter to Geometry COMP.

Summary

We achieved a lot in this chapter; we got familiar with many parts of TD, and finally, dove into rendering simple 3D scenes. We learned a lot about time in TD, used TOPs, and got more familiar with keeping things tidy and structured.

For the final TouchDesigner chapter, we will mostly intensely work on getting some beautiful 3D stuff done. If you've come so far, the rest will be easy, but there is a lot to come! We will learn a lot about light, materials, cameras, and rendering. Also, we will create some 3D user interfaces and visit a bigger scene that is supposed to bring together everything we learned.

11
3D Rendering and Examples

This chapter will finally explore some serious 3D rendering, multi-pass rendering, and procedural modeling. We'll go through several more large-scale examples of rendering 3D scenes and take a look at numerous techniques for modeling. In order to achieve this, we will talk a lot about SOPs. SOPs can seem to be complicated, but do not forget that what we are actually doing when we go about 3D rendering is interfacing OpenGL in a fancy, convenient way. So if you feel confused or overwhelmed by the principles or vocabulary, don't hesitate to look up beginner's literature on OpenGL, be it to get a deeper understanding of **Non-uniform Rational B-Splines** (**NURBS**), primitives, lights, or anything else in this context. The most common reference for OpenGL is the *Official Guide to Learning OpenGL*, often called the **Red Book**, which is available at http://www.glprogramming.com/red/.

Interactive and non-procedural tools

Before really building bigger networks for modeling, we should get familiar with a couple of the following tools/methods:

- The geometry viewer
- Grouping by selection
- The modeler

The geometry viewer

We saw the geometry viewer in *Chapter 9, Basic Visualization Using TouchDesigner*. When we model with SOPs, it's a good idea to have one pane in the geometry viewer mode so that we can keep track of what we are doing. Full documentation of the viewer can be found at `http://www.derivative.ca/wiki088/index.php?title=Geometry_Viewer`. If we create our familiar basic rendering setup that features a camera, a geometry, and a light COMP, the geometry viewer offers the possibility to interactively translate our objects in space rather than by entering numbers. We can, for example, switch its view to a quad-split by clicking on the **View** button at the bottom or by just pressing 5 on the num block. The num block holds all kinds of perspective shortcuts, so just try them out.

> A list with all the shortcuts can be found at `http://www.derivative.ca/wiki088/index.php?title=Application_Shortcuts`.

We can enter the selection mode (*S*) to be able to select the camera, for example, and turn on the transformation handles (*Y*) to transform our camera. We can get back into the view mode by hitting the Space bar. This way, we can obviously control our objects in a more intuitive way. Another very handy shortcut is *W*, which toggles between the wireframe and the shaded view. Usually, it tends to be somewhat cumbersome to control a camera's position without having a handle for what it's looking at. Luckily, a Camera COMP, as with all the other **Object COMPs**, has a **Look At** parameter. This parameter expects us to insert another Object COMP, for example, a Null COMP. A Null COMP is a very handy thing; it won't render and just serves as a kind of template object that lives in 3D space often referenced by other objects. So, by assigning the camera's **Look At** parameter to a Null COMP, we are not only able to interactively place our camera at any location in space, but also adjust what it's looking at by placing the Null COMP where we like. The result of this process can be seen in the following screenshot:

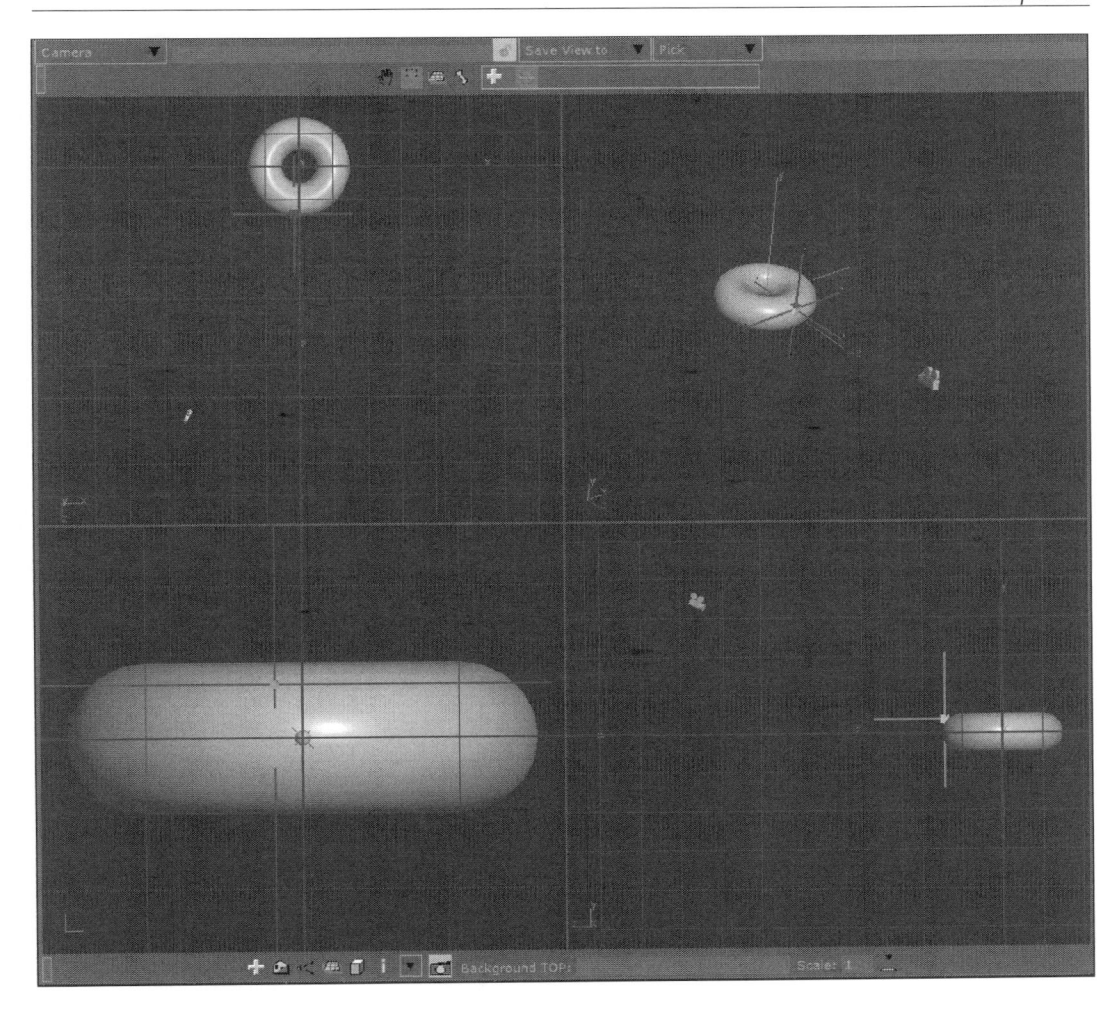

Another possibility to place our camera at a certain position that looks at a certain part of our scene is to adjust the perspective viewport to what we'd like to see in our renderer and click on **Save View to** and choose our camera. The same is true for lights.

3D Rendering and Examples

Grouping by selection

Grouping is a powerful tool to modify parts of your geometry. Very often, we like to have an SOP to only affect parts of the incoming data. For example, assume we want to extrude a square region out of a grid, or we want to put a noise on the point position of only half of a torus. Many SOPs have a Group parameter for exactly this purpose. If we create a group using the **Group SOP** that contains all the points that we would like to be affected, we can enter that group's name in a Noise SOP, for example, to process these points only. But how do we create a group? We have many options to create groups; for example, we can use a bounding box. In general, it's a good idea to stay procedural for group creation. This means that if we need a group that contains half a torus, we should use a bounding box as shown in the following screenshot and in the example placed at /project1/miscExamples/grouping:

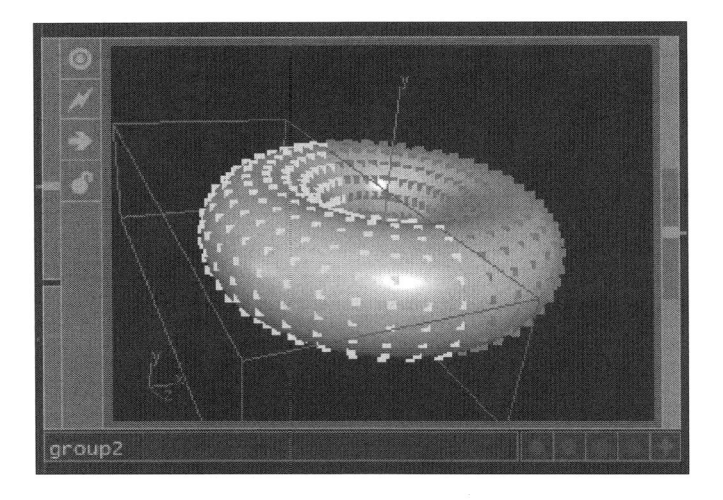

Sometimes, we need a more complex selection for which we can't come up with a pattern or any other definition. In that case, we can right-click on the Group SOP and choose **Select Geometry** to manually select points. A **Geometry Viewer** window will open in which we can select the desired points, and in the **Number** shelf of the Group SOP's parameter dialog, we can click on **Transfer Selection to Pattern** to obtain a group that contains these points. The interactiveness and freedom to directly choose what we want may be very tempting to make great use of this method. Beware though that as soon as we do some processing on the geometry entering the Group SOP, for example, reorder the points, resample the geometry, or simply increase/decrease the resolution of the torus, our selection will break. Using a bounding box, for instance, will still give expected results in the case of resolution or point number changes, since it's a geometric definition and not a purely numerical one.

The Modeler

The **Modeler**, also known as the SOP Editor, is another non-procedural tool that can be very handy. Typically, we won't do very complex modeling in there, so don't expect a full-featured 3D modeling suite. To access the Modeler, stop a **Model SOP**, right-click on it, and choose **Model Geometry**. The Modeler is especially useful to build simple primitives such as polygons, NURBS, or Bezier curves or surfaces to be then used as a building block for something else. A good example for this is located at `/project1/miscExamples/modeler` and shown in the following screenshot. We built a NURBS curve using the Modeler to revolve it and created a structure that resembles a wine glass.

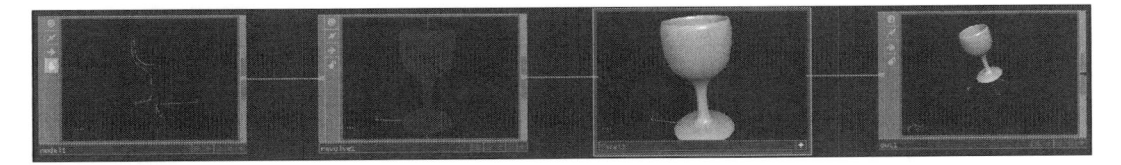

The Geo COMP

The **Geo COMP** holds the geometry to be rendered. It references the material to be used for rendering, has transform controls, and allows instancing. We don't need to build our SOP networks in there; we can also just send our final geometry in one of these via an In SOP. Also, sometimes, it's useful to have the material that is to be used inside the Geo COMP, to be referenced via `./phjong1`, for example. A Geo COMP can hold other Geo COMPs, which is especially useful since we can only assign one single material to a particular Geo COMP for rendering (although it can contain many MATs). An example of what can be achieved by this technique is the wheel asset that is located at `/project1/advanced/wheelAsset`, which is a more advanced example; but still, take a look at it for a second to get a more clear idea of the structure.

The Geo COMP might seem pretty useless at first glance, for example, its transform controls. Why not just put down a **Transform SOP** if we want to move things around? There is a huge difference between using the Geo COMP's transform controls and the use of a Transform SOP. The Transform SOP translates each point of the incoming geometry, while the Geo COMP transforms the whole model. The result is that there is no updated model to be uploaded to the GPU. So the bottom line is that the Geo COMP's transform is computationally really cheap. You can compare the different behavior at `/project1/miscExamples/SOPtransformVsGEOtransform`.

Instancing

Instancing is the idea of drawing a model that has already been uploaded to the GPU multiple times. Using instancing, we can, for example, render 500 cubes very fast. Similar to the differences in transforming points/a whole model, there is a pendant in the SOP world to instancing. A naive approach to getting 500 cubes would be the use of the Copy SOP. The downside of instancing is that there is a limited set of changes we can apply to each copy, whereas if we do the copying in the SOP domain, we have total freedom. Often, this limited set is enough though. One of the things we can define for each instance is the position. This list of coordinates has to be fed into the Geo COMP as DAT or CHOP.

Generating a CHOP that has a channel for location in x, one for y, and one for z, each sample of the channels representing the parameters of one instance, may seem cumbersome, but remember we can switch back and forth between OPs. So, we can create a piece of geometry whose points represent positions of the final instances. This principle is shown in the following screenshot and is placed at `/project1/miscExamples/instancing`:

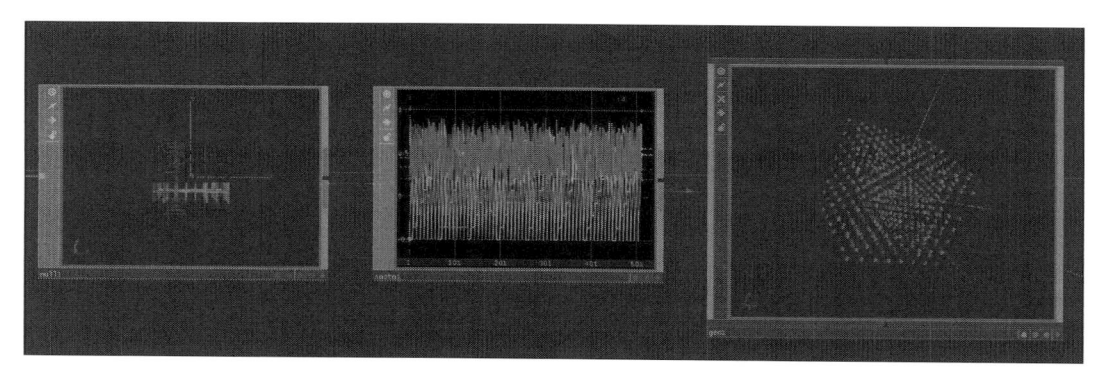

Which channel contains what information has to be configured on the instancing page of the Geo COMP. In the preceding example, the points' diffuse color has been processed with some noise, and the SOP to CHOP has been configured to also extract this information and use it as the diffuse color for each individual instance.

> It is important to note that a Render TOP must be used to take advantage of GPU instancing. Other viewers will cause TD to slow down due to extra CPU processing time; thus, turning the displays off can help a lot.

Camera, light, and shading

We just talked about camera placement, so let's now examine the basic rendering setup a bit deeper. We need to talk about what we can do with the following:

- Cameras
- Lights
- Materials
- Render passes

Cameras

The Camera COMP is pretty straightforward. You've already seen how to position it interactively and how to use a Null COMP to control its orientation more easily, but there are some more features you should be aware of. In COMP's `/project1/camera` folder, you will find some examples of the Camera COMP's capabilities.

> In any case, when experimenting with one or more cameras, be sure to take advantage of the camera's uniform scale parameter. This parameter is also available on a Geometry COMP and is used to scale the whole geometry up or down. In the case of the Camera COMP, it only affects how the camera is displayed in our geometry viewers, and it does not affect the rendering at all. Therefore, if you are working on a huge or tiny geometry and you can hardly see your camera, or the camera is ten times bigger than your whole scene, don't hesitate to scale it to your convenience.

A camera path

Moving an object along a path is possible for all Object COMPs, so for geometry, lights, cameras, and so on, we can, for example, make our camera move along a path defined by an SOP that may hold a curve, as depicted in the following screenshot. Notice, in the example, that the Modeler has been used to create a curve. Since the uneven spacing of the **Control Vertices (CVs)** of that curve would result in a speed variation of the camera while moving along the path, we converted the curve to a polygon with even vertex spacing using the Resample SOP present in the `/project1/camera/path` folder.

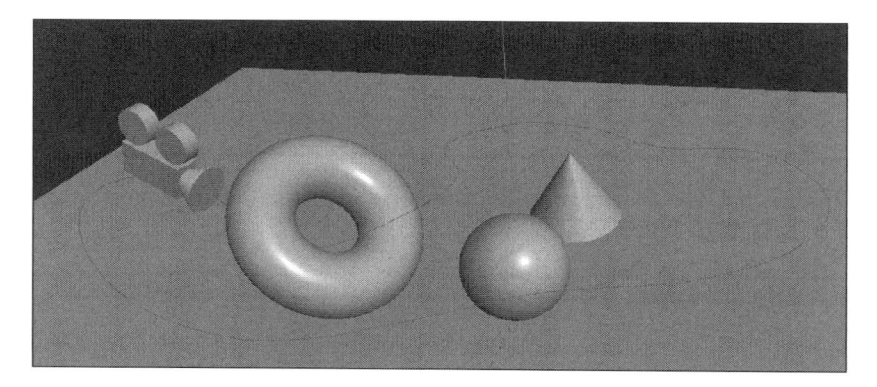

Cut and blend

The preferable way of working with multiple cameras is to use a Camera Blend COMP. In the following screenshot, you can see an example setup using three cameras. At the bottom, we have a Camera Blend COMP that is aware of our cameras via parenting. This technique allows us to both blend between different camera positions as well as cut between them.

Chapter 11

The Null COMP at the top is just a common `Look At` object, and is present in the
`/project1/camera/cameraBlendandCut` folder.

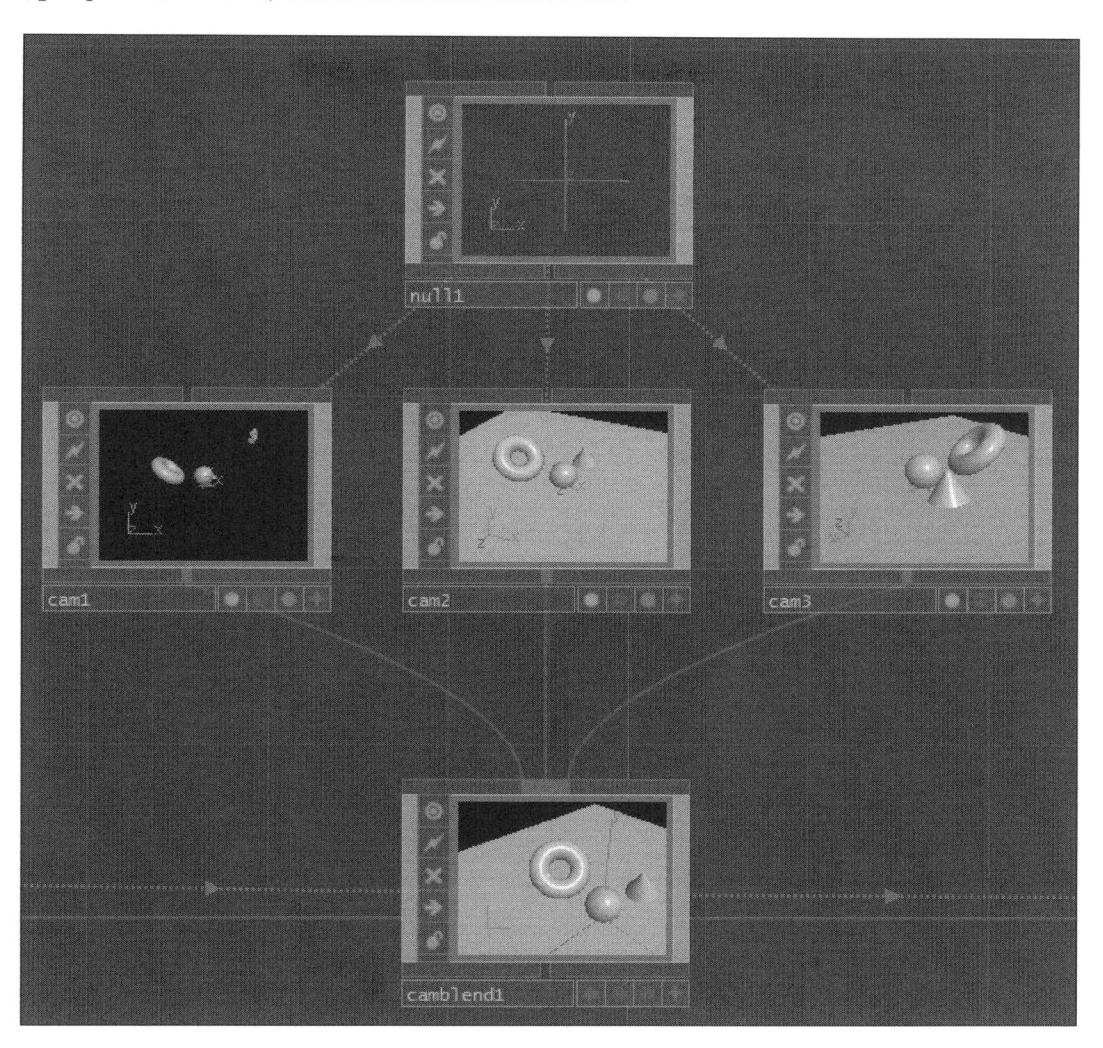

Fog and FOV

The other examples in `/project1/camera/` deal with **Field of View (FOV)** and fog. Fog can be generated on the background page of a Camera COMP's parameter dialog. A convincing result can be achieved if the background color matches the fog color. A fog map can be used to give the fog a more non-uniform appearance. In the following screenshot, you can see such a rendering that makes use of a shadow map:

In the COMP vertigo, you can see how the parameter FOV affects the distortion of the camera image. The well-known vertigo effect has been achieved by using a formula (located in the `script1_script` OP) to compensate the zooming that comes from the adjustment of the FOV. In the following screenshot, you can see a very distorted background and a fairly undistorted foreground, as is possible with the vertigo effect:

Lights and shadows

Lights drastically influence the look and mood of a scene. OpenGL offers the following several types of lights:

- Point light
- Cone light
- Distant light
- Ambient light

The `/project1/light/lightTypes` COMP shows the different effects that can be achieved depending on the type of light used. Depending on the type, the transform parameters have different effects. For example, a point light illuminates the scene in all directions; therefore, its orientation or rotation is unimportant for the lighting of the scene. Another example for this is the distant light; its position has no effect, only its orientation, since it's mimicking a very distant light, such as the Sun. It is always virtually infinitely distant. All this is true for the actual lighting of the scene, but as soon as we use shadows, it's different. Usually, we generate shadows in TD by just configuring the `Shadow Type` parameter of the Light COMP to our choice of shadow style. However, we can also do it differently as is done inside `/project1/light/ShadowsOldSchool`. What's in there is very similar to what the Light COMP is doing automatically if we choose to generate hard shadows. We have a second Render TOP that is using the Light COMP as a camera that renders the scene from the light's perspective. This Render TOP is configured to not output any color but just to draw into the **Depth Buffer**. A Depth Top is used to access it, and this, in the end, is used as a Shadow Map in the same Light COMP. So you see, what's in the frame of our Light COMP does matter a great deal if we want shadows. Also, in order to get nice-looking shadows, you should aim to use the resolution of the shadow map in an optimal way, meaning that they should appear as big as possible in the Light COMP's viewer. To prevent or treat artifacts, the Polygon Offset settings can be used. These are found in the Light COMP's **Shadow** page, or in the old-school scenario, we'd use that of the Render TOP.

3D Rendering and Examples

Another very useful possibility is the use of a **projection map**. If we provide an image/TOP to the Projection Map parameter of a Light COMP, we can, for example, achieve effects that remind us of a flash light as depicted in the following screenshot:

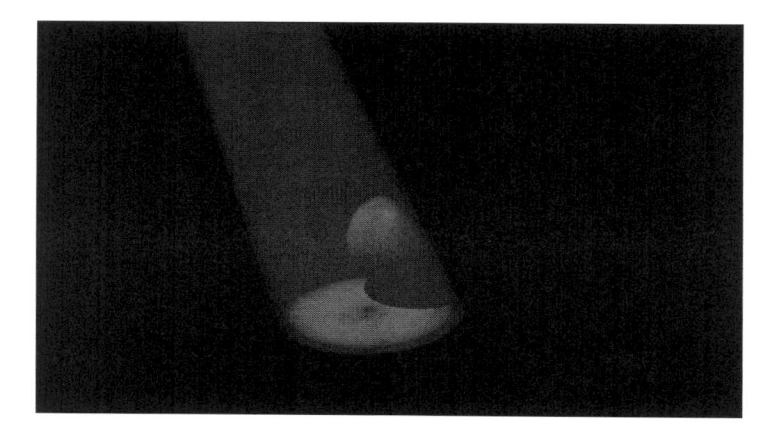

This example makes use of a transparent material and a second render pass; both are topics that we'll address next. However, when you are at `/project1/light/cone`, try playing around with phong1's parameters. The whole geometry inside the different light examples use this material. Material and light have a lot to do with each other. Here, you have the opportunity to see the material settings under a variety of lighting situations.

Also, a suitable projection map can simulate the presence of multiple lights as shown in the following screenshot and at `/project1/light/neon`. This can often lead to performance improvements since lights are rather expensive to compute. A small TOP network can simulate neon lights and feed into a Light COMP to achieve something like the following screenshot:

Materials

Materials (**MATs**) are what give our geometry some more character. These are actually **shaders**. A shader is a small program written in **OpenGL Shading Language (GLSL)** when dealing with OpenGL. TouchDesigner luckily comes with some shaders that expose their parameters to the user. Most often, we will tend to use the Phong shader, which offers the most functionality. If you want to look at the actual shader code or modify it, the Phong MAT has a button in its parameter dialog, **Output Shader**, and you will end up with two DATs and a GLSL MAT.

If you are coming from a regular non-real-time 3D environment, you might be a bit disappointed about having too few options here, but the next *Render passes* section will show you that the possibilities are nearly endless. We have already seen the application of a bump map or a normal map in the previous chapter; another very powerful feature is the possibility of an environment map, not to mention regular color maps. Here, you can see some examples of what can be achieved with some minor tweaking of the Phong MAT:

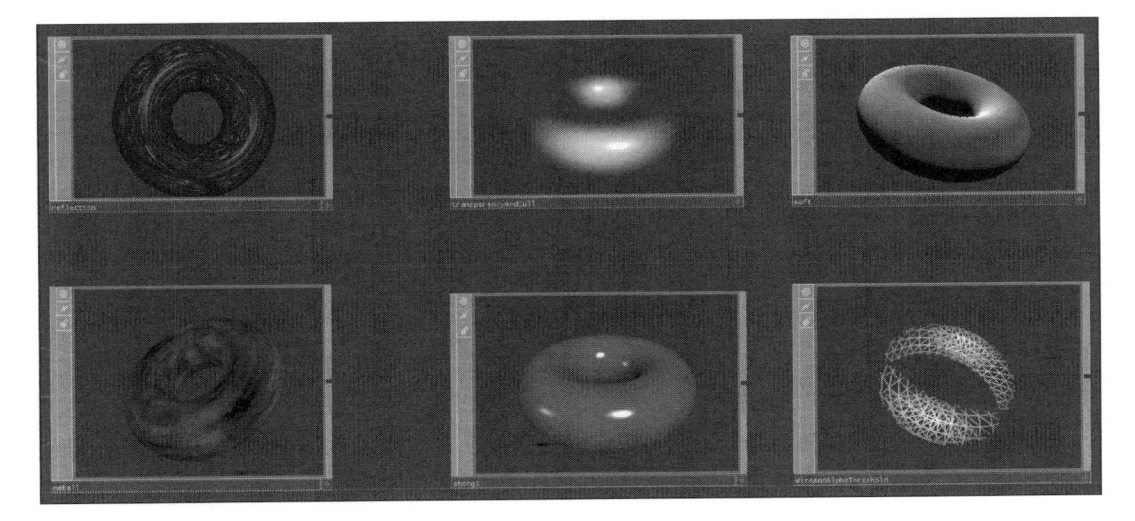

These examples are located at `/project1/MATs/PhongExampels`.

Transparency

When we want to achieve transparent geometry, one would think it's enough to give it a low alpha value. However, we have to put some more effort into transparency. First of all, we have to activate **Blending** for the material that's supposed to be transparent. However, OpenGL is, in general, not aware of the fact that our transparent object is in front of something that's supposed to shine through. We do either of the following:

- We tell OpenGL the order in which things are supposed to be drawn (the Draw Priority parameter of each Geo component must reflect the order in which things are supposed to be drawn).
- We tell the renderer to look up this order itself, which is computationally more expensive but sometimes necessary. This is a parameter of the Render TOP called order-independent transparency.

These two methods are shown at /project1/MATs/transparency; notice a subtle visual difference in the case of an object that reveals parts of itself through transparency, as shown in the following screenshot:

Two other options are related to transparency; both are settings for a Phong MAT: culling and the **Discard Pixels Based on Alpha** option. The latter one lets us define a threshold, and if a pixel has an alpha value lower (or if higher, see the **Keep Pixels with Alpha** setting) than this threshold, it simply won't be rendered. Culling lets us discard the geometry that does not face the camera (back-face culling) or the faces that are visible to the camera (front-face culling). This can be used to prevent artifacts when using transparency.

Render passes

If we want to apply some effects to a specific object in a scene but don't want to apply this effect to the rest of it, this calls for a second render pass. The **Render Pass** TOP is almost the same as a Render TOP but has two unique selections that make it easy to split up render layers while retaining or clearing some already-processed information. The idea is simple:

- We render our scene but don't render the object we want to process, for example, a sphere.
- We add a Render Pass TOP connected to our Render TOP. We configure this second renderer to clear the camera color, render our sphere, and inherit the depth buffer.

So if our sphere is hidden behind another object, it won't show up as desired, as shown in the following screenshot:

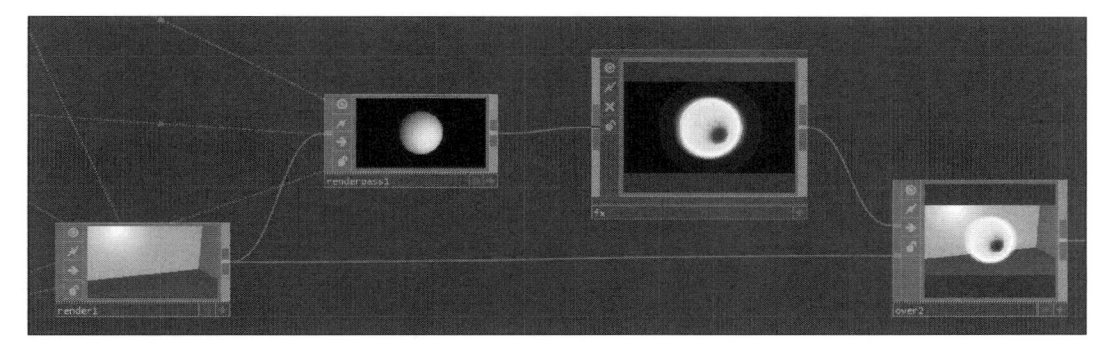

In the previous screenshot, you can see an example of this construction; it allows us to come up with arbitrary materials and FX very easily. Also, many more render passes can be added if needed.

Render picking and 3D GUIs

TouchDesigner's capabilities in regards to GUI building are immense. We have already seen some GUI magic, but there is much more. If we render a 3D scene, we have some tools that allow us to easily gain information about how a user interacts with it. The Render Pick DAT, the Render Pick CHOP, the Panel Execute DAT, and the Panel CHOP are our friends in this regard. To push things even further, there is a whole wiki page for the purpose of expanding our projects with multi-touch features at http://www.derivative.ca/wiki088/index.php?title=Multi_Touch.

3D Rendering and Examples

A basic setup for render picking can be found at `/project1/renderPick/PickingSimple`. This example demonstrates a very simple setup to allow a user to move a torus around. Note that the component's viewer active flag has to be set or the viewer has to be opened for this to work. If you imagine combining this technique with some basic UI elements, I think you know where we are heading. Quite impressive UIs are possible this way.

A basic mix of 2D and 3D elements can be found at `/project1/renderPick/pickingPlusGUI`. Here, we can pick one of the three donuts, causing an edge effect on it to illustrate the selection, and we can configure this picked geometry's MAT diffuse color with a basic GUI element from the palette, as shown in the following screenshot:

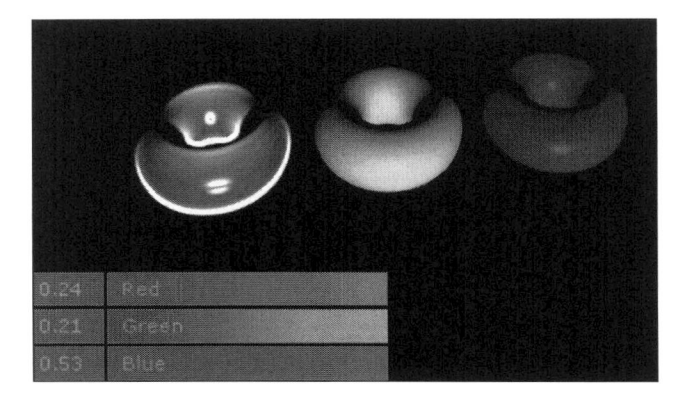

One other example that shows a bit more sophistication is located at `/project1/renderPick/pickingInstances` and is shown in the following screenshot. It's a building block for creating something like an interactive 3D mixing desk that features a couple of faders generated using instancing, so it's rendered pretty fast. A small amount of scripting is used in this example so as to not lose focus with the mouse, to generate a DAT with one row per instance, and to keep everything cooking if needed.

Of course, it's possible to use the values of these faders right away; a Null CHOP named **ValuesNormalized** provides all the fader positions in a range from 0 to 1.

This example features some pretty simple, comprehensible procedural modeling, so let's go over it in detail before things get a little more steep. Let's talk about the knobs of the faders, that is, all the SOPs in the slider's Geo COMP. For these knobs, we have a signal flow like this:

1. We create a box and use its scaling parameters to get the basic design in the right ballpark. Also, we reference the size and translate in the y parameter in order to have the box sit on the XZ plane perfectly. For this, we use the expression `me.par.sizey/2`.
2. We use a Subdivide SOP in which we subdivide only with a depth of 1 to get an edge on the top of our box.
3. We group the points on that edge in order to push them down via a Transform SOP.

At this point, we arrive here:

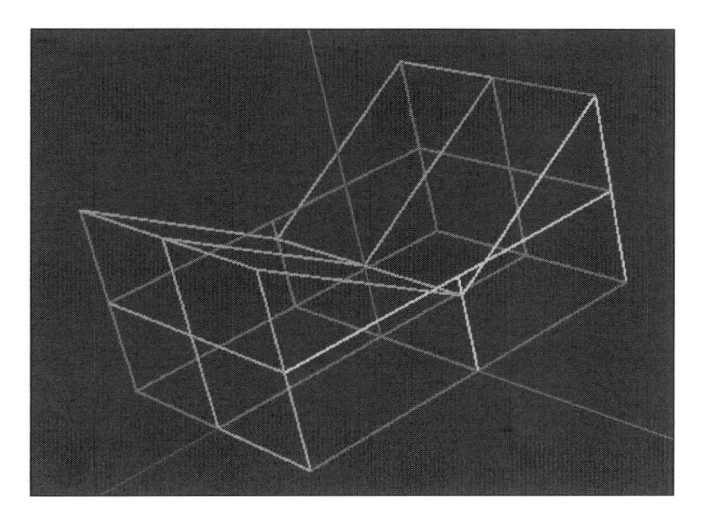

The previous image may look a bit messy; we pushed these points below other ones, generating a geometry that won't render properly. A shaded version is shown in the following screenshot that shows the artifacts:

This effect is called **Z-fighting** and comes up if two or more faces are at the exact same location in space. The renderer is confused about which one is in front. Anyway, we don't really care at this point since the final result won't show these artifacts; it won't have these coplanar primitives. Now, we perform the following steps:

1. We use a Facet SOP. The Facet SOP is one of the Swiss army knife SOPs. It's one of the many that we need to know very well. In this case, we use it to consolidate points with its consolidate parameter set to consolidate points slowly. This means that vertices at (nearly) the same location that might each have their own points should all reference the same point.

2. This last step made it possible to use the Subdivide SOP to smooth our surface (because otherwise, we would have many points very close to each other). This makes smoothing between them have little effect, which also solves our Z-fighting problem because the smoothed surface doesn't overlap itself.

After this, we use another Facet SOP to recompute our normals. Look at the following screenshot; you'll see that the updated normals really help to emphasize the detail we gained by the subdivision:

Chapter 11

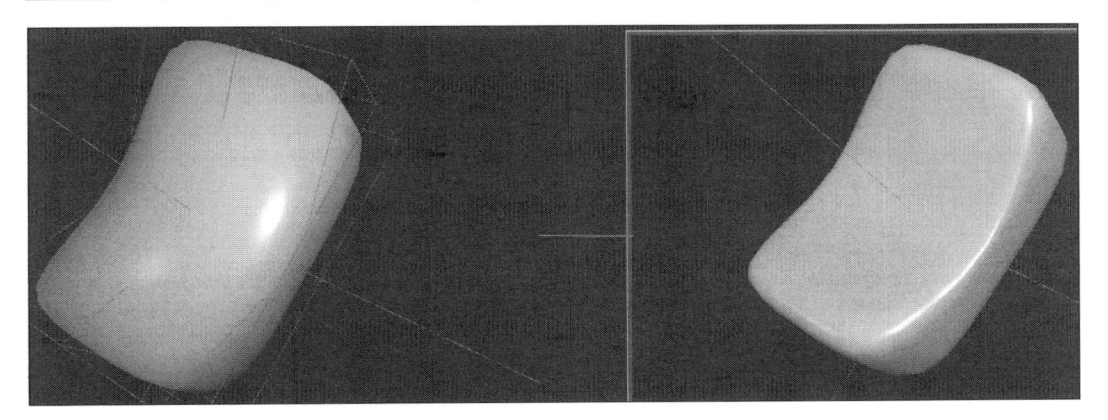

On the left of the previous screenshot, you see our geometry before the recalculation, and on the right you see the geometry after the recalculation of the normals.

At this point, we orient our model to face in the Z direction. This could also have been done at any step or in the Geo COMP. However, since the model upstream of the Transform SOP won't cook, we don't care about the performance difference between Geo-transform and SOP-transform.

Finally, we modify our **UV Texture Coordinates** using the Texture SOP. If we need to apply textures as color maps, bump maps, and so on, we need to come up with some kind of mapping to wrap our 2D image around our 3D body. Here, we use one of the most basic and intuitive variants of doing this. We just project our texture on the body from the Z direction. This action modifies the coordinates stored in the geometry as a vertex attribute (UV), which is then used by the material/shader to know where to put what pixel of our texture.

Finally, we render the result and use some instancing, DAT and CHOP processing, and render picking to get our sliders to move correctly.

> Take a look at the boxes on which the knobs sit, making the fader complete. Try to recreate this; also, this is a good point to read some documentation; make sure you understand what we have done so far.

Examples of procedural modeling

We can always import geometry from other applications via the file in SOP. However, often, it makes sense to model directly inside TouchDesigner to keep things procedural and to be able to make things react to sound, user interactions, or other incoming data. Procedural modeling, as with the other topics we have tackled, is a huge one, and there are many ways to achieve a certain aim. We'll cover a variety of techniques, embedded in some larger projects, which are supposed to demonstrate a condensed version of everything we have covered and beyond. On the way, try to look through other examples of the chapter file.

> All of the upcoming examples show some rather conventional scenery; things that might be achieved better in a traditional 3D modeling environment if real time is not required, or if so, may best be done in a game engine such as Unity. These examples should show you techniques. Coming up with wacky content is not covered here. Also, beware that if you master these techniques, it's a very solid basis for live shows or installations using TD with your content. Here, we try to lay a base for the endless things you can do with TD.

A speaker

In this example, as in the others, we'll try to keep things as procedural as possible where it makes sense. We won't import any geometry, although we might get a lot more detailed results if we take the time to model something in every detail. This example will demonstrate that without much effort, we can get a very pretty image of a speaker as shown in the following screenshot, rendered in real time and reacting to sound. The Speaker COMP is located at `/project1/advanced/speaker` and is shown in the following screenshot:

Structure

This example, as with all other sound-reactive examples in the file, gets its sound from `/project1/centralAudio`. So if you would like to hear what the model is reacting to, you'll have to turn up the volume in that COMP. The general setup is pretty simple; there are four Geo COMPs, as follows:

- **The speakers**: This is the only model that's actually animated. This COMP is using instancing.
- **The box**: This is a box with some holes where our cones will be.
- A bass reflex port; a shiny looking cone.
- A floor.

There is a DAT, `null1`, which is manually configured by its input Table DAT. It's the central point that decides how many and where the instances of the speakers are, where the holes in the box should be, and how big each of them shall be.

Modeling

Let's start with the speaker. We used a Tube SOP, and turned one of the radii way down to 0 to obtain a cone. This, in combination with a sphere and a torus, already gives us the basic shape. Now, how do we distort this, and how do we animate the speaker? We could just animate the position of the sphere and the height/scale of the tube. Note that these two operations can be done on the Geo COMP parameter level if we put these two elements into separate Geo COMPs. This way, this animation will computationally get very cheap.

However, a more organic-looking result can be obtained using the very handy Lattice SOP. The Lattice SOP allows us to deform complex geometry according to a 3D grid. We simply feed in the geometry to distort a rest geometry (the grid in its original form) and a distorted version of the grid. This way, we can deform a model in a complex manner just by moving a couple of points. In the following screenshot, you can see our model, the rest geometry in red, and the distorted grid in yellow:

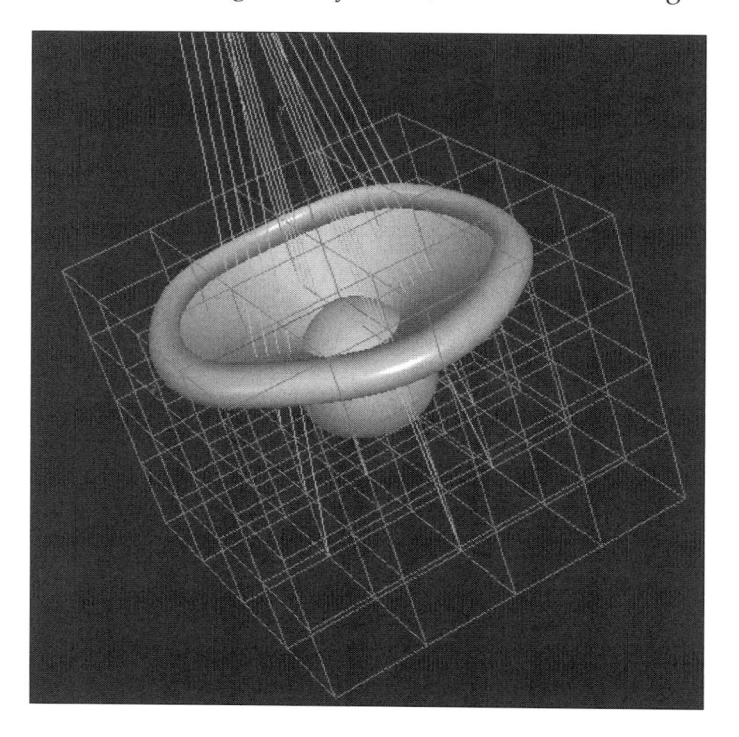

In this case, the texturing really matters; it finishes off our cone beautifully. The UV coordinates are again made via a projection; the textures themselves are mainly created using some Ramp TOPs.

Let's move on to the box; a Superquad SOP gives us a nicely configurable box-like shape as a starting point. This is then processed by a Boolean SOP; we need to get some holes in there. The shape that cuts our holes is produced like this; we use the same table as the one that is used for the instancing of our cone. This table is fed into an Add SOP as a points table. What we get are a couple of points at the same locations as the cone instances. Now, we use the Copy SOP. This SOP is very powerful, and among other possibilities, we can copy an incoming geometry to every point of the geometry that comes in at the second inlet (the template input). Finally, we add another tube that cuts out the hole for the bass reflex port.

Rendering

The actual rendering consists of a very small network with some helpful ingredients for getting a quite decent image. We added two lights and activated soft shadows. We use the **Screen Space Ambient Occlusion (SSAO)** TOP to get some ambient occlusion effects (that also cause some artifacts). After that, we use a combination of a Luma Blur TOP and the Depth TOP to render a cheap **Depth of Filed (DOF)** effect. In the end, like putting a slight amount of reverb and compression on a multitrack audio recording to glue things together, to give them the same coloring, it's sometimes a good idea to do some manipulation to the colors.

Just like CHOPs have a Scope parameter to influence only selected channels from the incoming multitude, we have a Channel Mask parameter on the common page of TOPs. Three different Level TOPs, each for one of the colors, let us adjust values such as contrast, gamma, and brightness for each color channel individually, giving the image a somewhat more coherent character. In the end, we add a slight amount of noise, simulating noise on a digital camera's image sensor and making the image a bit less sterile.

A waterfall plot

Visualizing the spectrum of incoming audio is a very common idea. As usual, there are many ways to do this, and we are going to take an approach that uses a TOP to distort an SOP. This technique might be useful often and allows us to define how our spectrum is drawn in a very intuitive way. The example is located at `/project1/miscExamples/spectrum`. Refer to the following screenshot:

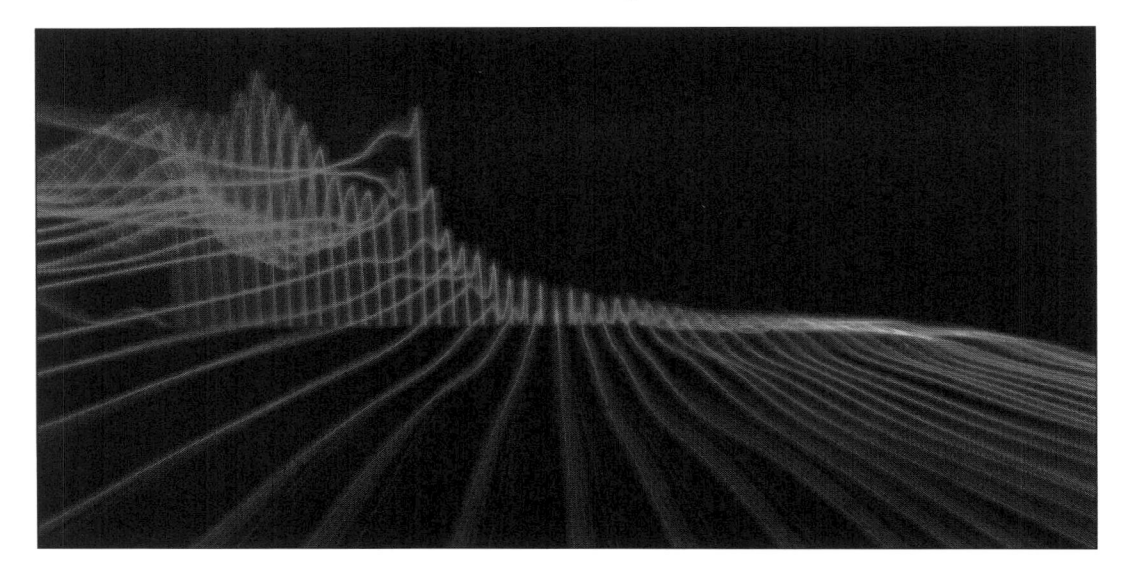

Structure

We select our central audio input again and then use the Spectrum CHOP to go to the frequency domain, obtaining the spectrum of the signal. A bit of CHOP processing is used to adjust the x axis to a visually pleasing, nearly correct, logarithmic mapping. After that's done, we go to the TOP domain, generating a line of pixels. A simple feedback loop including a transform TOP gives us an image in which brightness is intensified; the x axis represents frequency and the y axis represents time. A **TOP to CHOP** allows us to move back to the CHOP domain; from there, we move on to SOPs.

A variable inside local is used to determine the resolution of our grid and the whole processing, allowing us to easily balance speed versus resolution at any point in time. The resolution of the actual rendering and TOP processing of our output is only dependent on the Render TOPs' resolution, so this can also be changed easily.

Modeling

There is not a lot of modeling involved in this example; the main thing is to see that modeling might involve a lot of jumping around between OP families, exploiting the advantages of each family, or to put it differently, there are not a lot of SOPs involved here but still a lot of modeling, if you want to view it like that.

Using a Grid SOP as a basis for our modeling, we convert it to a CHOP in order to modify the data. After some minor processing, we use our TOP image, which is converted to a CHOP to replace the grid's Z-point position.

A fractal texture

This is a very short example that demonstrates how we can obtain an artistically interesting, seemingly high resolution texturing from a very simple texture. The example is located at `/project1/miscExamples/textureSpace`. Refer to the following screenshot:

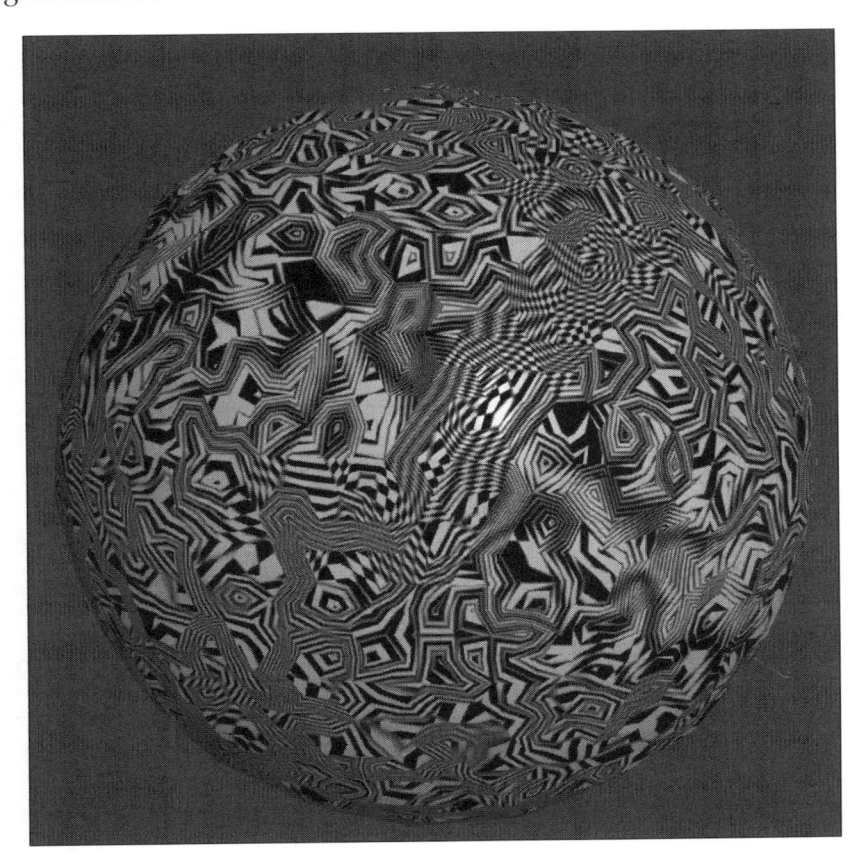

Modeling

TOPs are used to create a checkerboard texture. A sphere is generated and texture coordinates are applied using the Texture SOP. Next, we use the Point SOP to swap point coordinates and UV coordinates. We end up with a distorted-looking strange piece of geometry that lies in a plane. It lies in a plane because our texture coordinates are two-dimensional in this case. This geometry now has UVW coordinates that store our point positions in the meantime. Then, we apply some effects to that geometry's point position, in this case, a fractal SOP. Finally, we swap the UVW and point positions back, apply our texture, and end up with a fractal texture.

Liquid

Simulating liquids in real time in a convincing manner is a bit much to ask for. Nevertheless, we can get quite close. We haven't dealt with particle systems at all up to this point. The particle SOP is one of the most fun things to play with in TouchDesigner. Try modulating its parameters with sound, for instance. In this example, we'll try to use quite a small (for a liquid simulation) number of particles, and use some TOP processing to make the rendering a bit more liquid like. Still, it's a lot of particles, so if your machine slows down, try reducing the Particle SOP's **Birth** or **Life** parameters to decrease the overall particles. We'll try to smear the particles and add something like specular highlights. The example is located at `/project1/particles/fluent` and is shown in the following screenshot:

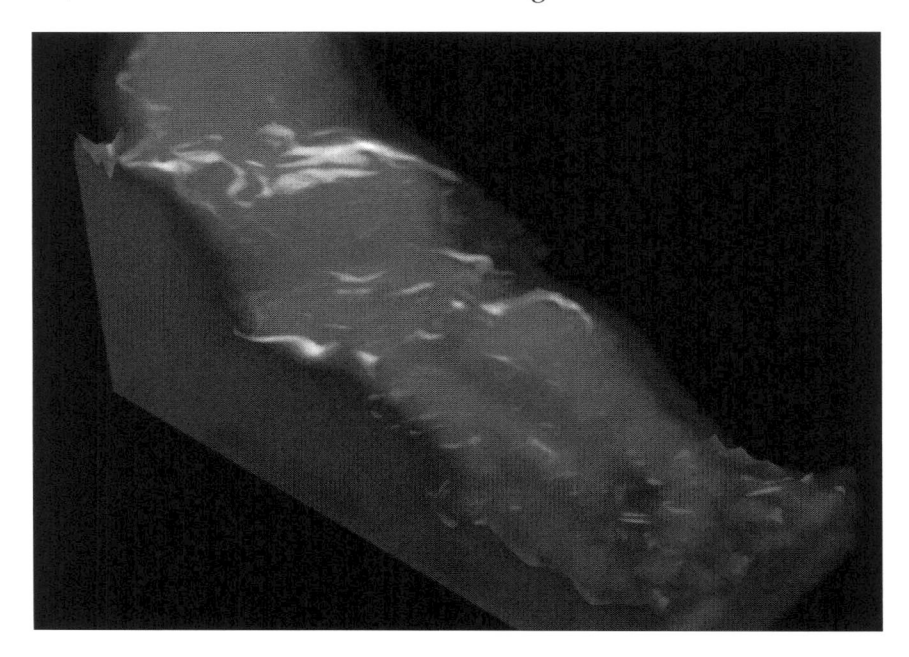

Structure

All of the modeling happens inside **geo1**. We model the rock in there and use it as the collision geometry of our particle system. From there, we fan out to two Geo COMPs, one for the rendering of our rock and one for the particle system. Also, render these two independently, since our particle system needs some processing. To get more particles, we use instancing. We just duplicate our particle system and offset it slightly. This way, we get a lot of movement with quite a few particles. Of course, this approach leads to strange symmetry effects if we overdo it. We still only have one particle system; it just appears twice.

Modeling

We first create a stair-like model, use it as a collision geometry, and put some noise on it to make it look a bit more natural. The Join SOP and the Skin SOP prove to be useful for a modeling approach that consists of placing simple geometry in the right place and connecting them. Certainly, a rock-like model can be made a lot more beautiful; the central thing here really is the particle system. This example is more about having fun with particles, so go ahead and have some fun with it! Another takeaway message is: we can't afford many particles in real time; we can't really simulate water, fire, and so on. However, we can get pretty close with some very simple trickery. You might think, "But wait, I saw real-time water and fire in computer games with astonishing quality!" Well, there is a lot of trickery (especially custom shaders, GPU computed particles, and CUDA physics) to explore.

Rendering

Here, we don't use a Phong MAT for the particle system. The particle system has been set to **Render as Point Sprites**, and so, we also use a Point Sprite MAT. This allows us to render each point sprite as a rectangular texture that faces the camera. Each point will have the same size with the possibility of scaling it by distance to the camera in order to make it also appear farther away.

The smearing of course is a feedback system again. An Edge TOP in combination with a Displace SOP gives us some liquid-looking specular highlights.

A house in a landscape

In the last example, we are going to visit a larger landscape with trees, a house, rain, lightning, and mountains in the background. We have mentioned already that if you don't want to modulate or modify all this geometry in real time, nobody on earth would model all this procedurally with TouchDesgnier. Modeling it procedurally in **Houdini** or just modeling it in any 3D modeling suite is also an option. However, this approach is possible and illustrates different techniques to structure a project, and the example features a small animation, render passes, generating convincing textures, a lot of modeling obviously, and much more. The example is located in a separate file, `house.toe`, and is shown in the following screenshot:

Structure

On the top layer, it might seem a bit too much at first; let's see what's happening.

The Geo COMP `scene` contains nearly all our geometry. There are a couple of Geo COMPs in there. All the materials for the Geo COMPs are also in there. Each Geo COMP contains its own MAT, so the one it is rendered with.

There are four COMPs: `lightningGEO`, `lightningControl`, `lightningLight`, and `null5`, all of which have to do with the lightning of course. The Geo one contains one of the two models that are not inside the Scene COMP.

The Rain COMP contains the second one; it's generating a particle system, serving as rain.

The Textures COMP generates all the textures. Mostly, this COMP isn't very spectacular, but don't forget to take a look at /project1/textures/brick. The textures for the house's walls are generated using 3D rendering of a brick-like structure. The Copy SOP and its stamping functionality are put to great use here. Using this technique, we can model very nice textures on the fly. Also, note that the renderer that generates the textures is locked, so it doesn't consume our processing power.

You might be surprised that there are three cameras and three Render TOPs (plus Render Pass TOPs). The main rendering uses cam1 and render1. The cam2 and cam3 objects, each with their corresponding Render TOPs, are rendering images to serve as environment maps for shaders (for the window and the roof).

Inside local, we don't configure a lot. We defined some variables and a module. Also, we added a local time to keep the animation working in case we decide to copy the scene into another project. Imagine if we copied it into a project with a standard length of 10 seconds; our animation would be truncated. This way, we just have to make our local time independent and it will keep working.

Modeling

Again, all the geometry is generated within TD. Some of the more interesting Geometry may be the roof, the path, the mountains, windows, and lightning. The roof, as the path, the mountains, and lightning are made using the Limit SOP. The Limit SOP is a bit like a CHOP to SOP, maybe a bit more intuitive since it just makes a line/tube that features all the samples in the input CHOP. The lightning uses the Limit SOP's output directly in combination with an L-System SOP (a handy SOP for building tree-like geometry; see Lindenmayer Systems in general). The roof is made up of a wavy line duplicated and skinned; the path is following the same principle, and uses a Line Thick SOP and extrudes the result

The window model is mostly made up of boxes and Boolean operations. To bring the reflectivity of the glass to live, some noise has been put on the normals. The door demonstrates how useful the Wireframe SOP can be in combination with its incoming geometry to give it a rounded finish.

Rendering

Notice that one of the light's position and dimmer parameter is coupled to the lightning. As you already know, we are rendering two more perspectives for use as environment maps, which might be a bit of an overkill. Some noise that is leveled up and down according to the lightning might suffice; we could save a lot of performance here.

A custom shader is used for the windows to make them reflect only on its glass regions and not on their frames. This custom shader is just the output of a standard Phong MAT; the line that controls the environment map contribution is multiplied by an incoming texture.

Again, we are using multiple render passes, one dedicated for the rain and one for the lightning. Some post-processing is done again to give the scene a more consistent coloring. Also, a very cheap pseudo depth of the field is made by just blurring the edges of the image. This approach really has nothing to do with DOF, but gives a similar impression for some scenes, is cheap to render, and doesn't produce artifacts (as a sharp edge blurring/bleeding into a blurred background).

Summary

This concludes our section about real-time visualization. Hopefully, the discussed concepts and examples have made you understand how to approach bigger projects. TouchDesigner is a very deep environment, and we are nowhere near to covering everything. We concentrated on the actual visualization in 2D and 3D; we didn't cover its capabilities in networking (the Touch In/Out OPs, the TCP/IP DAT, the WebSocket DAT, UDP DATs, and so on), multi-touch, projection mapping (see Kantan Mapper, CamSchnappr, and Vert Pusher on the forums for some mapping tools built into TD), inter-application communication (shared memory for example), audio processing, and a lot more.

The file that accompanies this chapter contains more than we had time to talk about, so explore it on your own to find out a bit more about SOPs. Also, never forget the OP snippets in the **Help** menu if you are lost about an OP's functionality; seek help in the documentation and the forums if you are unclear about anything.

12
Connecting Our Software to the World

We have talked a lot about programming Max patches, TouchDesigner projects, Max for Live devices, and so on. However, the really interesting stuff is what comes out of the speakers, the screen, or the projector. What about inputs and outputs to our programs other than microphones, cameras, speakers, and all the standard stuff? What about multispeaker setups, multi-touch screens, and the famous MIDI-controlled coffee machine? This is what this chapter is about. As you can imagine, this really opens up the horizon, both for our software and our imagination. So this is just be a broad overview, picking some examples of techniques and equipment we could use. In this chapter, we are going to cover the following:

- Interfacing analog synthesizers
- Arduino boards and how to receive voltage in Max and TD
- Multi-touch screens
- Interfacing other programs
- Dealing with exhibitions
- Exporting an application from Max

Analog synths and control voltage

Many people who work with Max/MSP also like analog modular synths since the idea behind the two is pretty similar: connecting boxes, tweaking parameters, and making sound. Analog modular synths use **control voltage** (**CV**) to communicate, send triggers, control pitch, and the like. How could we use a great sequencer that we just created in Max to control our analog modular synth? Well, there are a couple of options, some of which require the acquisition of additional equipment or software, but we'll stick to the most simple one: using our audio interface to send out CV signals (please take a look at the section about Arduino too; it also generates voltages and is a very handy tool for this task too).

There are two problems when using an audio interface for the generation of CV signals:

- AC coupling
- Maximum voltage

AC coupling essentially means that there is a high-pass filter or a DC-blocking filter, after the DAC, the digital-to-analog converter. Since CV signals often contain very low frequencies or DC, these would be filtered out. So there are two options to get this going: buying an audio interface that is AC coupled or modifying one that is. Although this is a simple task, depending on your skills in Electronics, this risks the danger of breaking the interface, and surely will corrupt any existing warranties. For example, MOTU is a manufacturer that offers audio interfaces that are DC coupled. The good thing is that we can always generate trigger CV signals since the rising edge won't be filtered out even if we use an AC-coupled interface. The maximum voltage your audio interface provides may vary. However, regardless of the specific audio interface, chances are that the maximum voltage it can output is way under the typical CV voltages. My own audio interface is capable of outputting about +-4.81 volts (measured using a multimeter). While many modules of analog modular systems use +-5 volt ranges, it's not unusual to find MIDI-to-CV converters that can output 10 volts. Since it's a common standard to perform pitch control using 1V/octave, this results in a pitch control over 10 octaves, which an audio interface typically won't be able to do.

So these are two quite limiting facts right? What we can always do though is create clock signals in Max/MSP, regardless of the audio interface. Alternatives to using an audio interface are MIDI-to-CV converters or specialized DAC solutions such as the ones the company Expert Sleepers offers.

In the following screenshot, you see a tiny Max patch that shows how one can generate CV signals using the audio interface:

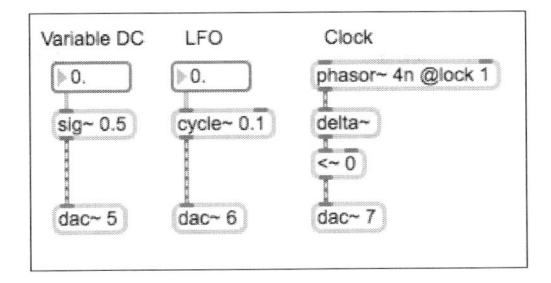

```
Variable DC          LFO              Clock
  ▶ 0.              ▶ 0.            phasor~ 4n @lock 1
 sig~ 0.5         cycle~ 0.1           delta~
                                        <~ 0
 dac~ 5            dac~ 6             dac~ 7
```

A very obvious thought when thinking about *Max/MSP + Modular Synth = ?* is routing each output of the synth into the computer and going from the computer to all the modular synths inputs. This way, we can do the patching inside Max, create presets of how our synth is patched, and so on. This is perfectly possible, but beware, it's not that simple. Again, there are two limiting factors:

- The number of inputs/outputs of our interface
- The I/O latency

The latency is a bit of a bummer. The problem is that if we connect a couple of analog synth modules in series inside Max, we are creating a chain of ADC/DAC conversions. So the more connections in series, the more latency we get. In many situations, we can live with that, so go ahead and try it if you have a modular somewhere around. A different solution for digital patching would involve an Arduino, some relays, and no DAC/ADCs. So let's take a look at Arduino.

Arduino and microcontrollers

To put it simply, a microcontroller is something like a very small computer designed to be used in embedded systems. The Arduino board is a small circuit board that features a programmable microcontroller. It's an open source project and comes in many different flavors. There are also options other than Arduino, but since this is so common, and we can't offer a complete microcontroller course here, we'll just stick to Arduino.

While Arduino can act on its own, without a computer controlling it, it's also the most common method of getting miscellaneous (non audio) voltage into or out of Max, TouchDesigner, and the like. This enables us to read sensors, control motors, and build custom MIDI or OSC controllers, and just opens up the wonderful world of physical computing.

Connecting Our Software to the World

In the following screenshot, you can see an Arduino UNO, which is one of the most common Arduino versions:

Original image at `http://arduino.cc/en/uploads/Main/ArduinoUno_R3_Front.jpg`

The real advantage of Arduino is that there are many so-called shields available that one can just stack on the board without any soldering, which offer things like an Ethernet connection. Without any shield, Arduino features a bunch of digital inputs and outputs and a couple of analog ins and outs, a USB connector to program the board and for communication, and a couple of other connectors. Refer to `http://www.arduino.cc/` to get more information, specifications, and a lot of documentation and examples.

So how is the communication between an Arduino board and Max established? First of all, there is a project called **Maxuino** (`http://www.maxuino.org/`), which offers Max patches and Arduino sketches that communicate without us having to program a lot. Here, instead of describing this project, we will just take a look at how to read out a potentiometer in Max using the `[serial]` object.

An Arduino example project

We plan to get a potentiometer, wire it up to Arduino, and control some parameters inside Max with it. Hooray! We won't get 7 bits, that is 128 values, as we have when using MIDI; we can get 10 bits, that is 1024 values; what a resolution! This really pays off for certain parameters when using it to control FM synthesis for example.

First, go to the Arduino web page and download and install the Arduino software. If you are on Windows, you'll also have to install drivers, so go to Arduino's **Getting Started** page at http://arduino.cc/en/Guide/HomePage.

There, you'll also see that you have to tell the software what serial port and board you are using. Next, let's have a look at the hardware.

Hardware requirements for the Arduino project

What we need is Arduino, a linear 1k Ohm potentiometer for example, some wires, a soldering iron, and a USB cable to hook up Arduino to the computer.

We'll solder three wires to the potentiometer, one on each pin. Now, the middle wire will go to an analog in, and the other two will go to 5V for an Arduino UNO (take care, have a look at the maximum input voltage your board can take!), and to the ground. Which pin of the potentiometer goes to the voltage source and which to the ground only inverts what we get from the potentiometer. Since we can just invert it again in the software, one could say it doesn't matter. We plug the Arduino into our computer and finally end up with something like this:

Here, the Arduino DUE has been used and not the Arduino UNO, so it looks a little different.

Using the software package **Fritzing**, from `http://fritzing.org/`, we can sketch our wiring before connecting. In the following screenshot, you can see the wiring, using an Arduino UNO:

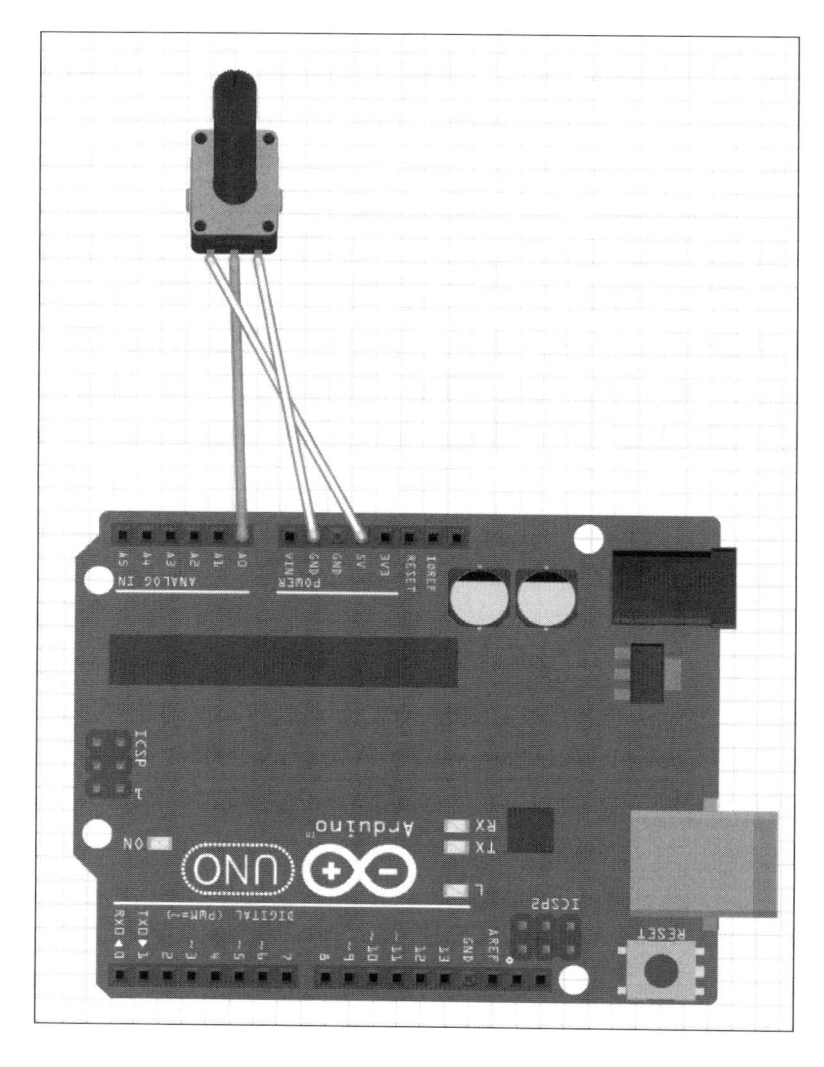

This can help a lot when we plan more complex wirings before soldering.

Chapter 12

> Soldering is easy. However, if you have never done it, you should definitely get some information, maybe watch some videos online, or ask somebody to help you. The real danger is, even if you have never done it, you will be successful anyway, you will achieve your targets, and you will be able to solder within minutes, but in a very frustrating way. There are some simple and not at all obvious tricks that make soldering very convenient, and if you don't know them, you might be tempted to think that you can solder, but soldering is a very tedious task.

Alright, now let's turn to the software side of things.

The Arduino code

As soon as you get Arduino running and configured on the port and board, we can start programming. Here, we will use an example sketch that comes with the software and rather care for the Max side of things. In the Arduino software, go to **File | Examples | 03.Analog | AnalogInOutSerial** to open the example sketch. What's a patch in Max is a sketch in Arduino; it's simply the Arduino speak for code that can be compiled and uploaded to the board. Upload the code right away by pressing the little arrow button in the Arduino interface. The code is well documented, so you'll hopefully see what happens pretty fast. Let's quickly look at parts of the program to see what really matters to us. Note that there is an Arduino package for Sublime Text, which makes writing, reading, or modifying the code a lot easier.

On line 24, you will find the following code:

```
const int analogInPin = A0;
```

Here, the analog pin is chosen, so we have to connect our potentiometer to pin 0 or change this line.

On line 32, you will find the following code:

```
Serial.begin(9600);
```

The preceding code starts up the serial communication with a baud rate of 9600 baud. This, roughly speaking, sets the speed of the connection. The baud rate is related to but not the same as the bit rate. This is also important since sender and receiver have to be adjusted to the same baud rate. So, as we will see, we will have to tell Max this value if we want to receive information in Max.

Have a look at lines 44 to 47:

```
Serial.print("sensor = " );
  Serial.print(sensorValue);
  Serial.print("\t output = ");
  Serial.println(outputValue);
```

Connecting Our Software to the World

This prints out the data to the serial port. The variables `sensorValue` and `outputValue` are assigned a bit earlier in the code. The point here is that we concatenate messages, and note that the last line here, that is 47, says `serial.println` not `print`, and this means that we print a new line after this. We will make use of this in Max later. Also, note that this code not only reads an analog pin and prints the value to the serial port, but it also outputs voltage to an analog out. In our example, we are not particularly interested in this, and we are not really interested in receiving the analog output value in Max. You might consider deleting some of the code if you don't need this functionality, and you might adapt the code to use our beloved OSC syntax. At the moment, this code sends something like this:

```
sensor = somevalue   output = somevalue
```

This might not be the most handy thing when dealing with it in Max. Let's change it to something like this:

```
/potentiometers/1 somevalue
```

The preceding syntax will be a lot easier to handle inside Max, especially if you add more potentiometers, switches, and so on. We can see what comes out of Arduino if we open Arduino's serial monitor by going to **Tools | Serial Monitor**. This way, we can check nicely whether our soldering, uploading, and the whole Arduino business worked out and whether we can now turn to Max. You should see something like this:

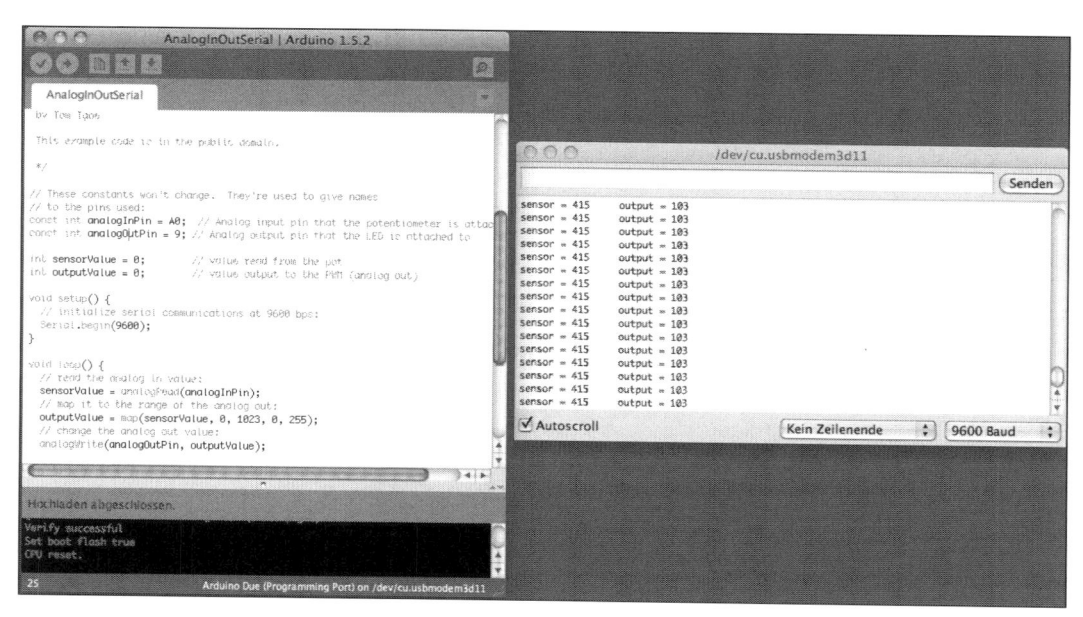

Try turning the potentiometer and see whether the values make sense. If they do, we can turn to Max and see how we can get the values into our patch. Refer to the following screenshot:

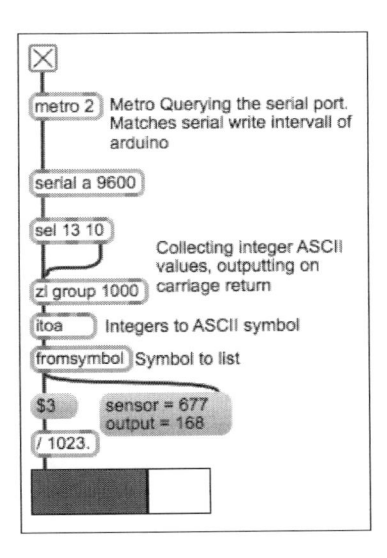

[metro 2] Metro Querying the serial port. Matches serial write intervall of arduino
[serial a 9600]
[sel 13 10]
[zl group 1000] Collecting integer ASCII values, outputting on carriage return
[itoa] Integers to ASCII symbol
[fromsymbol] Symbol to list
[$3] sensor = 677 output = 168
[/ 1023.]

The patcher depicted previously should receive our values, but if not, note that there is a small pitfall.

> Before we start receiving the values and dive into Max, note that it's not possible for two applications to read the serial port at the same time. An application can open and close ports, and if an application fails to close a port properly, bad things can happen, such as crashes, or another application may not be able to connect to the port. During the development of a sketch that should communicate with Max, since we switch back and forth between Max and the Arduino software, we are asking for problems a bit. One way around these problems, which I prefer over serial communication, is the Arduino Ethernet shield. Using this shield, we can just get all our data into Max via UDP and avoid these problems.

So, there is the [serial] object. Since we just discussed this, there are the open and close messages to open and close the port. Also, there is the autoopen attribute (which is on by default), which handles opening and closing automatically. We have to tell [serial] which port we would like to use and what the baud rate will be.

The rest is simple; we just collect the integers that represent the **American Standard Code for Information Interchange (ASCII)** characters, and output the group on reception of a carriage return (ASCII value 13). We then convert this group to characters and end up with our decoded messages.

In TouchDesigner, as in Max, the syntax of the messages that we send is kind of cumbersome. Nevertheless, let's see how to extract the sensor value of the message as it is. We'll use the serial DAT to receive the messages. We could use Python to get the value, but here, we'll use a handy little trick to parse tables. If a table has values in cells that contain too much information and we want a finer table resolution, so that one cell would contain the word sensor and one would contain the actual value, we can do a conversion. We convert the whole table to text, and convert back to a table again using the space cell-split character. In the following screenshot, you can see the final TouchDesigner version of receiving the values:

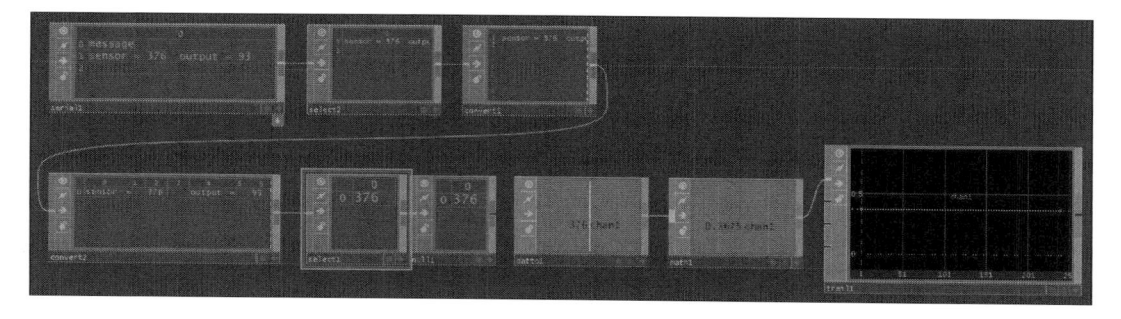

So you see, it's not that hard, and if you have mastered this exercise, you are ready to build some small OSC controllers!

Pure Data

Pure Data (PD) is very similar to Max, so if you are good at Max, you can be good at PD too if you make some time for it. While it doesn't look as polished as Max does and it might seem to have a lot less features, don't underestimate it. Pure Data also has many advantages over Max/MSP, so it's a good thing to have some experience with it. Some of the main advantages over Max include:

- It's free
- It's open source
- It runs on Linux
- It's very lightweight
- We can use `libpd` to use PD patches on Android or iOS for example

So PD really has some very convincing features. When you are accustomed to working in Max, changing to PD might be a little frustrating, simply because in the back of your head, you know that you could be quicker in Max (just because you know Max and you don't know PD), but don't blame the tool. One of the biggest advantages might be its ability to run on Linux. This opens up possibilities such as running a patch on a Raspberry Pi or similar small computers. We can easily prototype an effect in Max, translate it to PD, put it on a Raspberry Pi, and build a nice little box around it to end up with a standalone device that only does signal processing. Here are some links to get you going:

- http://puredata.info/docs/tutorials/PdForMaxUsers
- http://www.raspberrypi.org/
- http://beagleboard.org/bone
- http://www.udoo.org/

Multi-touch screens

As soon as you have mastered TouchDesigner and Max, multi-touch screens shouldn't be much of a problem for you. Since Microsoft Windows 7, we have native multi-touch that is piped to any application. Max can't do anything with multi-touch, but is OK with single-touch events. So if you have a touchscreen, you can just fire up your Max patch GUI and start playing around with it. If you'd like to use multi-touch, one way to do this is to build an interface with TouchDesigner. Inside TD, we have no problems whatsoever using any standard multi-touch screen, and we can just send our controls to Max via OSC if we need to control a Max patch.

How is multi-touch used inside TD? We can just use a regular Container COMP, and it will react to multi-touch input just as it would when we click on it with the mouse. However, there is also multi-touch in DAT that gives us either raw data or a table that shows us all touch events with an index number per finger as follows:

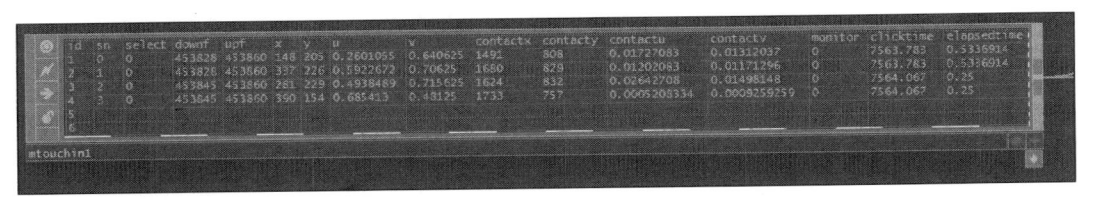

This table can, for example, be used to drive a Render Pick DAT if we wish, to build 3D multi-touch interfaces.

> A complete example of using multi-touch in combination with render picking can be found at http://www.derivative.ca/Forum/viewtopic.php?f=36&t=5560.
>
> For the sake of completeness, there is a Max external called **Fingerpinger**, which reads multi-touch information from trackpads. It can be found at http://www.anyma.ch/2009/research/multitouch-external-for-maxmsp/.

The TUIO protocol

When working on multimedia installations, it's very likely you will encounter the TUIO protocol. It is most known for its use of the famous **Reactable** synthesizer and the software **reacTIVision**. In case you not only encounter TUIO but also reacTIVision, you will also encounter the famous marker image depicted in the following screenshot:

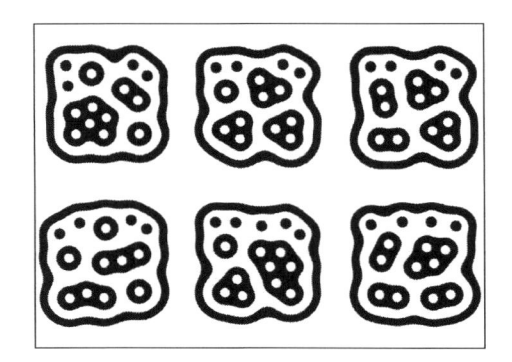

Original image at
http://reactivision.sourceforge.net/images/reactivision02.png

The reacTIVision application is software that allows us to make use of the so-called markers or tags (depicted previously) to identify objects we film with a camera. There is lots of documentation online, so we don't need to go through all the details here. If we'd like to make use of these markers, we just have to install the reacTIVision software and run it; what do you think we'll get out of it? TUIO via UDP. TUIO is a protocol (that utilizes the OSC protocol), which is used to talk about 2D and 3D coordinates of single or multiple objects, their IDs, appearance, and disappearance. It's very similar to what a touchscreen would tell us about us touching the screen, with the additional functionality of being able to communicate 3D coordinates and a lot more (angle, dimension, velocity vectors, and so on).

So this is the most used method to talk about multi-touch gestures in a wider sense. Both in Max and in TouchDesigner, we can receive and decode TUIO pretty quickly; an example patch and even an external for Max can be found at http://www.tuio.org/?software and an example tox for TD is available on the TD wiki at http://www.derivative.ca/wiki088/index.php?title=TUIO.

When working on a TD project or Max patch that's supposed to receive TUIO information, be sure to check out the TUIO simulator, which can also be found on the TUIO website. It enables you to simulate a device that is sending TUIO data to the patch you are developing, so you can see whether it behaves well.

Interfacing other programs

Sometimes, we need to interface other programs either because they fulfill our needs for a certain task so well that we just don't need or want to program something ourselves, or because they can do things we just can't do in Max or TD. A very likely scenario is the communication with other multimedia applications such as vvvv, processing, or a DAW-like Cubase, or Pro Tools. We are now going to list some ways of interfacing these programs and think about what we would prefer over what and why.

Open Sound Control (OSC)

You already know **Open Sound Control** (**OSC**), so we won't talk a lot about it here. Typically, we use it on the UDP layer, and it will be our first choice for communication between different pieces of software and if the data we want to transfer is not audio or video but messages. Communicating via the network has a huge advantage in that there is nearly no effort needed to change from a scenario in which both pieces of software (Max and TD, for example) run on the same machine, to a scenario in which we use one machine per application. The problem, which luckily slowly diminishes, is that some applications don't support OSC.

MIDI

MIDI is such an old trusted protocol that every serious multimedia application supports it. Also, the availability of hardware MIDI controllers is a big plus of the MIDI protocol. Due to MIDI's lower data rates, higher latency, and lower resolution, OSC is preferable over MIDI. Anyway, sometimes, we need to communicate with an application on the same machine using MIDI. Here, a couple of free software solutions are available for Windows, such as MIDI Yoke. On Mac, the audio MIDI setup can be used to activate the IAC driver, resulting in a virtual MIDI device that can be used for inter-application MIDI communication. One advantage of MIDI over OSC is that we have standardized widespread syncing methods, such as **MIDI Timecode (MTC)** and MIDI beat clock.

Keystrokes and simulated user activity

Sometimes, we need to take desperate measures. This is the case if we need to communicate with an application that just doesn't understand any language we speak. It does not know OSC or MIDI or any other protocol that we might be able to generate. It might be an application that just isn't made to be communicated with. This is the point where we have to use aka.keyboard and aka.mouse. More information on these can be found at http://www.iamas.ac.jp/~aka/max/. A situation in which this might be the quickest solution would be if somebody asks us to program a patch that would drive a PowerPoint presentation via clapping. It's really easy to make Max generate a keystroke with these externals and we don't even have to think about if there is a different way of communicating with PowerPoint.

Audio and video

We often need to send audio between applications. The simplest and a bit dirty way is to do physical feedback, meaning we go out of the audio interface and back in. If we use digital inputs and outputs, such as SPDIF, Toslink, and ADAT, we don't even have a loss in quality. This admittedly awkward solution has the advantage that we can directly use the audio interface in both applications, meaning we have full access to all inputs and outputs in each of them. The usual solution to the problem of interchanging audio signals is the use of software, such as Jack Audio or Soundflower. While this is nice in theory, it's an additional piece of software that has to be configured correctly, which has to run stably and start before the other applications. However, as soon as you have an external audio interface, you most likely have a digital input and output, which probably is unused most of the time. So keep in mind that you can scratch that additional piece of software if problems arise.

It is also possible to send audio over networks. In Max, we can do this via the transformation of audio into Jitter matrices. We can use [jit.net.send] and [jit.net.recv] to then send the information via TCP. In the following screenshot, you see an example of how this can be done:

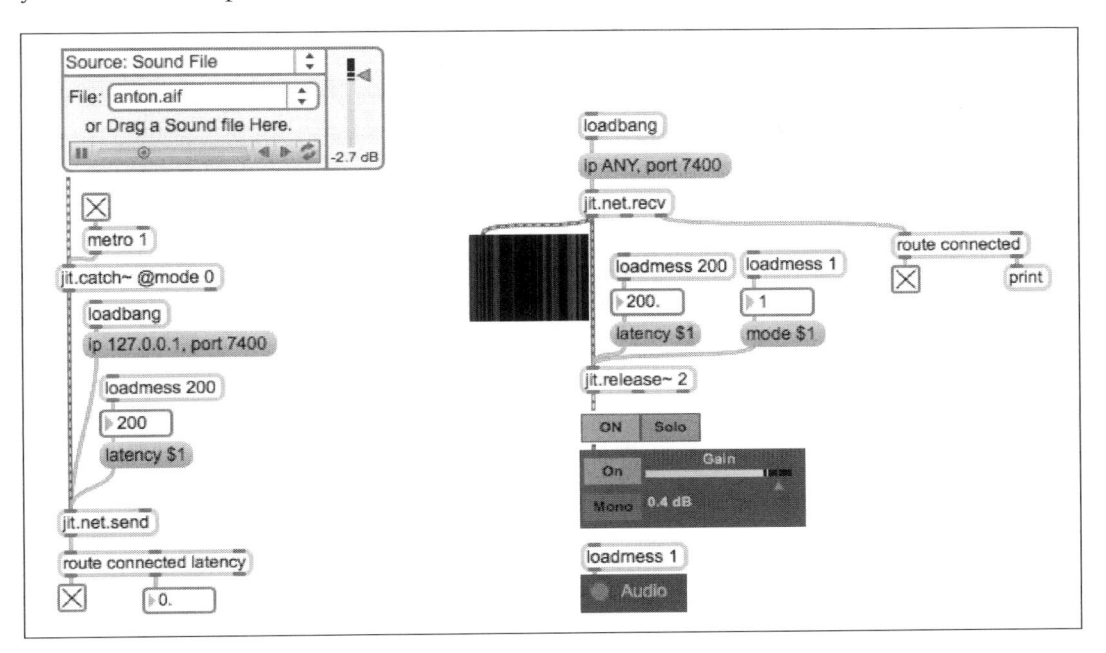

Since this information can theoretically also be decoded by other programs, we can also use this technique for inter-application data streaming. One example of an app that can decode Jitter matrices that are sent from a jit.net.send object is vvvv. Matthias Husinsky wrote a vvvv node for this purpose, which can be found at http://vvvv.org/contribution/maxjitter-matrix-nodes.

Another desire regarding audio streaming might be to broadcast. We might want to stream our audio jams and make it possible for people around the world to listen to the stream using regular stream players such us Winamp or VLC. An external for Ogg/Vorbis streaming can be found at http://www.nullmedium.de/dev/oggpro/.

A very efficient way to communicate between applications is shared memory inside TouchDesigner. In the commercial version of TD, we find the shared memory in and out TOPs, CHOPs, and COMPs. Some efficient ways of communicating with a DirectX program, such as vvvv, are the DirectX in and out TOPs.

Two all-round tools for GPU-accelerated video streaming, so essentially texture-sharing, are Syphon and Spout, which can be found at http://syphon.v002.info/ and http://spout.zeal.co/.

Multispeaker setups

We haven't discussed multispeaker setups at all. In fact, most of our audio examples were only mono. While stereo is just straightforward and sends signals to multiple audio outputs too, what if we'd like to have some more sophisticated control about the spatialization in a, say, four-speaker setup? This can get really complex, so we rely on some externals here.

There are multiple techniques to approach the problem of how to perceptually position an acoustic phenomenon in 3D space. One of them is called **ambisonics**. For ambisonics, the following three different libraries are available:

- http://www.mshparisnord.fr/hoalibrary/en/downloads/max/
- http://spatium.ruipenha.pt/max/
- http://www.icst.net/de/forschung/download/ambisonics-externals-for-maxmsp/

In the following screenshot, you can see a patch contained in the ICST Max/MSP package. It illustrates the library's capabilities in distributing two sounds over eight speakers, but these are not the limits of the system.

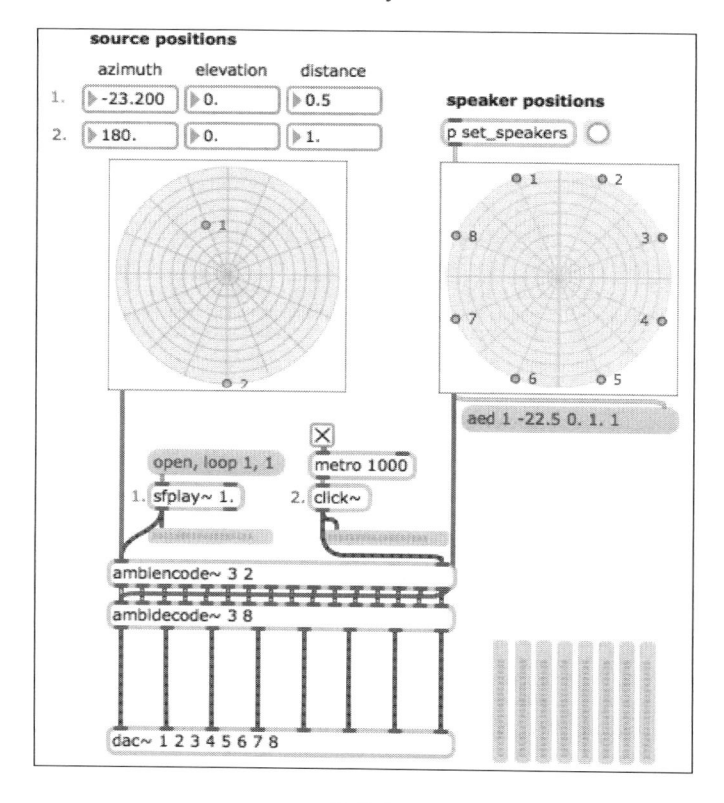

As you can see, we can inform the system about our speaker setup and move around our sound sources in space. Although we can only see a 2D representation in the previous screenshot, 3D placement is also possible.

Exhibitions

Often, Max and TouchDesigner are used in exhibitions. The following are some main points we often have to be careful about when preparing, planning, and finally producing a multimedia piece for an exhibition:

- **Communication**: Communication is the key. In an exhibition, most of the time, there are a lot of people involved and we will want to know everything we can.
- **The room, cabling, and so on**: The room, the furniture, and the cabling are factors that are very crucial. If possible (but often not), visit the room before you plan your exhibit. If you need to design furniture (for a computer screen, for example), think about cable lengths, or start up some CAD software to plan everything thoroughly. If you have done this, you also have a proper plan in your hand, which can further improve communication with exhibition designers for example.
- **Making things robust and secure**: In public exhibitions, robustness and security is very important. The user should have no obvious possibility to sabotage our installations. There shouldn't be the possibility to easily turn off our screens, for example, and everything should be stable in a physical sense, so we don't have to do a lot of maintenance. Security is a different topic; talk to the project managers or other responsible staff; just to give you an example: it's very likely you can't use rough sawn wood surfaces, even in places where it's unlikely they are going to be touched.
- Starting up and shutting down
- Maintenance
- Migration

Starting up and shutting down our system automatically is probably not necessary, since the exhibition staff could do it for us. But it's nice, both for you and the staff, if you make sure that the computer that controls your exhibit is not going to be touched unnecessarily. If we need or want our system to start up automatically, we have to hope that our BIOS in case of a Windows machine supports this. But even if it doesn't, it would be nice if the museum staff just have to push the power button in the morning, and our patches start up automatically.

This can be done using a batch file under Windows. Such a batch file could look like this:

```
TIMEOUT 60
Start "" "X:\PathToMaxRuntime\MaxRT.exe" X:\PathToMaxPatch\myPatch.maxpat
TIMEOUT 30
Start "" "X:\PathToTouchDesigner\touchdesigner088.exe" X:\PathToToe\MyProject.toe
```

These are just four lines; don't insert line breaks between the app name and filename. What this does is if this batch file is called, it first waits for 60 seconds (or a keystroke), then starts the Max patch of our choice, then waits another 30 seconds, and lastly launches TouchDesigner. This waiting time is useful since if we launch the script on startup, we have to wait for our computer to have settled and really be ready for use. The same is true after starting the Max patch. Typically, we'd like to start up an interface or visualization in TouchDesigner, which should really be fullscreen. We don't want any Max patch to suddenly appear because it took too much time to start up. The TIMEOUT file helps us here.

This batch file can then reside in the Autostart folder (in the Start menu) to be executed on startup. A nice alternative to this is the free application **Restart on Crash**, which will both launch programs on startup and also watch them, so if they hang or crash, it will just restart them automatically.

Now, how do we shut down the computer at a specified time? There are many possibilities and small programs that could do this for us, but a nice way is to use **sy** inside TouchDesigner for this if we are using TD anyway. Now, we put the following small Python script inside a DAT:

```
import subprocess
subprocess.call(["shutdown", "-f", "-s", "-t", "60"])
```

When we run this DAT on a Windows machine, the machine will shut down in 60 seconds. The clock CHOP can give us the time, a little math and logic can check whether it's late enough, and a CHOP that executed DAT can fire our script, as shown in the following screenshot:

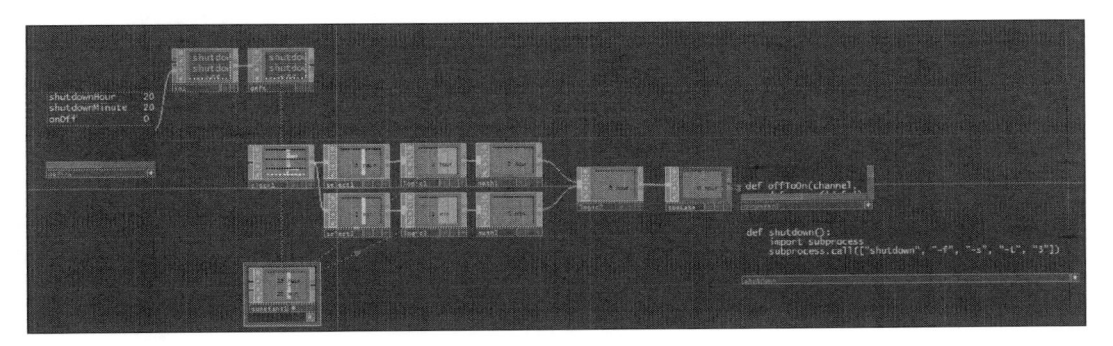

Sadly, in Max, we lack such direct access to the operating system, but there are externals such as **DOShack** and **aka.shell** to the rescue. These allow us to issue commands to the OS, enabling us to shut down a computer using Max.

Finally, maintenance is something we have to keep low and practical. Some **Virtual Network Computing** (**VNC**) software will help us to do maintenance remotely if there are any problems with our software and will even allow us to upgrade the system later.

Migration is also an important topic if we want to distribute our code. So, we will talk a bit about it, first and foremost, the case of exporting an application that should run on other systems. When designing a multimedia piece for an exhibition, we will often partly develop programs on our personal machines, and then migrate to the machine that will finally stand around in the exhibition. This migration process is a source of errors and should happen as early as possible. The ideal case being, to develop the whole program only on the machine it will run on, eliminating migration completely.

The Max projects feature helps us to manage files, and checks for dependencies, so this is ideal for the preparation of migration. Honestly, I personally use the projects feature to keep things tidy, but ultimately, I use the path message in `[thispatcher]` to load files. This is very similar to the TouchDesigner system. In TouchDesigner, we allow TD to create a project folder and then use `project.folder+'/image/myImage.png'` to access a picture in the `image` folder via Python. This way, we are independent of the location of the whole project folder. The same can be done in Max; we can allow Max to manage our project folder, but access items explicitly using the path message as follows:

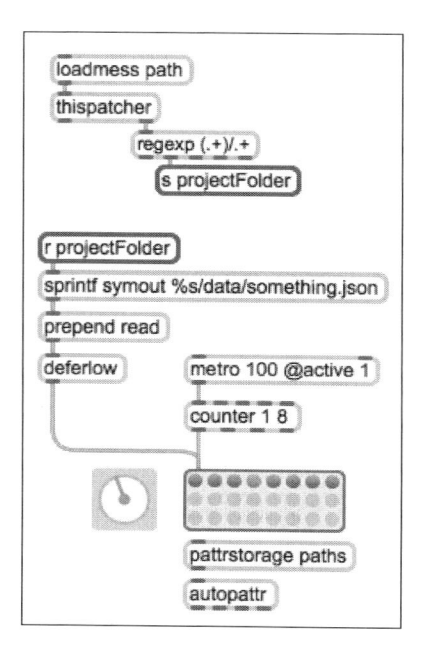

```
loadmess path
thispatcher
    regexp (.+)/.+
    s projectFolder

r projectFolder
sprintf symout %s/data/something.json
prepend read
deferlow          metro 100 @active 1
                  counter 1 8

                  pattrstorage paths
                  autopattr
```

You might wonder what we can win when doing things like this. The big advantage is that we can use any folder structure. At some point, we might not be happy with the structure that is proposed by Max's projects. We probably need to deal with a lot of data and have to come up with a more sophisticated folder structure to keep things tidy and useful. Think about having a hierarchical folder system for samples for instance.

Exporting an application

If we want to distribute our patches to people who don't have a Max license, we can just send our patches and tell them to install Max anyway, so they can open the patch with Max Runtime or the demo license. If we, however, don't want them to be able to edit the patcher, we are going to build a **Max collective**. A Max collective may include many patchers, files, and folders. To run it, a valid Max installation is still necessary. Alternatively, we can just build a **standalone application**, which will not require Max or Max runtime to be installed. Since the processes of creating a standalone and a collective are very similar, we will concentrate on building an application. One factor we always have to be careful with is the operating system compatibility. A Max collective has the advantage of being platform-independent, as a patcher is. If we use any externals though, we need to make sure we include Mac and Windows versions to keep things compatible. On the other hand, if we build an application, we have to build it on the OS it is supposed to run on anyway, and of course, it will not be platform-independent. We will end up with a `.exe` file when working on Windows and a `.app` package on Mac.

If we wish to export an application from a patcher, we just open it and go to **File | Build Collective | Application**. We are presented with what's called the **Collective Editor**, as shown in the following screenshot:

This dialog's official documentation can be found at `http://cycling74.com/docs/max6/dynamic/c74_docs.html#collective_editor`.

If we just push the **Build** button now, we can choose either collective or application, save it, and we are done. This is the most straightforward route to making an application out of a Max patch. What about dependencies of the patch, such as externals and sound files? The build process will try to manage this to the best of its abilities, so it will look for abstractions, externals, and the like. However, as soon as we require files in the patcher that are not referenced in a hardcoded way, for example, we plan to load different sound files into buffers via messages; the build script won't know about it.

This is why we have the option of adding files and folders. If we do add a file, for example, you will see that our script will be expanded as shown in the following screenshot:

```
Script
open thispatcher
include SSD:/PROJECTAS/SAMPLES/2SEC/2011_10_28-16_45_47.wav
```

The script we see previously says that we want to use the current patcher that we wish to open on application startup, and that we want to include the `2011_10_28-16_45_47.wav` file. Often, exporting an application is an iterative process; we export, see what we messed up or find a bug, correct the patcher, and export it again. Therefore, it makes a lot of sense to save the script alongside the patcher, especially if there are a lot of files we need to include.

When this is done, we'll have an app or exe, but there will be a lot of little details we won't quite be satisfied with. What about the icon of our app? Why is the Max window opening with our app? We'll have to configure our patcher, our Script, and our resulting app or exe a bit more.

First of all, there is the `[standalone]` object. We can just put it in our patcher and look in its object inspector to find these options:

standalone	
Audio Support	☑
Can't Close Toplevel Patchers	☑
Database	☐
Disable Loadbang Defeating	☐
Enable All Windows Active	☐
Enable Overdrive	☐
Extensions	☑
MIDI Support	☑
Make Application Subfolder Search Path	☐
Preferences File Name	"Max 6 Preferences"
Search for Missing Files	☑
Status Window Visible at Startup	☑

Here, we can uncheck the **Status Window Visible at Startup** option to hide the Max window. Obviously, there are many other options; some can greatly reduce the size of our applications, such as when we uncheck audio and MIDI support if we don't need it. Two settings are a bit less obvious in what they mean, but quite important: **Make Application Subfolder Search Path** and **Search for Missing Files**. If **Make Application Subfolder Search Path** is checked, the app will add the whole folder in which the app resides to the search path. This is nice as long as we have our app inside its own folder as is often the case on Windows systems. On Mac, an app typically just resides inside the `applications` folder. Therefore, the whole `applications` folder is then added to our app's search path, which at best, makes our app's startup slow, and at worst, produces conflicts. We just don't know the `applications` folder of a potential user.

The **Search for Missing Files** option seems like a setting that should always be turned on. However, it's really handy in development, so we can check whether everything is contained in the app's collective. If this is on, the search path will also be used for the missing files.

Customizing an application

To customize an app's look, a combination of the patcher inspector and the `[thispatcher]` object can be used. We can prevent the resizing of the patcher, set our app's window floating, and hide the scrollbars and the title bar, as shown in the following screenshot:

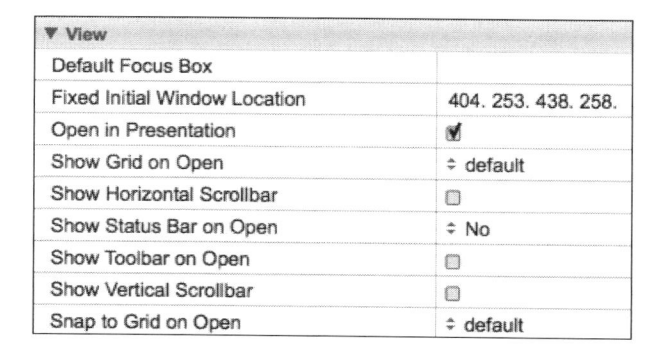

▼ View	
Default Focus Box	
Fixed Initial Window Location	404. 253. 438. 258.
Open in Presentation	✓
Show Grid on Open	≑ default
Show Horizontal Scrollbar	☐
Show Status Bar on Open	≑ No
Show Toolbar on Open	☐
Show Vertical Scrollbar	☐
Snap to Grid on Open	≑ default

The **Fixed Initial Window Location** parameter can simply be set by dragging the patcher's window into place, resizing it to our preference, and navigating to **View | Define Initial Window Location** instead of trying out numbers.

A couple of messages to `[thispatcher]` at startup make our app floating, prevent resizing, and remove the title bar. Refer to the following screenshot:

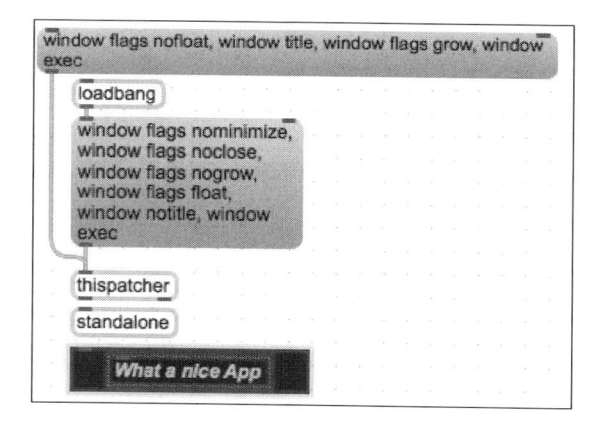

Since this initialization of the patcher restricts us (no resizing, no scrollbars, and so on), it's a good idea to place an emergency exit in the upper-left corner; a message box that allows us to resize this turns off floating and gives us back a title bar.

Chapter 12

If we render out a patcher without a title bar, a user won't be able to move the window. Sometimes, we don't want the user to be able to reposition a patcher window, but most of the time, this will just be annoying. What if we really don't like the look of the OS title bar but still want the user to be able to reposition the window? Here, [panel] comes to the rescue. It has an attribute called `Drag Window`, which if enabled, allows us to drag around the patcher window if we drag the panel. This way, we can just design our own titlebar. So, although it might seem unfamiliar, what you see in the following screenshot of a patcher in front of a grey desktop. At this point, remembering the shortcuts to switch between the locked and unlocked mode (*command/Ctrl + E*) and between the presentation and edit mode (*option/alt + command/Ctrl + E*) really pays off; otherwise, you'll always have to go to **View |easily get stuck.**

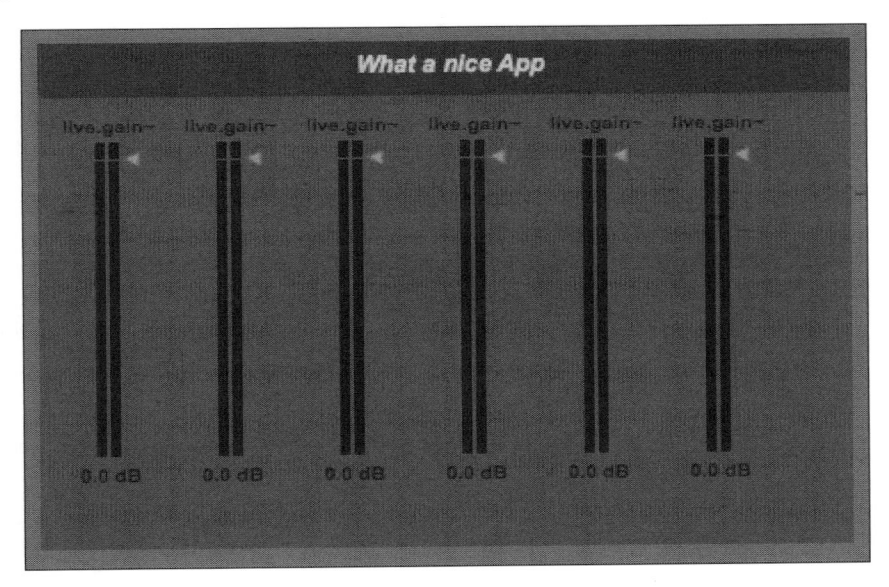

Finally, we probably want to give our app an icon. On Mac, we will need to convert an image into a `.icns` file; on Windows, we'll need a `.ico` file. On Mac OS, we have a preinstalled app called **Icon Composer**, which easily allows us to create a `.icns` file; on Windows, GIMP can be used to create a `.ico` file.

To configure our build script to set the application icon, we just have to add `appicon` and a path (in quote marks if it contains spaces). Refer to the following screenshot:

```
Script
open thispatcher
appicon SSD:/PROJECTAS/ICONS/myIcon.icns
```

Sometimes, we also want to customize the menu bar of our application. The [menubar] object allows us to do this easily. Refer to the following screenshot:

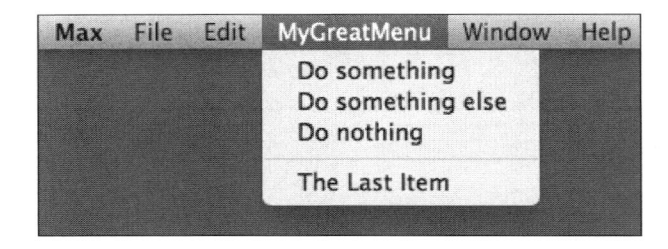

A very good resource to get information about how to achieve even more customization, how to protect an exported application, and how to make installers for our applications (which are not needed in most cases but can be nice) can be found at http://defectiverecords.com/expo74/standalones.pdf.

Collaborative work

Being able to work collaboratively in Max or TD is important. There are a couple of points that really make things a lot easier if we work as a team, and although they may seem trivial, let's think about these for a moment.

Imagine we develop a project that features audio and video, and probably some electronics too. We can't develop everything at the same time, and while we are probably responsible for audio, somebody else is doing video input and output, and a third person is doing electronics. That's the setup and it's not a very unlikely one. What is also likely to happen is that the components, so audio video, and electronics meet at a point in time, at which they are somewhat mature. So what we really need to know is how the different parts will communicate, and when it is likely that we will be able to try out this communication. The *when* is particularly interesting here, since in many cases, we might need to build a small patch that simulates the input we will get from the guy's electronic devices for example. Depending on his development timeline, we will invest more or less work to accurately simulate the data.

A different matter is data organization. We can't work collaboratively if we don't use abstraction. Parts of a program have to feature a certain amount of modularity or we will either get lost or lose a lot of time. Similarly, documentation is important. We need to allow our colleagues to know what a certain piece of code means; we need to document our to-do's and any known bugs. A very good practice in regards of documentation is color coding our patches and TD projects. Hopefully, you are already accustomed to coloring up your programs, so you find things a bit faster. Why not talk about your coloring schemes with your fellows and declare certain color standards for certain collaborations? Also, setting up a small Wiki can help a lot to document a project, to communicate, and to fix standards and protocols that are used in a project.

Regarding abstraction and file management, Git and Github are extremely powerful tools for version management collaborative programming in general. However, even Dropbox or similar services can be used to keep a team's resources synchronized. A very handy and slightly hidden feature of Max along these lines is the Max preference **Resolve Search Path Aliases**, which is off by default. If we activate it, we can put an alias to a Dropbox folder into the Max packages' folder, so we can use common clippings, abstractions, code, and all the Max goodness in sync with others or the multiple machines we might be working with.

Summary

We have now tried to get an overview of what to actually do with our patches and programs. We have seen how to access other electronic devices using microcontrollers; we have looked at how to publish our programs as applications and thought about how to prepare to leaving our patches alone in an exhibition. There are many devices, gadgets, and interfaces we didn't discuss, such as the Kinect, Leap Motion, Oculus Rift, and so on. Mainly, we did not talk about these because there are only very few possibilities how we could interface these. Either they support a protocol we know, or we see whether we can find an external or application that generates a protocol we understand. For the Kinect in Max, it would be the latter case. There is an application called Synapse, which can send OSC to Max. In TD, on the other hand, we have dedicated OPs for the Kinect. This is more or less true for all of these gadgets. A little research will most often lead us to some way of interfacing them.

This concludes the journey into the technical aspects of multimedia programming using Max and TouchDesigner. I want to wish you lots of inspiration for all the projects ahead, and hope that the technical skills presented in this book form a solid basis for your own experiments and research in the field of digital audiovisual expression.

Index

Symbols

2D composting example 278-280
3D GUIs 329-333
3D rendering
  about 302-304
  data, SOPs 308-314
  material, assigning 306, 307
  SOPs 304, 305
[autopattr] object 75
[deferlow] object 82
[jit.gl.material] object 213
[jit.matrixset] object 211
[live.number] object 229
[live.object] 227
[live.path] object 227
[loadbang] object 58
[loadmess] object 58
[matrix] object 78
[multislider] object 114
#n notation 66, 67
[noise] patch 58
[numbox] object 148
[onepole] patch 58
[param] object 186
[pattrstorage] object 74
[preset] object 74
[print] object 47, 48
[swatch] object 208
[thispatcher] object 87
[toggle] object 148
@transport attribute 80

A

abstraction 187
abstraction, Max
  about 33-36
  advantages 35
abstraction, project 265
additive synthesis
  about 112-114
  DSF 114-116
After Fader Listening (AFL) 134
aka.shell 363
ambisonics
  about 360
  libraries 360
American Standard Code for Information
        Interchange (ASCII) 354
Amp heading 224
amplitude modulation
  about 91-93
  tremolo 95
  versus ring modulation 94
analog synths 346, 347
animation COMP
  used, for nonlinear work 296
Animation component
  about 294-296
  animation COMP, using for
    nonlinear work 296
  URL 294
Animation editors
  URL 294

application
  customizing 368-370
  exporting 365-367
Arduino
  about 347
  advantages 348
  example project 349
  PD 355
  URL 348
Arduino code 351-354
ARGB 208
arguments 40-42
Attribute Create SOP 308
attributes 43, 45
audio 358, 359
audio file playback 128-131
Audio in/out, Max for Live 222
audio interface, using
  issues 346
audio principles 89, 90
audio ramp
  about 300
  advantages 300
audio-reactive video 272-277
audio status window, Max
  about 24-27
  audio 25
  CPU utilization 27
  driver 25
  function calls 27
  In Audio interrupt (Scheduler) 26, 27
  input device 25
  I/O Vector Size 25
  output device 25
  parallel processing 27
  sampling rate 26
  Scheduler, in Overdrive 26
  signals used 27
  Signal Vector Size 26
audio synthesis
  about 90
  additive synthesis 112-114
  amplitude modulation 91-93
  feedback 96-98
  filtering 116-118

frequency modulation 98-100
poly~ object 106-108
subtractive synthesis 116-118
waveshaping 126-128
auto-compile button 185
AutoHotkey 32
AutoIt 32
autoopen attribute 353

B

bang 13
Base COMP 260
basicControl COMP 293
basics, TouchDesigner 235
Blending 328
bpatcher, for MIDI input 62-64
break watchpoints 84
buffers 186
by index method 257
by name method 257
bypass flag 247

C

camera path, cameras 322
cameras
  about 321
  camera path 322
  cut and blend 322
  fog 324
  FOV 324
  lights 325, 326
  shadows 325, 326
Channel Operators. *See* CHOPs
Chebyshev polynomials 128
CHOPs
  about 240, 254-257
  URL 240
clap detector 14
classic approach 118-120
clippings, Max 36-38
clone immune flag 246
clones, project 268
CNMAT
  URL 284

CodeBox 188, 189
collaborative work 370
compare flag 305
compile button 185
component, for movies 289
components 259, 260
compressor 154-156
COMPs 238
construction 46
Container COMP 260
contents 47
Control Vertices (CVs) 322
control voltage (CV) 346, 347
conventional mixing 134
convolution 165, 166, 171, 172
cooking flag 247
CPU utilization 27
cut and blend, cameras 322

D

data
  about 186
  collections 67-69
  receiving 64-66
  sending 64-66
DATs (Data Operators)
  about 242-245
  URL 242
DAT table
  URL 263
debugger 83, 84
debugging
  about 82
  debugger 83, 84
  optimizing 84, 85
  ways 83
delay, Jitter matrix 210, 211
Depth Buffer 325
Depth of Filed (DOF) 337
different effects
  amplitude 122
  frequency response 122
  time 122
Digital Audio Workstation (DAW) 12
Digital Signal Processing (DSP) 89

Discrete Summation Formula. *See* DSF
display flag 306
display parameter 281
dissection 46
DOShack 363
DSF 113-116
dynamics
  about 149
  compressor 154-156
  expanders, working with 151, 152
  limiter 152-154
  noise gate 149, 150

E

edges 312
efficiency 190
envelope following 149
environment variable 269
equalizer
  building 120
event priority 82
example project, Arduino
  about 349
  Arduino code 351-354
  hardware requirements 349-351
examples, Gen
  about 190
  Karplus-Strong synthesis 191-195
  mass-spring system 196-198
  scattering junction 198-203
  waveguides 198-203
exercise_solution 254
exhibition, key points 361
exhibitions, multispeaker setups 361-364
expanders
  working with 151, 152
Exponentially Swept Sine (ESS) 167
exporting 244, 254-257
externals, Max
  about 23
  installing 30, 31
  URL 23
extras, Max 36

F

Fast Fourier Transform. *See* FFT
feedback 156
feedback, audio synthesis 96-98
feedback, frequency modulation 103, 104
feedback, Jitter matrix 210, 211
feedforward 156
FFT
  about 23, 143, 167-169
  convolution 171, 172
  data, playback 175
  data, recording 175
  filter 172, 173
  freezing 173, 174
  spectral reverb 173, 174
  spectrum, drawing 169-171
  transient detection 176-178
Field of View. *See* FOV, cameras
file preferences, Max 30
filtering 116-118
filter theory 121-125
Fingerpinger
  URL 356
finished code, organizing
  abstractions 33-36
  clippings 36-38
  extras 36
  packages 38
  projects 39
  prototypes 39
Finite Impulse Response (FIR) 122
Fixed Layer parameter 275
FM
  controlling 100-102
fog, cameras 324
forums, Max 22
FOV, cameras 324
FractalNoise 280
fractal texture
  about 339
  modeling 340
freezing
  URL 222
freezing, FFT 173, 174
frequency modulation
  about 98-100
  feedback 103, 104
  FM, controlling 100, 102
  phase modulation 104-106
Fritzing
  URL 350
Full Scale (FS) 90
functionality, Max
  Max object 39, 40
functions 227
FX
  about 146
  dynamics 149
  reverberation 157-161
  stutter 147, 148
  using 215-217

G

Gen
  about 183, 184
  advantages 183
  and Max, comparing 185-190
  features 183
Genexpr 188, 189
Gen versions
  about 184
  gen~ 184
  jit.gen 184
  jit.gl.pix 184
  jit.pix 184
Gen workspace
  about 184, 185
  Max and Gen, differences 185-190
Geo COMPs
  about 319, 335
  bass reflex port 335
  box 335
  floor 335
  instancing 320
  speakers 335
geometry manipulation 214, 215
geometry viewer
  about 316, 317
  URL 316
granular sampling 143-146
Graphics Processing Unit (GPU) 209

grouping
  by selection 318
Group SOP 318
GUI
  and Max patching 39
  creating 262

H

hardware requirements,
    Arduino project 349-351
Hello World
  about 237
  CHOPs 240
  COMPs 238
  DATs 242-245
  MATs 241
  SOPs 240
  TOPs 239
Hello World program
  [print] object 47, 48
  construction 46
  contents 47
  creating 45
  dissection 46
  message box 48, 49
  MSP-Hello World 50, 51
help, TouchDesigner
  obtaining 234
hierarchy, project 263, 265
HIRT (HISSTools Impulse Response
    Toolbox)
  URL 30
Houdini 342
house, in landscape
  about 342
  modeling 343
  rendering 344
  structure 342, 343
hysteresis 178

I

icon 289
Icon Composer 369
impulse response, room
  taking 166, 167
Infinite Impulse Response (IIR) 123

information hiding 73
instances
  managing 109, 110
instancing 320
interactive tool 315

J

Jack Audio
  URL 300
jit.gl.asyncread object 213
jit.gl.gridshape object 212
Jit.gl.handle object 213
jit.gl.pix object 190
jit.gl.render object 212
jit.qt.grab object 205
jit.qt.movie object 205
Jitter
  about 16, 17
  data format 17, 18
  OpenGL, using 212-214
Jitter data
  inputting 205-207
  outputting 205-207
Jitter matrix
  about 208
  delay 210, 211
  feedback 210, 211
  processing 209
jit.window object 212

K

Karplus-Strong synthesis 191-195
k-dependent coefficients
  (1-k) 202
  (1+k) 202
  -k 202
  k 202
keystrokes 358
knobman
  URL 78

L

lights, cameras
  about 325, 326
  types 325

[377]

limiter 152-154
Linear Time Invariant (LTI) 122
links
  about 252, 253
  URL 251
liquids
  about 340
  modeling 341
  rendering 341
  structure 341
Live API 226-228
Live Object Model (LOM) 226, 227
local, project 267
lock flag 247
lookahead 154
Low Frequency Oscillator (LFO) 108

M

M4L. *See* Max for Live
mass-spring system 196-198
material
  assigning 306, 307
Materials. *See* MATs
Matrix 17
MATs
  about 241, 306, 327
  transparency 328
  URL 241
Max
  32 bit 21
  64 bit 21
  about 7-10, 21
  advantages 10
  and Gen, comparing 185-190
  and TD, connecting 284-287
  finished code, organizing 33
  Jitter 16, 17
  Matrix 16, 17
  modular basis, for expressions 10, 11
  using 11, 12
  Video Processing 17
Max and Gen, differences
  abstraction 187
  buffers 186
  CodeBox 188, 189

data 186
efficiency 190
Genexpr 188, 189
parameters, through param 185, 186
subpatchers 187
Max for Live
  about 219
  Audio in/out 222
  fundamentals 219-222
  Live API 226-228
  MIDI in/out 222
  parameter modulator, example device 228, 229
  parameters 224, 225
  saving 224-226
  synchronization 223
Max GUI
  about 51, 52
  installing 52
Max, help
  externals 23
  forums 22
  Max-integrated help system 22
  obtaining 22
  other resources 23
Max-integrated help system 22
Max, message domain 12, 13
Max/MSP forums
  URL 22
Max object
  about 39, 40
  arguments 40-42
  attributes 43-45
Max patching
  advantages 9
  and GUI 39
Max, setting up
  about 23
  audio status window 24-27
  externals, installing 30, 31
  file preferences 30
  MIDI setup 28
  object defaults 29
  preferences 28
Max Signal Processing (MSP) 14, 15
Maxuino
  URL 348

me.digits expression
    used, for individualizing
        replicants 282, 283
message box
    about 48, 49, 70
    URL 70
message ordering 60, 61
microcontrollers 347, 348
microscopic timing 60, 61
middle mouse-click info box 245
MIDI 358
MIDI beat clock
    URL 80
MIDI in/out, Max for Live 222
MIDI setup, Max 28
MIDI Timecode (MTC) 358
migration 363
Miller Puckette
    URL 203
mixing
    about 132, 133
    conventional mixing 134
Modeler 319
modeling, fractal texture 340
modeling, landscape 343
modeling, liquids 341
modeling, procedural modeling 336, 337
modeling, waterfall plot 339
Model SOP 319
Model-View-Controller (MVC) 76
modular basis
    for expressions 10, 11
modules 276
modules, accessing ways
    URL 277
modules COMP 276
MSP-Hello World 50, 51
multispeaker setups
    about 360, 361
    exhibitions 361-364
multi-touch features
    URL 329
multitouch screens
    about 355
    TUIO protocol 356
    URL 356

N

noise gate 149, 150
nonlinear work
    animation COMP, using for 296
non-procedural tool 315
Non-uniform Rational
        B-Splines (NURBS) 315
normals 308
Not a Number (NaN) 28, 185
nullDisplay TOP 263

O

Object COMPs 316
object defaults 72
object defaults, Max 29
Ogg/Vorbis streaming
    URL 359
OpenGL
    used, in Jitter 212-214
OpenGL, in Jitter
    FX, using 215-217
    geometry manipulation 214, 215
    shaders, using 215-217
OpenGL Shading
        Language (GLSL) 234, 327
Open Sound Control (OSC)
    about 64, 357
    URL 284
operators
    about 245
    bypass flag 247
    clone immune flag 246
    cooking flag 247
    lock flag 247
    viewer active flag 247-249
    viewer flag 246
OP families
    converting between 290
optimizing 84, 85
other programs, interfacing
    about 357
    audio 358, 359
    keystrokes 358
    MIDI 358

[379]

Open Sound Control (OSC) 357
simulated user activity 358
video 358, 359

P

packages, Max 38
palette, project 266
pane bar 257
panes
  about 257-259
  URL 257
parallel processing 27
parameter dialog
  about 249-251
  Comment 251
  Copied Values/Clipboard 251
  Expand/collapse parameters 251
  Operator Help 251
  Operator Info 251
  Python Help 251
  Show non-default parameters only 251
  Switch Language 251
  URL 249
parameter modulator 229
parameters
  through param 185, 186
patcher
  about 7
  initializing 57-60
patcher loading 109, 110
patches
  pattr family, communication system 74-78
  structuring 70-74
patches, reusability
  information hiding 73
  interface 74
  protocol 74
pattern matching
  URL 287
pattr family 74-78
pattrstorage object 75
pattr system 74-78
PD
  about 354, 355
  advantages, over Max 354

references 355
Perlin noise 280
phase modulation 104-106
Phong shading 213
physical modeling 191
point attributes 308
poly
  as cascade 161-165
polygon 308, 312
poly~ object
  about 106-108
  instances, managing 109, 110
  patcher loading 109, 110
  polyphony 110, 111
  voice allocation 110, 111
polyphony 110, 111
Praat
  URL 195
Pre Fader Listening (PFL) 134
preferences, Max
  about 28
  Debug | Probing | enable 28
  Font | Native Text Rendering | enable 28
  Patching | Grid Size 29
  Patching | Segmented patch cords | enable 29
  Patching | Show Grid (default for new patchers) | enable 29
  Scheduler | Refresh Rate 29
primitive 308
print object 47
procedural modeling, examples
  about 334
  modeling 336, 337
  rendering 337
  speaker 334
  structure 335
project
  structuring 259-261
projection map 326
projects, Max 39
project, structuring
  abstraction 265
  clones 268
  component example 268

[380]

GUI, creating 262
   hierarchy 263-265
   local 267
   palette 266
properties 227
prototypes, Max 39
Pure Data. *See* **PD**

R

Reactable 356
reacTIVision application 356
Red Book
   URL 315
render flag 306
rendering, landscape 344
rendering, liquids 341
rendering, procedural modeling 337
Render passes 329
render picking 329-333
replicants
   individualizing, me.digits expression
      used 282, 283
Replicator COMP
   about 280-282
   me.digits expression, for individualizing
      replicants 282, 283
   URL 280
representations, system
   differences 9
reset button 185
Resolve Search Path Aliases 371
resources, Max 23
Restart On Crash and ReStartMe 32
reverberation
   about 157-161
   convolution 165, 166
   impulse response, taking 166, 167
   poly, as cascade 161-165
rgba values 275
ring modulation
   about 91
   versus amplitude modulation 94
root, component
   URL 268

S

sample accurate sequencing 178-180
sampling
   about 128-131, 138-143
   granular sampling 143-146
sampling rate 26
scattering junction 198-203
scheduler
   URL 82
Screen Space Ambient
      Occlusion (SSAO) 337
scripting 86, 87
scripting prologue 236, 237
Script parameter 281
select OP 253, 254
setup tips, Max 31-33
shaders
   about 327
   using 215-217
shading 321
shadows, cameras 325, 326
Shadow Type parameter 325
signal routing 132, 133
simulated user activity 358
SMPTE LTC 299
Soften parameter 279
SOPs
   about 240, 304, 305
   compare flag 305
   data 308-314
   display flag 306
   render flag 306
   template flag 305
   URL 240
Soundflower
   URL 300
speaker, procedural modeling 334
spectral flux 177
spectral reverb 173, 174
spectrum, signal
   drawing 169-171
Spout
   URL 359
starsBG COMP 279

structure, landscape 342, 343
structure, liquids 341
structure, procedural modeling 335
structure, waterfall plot 338
stutter 147, 148
Sublime Text package
  URL 190
subpatchers 187
subtractive synthesis
  about 116-118
  classic approach 118-120
  equalizer, building 120
  filter theory 121-125
Surface Operators. *See* SOPs
synchronization
  about 297-299
  audio ramp 300
  SMPTE LTC 299
  UDP 301
synchronization, Max for Live 223
synthesizer example 56, 57
Syphon
  URL 359

T

TD wiki
  URL 357
template flag 305
Template Table parameter 281
text editor
  assigning, to TouchDesigner 269
Texture Operators. *See* TOPs
this patcher 86, 87
threshold parameter 279
time
  Animation component 294-296
  dealing with 291-294
  synchronization 297-299
time dependent OPs
  examples 293
timeslicing
  about 254-257
  URL 255

timing, in Max 78-82
tools
  geometry viewer 316, 317
  grouping, by selection 318
  Modeler 319
TOPs
  about 239
  URL 239
TOP to CHOP 338
TouchDesigner
  CHOPs 254-257
  components 259
  exporting 254-257
  Hello World 237
  links 252, 253
  need for 234
  operators 245
  panes 257-259
  parameter dialog 249-251
  scripting prologue 236, 237
  select OP 253, 254
  text editor, assigning to 269
  timeslicing 254-257
  wires 251-253
TouchDesigner (TD)
  about 233
  and Max, connecting 284-288
Transform SOP 319
transient detection 176, 178
transparency 328
Transport Control Protocol (TCP) 284
tremolo 95
trigger attribute 127
TUIO
  URL 357
TUIO protocol 356

U

UDP 284, 301
UI, TouchDesigner 235
USB (Universal Serial Bus) 64
UV Texture Coordinates 333

V

ValuesNormalized 331
varbp 87
vertex 310
video 358, 359
viewer active flag 247, 249
viewer flag 246
Virtual Network Computing (VNC) 363
Virtual Studio Technology (VST)
    plugin 226
voice allocation 110, 111
vvvv node
  URL 359

W

Watchpoints 84
waterfall plot
  about 338
  modeling 339
  structure 338

waveguides 198-203
waveshaping 126-128
wires
  about 252, 253
  URL 251

Z

Z-fighting 332

Thank you for buying
Multimedia Programming Using Max/MSP and TouchDesigner

About Packt Publishing

Packt, pronounced 'packed', published its first book "*Mastering phpMyAdmin for Effective MySQL Management*" in April 2004 and subsequently continued to specialize in publishing highly focused books on specific technologies and solutions.

Our books and publications share the experiences of your fellow IT professionals in adapting and customizing today's systems, applications, and frameworks. Our solution based books give you the knowledge and power to customize the software and technologies you're using to get the job done. Packt books are more specific and less general than the IT books you have seen in the past. Our unique business model allows us to bring you more focused information, giving you more of what you need to know, and less of what you don't.

Packt is a modern, yet unique publishing company, which focuses on producing quality, cutting-edge books for communities of developers, administrators, and newbies alike. For more information, please visit our website: www.packtpub.com.

Writing for Packt

We welcome all inquiries from people who are interested in authoring. Book proposals should be sent to author@packtpub.com. If your book idea is still at an early stage and you would like to discuss it first before writing a formal book proposal, contact us; one of our commissioning editors will get in touch with you.

We're not just looking for published authors; if you have strong technical skills but no writing experience, our experienced editors can help you develop a writing career, or simply get some additional reward for your expertise.

Multimedia Programming with Pure Data

ISBN: 978-1-78216-464-7   Paperback: 350 pages

A comprehensive guide for digital artists for creating rich interactive multimedia applications using Pure Data

1. Carefully organized topics for interactive multimedia professional practice.

2. Detailed reference to a large collection of resources in the open source communities to enhance the Pure Data software.

3. Visual explanation and step-by-step tutorials with practical and creative multimedia applications.

Cinder Creative Coding Cookbook

ISBN: 978-1-84951-870-3   Paperback: 352 pages

Create compelling animations and graphics with Kinect and camera input, using one of the most powerful C++ frameworks available

1. Learn powerful techniques for building creative applications using motion sensing and tracking.

2. Create applications using multimedia content including video, audio, images, and text.

3. Draw and animate in 2D and 3D using fast performance techniques.

Please check www.PacktPub.com for information on our titles

[PACKT] PUBLISHING

Managing Multimedia and Unstructured Data in the Oracle Database

ISBN: 978-1-84968-692-1   Paperback: 504 pages

A revolutionary approach to understanding, managing, and delivering digital objects, assets, and all types of data

1. Full of illustrations, diagrams, and tips with clear step-by-step instructions and real-time examples.
2. Get up to speed on all the aspects of this new technology.
3. Learn how to work with rich multimedia and control it.

Moodle 2.5 Multimedia Cookbook
Second Edition

ISBN: 978-1-78328-937-0   Paperback: 300 pages

75 recipes to help you integrate different multimedia resources into your Moodle courses to make them more interactive

1. Add all sorts of multimedia features to your Moodle course.
2. Lots of easy-to-follow, step-by-step recipes.
3. Work with sound, audio, and animation to make your course even more interactive.

Please check www.PacktPub.com for information on our titles

9696665R00223

Printed in Great Britain
by Amazon.co.uk, Ltd.,
Marston Gate.